Digital Doesn'
(and other adv ıeresies)

by Josh Sklar

Edited by Ruth Mills

First published in 2014 by
Heresy Press, LLC
a division of Heresy, LLC
Austin, Texas
http://heresy.co

Heresy is a virtual ad agency of award-winning creative professionals providing execution and strategy for companies and brands of any size. It offers solutions in digital strategy, brand strategy, creative direction, technical direction, content development, campaign development, site design, app design, and execution across all media.

Additional services focus on helping traditional advertising and marketing professionals better understand digital platforms and emerging media. They include: workshops, master classes, mentoring and coaching, interviewing/screening candidates, performing evaluations of staff and process, discovery, recommendation reports, and writing/coordinating RFPs for projects that are principally digital.

Heresy is an independent shop headquartered in Austin, Texas with talent located all over the world.

Digital Doesn't Matter on:

- The Web: http://digitaldoesntmatter.com
- iTunes App store: search for "Digital Doesn't Matter"
- Facebook: https://www.facebook.com/DigitalDoesntMatter
- Twitter: https://twitter.com/chiefheretic

ISBN: 978-0-69-222685-8 (paperback)
eISBN: 978-0-692-22686-5 (ebook)
Library of Congress Control Number: 2014911479

Television on cover from the collection of EC Gee

Digital Doesn't Matter (and other advertising heresies)

This book is dedicated to my father, Sheldon, for his unwavering faith in me, my whole life;

to the bittersweet memory of my ever present sons, Noah and Zach;

and to the salvation and joy their little brother, Ethan, continues to bring to their mother and me.

Contents

Foreword

by Jeff Goodby, Co-Chairman, Goodby, Silverstein & Partners

To begin with, a warning.

As soon as I am finished writing this foreword, it will be obsolete, as quaint as metal type and the IBM Selectric. That's how fast this stuff is changing right now.

And yet, this piece – this whole book – must be written. Because the movement toward digitizing all of our interactions with the world, and the effect this has all had upon our understanding, are perhaps the most important issues of our day. They will play out aggressively in the world of advertising, changing it until it is unrecognizable.

Yes, there are some major banana peels on the sidewalk ahead. Advertising will flourish, but will it require the arty, storytelling types that have populated it in the past? What will the Bill Bernbach or Dan Wieden of 2020 look like? And just how do you get across this digital divide?

Bob Greenberg of R/GA, who has been about as adept as anyone at understanding the digitization of advertising, once told me, "Jeff, it's hard. It's exhausting, in fact. But when you get the right reflexes, and want it to happen enough, it gets easier."

In the spring of 2005, my partner, Rich Silverstein, and I rented out the airy studio of a local photographer and pulled together the creative department of Goodby, Silverstein & Partners for what we knew would be a rather controversial meeting.

A few months earlier, Derek Robson, freshly arrived from Bartle Bogle Heggarty as our managing director, had inconveniently pointed out to us that the creative staff's specialties no long matched up well with the jobs in front of our agency.

Okay, it was actually worse than that. Derek estimated that more than 70% of what we did could be characterized by the new-fangled term, "digital" – meaning that our output was suddenly not the traditional TV commercials, print advertisements and outdoor boards we were known for.

Why was this a problem? Well, because only 30% of our staff thought of themselves as people who were trained at such forms and, disturbingly, even liked them. The majority of the agency's work – the work of the future, in many ways – was being done by a small minority of the staff.

Worse, the rest of the creative personnel had cultivated an attitude of superiority, feeling that the traditional work they were doing was the true center of the agency's gravity. They were the keepers of craft, they thought, the true practitioners.

It was a situation that could easily have forced layoffs and a complete realignment of all personnel. But we decided to approach it head on, to presume that people could change.

We showed the staff some examples of work from other agencies that, we thought, could not have come from our place as it was currently constructed. Thus, I told them, we had to change.

"It will no longer be acceptable here to think of yourself as strictly a digital or traditional advertising person," I said. "You must be a bit of both.

"This will take active study and open minds. If you are currently designing digital experiences, we want you to learn how to tell stories, shoot film and design in ways digital people currently do not. If you are a traditional type, we want you to learn how Internet design works, so that you feel comfortable in that world.

"Do we expect you to magically become this new person immediately? No. But we do expect you to work toward it. And if you are not comfortable with this effort, you may be working at the wrong agency."

Okay, it may have been a little melodramatic, but it had its effect. Indeed, some people – mostly traditional types who thought we had lost our way and would never again kern type or finesse an edit – got their portfolios together and left. But the ones who stayed went on to become the most awarded agency in the world just four years later.

It makes a good story and that would be the end of it, if it weren't for forces in the world right now that threaten the more noble aspects of this new creativity.

Before I expand on that, let's remember that things like this have happened before. In 18th-century England, the new moveable type created a mass commercial market for books, and put an end to the patronage system under which rich guys supported literary endeavors. In the wake of that, many people feared a sudden explosion of hack writers that simply served popular tastes. And there were those, sure. But soon there was also Samuel Johnson, Charles Dickens and Graham Greene.

In the fifties, Marshall McLuhan wrote about our fears that the invention of television would just be a lame version of the theater, and render the latter obsolete. But that was before we learned they were two rather different things – and that *Friends* probably wouldn't put Broadway and the East End out of business.

We are currently experiencing new things about the crossing of the digital divide that are extremely disturbing, in much the same way. Newness can be disturbing.

In this case, the threat comes from Google's ingenious combining of advertising and search, probably one of the biggest moneymakers in human history. Suddenly, the hive seems to know what we want and love and someone, somewhere is placing extremely targeted advertising alongside our content experiences. As Jaron Lanier has put it, "At the end of the rainbow of open culture lies an eternal spring of advertisements. Advertising is elevated by open culture from its previous role as an accelerant and placed at the center of the human universe."

Sadly, as ads become supremely and perfectly targeted, they don't have to be all that good. The charm and humor that makes people seek out our creations becomes less and less of an imperative. Content, likewise, seeks the lowest common denominator as well, being just good enough to deliver the audience to the anemic advertising.

Listen, over the next decade or so, I'm not sure whether advertising is going to be a good place to end up. What drew me to it, and made it hard and admirable, even, is slowly being leached out of it. We are not just at a commercial crossroads, but at a moral one. We are moving from a world in which products were openly embedded in stories and from creations that, at their best, charmed us all, to one in which we – as citizens of the cyberworld – are silent servants of the commercial urge and the things we love are invisibly used against us.

The Internet could very easily become a place where advertising is something flatfooted and unwelcome that scrolls or pops up as we pursue our interests. It will be incisively targeted, and we will get as much of it as advertisers think we can stand without leaving a site. If that sounds a lot like a more scientific version of the old commercial networks, that's because it *is*. Commercial TV treated us like idiots, too, much of the time, and thus it is dead.

But there is hope. Brands have people talking back to them now. They have to pay attention. Companies have no choice but to be better citizens of the world.

And that is where you come in.

The things you make over the next decade, and the paths taken, will determine whether we all breathe on the single coal of humor and beauty left in advertising and expand it to be something people gravitate toward, actually like, and talk about – or simply resign ourselves to a Google world in which search and advertising are one and the same and the commercial urge happens invisibly, placed there by seemingly well-intentioned films and diversions that learn our desires and then happen to place the utilitarian objects that might fulfill them magically into our ken.

There are a couple of ways such a world might look, and both of them may come to pass.

The first is a much more explicit intersection between network television and the Internet. What if the television series of today were posted on corporate web sites, rather than on independent media networks? For instance, you might go to the Cadillac site to watch *Mad Men* or to American Apparel for *America's Got Talent*. One can imagine such a world replacing television as we know it now. To see the series, you'd have to watch one or two of the host sites' messages. The host's products could be embedded in the featured shows, and it would be easy to link to shopping and information.

It is an opportunity that will favor those who know both the traditional and digital advertising worlds. Paired beside destination shows, amidst the freedom of the online world, there would be big pressure on the advertising to be welcome and entertaining – which, we hope, will be the watchwords of the advertising future. The feedback on the show, the site and the advertising would all be intertwined.

A second world might be the more likely scenario in which farsighted brand people realize that annoying pop up or sidebar ads alongside "related" content often do more damage than good – largely because the Google search model invites (even rewards) mediocrity. Instead, these people will demand deeper Internet experiences that viewers will seek out and discuss. Making these things will require storytelling skills, a sense of humor, design sensibilities, filmmaking abilities, musical talent and an understanding of human nature. At their best, these creations will be like digital novels, with layers of meaning, and deep involvement. People will embrace them, critique them, shape them. That means the creators will have to transcend the old labels of traditional and digital advertising. They will be inventing the future.

As an advertising person, trust me, you want to be one of these new creative people. As a consumer of media and products, you want to reward the brands that please you in these ways. As a reader of this book, you will learn a lot about how to navigate these waters.

And believe me, it will decide whether advertising is interesting ten years from now. In the larger sense, it will decide whether Google is the new Blu-ray or, well, Google as we know it.

The time has come, as Hunter S. Thompson once urged, "to chase them like rats across the tundra."

Or else.

Introduction

These days, the medium is irrelevant. Whether it's television, print, direct, or digital doesn't matter. None of them matter. There should be a focus only on appropriately using the vehicles to tell a convincing brand story or get a marketing communication message out, and it doesn't matter whether that is done through a 30-second TV spot or GPS-based augmented reality mobile app or billboard or competition or point-of-purchase display, banner display ad, piece of direct mail, or social media campaign. If an advertising agency goes on about integration, that means it is rooted in a traditional model that holds above-the-line (television, radio, print) or below-the-line (direct) as the core of its strategic offering and everything else as a "nice-to-have" add on.

When people in the business fixate on the platform for the idea rather than on an idea that can be extended creatively and intelligently through any channel, they run into conflict over ownership and territory and lose the ability to be flexible and create something bigger and more memorable. In other words, they become small-minded and drop the notion of The Big Idea. They become tactical. They care more about specifications and requirements than storytelling. They are no longer medium-agnostic; they have a vested interest in working within particular media that they do best but that may not be best for the goals of the client.

"When you consider the fact that traditional budgets are getting slashed, that interactive budgets are expected to grow significantly in the next five years, and that technology is becoming more and more integral to marketing, we see digital becoming the backbone of marketing and technology becoming so vital that everyone needs digital capabilities. Everyone is coming from a different strength. Everyone is trying to add the other's capabilities. The market is now ready to take a big step to join, and in some cases even replace, traditional agencies in leading marketing strategy for top brands." Sean Corcoran, *The Forrester Blog for Interactive Professionals*.

Fortunately, today more and more agencies, big and small, have recognized that to not embrace and absorb digital and to not have it as the red thread that runs throughout every part of your marketing communications business is pure folly. To continue to relegate it to a corner of the office that is called on only after everything has been baked by the stars of the show—the TV creative—is a huge mistake that has undone many a large account. With audiences shifting their attention and their thought processes more and more over to their smart devices, social news aggregators, and mobile apps, it has become very clear that there is a great deal to be learned about audience behavior by observing them in these new experiences. There is a good deal of opportunity that can now be realized if customers and prospects are driven into these data-rich environments, where a little sociology, psychology, and analysis can go a long way to achieving results favorable for the targets, the brands, and the agencies.

But if you work in the advertising industry today, you know something's wrong. Seriously wrong. Of course, if you're one of the many who no longer work in it, this is definitely not news. But if you've joined in the last decade, you may be wondering how anyone ever thought of the field as glamorous or sexy — and you're probably feeling it can't always have been this way. Where creative and strategic professionals are treated as if we are part of a mindless production assembly line. Where all of the important directions come from the advertiser and a group of specialists and consultants, with the agency left to execute their vision and buy the media. How could the likes of David Ogilvy, Bill Bernbach, Rosser Reeves, William Backer, Mary Wells Lawrence, Lee Clow, David Droga, and Alex Bogusky have become famous advertising giants in an environment as bland and uninspiring as what most of us now find ourselves working in? What would have even interested them in a career in the business?

Don't worry, you're crazy for working in advertising, but you're not going mad. For some of the most highly artistic, clever, and interesting people on the planet, advertising really used to be an oasis where they could have *real jobs* while being able to creatively express themselves. What other profession could tolerate the numbers of imaginative souls who want to be more than armies of Walter Mittys daydreaming within 8-to-5 offices?

Over the past 25 years or so, there have been a number of monumental events that have dismantled, rebuilt, and now finally threaten the existence of the agencies in which many of us have made not just careers, but our homes. What had been a reliable base of long-term employment with well-worn paths to senior advancement for a variety of skill sets is becoming something that gives stability to most only on a project-by-project basis. *No one* is safe from the inevitable reduction in force (RIF) that uproots the highly paid, experienced, and deeply loyal, along with the entry-level hopefuls. If you think you're safe, don't walk out of the executive meeting room at the wrong time, or you'll find your name on the whiteboard along with the other soon-to-be-former employees.

Some of these events are the unwitting doings of the same people who would now do anything to save the agencies' cultures and the business at large, but most have to do with the same problem that is ruining many industries (such as publishing and music) that have creativity at their center: financial geniuses trying to wring every halfpenny they can out of the product before they move on to consume something else, with no concern for what existed before they got involved or why it was successful. Certainly, they've spared no thought for the craft they do not practice and the droves of people now left without jobs.

Don't run off to Hollywood with your steamer trunk filled with half-finished scripts just yet, however: fortunately, this problem is happening at the very same period that technology has allowed us to overcome the requirement of a large capital investment to run and operate an agency and when nearly everyone, especially the audience, has adapted to working and playing through digital screens. There are enormous possibilities today and even greater opportunities in the near future for the very same groups of unique thinkers and strategic visualizers who, before, had no choice but to join and/or follow a standardized agency structure with very clear revenue capabilities based on a limited range of service offerings. There's no reason for that to remain the case. So if agency-shattering change is here, why not turn it into long-overdue positive change and reinvent the business in favor of those who have a passion for it?

The alternative is to watch our jobs get absorbed into the marketers' organizations or to turn off our brains along with our expectations, self-respect, and desire to do the work. I don't need Advertising to remain an inflexible entity steeped in tradition above results, and I'm fine if the times dictate tremendous change and upheaval. Advertising needs to evolve and embrace the new audience mindsets, the ways brands can interact, the new channels for content, day- and time-parting, and everything else that is new, interesting, and a fact of life. And we all also need to evolve. What I'm not OK with is having bean counters and procurement officers — who have no understanding or regard for a necessary, effective, and valuable set of skills and talents — throw it all away in exchange for marketing automation, third-world production facilities, and cookie-cutter clichés that are deemed "good enough."

When there is only a handful of owners of every major ad agency network in the world, the deck is stacked against success for marketers, and this situation ensures endless agency reviews, resulting in clients frequently moving from one holding-company agency to the next. This makes it look like they're getting something different, but today, it really only means that the holding company still gets paid.

It would have been fairly easy — and cathartic — to sit down and write a long rant about how much the advertising business has changed for the worse since people my age (45) were drawn into it and then relate ideas about how it can be fixed before it collapses. But who cares about the opinion and feelings of one person out of the hundreds of thousands in the industry? Instead, I wanted this book to identify and solve heady industry-wide problems, so I decided to approach it the way any good advertising professional would take on a creative problem: with instinct, experience, and a great deal of research, speaking directly to the people the message is trying to reach to ascertain their pain points, needs, wishes, and experience with the issues. I may be a creative director and, therefore, know *everything*, but I felt this project was too important to be driven by ego. (Luckily for me, there are plenty of other projects that aren't.) Instead, I wanted the wisdom from the collective experience and talent of the best and brightest in the business, so I crowdsourced a good deal of the content.

My former ad agency colleague John Lambie aided in the effort, and we reached out to the hands-on leaders of agencies within the big six marketing communications holding companies of WPP, Omnicom, Publicis, IPG, Dentsu, and Havas. We also used our networks, life-long knowledge of the business, and referrals from executives to speak to successful brands, independents, collectives, crowdsourcers, individuals, influential industry bloggers, and respected trade journalists across six continents. I felt it was important to have a comprehensive cross-section of the industry from all perspectives around the world and to speak with people who went through the momentous events and upheaval; who tried or observed first-hand the different attempts by agencies and advertisers to weather the changes and fractures; and who have succeeded, such as the greatly respected author of our foreword, Jeff Goodby, and his senior team members at Goodby Silverstein & Partners.

I have worked in the industry since the mythical time of the early 1980s in a variety of positions ranging from programmer and SysOp of the very first social networks, dial-up bulletin board systems (BBSes), to pre-press operator to typesetter to graphic designer to offline video editor to commercial director to copywriter to creative director to regional agency CEO and global chief creative officer for WPP-owned agency networks around the globe. If it helps as a measure of credibility, like everyone, I've won shelves full of industry awards during that career. My last gig was global digital creative director and director of digital strategy on the Dell account; my most successful run was in the 1990s helping establish Nokia as a brand through the power of the earliest days of online, interactive advertising. I have seen the agency world dramatically morph from a demanding place that offered sanctuary and the best imaginable platform for expression to one where even Type-A personalities have no long-term prospects based on anything more than luck and politics.

Today, I sit in my home office and run a virtual branding and marketing agency comprised of the people I worked with for years in the "big" agencies around the globe, serving clients I have mostly never met that range from startups to the Fortune 50, equally spread out around the planet. It's called Heresy, and we're all about going against the ingrained status quo by practicing what we preach — and discuss — throughout this book. It's a brave new world for all of us, and I'm thoroughly enjoying the change in quality of life it has meant for me, all of the people I work with, and the pride we can take in our work again.

How the Interviews Were Conducted

I sat in very senior meetings in holding-company-owned global agencies and large client marketing organizations and listened to the Powers That Be describe how agencies should address the changing marketplace and technological advancements. What I heard again and again sounded very much like the past, not the future. It sounded reactive, and it looked like the sole driving need was to create as high a margin as possible and to *appear* attractively efficient. Meanwhile, more and more, I was forced to lay off talented and loyal people during perennial hiring freezes and told to do what the client wanted, not what they needed. Contract workers outnumbered the surviving full-time employees, staff were correctly concerned on a daily basis that they'd be laid off, clients complained of not having enough support and of the agency not being forward thinking and consultative, and the many who tried to do the right thing tended to be wasting their time. Time that extended into nights, weekends, holidays, sick leave – 80-120 hours a week, week in and week out, year after year. What was once considered an *Office Space*-like infrequent request of "Ummm, I'm gonna need you to go ahead and come in on Saturday. So if you could be here around 9, that would be great." has become the expected norm.

These are problems that people in the agency world talk about constantly, but only amongst ourselves. I felt it was time to say it all together and out loud, along with solutions for surviving the not-so-silent owners that have gobbled up most of the industry. It seemed the best way to do that was to have the same heated conversations we always tend to have, but this time on the record and for everyone, which led to 135 interviews conducted from July of 2012 through May of 2013 (with John Lambie who did a bunch of them and coordinated many more), and although that was the longest part of the process of creating this book, those talks were easily the most enjoyable part and didn't feel time-consuming as we continued to explore new ground, hear each interesting and revealing anecdote, or bond over all-too-similar experiences.

Before conducting the interviews, I wrote a detailed outline to serve as the backbone of the book. Then, John and I followed it to conceive a general guide of 30 multi-part (and I mean *multi*-part) questions that we then adapted to be specifically relevant to each of the 15 different roles we initially identified:

1. Account Management
2. Agency Education
3. Agency Management
4. Brand Stewardship
5. Creative Direction
6. Data Analysis
7. Marketing Strategy
8. Media Strategy
9. New Business Development
10. Recruitment
11. Social Media
12. Strategic Planning
13. Talent Development
14. Technical Direction
15. Trade Journalism

In the future, we may add Producers, Project Managers, Editors, Developers, Media Buyers, and others, as interest and time allow.

Some people opted to write down detailed answers to several of the questions, but with most, we simply used the questionnaire as a starting point for a spontaneous dialogue about the topics touched on in the questions, and we went wherever the conversations naturally took us. The questions were structured in a way to follow the detailed outline that would explain why so many talented people were/are drawn to advertising as a career; relate when things began to change and why; express how all of that has affected the people doing the work; explain what can be done to right the ship before it sinks; and give examples of the optimistic new opportunities out there for all of us. It was my hope that by following the outline and the questions with the interviews, the book would essentially write itself. (Too bad nothing is ever that easy.)

For a sense of how we introduced the topics, here are four of them:

1. *When did digital start to have an effect on your job?* When did you start asking your agencies to incorporate it, or when did they start suggesting it? What was your response (did you try to talk them out of it, or did a light go off)? Was it an isolated strategy or integrated at that time (e.g., some in branding considered the Web a discrete area that did not have to fall within the brand guidelines)? Can you describe it and how people in your organization reacted? Did you have

to struggle against any other people in the company who perhaps didn't agree or wanted to completely minimize the effort (e.g., no digital call to action on the press and TV ads because they will ruin the integrity of the art direction or those who didn't want the budget sliding away from TV production)?

2. *What do you feel has been lost by this explosion of technology?* Has the craft suffered, has the creative product suffered, have your fellow creatives suffered?

3. *When working with clients today, do you fear that they know more about digital advertising and marketing tactics and technologies than you do?* Do you have any stories about being unable to answer a client's questions and feeling inadequate, over your head, unqualified? How do you handle situations when you're going to have to check with others, yet you don't want to come across as uninformed? How have you learned to adapt to coming up with answers, strategies, directions, etc. on-the-fly in client meetings?

4. *Where do you see all of this heading?* What do you believe the future of advertising and marketing holds for you and your staff? For the client? For the audiences?

Since we spoke with many seriously busy executives, we sometimes had as little as twenty minutes to cover the topics that they were most interested in. However, with some interviewees, we ended up in such engaging discussions that we often spoke for a few hours and a few times even had follow-up calls. On average, each conversation lasted an hour and a half.

After the interviews concluded, the digital audio was transmitted to our team in the Philippines who magically transcribed them into Word docs over a period of around 10 months. When put together with the written responses, this gave me more than *5,000 pages* of fascinating source material to work through. But first, I had to check the original recordings against each of the transcripts to make sure the transcriber understood the use of idiom and industry jargon, the subtle jokes (or those without cultural equivalent), and make the inevitable numerous corrections. Since we spoke with people from around the world, some of the accents and colorful language proved nearly as challenging to suss out for them as the quality of the recordings (especially the ones over Skype).

I wanted to make sure we could cull the best material for a general book, with the most interesting and useful insights from all of the people we spoke to. I also wanted to focus on two roles in particular: the head of the agency and the senior creative leader. The idea was that the tablet app version of the book that I produced simultaneously with the manuscript can continue to grow and never need be out of date, and more content can be added from the other roles over time (or all at once, if there is demand), with the print version standing on its own.

I decided to keep the content as quotes so you can "hear" them in their own words and really understand the common experiences and the nuanced differences. Certainly, not everyone agreed with us or subscribes to the premise that the agency world is collapsing with digital as the catalyst (or that it's even collapsing at all), and I wanted to make sure they were represented as intelligent counterpoints to think about.

The book's title, *Digital Doesn't Matter,* is meant to be ironic. In the early days of "new media," "interactive," and "digital marketing," that was the oft-heard refrain and dismissive excuse for minuscule budgets and meager representation in the marketing mix. In the strategic, creative, and financial estimations at that time, digital simply didn't register.

Now, with over a billion people on Facebook, mobile app mania, and the digitization of TV, newspapers, magazines, radio, and even outdoor – plus a multitude of exciting new media touch points — it seems everything is digital. The term "digital" has become so ubiquitous, it's practically redundant. Yet many agencies still partition it in its own silo instead of making it a natural, organic aspect of the strategic creative process.

The book is divided into four parts that take us through:

- *The Good Old Days* – why many of us gravitated toward the industry and devoted our lives to it
- *Things Fall Apart* – when things began to "go off the rails" (sadly, a common refrain heard in advertising that relates to many aspects of the business)
- *Digital Takes Over* – how digital media and its practitioners were regarded for much too long and why this treatment is symptomatic of deep problems within the business
- *The Future of Advertising* – and finally what we can transform it into if we collectively agree that the entire system is broken and driving talented old hands and fresh blood alike far away from advertising as a career and into fascinating new media business possibilities.

There is a linear storyline that can be followed from start to finish, but feel free to dip into the sections that intrigue you the most, especially considering the number of pages. In addition to being a snapshot of people's views around the world preserved during a critical transitory period of the Advertising industry, the book is meant to serve as a guide and resource to what is happening now, how it came to pass, and what can be done. So if you already lived through the depressingly dark days of fragmentation, you might jump past that to what people are doing today. The tablet app version of the book is certainly meant to be consumed in any number of ways including applying a filter to drop out chapters that are not relevant to you, reading from the point of view of a particular role in the business (whereby the book will automatically rearrange its order to suit the perspective), searching for topics, reading as a coffee table book (i.e., only the chapter sidebar content exclusively available in the app), and so on. It will also continue to be updated and grow. The way we conceive of creative solutions to our clients' issues shouldn't be cookie cutter and linear, so why should a book about the industry be?

Who the Book Is Intended for — and Why You Should Read It

This work is meant for anyone who is associated with or has interest in any area of marketing: advertising, media, public relations, branding, and so forth. It doesn't matter if you are involved on the marketer or agency side of the coin or are a vendor or pundit. The factors discussed in the book are having a major effect on all of us, and it's important to at least be aware of what's happening and why if you want to avoid being surprised at being without a job or any prospects. Things are moving fast, so why not learn from the people who have already gone through everything you're facing or likely to face soon, be prepared and armed with a way forward?

If you're as frustrated as many of us, you may even want to help start a revolution that accelerates the morphing of the old models into exciting and intriguing new ones to help retain talent and finally re-attract the fresh blood that has been avoiding advertising of late and rushing instead to places like Google, Facebook, Pinterest, Foursquare, and startups of every stripe.

As with climate change, it's easy to think that the world will keep turning, and all of this worry about the collapse of the advertising business is nothing more than Chicken Little Syndrome. In the pages of this book, you will be able to follow along with what things used to be like versus how they are now and how it came to pass, as told by the people who were and are there. These aren't pundits and personalities trying to make a name for themselves with sensationalist reporting. These are the people who have already established their reputations, who have been and are currently running the most successful, largest and most interesting agencies and brands out there — and they are saying things are *not good*.

If we do not take the time to understand what has happened and what the situations were that led us here, if we just allow nature to run its course, then the millions of people employed in the large agencies that are responsible for over 90% of the more than $500 billion spent in advertising each year are going to find that the assembly line is not a temporary situation while things shake themselves out. Things will only continue to erode, as more and more of the strategy is decided outside of the "agency of record" and as roles become commoditized to the point that... there is no point. Anyone can do them. Not as well. Not as fast. But cheaper — and more and more often, that's all the bean counters who control both the agencies and the clients care about. Don't let that happen. Instead, read what well over a hundred of the most experienced advertising luminaries have to say about the state of our industry today, see what they've done to keep their agencies relevant and successful, and consider what you might be able to do to change the direction we're going in — before it's too late.

Part I:
The Good Old Days

If you entered the business more than 10 years ago, these three chapters are intended to remind you why you likely chose to go into advertising in the first place. They describe what we loved about it and why we valued the life (enough to always sacrifice our personal time while still wholeheartedly believing that we had a great quality of life directly linked to being able to work in such a satisfyingly creative field). We discuss the importance of agency cultures before the holding companies bought everyone up, took over, and forced their rigid, unconcealed $, £, €, and ¥ agenda upon the majority of the industry.

For those more recently involved, Part I explains the importance of the business for the first many decades of its existence as an industry and relates that to what we should try to get back to since we have now drifted far afield of where things used to lay.

Chapter 1: Breaking In

Way back when, in the 20th century, if you were blessed with the talent of a highly creative imagination, you might have found it to be an itch rarely scratched outside of the occasional hobbyist weekend spent painting, writing, or daydreaming. Never mind trying to explain it to your disapproving parents, the fact is there were very few jobs available that allowed for both continual expressions of creativity and at least one square meal every day or so. Making a living as a starving artist, author, or musician was nearly impossible (hence the adjective "starving" although it's true that post-death a few people *did* apparently do quite well; and getting a job in Hollywood (and Bollywood) has always been less about talent and more about the people you know, with a liberal dose of blind luck and timing mixed in. Fortunately, a bastion was available for those of us otherwise doomed to careers filled with sales figures, inventory controls, or hard labor: the stimulatingly volatile world of advertising.

Despite what may have been seen on popular TV shows ranging from *Bewitched* (1964-1972) to *Mad Men* (2007-2014), the advertising industry is more than an environment to practice sexism and drinking before lunch. It is even more than being paid to travel to exotic location shoots (that *everyone* insists be written into the scripts) and acting like a big shot around square, office-grounded friends. Advertising is the only profession that provides a sincere outlet for writers, designers, illustrators, and creative strategists from all backgrounds while paying our bills and even providing a bona-fide career path to the top for those ambitious enough; that includes those who enjoy being around or part of a creative team but who don't have the hands-on talent. If you are entrepreneurially minded or simply disheartened working for people who don't "get it," you even have the option of creating a business of your own.

This industry not only gives a home to all of these otherwise frustrated lost souls and brings us together, it pays for our homes and our kids' college tuitions (where they thankfully learn to be doctors and lawyers instead of ad execs) and it gives us freedom to work however we want — these days, more than ever. Over the years, it deserves a lot of credit for saving the minds and talents of so many good people who might otherwise have spent their free time banging their heads against a wall or desk in interminable frustration and, in their fertile imaginations, eternal damnation.

Many of the most experienced ad executives in the world were attracted to the industry for this same need of being free to practice creative problem solving and to unleash his or her unique vision, whether they knew in their bones what they wanted to be or they just happened to blindly stumble upon the business.

$$\backsim$$

Global CEO of Y&R, David Sable, recalls, "I got into the industry actually, believe it or not, when I was a senior in high school. This is 1971. I went to a very progressive high school in New York and they piloted this work program, which now you see in a lot of schools. The idea was that you were supposed to do something and you couldn't get paid and you were supposed to add value to your life, your career, to give you an idea. The truth is, back then they wanted everybody to work in a laboratory or something like that. I'd always been the creative guy in school; I'd always been into drama and writing and all this stuff, so I went to work in an ad agency.

"It was a small, very hot, at the time, New York shop. Very retail-oriented, with some really cool clients. It was a lot of fun. It was typical – I don't want to say 'traditional' – it was typical. It was what an ad agency should be. It was like what any good creative agency is today, whether it's digital or not. It was just a few guys sitting around coming up with ideas and executing them. We did everything from newspaper to television to print to outdoor to events. Full service. If there'd been digital, we would have done digital. We all would have been in the middle of it, without a doubt. We did some pretty clever stuff. Digital is bullshit; digital is just another thing.

"Television commercials used to be live. Then, when people realized you could do different things if you filmed it, they went to film. So, we went back to doing live commercials for a department store called Ohrbach's in New York. It was famous in those days. It was on 34th Street, owned by a Dutch company. We did live fashion show :60s spots, every morning on the *Today Show,* and it was huge. Since buzz and word-of-mouth have been only created recently, they didn't exist then; it got whatever the equivalent was then. Everybody talked about it. It was an interesting company, it was written about. Basically, they were out, and the client came in with something, and I just went in and did it. I trafficked something and wrote it and designed it, and they freaked out that I did it. That's what hooked me. I just stayed in the business and I loved it. And I still love it."

∽

Åsk Wäppling, *Adland* Founder and CEO, "The industry itself didn't attract me, since it was of full of tossers, wankers, and sexist old men who wanted to hit on me all the time. But the process of solving a problem was very interesting to me. When I went to college, I was a Sherlockian and it was all a bit of a mystery: you put these pieces together, you solve the problem. That was really fun then and you'd do it as a creative output.

"Before I went to Parsons, I went to art school, and that was the only thing I could do. I was like, 'I don't know math, I don't know engineering, I don't know world history. I know how to draw.' That's how I felt. Then I started reading *Sherlock Holmes,* and I discovered that all I really wanted was to solve problems, and that's what you do in advertising. They come to you with a problem. They tell you, 'OK, we gotta do *x*,' and how do you solve that problem? That is a bit of a Sherlock Holmesian mystery. You find out everything you can find out about the target market and the people that you're going to sell stuff to. And you solve the mystery.

"I've always been addicted to advertising. Like, seriously addicted. When I was a kid I would make audio tapes for my grandmother because I couldn't write, and I would stop in the middle of recording the tapes because an ad would come on the TV. I would repeat everything that they said on the ads. I see the same thing in my kid so it's obviously some sort of genetic disorder.

"She won't watch the TV at all, but when the ads come on they have her attention. It's something that we do in those 30 seconds. It's the boiling down of the story until it's 30 seconds that really catches people's attention. I don't think I was discerning in the same way that I am now, though. I'd watch the Tide ads and the really popular Procter & Gamble shit actually worked on me."

⁓

Chris Kyme, Hong Kong-based CEO of creative services agency Kymechow, former Regional Creative Director for FCB and former Executive CD of Grey Worldwide, "I did not go to college and had no help with anyone directing me on a career path, but I knew I was creative and went in search of advertising. I got a job in the mailroom of FCB London and worked on getting to know people until I eventually got a chance as junior copywriter. I was bullied and beaten up over my writing craft, and it was not until after about two years that I could honestly say I was a copywriter."

⁓

Edward Boches, Mullen's Chief Innovation Officer and Professor of Advertising at Boston University's College of Communication, "I've been doing this 35 years. I fell in love with media, when I was probably 14 years old, with the printed, oversized pages of *Look* and *Life* magazines. I either wanted to create that kind of content or to be the next Orson Welles. By the time I was 16 or 17 years old, I wanted to be the next Walter Cronkite. When all was said and done, what was left was my love of media, content, and communications. So, I went to Boston University and studied film, then journalism, and then a little bit of everything. I went from a newspaper reporter to a corporate speechwriter to public relations to the advertising industry at Hill Holiday. Then, 30 years ago, to Mullen when we had 12 or 14 people and when one person could basically do everything: press releases, creative advertising, radio, all of that kind of stuff.

"For someone who's a little bit ADD and Type A, you need a non-stop positive reinforcement for your ideas, as opposed to writing a book and taking a year and half to find out if anybody likes it. Advertising was the perfect business, and it was fun, intense, collaborative, creative, and a great outlet if you had a need to make stuff. In the early days, for me, anyway, it was a great business."

⤸

SapientNitro's Executive Creative Director in the Asia Pacific, Andy Greenaway, "I initially wanted to be an illustrator and got a place at Bath Lane Art College in Newcastle Upon Tyne, UK. In the foundation year, you had to do everything. One of the subjects was advertising. The lecturer who ran the class, a Tom Selleck lookalike called Alan Oager, was inspirational. The classes were exciting and exhilarating. I quickly dropped my aspirations to be an illustrator and specialized in advertising in my second year. I spent half my time traveling down to London on a coach and showing my book around the top agencies, quite often making my way back to Newcastle with my tail between my legs after my book had been torn to shreds.

"In those days, you could only get a job as a team. The agencies wouldn't hire fresh-out-of-college individuals. The problem was, I'd fallen out with my partner and was solo. Luckily, I heard through the grapevine that a job was going at Ogilvy & Mather Direct. I went alone and got the job. It wasn't my intention to stay there in direct marketing for long, but… they gave me so many pay raises, so regularly, I couldn't afford to jump across to the advertising side (after two years, my colleagues on the ad side were making £12K a year. I was making £25K)."

⤸

CEO of Forrest Personnel in Australia and former President of Asia-Pacific for Wunderman and numerous other global ad and branding agencies, Mike Langton, "I went into advertising after studying to be an economist, and finding there were no jobs for economists because the economy [in South Africa] was so bad! I heard about a training scholarship for ad people. The dad of an ex-girlfriend in the mid-'70s had been the CEO of J. Water Thompson in South Africa. The family had bought JWT from Cape Town to Cairo during the Great Depression and they still owned most of that. They had plenty of money, and he had this extraordinary job and lifestyle, so I thought, 'If there're management traineeships going in advertising, I'm going to try for one.'

"Back then, people didn't talk about the Halcyon days of advertising because everybody thought that they were *still* in the Halcyon days. Every agency had a pub and every Friday night everyone was getting shit-faced and hooking up with each other or crashing their company cars on the way to the next media party. It was pretty wild and crazy and I figured that I could make a difference by being better educated about the business and by running the businesses more professionally than the half-crazed buggers who seemed to run most ad agencies. 'Okay,' I said to myself, 'I'll run with this.'"

⌇

M&C Saatchi Sydney's Creative Group Head, Andy Flemming, "I was 17, and a guy from an advertising agency came into a media college I was in and stuck a product to the table. He basically gave us layout pads and fucked off for half an hour saying, 'When I come back I want you to have an ad.' It was the absolute purity of creation that I got off on.

"Within about a week, I contacted (I was probably naïve) some of the most powerful people in advertising in London. I just kept calling the fuckers until one of them agreed to see me. I exposed the guy to possibly the worst phony ad you've ever seen. It was so bad that he actually gave me two extra days and said, 'Look, please. Just take these, go home and think about them.' I loved the idea that you walk in on a Monday morning with a blank sheet of paper and at the end of a day, or one or two weeks, or a month, you'll create something that hopefully will get made and will provoke a reaction from someone. That's the dream, anyway.

"I was in London for a while in the late '80s, when advertising was the glamour job and there were hundreds and hundreds of people like me wanting to break in. So, I was sitting in the back office, doing work, often nothing, and getting paid fuck all. I saw myself possibly doing that for the next few years until maybe I got a breakthrough. From there, I got a job in Hong Kong when I was twenty-three. Then I moved to Singapore for four or five years, then Melbourne and up to Sydney. What drives me to do all of this is the dream that an idea we come up with can actually pass all boundaries and move someone across the other side of the world, as we've seen in great viral ideas. The very best ones are shared, literally, worldwide, and that's the power a good creative can wield; it's a wonderful thing.

"Creative people have so many more options now. It used to be that really brilliant creative people only had three:

- **Number one** was *fine arts*
  where you could be a painter or a serious writer.
- **Number two** was the *commercial arts*
  where you could write for TV or be an art director.
- **Number three** was *advertising*.

"That's not to say that there aren't brilliant people in advertising or that everyone in fine arts is brilliant. As a rule though, that's the way it's stratified. Well, now, there's a whole other layer that a lot of creative young people prefer to traditional advertising.

- **Number four** is the *digital world*."

﹏

Dirk Eschenbacher, former Regional Creative Director for Ogilvy & Mather Asia Pacific and current Founding Partner, CMO and creative director of ZANADU, "I started with street graffiti, as an adolescent. From there, I realized that I always wanted to have something to do with design, but I didn't want to just be a designer. I went to art school and then went on to marketing management. After graduation, I went to work at a B2B German advertising agency and started a digital department there.

"Then, beginning in '93/4, I made my first web site. In the beginning, I coded a few pages in HTML, but, very early on, quickly split the designing and the programming: the conceptual and the technical. In the beginning, it was all merged. We had to do everything. It was never really called 'digital.' At that time it was the 'Web' more than the word 'digital.'"

And that's how people looked at it back then. As a mysterious and largely irrelevant single channel that was not going to help move the brand recall or sales needles. It was thought to reach such a small percentage of the overall target audience that it became the one medium that not only did not have official branding guidelines, but where the brand gatekeepers did not enforce their rules at all. That's how little the Web was regarded by the mainstream marketing world. It was considered a greenhouse where nerds might experiment and nothing more."

⤺

Neil Leslie, Creative Director, South East Asia at Edelman Digital, "I always wanted to work in advertising. Ever since I watched the Challenger disaster on TV as a nine-year-old and decided being an astronaut might not be such a good idea.

"Uninterestingly, I chose my subjects in high school with the aim of achieving a marketing degree before beginning my advertising career as a strategic planner with DDB/Tribal in Singapore. A start for which I am eternally grateful as I learnt a great deal there that serves me well to this day as a senior creative."

⤺

President of Tribal DDB Worldwide Asia Pacific, Head of Tribal Worldwide Singapore and TEDxSingapore Lead Curator, Jeff Cheong, "I can stop being a creative, but you can never take the creative out from me. I was a bus away from being an architect. If I had boarded the bus back then, I would have become one."

⤺

Peter Moss, Creative Director for Leo Burnett Switzerland and former Group CD for Ogilvy New York, "I seriously didn't even know this industry existed. I assumed when I saw a Cadbury's Creme Egg commercial on TV, it was Cadbury's that made it. I didn't know there were these people sitting in rooms, thinking about this stuff.

"I had a friend working at MTV back then so I went over there and made some very small observations like, 'Do you people not have email?' They said, 'What are you talking about?' They put me on this little retainer. It was the equivalent to about HKD10,000 a month (£1,000) ,and that was it. I used to go in and make the computers work for them because you could not just have them on the desk for Microsoft Word, right?

"While I was doing that, I got friendly with some of the VJs there, one in particular that I used to go out with, and I started writing his shows because he thought I was funny. After about six months, I got offered a job as a Promos Producer at StarTV for the movie channel. That night I was so excited about the news I went out for a drink and, funnily enough, met Andy Greenaway and Craig Smith in the Fringe Club. I'd just got this job as a show writer and they said to me, 'We're looking for writers.' I said, 'Well, I can write.' (I could write in the computer language Pascal, but I never got specific with them). And that's how I got in for an interview. A bit of an odd one, actually.

"I remember going in to see Andy Greenaway and he asked, 'Have you brought your book [portfolio]'? I thought he was just joking around; I didn't know what a 'book' was. But he was very good to me and he set some very challenging silly assignments; and I went off to the pub and faxed them all back within the hour. Eventually he got fed up with me badgering him and gave me a job as a junior writer.

"That was it. All my Christmases came at once, when I realized that I was actually involved in *advertising*, albeit direct advertising, which wasn't the sexy bit back in the day. But that was a real revelation to me. And I stayed at Ogilvy until recently (much has changed)."

~

Scott Morrison, CEO of The Bauhub, headquartered in Toronto, "I was fortunate that I started in the advertising game and the design field when I was 16 years old. I had a summer job working in the film industry and I got to work in the art department a couple of days a week. I learned how to use computers there. Back when I was 10 years old we had a Commodore 64, and I learned to program on it. Then we got an Amiga 1000 and I remember someone saying to us, 'Oh, my god, one megabyte of RAM. What are you going to do with all of that?'

"I was programming on it with my friends when I was in grades seven and eight and by the time I was in high school, one of my friends' dads who worked in the film industry taught me how to use ProDraw and ProPaint on my Amiga. With that knowledge, I started working on movies and TV shows as summer jobs doing art department work, and by the time I was 16, I was a production assistant on my first show. By 17, I was doing computer artwork on movies and TV shows for the art department. The first year, I was just a gopher. I spent the whole year learning more about computers and by the next, I was working in the art department on *Kung Fu: The Legend Continues.*

"I was the only person in the department who knew how to work with graphics on a computer. All the other people were laying out sets using drafting tables and stuff. It was the early 1990s, so the Internet and email were only just becoming ubiquitous. The crew was still printing out production schedules and handing them to everyone. Nobody even PDFed anything back then. Everything was still print and paper. Computers were being used, don't get me wrong. It wasn't like there were no computers in 1993, there were. But there was nobody in our department experienced to do computer artwork."

⤿

Former Managing Director of M&C Saatchi Australia, Dave Whittle, "I joined the industry in the first place because I was passionate about two things: technology and marketing. I didn't know which area to focus on until I discovered that advertising provided the opportunity to pursue both.

"I went to Deakin University,[1] and they had just started the first class of Electronic Commerce as a Major. It was part of my marketing degree. It was in the early days back then, around 1995, but was pretty inspiring and interesting. That's what got me into it originally. I was aways a bit geeky. I remember vividly being at school and we always had to write out notes on books that we studied. And I remember this one geeky kid who said, 'I just scan my books in and that creates all the notes.' I was really curious about that.

"It was primitive in that you could scan any piece of text and turn it into your Word document through OCR [optical character recognition]. But I thought, 'This is amazing. This is going to save me hours and hours and hours.' I realized that technology could deliver massive efficiency and save time so you could really do things that you might enjoy.

"The other thing that happened is I remember there was a little computer lab that was pre-Internet and pretty low budget and I remember people started to fight over the computers. One of the geeks took control of the situation and pinched all the mouse balls. Remember the first mice had a roller ball inside them? Because he got bullied by the jocks, this genius geek decided to control the supply of computers. They would come in and bully him off the computer so he decided, 'Stuff you. I'll just take all the mouse balls. You

---

1   One of Australia's leading universities.

can go ahead and have the computer... but you can't operate it.' It was that moment that I saw the geeks were the kings.

"In my final year at uni I was desperate to get a corporate job, though none of the big corporations would hire me. They'd all rejected me, so I began telling everybody I met what I was passionate about and asking them if they knew anybody who was passionate about the same stuff.

"Within two weeks, two completely unrelated people answered, 'Sure, I know somebody like that. His name's Paul Cross.' Paul had finished his MBA at Melbourne University, worked with Evan Thornley at Looksmart and then decided to set up Australia's first interactive media buying agency. I tracked Paul down, convinced him to meet and he ended up offering me a job. Paul paid me about $300 a week and I eagerly worked 30-40 hour weeks part time while finishing University – and that was my first job in the industry."

∽

Martin Howard, Senior Graphic Designer at Tennyson Group in Queensland, "I was an illustrator and a layout designer in the pre-computer times where all the layouts had to be hand drawn. I was artistic and I was lucky to find a vocation that enabled me to use those skills and get paid for it. That was as simple as it was. That was my initial introduction to it, but as I got more involved, I was more interested in why people liked certain layouts, why others didn't do as well, why some were profitable, why some were very popular with the client but not with the public – that all drew me into the psychology and the methodology that some of the practitioners were looking at. And here we are."

∽

Tobias Wilson, Managing Director at @ccomplice and Leadership Council Member for the Internet Advertising Bureau (IAB) in Singapore, "Growing up, I wanted to be in advertising or a stockbroker. I'm very glad I chose the career path I did. The problem is that everybody's been picking their asses for so long, and the big guys have obviously been snapping up a lot of agencies and putting them all at the mercy of the shareholders. It has lost a lot of its sexiness because it has become about the dollar. I take a lot of staff from bigger agencies who're charging bundles for their work and snowballing their staff into working 7:00 a.m. until 12:00am three or four times a week. They're creating sweatshops.

"There's nothing sexy about a sweatshop. We should bring sexy back. Advertising should be that cool sexy thing, like it used to be."

～

Founder and Creative Partner of Goodfellas and former Y&R Brands Executive Creative Director, Patrick Low, "Since I could pick up a crayon, I couldn't stop drawing. I drew everything I saw: cars, trains, bulldozers and anything that interested me. When I completed my secondary education, I went to the Nanyang Academy of Fine Arts hoping to become an artist. However, after two years at Nanyang, and two more in mandatory military service, I decided to become a commercial artist meaning art director or designer in those days. So I enrolled in an Advertising Art program.

"Upon graduation, I was offered a job at Fortune Ad, the largest Singaporean advertising agency at the time, where I worked on Mitsubishi, IKEA and DBS Bank as an art director. After three and a half years, I joined Ogilvy for more opportunities to work on TV commercials."

～

The Wall, 1995 TV spot for Nike by Wieden + Kennedy, Amsterdam. CLIO Awards 1995 Grand Clio winner. Creative direction by Susan Hoffman, copy by Bob Moore, directed by Joe Pytka. http://youtu.be/dXH7cPlaMB8

Nike's Jordan brand Marketing Director, Sukwan Chae, "The ad that really captured and pulled me into this field was in '94, during the World Cup. Nike had this campaign called *The Wall* and it was an ad where a football was basically traveling off the walls of billboards, ginormous billboards, in all the key cities: London, Milan, Berlin, and it was Times Square, and then down to Rio. Something so simple, yet very powerful, about that ad spoke to me about the power of sports. People can say, 'It's just a TV commercial where balls are flying all over the world,' but there's something powerful about how sports, how football, was elevated in that global way.

"In downtown Shibuya, Japan they recreated one of the huge billboards right outside of Shibuya Station. I remember that moment when I got out of the station. I turned left and I saw it. There was something about that statement, that giant ad of Ian Wright and the words, *Just do it*. It captivated me and it got me into it.

At Nike, we use the word 'irreverence,' and that's truly what Nike's about. It's the culture of when you believe in something, you push it – and it's not something that's just limited to athletes, but anybody who puts their mind to it. Our corporate mission says to provide inspiration and innovation to all athletes. 'Athletes' has a little asterisk (*) on it that leads to the statement, 'If you have a body, you're an athlete.' The word athlete can come across as something very elitist. Actually, it isn't, because having a body doesn't mean that you have to have a muscular body. If you have a body, you're an athlete, therefore you can dream and you can play sports. That's the beauty of life. That's the 'just do it' spirit that makes Nike different. It's the inspirational messaging. These three words: *Just do it.*

"Then there was the whole Michael Jordan idea about how he really symbolized Nike. The list of those inspirational athletes goes on and on, whether it's in the USA, where there's Michael Jordan, Charles Barkley, John McEnroe, Andre Agassi or somewhere else. When you think about what brings all of these people together, there is a common thread. It's that they speak their minds and they do what they believe they need to do to achieve their goals. That very powerful message resonates with me.

"The image on the billboard, and on the posters on the streets, had an illustration of a ball that was popping out of the executions. There were a lot of details, and I said to myself, 'Wow, they're creating these billboards all around the world, bringing that sentiment true to life.' I think a big thing is that I was already a very big sports fan. It's a little bit of a combination, but in that moment, I would say I determined I'd like to create something that could affect people like that ad did to me.

"I had that picture for a while, then I lost it and I was really, really gutted. When I joined Nike in Oregon, I saw they had advertising databases. It was getting into Fall, so it was starting to rain, and I spent a lot of time after work on the database going through all the ads in the past and it was awesome (and I was single at the time). I remember coming across a print ad of that billboard in Shibuya, an ad of an ad. I remember finding it and getting a feeling of '*Wow.*'"

Rob Martin Murphy, Co-founder and Creative Director of Betabüro in Germany, "Having my old man in the business was the thing that got me interested in advertising. I got exposure to it as a kid growing up by visiting agencies on Friday nights or going in there at certain times. I felt the atmosphere of the place and vaguely understood what has happening because I was told the process from an early age. I understood clients come in and then we do strategy and briefs and ads. I had been walking in these agencies feeling, 'This seems like a really cool place to work.'

"Then I started thinking from quite a young age, 'That's what I like. I'd like to write ads.' I actually thought it'd be cool to come up with ideas for ads. That was it. It was, 'If that's the case, how do I go about doing that?' Which was, as you did then, to go and do AWARD School.[2]

"Because I knew I wanted to get into advertising I didn't go to university. I pretty much applied to get into AWARD School and did it and afterwards, armed with a book, knocked on doors and had interviews until someone foolishly gave me a job. And that was pretty much it."

⌁

Mike Fromowitz, former Executive Creative Director of BBDO NY and past Chairman/ECD of Batey Ads, "I got into the industry after I realized that being an artist (painter) was going to be tough life with very little money in the pocket. The life of an artist when you are a kid is tough. I was making pocket change singing folk songs in coffee house and selling popcorn and ice cream at hockey games.

"After selling only two paintings in a gallery art show, I concluded there needed to be a shift. I was attending art college at the Ontario College of Art & Design (OCAD) at the time, and hooked up with the head of the Advertising & Communications Department. He convinced me to move from painting classes to advertising. I fell in love with it then and there. He made me realize that advertising involved everything from music, art, design, type, film, photography and beautiful female models. I got my first job in Montreal, Canada, but when the French Quebecers tried to separate from the rest of the country, I decided to get myself back to Toronto.

"I spent 10 years working in some of Canada's largest ad agencies working my way up from junior to senior art director. Agencies pissed me off mostly because they never kept their word, even though they signed me

---

2 AWARD is a special course run for people who want to become copywriters/art directors in the advertising industry, with tutorials taught at advertising agencies by the professionals.

up with contracts. I was considered one of the top art directors in the country and was getting tired of what I thought was mundane work being done in the country and started looking abroad. I had no idea where I wanted to go. I do remember plenty of offers coming in from all over the USA.

"It was 1983, and I was lying on the beach in Antigua when a huge, muscular, good-looking man came up to me and said I had a long distance call from New York. I was on a plane two days later, flying there, thinking O&M [Ogilvy & Mather] was offering me a job in New York. I met with my boss-to-be, Michael Ball, then had a 25-minute meeting with David Ogilvy who worked to convince me that 'Asia was the next frontier' and that it would be 'exciting' and 'rewarding.' Needless to say, it wasn't a job in NYC; it was a job in Hong Kong. My first instinct was to hit the road. Why in the world would I ever want to go to Hong Kong – *that was in Asia* – and what kind of advertising did Asians do besides Kung Fu posters? That was no place for a professional ad guy!

"It took my wife several weeks to convince me that it would be an adventure, and hell, if I didn't like it, I could always come back. I took the job of creative director for Meridian Advertising, a small sister agency owned by O&M that took on conflicting clients (O&M had Hennessy Cognac and Meridian had Remy Martin). It took about three months to get used to the place after a severe typhoon tore into the place and wiped out every sixth tree in the colony.

"The office was crap when I arrived. That scared me too. Had I come out for a look see first, I would have said 'no way' and come home. The ceiling heights were 6' 2" and the Managing Director, a big South Afrikaner, kept banging his head on the light fixtures in the narrow brick-walled boardroom.

"The place had only about 12 people. Typesetting in English was sent out and set by a Chinese typesetter who spoke no English. I introduced the removal of 'leading' between all the letters of the typeset copy. An art director with a very sharp scalpel did it at our place. Imagine having to sit for hours cutting out fine amounts of white space between letters! I made them do it. Back then ads were all put together with paperboard and glue. There was no 'digital' at the time, of course. At least, I hadn't seen it yet. That was going to change.

"I was on a flight to London, England for a TV shoot, and a friend took me to an engraver's studio. He said there were amazing things going on in the world of retouching that I should know about. I followed him. The owner took me up to his second floor and opened the door to show me a room filled with photo retouchers. They were all sitting at their desks using scalpel blades to cut into several layers of photo film. It was extraordinary. He must have had about 30 of them and they were the number one photo-retouch service at the time.

"He took us downstairs into a single room with a big TV screen. They brought up a photo of Guinness Beer in a glass. Zoomed into the head of the beer, located a black mark, and said 'Watch how easy it is now to remove this mark from the head of the beer.' They did it in an instant, and I was amazed. That was my first recollection of the digital world creeping in to advertising.

"When I returned to Hong Kong, I was told that the Managing Director quit the company – the third one in a year to do so – and that now I would have to be the Managing Director as well as the CD. At first I said no to the offer, but when I was told that things would look bleak to our clients if we had to pull in another MD, and the clients knew me already – I was the most senior guy there after one year! In the end, I took the job but decided the title would be Chairman instead, as I had planned to hire a Managing Director to run the day to day. That never happened.

"During that time, we were still a small ad agency, and I was determined to change that by building up the agency's creative product and reputation. The company had changed its name to The Ball Partnership, when Michael Ball bought the company from O&M. I had been offered the choice of staying with O&M or joining Michael. I chose to go with Michael Ball. It was Lee Clow who said, 'It's more fun being the pirates, than the navy.'

"I focused on print ads as we had too little TV work. There was no 'digital' at the time. We began making ads that mattered and focused on getting the work recognized by the press. We entered every award show recognized by my peers, and PR became 50% of the task. By 1989, The Ball Partnership (the little office in Hong Kong) became *Advertising Age*'s International Agency of the Year (runner-up, but still highly recognized). We were cruising and winning everything in sight.

"What's important here is that our clients were proud of the work we were doing for them. Selling the work became much easier too. They listened to us because they saw big ROI.

"Back then, I would call up a client and tell him we were working on a campaign that he will love, that will be great for his business. I did some pre-sell, of course, setting the stage.

"Today, things are different. The client is now a junior-level marketing person fresh out of university that reports to an intermediate-level marketing person who knows squat that reports to a senior marketing executive who reports to the Marketing Director of the company.

"Save for the Marketing Director, none of these people can say 'yes' to anything. They sure can and do say 'no' to ideas presented to them. It's the fear of saying 'yes' and getting into trouble for having made the wrong choice. This is the number one killer of creativity today.

"In those days, there was no digital. Today everyone wants digital because they believe they need it, and that everyone is doing it and that's all that's written about in the press, or so it seems. Clients back then were more focused on 'what's the big idea' than they are today.

"Many of us have to brace ourselves when we read the newspapers each morning. It's been nothing but grim economic news. Amid roiling financial markets, a who's who of brand marketers are making moves to slash marketing spending or at least apply tougher financial discipline on what they spend. For marketers and their advertising agencies, changing economic and social developments demand a new approach to connecting with audiences and with consumers. They are thinking about marketing and communications in a radically different way. This is frightening to ad people who are afraid of change.

"On the radar are media cost-efficiencies, the fragmentation and proliferation of media, the erosion of mass markets and the rise of niche markets, the empowerment of consumers who now have an unrivaled ability to edit and avoid advertising, a consumer trend toward mass customization and personalization and the emergence of experience-based communications.

"We are seeing change that is transformational, not evolutionary. Marketers can no longer rely on TV, press, outdoor or Internet advertising alone when what is needed is powerful, holistic communication and consumer connection. The press and the Web are filled with editorials on the subject. One headline sums it up: 'To engage only traditional media today, will subject marketers to declines in efficacy and threaten their results.'

"Have you noticed? The advertising industry is changing. The convergence of television viewing and Web browsing, blurred lines between advertising and programming, and increased consumer control over access to programming and commercials are trends making that change happen. Consumers are increasingly in control of how they view, interact with and filter advertising in a multichannel world. Many continue to shift their attention away from TV, adopting more personal computer time."

⤳

Steve Hall, Publisher and Editor of *Adrants* and former Contributor to *Playboy* Magazine's *The Smoking Jacket*, "You could align the types of issues that this industry has with the types of problems that Hollywood probably has because there aren't a whole lot of industries where creativity is the product. But it's also a business and so you have the financial people and the number cruncher people trying to run the show just as much as the creative people are trying to run the show. The two never really go together because any true creativity is just that, true creativity. It's art for art's sake. You either appreciate it or you don't.

"In advertising, of course, it's *commercial* art. It's art for a purpose. It's art to make money. People go into advertising because it used to be an interesting profession. They want to be creative. In the back of their minds, they're writing a script or they're writing a blog or they're making a video. They're exercising the true creativity side of their brand. The starving artist scenario is to go out and be as creative as you want, but if nobody buys your creativity, what's the point? I didn't work on the creative side, but I worked in account management, in media, in small agencies and big agencies, so I saw it upfront. How it works, the interplay between the clients and the creative and the account manager, all of it.

"It's a little frustrating that advertising is on par with, say, a used car dealer and ambulance chaser now. We're looked down upon quite a bit."

⤳

Nimal Gunewardena, Chairman and CEO of Sri Lanka's Bates Strategic Alliance and Burson-Marsteller's Strategic Alliance PR, "Straight out of school in the '70s, my first job was in advertising at the feet of a local ad guru. Sri Lanka did not have TV when I started so I cut my teeth on writing and composing for radio. I worked on my professional qualifications in marketing (CIM) and spent 10 years in brand and marketing management with a multinational called Reckitt & Colman, and a two-year stint in an international job over in New York City.

"Finally, I went back to my first love, advertising, to head up JWT in Colombo back in Sri Lanka. Three years later, I founded my own IMC agency, which became the affiliate of Bates and Burson-Marsteller, now over 20 years ago.

"Being an affiliate has worked well for us and I've had the leeway to build the agency true to the original IMC vision, reaching out to our networks and others for the various expertise we needed. Just as we pioneered PR two decades ago, the new frontier now is digital. We've built long-term client relationships and retained key staff with loyalty. We've attracted qualified savvy youngsters to drive the new media."

⌒

Jim Speelmon, Client Services Director, Razorfish Hong Kong, former Vice President of Product Development for UniQlick, "I applied for a job and ended up going to work at Dalin Smith White in Salt Lake City, which was the forebear to Euro RSCG DSW Partners. Their early clients were Netscape and Novell Networks. I got hired to run consumer content on the Intel account. I did the Pentium III launch, which we called the *Outfitter Service*. I had to coordinate with clients and agencies in all of the geographies.

"We were doing a final review and Andy Grove was looking at it and he said something about not really being that keen on a background color, could we change it? I said, 'Well, of course we can change it if it's that important to you. You need to be aware though, that it will require that you delay the launch of the Pentium III by a couple weeks in order to complete the reshoot.' Everyone, including my bosses and all of the clients that I dealt with usually, was having a heart attack because, 'Oh my god. Somebody said *no!*' I figured you don't become Andy Grove by being stupid. He wanted to know if we could change it and the answer is, 'Yes, we can, but if we do then here are the consequences.' That is something that is sorely lacking in the industry today. Most of what I did was listen to the people on the service side, interpret what they were saying and explain it to the developers."

⏤

Former Executive Regional Director for Dentsu Asia Digital Division and Managing Director of Dentsu Möbius, Angeli Beltran: "Fortunately, there was an opportunity at American Express. American Express was the pioneer for everything direct marketing and they were looking for an intern. That's where I learned about DM [direct mail], database marketing, loyalty and CRM [customer relationship management] and that's where I had this epiphany that, 'Aha! This is exactly what I want to do!' It was the best marriage of science and creativity because you'd have both at the same time and it works; you get a response. You get to contact the customers and you can improve on those responses. I *really* enjoyed that part of the business and when I left school I pursued it. It was early days of direct marketing in the Philippines and I joined my boss in American Express then went to Ogilvy to set up Ogilvy & Mather Direct. In fact, I was employee number four in the Manila office."

⏤

George Tannenbaum, Executive Creative Director of R/GA NYC, "I often think that before you hire someone in this business you have to go to a grocery store with them or a spice market or something like that, because in my father's agency there was always a general excitement about the products: what kind they were, how they were packaged, how they were put on a shelf, what they do, how they're talked about and how they looked and felt. You either have it or you don't. You're either excited by consumerism or you don't know consumerism.

"In my father's agency there was always that excitement there. They were doing something amazing and the idea of having it on TV seemed awfully cool to me as a kid – and still does to tell you the truth. There's still a thrill when you have something on TV or in the newspaper. That hasn't changed for me. People like me get excited when new computers come out or new car models or even a new cereal and they have a gusto, a sense of excitement, about products and consumption that are important for this business.

"It could be a of function of age because I'm with fewer young people, and I say this figuratively, but today there seems to be more of an academic approach to solving creative problems than a visceral one and some of that excitement is gone, which is unfortunate."

~

Steve Elrick, Executive Creative Director at BBH, "I elbowed my way into this industry and found a place because it was, and still is, something of a meritocracy. Talent will win out. Sure, some majorly talentless pricks will get on and do well too, but that's probably the story in any business. There's that slightly unfashionable old-school belief I have that real talent amplified by a massive amount of hard work will get you somewhere. That's George Lois' big message too. Old school – sorry, I just summed up *Outliers* by Malcolm Gladwell.

"I was a young, working-class kid, from a small town in the North Of Scotland. I liked to write. For a while I wanted to emulate my oldest brother and become a journalist. Didn't happen. So I slid into getting a job as a copy-writer and it felt *right* somehow. As Vonnegut would say: *and so it goes.*"

~

And so it went for a very long time, but has necessarily gone in a different direction today and for the foreseeable future. The general culture is still largely a meritocracy, but the purpose has shifted from using the knowledge to arrange a solid structure for holding together a talented team with a "the sky's the limit" outlook, way over to simply making sure the best people available within the budget are running the campaign or project until it is over. When the assignment has concluded, whether it's six weeks or six months, it is more common than not for the team to be disbanded all the way out of the agency and into other jobs. If the client switches agencies, then entire swaths of dedicated full-time employees will find that outside of a bit of severance, there is little to distinguish them from the legions of equally hard working and equally unemployed contract workers who didn't have health benefits.

That dramatically changes the dynamics for what makes advertising an appealing career and for the types of people it attracts. Most of us who dedicated ourselves to it in the past did so because we had an itch, a need, to use the right side of our brains as much as possible; and if you're someone with a rich imagination and a different way of looking at the world, you're very likely to have trouble doing things in the expected fashion. Many of advertising's success stories entered the industry using a variety of techniques ranging from: hanging around with people in the business and simply asking for an opportunity, to being recognized for having a unique take on the things around them and being given a shot, to proving themselves by putting together some work and pitching it to a client or creative director, perhaps unasked. The beauty was (and still can be) in how like-minded people recognized that itch in one another and gave him or her the chance to scratch it; and to help the novice learn how to channel gut and instinct into something usefully memorable and effective, honing their raw talent into a razor sharp commercial craft.

Chapter 2: When Advertising Was a Hands-on Craft

Before computers could read our minds and provide us with everything we'd ever want, there were those who had the job of building brands and creating messages in any number of forms that might capture someone's limited attention for a moment. The processes, tools, skills, strategies, and talents employed to conceive and execute them were all perfected over years of trial and error, research, study, and actual doing. These are the crafts that used to be held in high regard within the agencies, amongst competitors and are what marketing organizations used to seek out and happily purchase to reach their business goals. Most everyone understood what the end game was and strived to play their role to the best of their ability — and personalities — to bring about the client's stated desired results.

It may have been as clear cut as that, but there was still a true art to the way people thought about and then executed each part of an ad, no matter the medium. Instead of worrying about whether something would be able to load and be seen by the specific target audience or concerning ourselves with how they might interact with or share it across multiple screens, we used to focus on what we were saying and how we could bring the message to life in unexpectedly brilliant forms, using our inspiration, ingenuity and hands. There were complex and refined tools for each part of this job and experts who could use them to produce creatively innovative messaging magic that did the trick for the bottom line and the brand.

Photoshop, Illustrator, HTML5, CSS3, After Effects, and the rest are all powerful modern instruments, fundamentally no different than what art directors, editors, and designers were using before everything physical became obsolete. We should have no issue with the march of technology when it comes to craft unless it makes us too lazy to execute with finesse, polish, style, artistry —whatever you'd like to call that quality that separates great from okay — since some may think, "What's the point of spending hours manually making something fantastic if the program can do it automatically to an acceptable degree in much less time?" Because time is no longer anyone's friend. No one in this field is given time for anything anymore. No time to do research and planning, no time for a long-term strategy, no time for development, no time to put together partnerships, no time for testing, no time to get a campaign rolling and give it a chance to get some momentum, no time for a good job. Sadly, even very little time for family and friends outside of the business.

We've so thoroughly convinced our clients that computers can help us do things so much more efficiently that they now believe timelines can be compressed to a fraction of what they used to be. Many have expressed, with the hard-headed logic of the person footing the bill, that if it takes three months to produce a television commercial it should take only a month to create a full digital campaign. There is an almost willful ignorance to stubbornly not understanding the complexities that go into virtual deliverables because they have no literal weight to them. As if you can just type instructions for what should happen and the devices "make it so" instead of requiring a number of specialized disciplines and crafts people to work together; sometimes dreaming up and building things that have never existed before.

Fundamentally, nothing has changed. Clients still have goals and agencies still have the experts and the tools they can use to realize them. However, in reality, as pressures of finance, time, and perception force agencies to do a "just good enough" job, these commercial artists and keen thinkers are likely to not be required, even if they could stick around and stomach lowering the bar to the new regulation height.

～

Paul Kwong, former Group Creative Director for Saatchi & Saatchi New York and former Creative at McCann Erickson NYC, APL NYC, and GSD&M, "In the old days you had to hand draw your own typefaces directly onto comps. Everything was done by hand: marker coloring, greeking, drawing, etc. Your best friend was a copy machine that blew things up or shrunk images, but usually only up to 127% or down to 64% .

"There was a real sense and learning of design and telling a story via colors, type, images, etc. Yes, great work is being done today, probably the same amount as always. What's missing are folks who really understand how to design or art direct.

"Picking a font or color that just happens to be loaded on your computer is not designing. You've got to find the right typeface with a particular serif, or thick and thins, that really helps tell the story of the piece you're working on. Knowing how to kern type wouldn't hurt either. Anyway, there's a lot less craftsmanship nowadays. Things are more forgiving in this digital world. The more raw or spontaneous or less manufactured something is, that's good."

～

Mike Fromowitz, "The Art Director had to have trade skills that included knowledge in typography, the printing process, photography, illustration, marking up type, mechanical art production, and more. These were not skills that just anybody could do."

⤳

Andy Greenaway, "The principles of communication are the same as they've always been. It's the channels, technology and intensity of engagement that has changed. I still think the best way to generate ideas is with a big, fat marker and an A2 layout pad. Trying to generate ideas on a computer screen limits your thinking. That's not to say that the type of thinking should be different. As we all know, it's not about two-dimensional ideas anymore (like a print ad). It's about generating multi-dimensional ideas that can be delivered through multi-channels.

"Some of the old direct marketing skills are as relevant now as they ever were. However, I don't see many people around with those skills. The last people to wield the classic DM techniques of the '80s are from my generation (oldies). I call them last of the Direct Marketing Jedis. An awful lot of training needs to be brought back into the industry. Teaching the young 'uns how to write copy that sells, for instance, is an imperative, I believe. That said, some people are in a delusional bubble and they'll just disappear.

"At O&M Direct, I had to do everything: art direction, visuals, which were done with markers, and my own mock-ups. In the DM business there was a lot of long copy stuff, so when it came to typesetting you had to work out the word count, type size and leading all by hand.

"I started in the business in 1985. Macs didn't come into our office until 1990. In fact, we had hired a typographer who convinced the agency to invest in a £250,000 machine to do typesetting and bromides. The thing came with about a thousand glass plates that had type etched on them in different sizes.

"He was dismissive of the Mac and tried to convince all of us the quality was terrible. He lasted one more year in the agency and the equipment he'd bought was sold for £10,000.

"The typesetting studio we used to use only lasted another five years after the introduction of the Mac. John, the owner of the studio, had to trade his Porsche in for a Ford. He eventually closed down his business and opened a sandwich shop.

"The thing I loved about the old world was you had time. A client couldn't demand an ad in one hour because it was physically impossible to do. Typesetting took at least three days. Photographs had to be processed, which took two days. If you needed retouching, it would take a week, because all the retouching was done by hand."

⌒

Jeff Cheong, "I still pitch with my copic markers and it brings a certain freshness to the game. I've worked with a few traditionalists. They have honed their craft and that's something a lot of young creatives lack. It's about finding their niche and bringing them to the new world. Many of them are still relevant in this day and age, and the greatest joy is to see how they have lifted the quality of the work with razor-sharp copy and superb craft.

Copic Marker System by Too, Japan.

"There is also still some magic in presentations given on boards. The audience is focused on you as you pace up and down, although, sometimes, in order to demonstrate a technology, you'd need the audience to participate to appreciate it. That's where we go all out to build a prototype.

"I see presentations as the training ground for my younger team. There are various methods and theatrics we use. In my agency no two presentations are alike. I would not allow that to happen.

"Teamwork and chemistry show through the presentation. I believe that's where the clients see the soul of the folks that will be working on their business."

⎯

Paul Kwong, "I'm sure the lack of knowledge or maturity is the same as it's always been. It's just now there's no time to slow down the process or take time to teach younger folks. Who even gets to go to lunch anymore? It's the lack of time and the speed which things are promised and expected, due to technology, that is causing a lot of the teaching and learning curve."

⎯

Chris Kyme: "In those days everything was crafted. Ideas were always presented as roughs, and once a print concept got approved it was passed to the typographer. We worked so hard on small details. The same with TV. We worked on as many concepts as possible based on a brief for about two weeks. Once an idea was given go ahead to show a client, I would take about another week crafting a script, word by word. I still love writing a good piece of copy. I used to spend three or four days getting the opening paragraphs just right."

⎯

Rob Martin Murphy, "Those were the days we would write the script, video and audio in two columns on a piece of paper and then hand those scripts over. That was '90 or '91. Some people might've wanted to type their stuff, but I remember I was writing it on paper and then the assistant would type it. We had a typographer who had all the Macs and stuff there in his office. It was that crossover period.

"Jump about two years to '93 to '95. At some point there, you were doing your own scripts. It was after the mid- to late '90s when you started to have your own computer to do your own stuff.

"It's funny. Talking about computers, my old man was at the Campaign Palace in Sydney when they had the Apple account. He was there from '82 to '84 and I remember walking into their offices and seeing the Apple Lisa and the //e. The creative department might've had them there as things to know about and tinker around with, but they weren't using them for doing any of their work. It was quite a nice little aside, put over there on the mantelpiece."

∽

Åsk Wäppling, "Sherlock Holmes is the logical dude and Watson is a bit of a hare-brain in most variants. I was more Sherlock Holmes. If I received a brief on something I would disappear into a library somewhere in the city for hours to just research the hell out of stuff. There weren't planners back then that were giving you that. In some ways that was better because planners filter through things and you may lose inspiration.

"I remember when I was in school in London they always put out all the newspapers in the morning and we read every single one. In the UK the newspapers are very different politically so you read tabloids, you read broadsheets for tourists, and really we had to read all of them. That's what we did or else you wouldn't know how to talk to your potential customer. That's what we did every morning and I did that as a habit everywhere I worked. I worked in Holland and I read the newspapers there every morning and everybody wondered aloud to me, 'Why do you keep doing that?' I'd answer, 'If I don't I won't know how to talk to people. I won't know what's on their minds.' Today it seems like people are only reading the headlines."

∽

Design and Illustration Lecturer at Texas State University and Associate Creative Director at Heresy in Austin, Larry Goode, "One morning in 1988 I walked into my office at the design firm where I was working and strategically placed on my desk (next to the drafting table) was an Apple desktop computer (Mac SE?). Apparently the partners of the firm thought that because I was one of the youngest members of the staff, I would have a natural inclination to work this new wonder machine. Back then there was no manual or online tutorials nor anyone to ask advice. It was completely new territory and I was the leader of the digital way in our office. Once I figured out how to turn it on I opened the only program on the machine, Aldus FreeHand 1.0. I made a circle and filled it black. Oh, the joy!

"Today this sounds like the simplest thing that can be achieved using any number of applications, but in 1988 it was like discovering fire. The day before my entry into the computer age I would have had to make the same circle using either a ruling pen or cut overlays with a compass.

"For the designers' edification whose career started in the mid-'90s, all printed pieces required what were known as 'mechanicals': Letramax board with overlapping plastic sheets that designated areas of color, photo stats logos, black and white photos and type headlines that were held together with tape, wax, and spray mount – all covered with pencil instructions. Indeed there were many nights that I went home covered in a thick layer of sticky wax and spray mount (carcinogens be damned).

"The production of mechanicals was a laborious process that required a thorough knowledge of the printing process and how to nudge temperamental press operators into getting the color variation you wanted (I found a six-pack or donuts did the trick).

"Also there was the issue of type. The writer delivered the copy in typed pages and the designer had to go through the copy line by line, designating the font, point size and leading, italic, bold and roman, and so forth. The marked-up copy was then sent to the typesetter who output the finished pages, called 'galleys,' to the designer who pasted them onto the mechanical boards.

"If you had color photos then the photos were sent to the color separator who output four pieces of film (cyan, magenta, yellow, and black) and the printer stripped them into the film made from the overlays on the mechanicals. Then plates were made from the film and the final piece was printed from the plates.

"Whew! Heaven forbid there was a typo in the piece. I lived in fear of seeing typos or wrong phone numbers at the press check. In any event, this illustrates the amount of work just in the production of a printed piece, never mind the design part that the mechanicals had to bring to life. There were a thousand other details, such as bidding the job, traveling to the printer in another state or country for press checks, physically getting the client proofs for approval while the grumpy pressmen are waiting to go to lunch. Printing something was a skill that few people possessed and, in the age of desktop printing, has been lost.

"Then there was the design process in 1988. Like today there were walls covered in sketches produced on tracing paper in pencil. However, unlike today, the concepts had to be nailed down at the pencil stage because there were no computers to refine ideas instantly for evaluation.

"The computer caused unexpected pitfalls at first. One of the first things I remember was bending type in funny shapes. Modernist rules of type aside, and before the excuse of post modernism, it was just plain fun to mangle type.

"My employers thought it was a thing of wonder, and for a while our design was at the mercy of FreeHand. We often confused good design with the ability to do anything crazy with type. Even today with my students I see the same common mistake of jumping onto the computer with a half-developed idea and thinking that a piece of design that looks finished because of the preciseness of the computer is the best solution to solve the design problem.

"It was fortunate that we only had five fonts to work with, which limited our type folly. After that, many of the computers purchased for the office ended up gathering dust on the floor under the designer's desk. The old-guard designer was still grasping at the familiar and comfortable drafting table, t-square and triangle.

"It became apparent that the reason our firm bought as many computers as they did was to impress clients with our ability to think far ahead of the competition. They even had impressive information graphics for their self-promotion brochures showing flow charts of all the computers and printers in the office. Just *having* the computers became more important than *using* them, the way it was with corporations and early web sites.

"The real potential of the computer in our office was not realized until a few years later when a new crop of young designers, yet to have old-school design skills set in their bones, dusted off the computers, found them wanting, and then demanded newer and faster Macs.

"There were many things I miss about the old days before the introduction of the desktop computer. I miss the wonder that non-designers would have when I told them that I was a designer and I knew how to get things printed. It was a sort of magic to most people. Today, of course, everyone can print anything with ease, be it on personal printers or at the local print shop using digital printing.

"Then there was the issue of time. I miss the amount of time we had to develop concepts in pre-email, file-transfer days. I don't call today the 'digital age,' I call it the 'hurry up because if you didn't design it and print it today, then you are a bad designer' age. Who cares what it looks like if it made the client happy? *Just finish it **now!***

"Of course in 1988 there was bad design, as much as today, and clients that wanted it in a hurry. Because of the nature of the business in the '80s, we could create time. Presentations had to be put together by hand which took time; packages had to be shipped, which would take at least a day or two; production might grind to a halt because the typesetter had the flu. We had time to make more time by manipulating these events and therefore have more room to consider and refine the design and production. Clients were used to the ample amount of time it took from signing the contract to seeing the first round of concepts. However, the client of today, because of the instantaneous nature of the computer and the information infrastructure, expects faster, but still great work to be delivered. The old adage, you can have two of the three— fast, cheap, and good – no longer applies. With the advent of digital, it seems three out of three is the expected norm.

"Being a designer or art director today is a tough gig. It is like doing great work on a tiny ship in an ocean of bad design and advertising, and trying to be noticed. The Designer, art director, creative director can barely be heard or found in the fast-good-AND-cheap new world. Because everyone claims to be a designer and can print or upload anything, a huge amount of bad design has overwhelmed the aesthetic of the general population. In 1988, the person in the street, subconsciously or consciously, could probably sense the difference between good and bad design or between effective and non-effective design. Today, the sense of good design has been lost.

"The paradox of today's information age is that the speed of producing design has gone up, but this faster pace has increased the amount of useless and counterproductive advertising and design that blot the landscape. The public is pliable and is accepting design and advertising as neither good nor bad. Like a worn-out building, they're now a part of the landscape."

〜

Patrick Low, "I was fortunate to have seen and experienced the advent of the digital revolution. In those days, we had finished artists in the studio doing paste-ups on FAs (finished art). Elements of the print ad were pasted on boards with glue called Cow Gum. The copy had to be typeset and printed on bromide paper and then pasted on the board together with the other elements, including photographs and illustrations.

"Headlines could also be typeset, but special fonts required transfers called Letrasets. Needless to say, you had to use the right point size. Then there was the art of typography, which involved details like kerning and leading. Today, we can do all that with a few clicks on our computer keyboard. Back then, we had to cut the typesetting with a knife and move the letters or sentences with the aid of some Cow Gum and lighter fluid. This laborious process might have taken a week to produce an ad that will normally take an artist a few minutes on a Mac.

"In fact, one of my first jobs at Ogilvy back in 1982 was on a poster campaign for Philips. One of them featured a giant vacuum cleaner in the sea moving menacingly towards the Singapore skyline. To create the poster, I had to position the shot of the vacuum cleaner onto the skyline image using photocopies and tracings. Then with the elements in position with the help of scotch tape, I had to send it together with the transparencies to a retoucher who would piece them together with a brush. The whole process took two weeks.

"In TV commercials, the most significant change has been in postproduction. I remember having to travel to Australia to post my films. It was great for collecting air miles, among other things. The Steenbeck was the machine editors relied on to cut their films, and it literally cut them. Strips of films were hung beside the Steenbeck to be re-cut frame by frame, a process that took days instead of hours, with editors relying more on intuition than technical skills. We had no clue how dissolves and other simple effects would work in the editing stage until it was finished.

A Steenbeck flatbed film-editing suite. By DRs Kulturarvsprojekt from Copenhagen, Denmark

"The transformation was quick, though. I remembered editors swearing that they would never switch to digital, but six months later when I went back to Australia for another job, I saw the editors working on their Macs next to their retired Steenbecks [film-editing suites].

"It took about two weeks of postproduction to complete a 30-second spot. Today, we can do it in minutes on a desktop. We can also view simple effects like dissolves instantly.

"When we finally finished the film that took hours in an online suite, it had to be transferred to a huge tape called a Betacam SP, which was the professional video tape format. This bulky tape could only be played through a bulky Betacam SP player.

"There was also the audio bit, which I miss most now. When we recorded music, we had real musicians in a studio instead of music created by computer software. Imagine my disappointment when I arrived at the studio in Sydney one day and found the musician typing on his laptop instead of playing the keyboard.

"Looking back, besides the live musicians, the things I miss most were the traveling and sightseeing."

Founder of Digital Caffeine and former Creative Director for AOL's advertising.com and Vivendi Universal, Susan Kim, "I do think it's still mostly about problem solving. It's just sometimes the deadlines can be so aggressive, and I am talking more about the developers and creatives, but the deadlines can be so aggressive, we end up focusing on the wrong thing. You want to solve a problem, but instead it's, 'I just have to get this done.' Not because it's something that's great that you want to proudly put out there, but because there's a deadline – and no one likes to work like that.

"We want to solve real problems. When you just have these crushing deadlines over and over, when you've got to get this out, when you've got to get this web site done, you are going to be more concerned with getting it finished, not how effective it's going to be for the client or the people using it.

"Most account or sales people didn't have the respect, the knowledge, the understanding, or even the concern about what it took to pull off a digital campaign versus print or TV. That is one constant that will always be with us. It was there in the early digital days, and it certainly hasn't changed at all, except I feel like it's even speeded up more because you can only make a TV commercial so fast. You know, there are actual logistics like getting director, casting, editing. Whereas with digital you can make a complete piece of crap fairly quickly."

☙

Executive Creative Director of Y&R Austin, Diane McKinnon, "David Sable, the CEO of Y&R Brands, writes that 'Everything is digital, but digital is not everything.' With some of the younger creatives and people coming into the business, there is a default attitude of the technology overtaking everything where, really, it's the technology that is in service of the relationship.

"There's a default position that the technology is the driver versus the experience and the relationship. The technology is really just a means by which we experience the relationship. It's not the relationship. It's the nature of youth and change that you think what you're doing and what you're bringing is going to revolutionize – and some of it does. But it still has to do with creating an emotional connection between your brand and the consumer. This is where the big agencies still want to stand on some aspect of their tradition or their provenance. The technology is the means to that, and if you've become over obsessed with how the technology works, and are not focused on the end game of what the relationship is, then the technology doesn't really serve you well."

⤸

Barry Wong, former Executive Creative Director for MRM Worldwide China & McCann Worldgroup Beijing and current Founding & Managing Partner of nhammm Co.Ltd, "The advent of technology has led to a couple of different observations in my own experience. I couldn't quite put a finger if it has been for the positive or negative. Maybe a fair statement is, 'You win some, you lose some.'

"Why do I say that? There is quite an apparent creative divide that happened with the increasing use of technology. Traditional folk who don't get it don't want to immerse to try and get it. They're constantly thinking that digital is just an 'oh, by the way.' The digital folks who get it think the traditional folks who don't get it are dinosaurs. As such, very rarely do you find creatives who come to the table with an open mind holding agnostic views.

"Good creatives with craft that spans the spectrum still exist, but it's a needle-in-the- haystack situation. Traditional creatives don't really try to make an effort to design for digital, always imposing a traditional mindset of a poster, an editorial, a TVC – hardly usable for digital channels. Conversely, the digital creatives have forgotten about the true beauty of craft, often adopting a constrained style. Has the craft suffered? Hell, yeah it has."

⤸

Steve Elrick, "Learning my craft was learning it from the ground up: small space ads, brochures, direct, everything smaller agencies turned their hands to then, and everything that filtered down to the junior creatives. I was glad to get the opportunity to do it, and that stuck with me. Much later in Hong Kong, for instance, my partner, Phil Marchington, and I were a senior team, but we grabbed hold of every brief in that agency if we thought we could add something. We usually did. We got better by *doing*.

"The craft of writing was writing and trying to learn from the people who were shit hot at it. How could you *not* learn about writing when Neil French was your boss?"

Paul Ruta, independent writer and creative director from Toronto and former Creative Director for M&C Saatchi in Singapore, "The smoke-signal guys (SSGs) and the hollow-log guys (HLGs) were at it again, bickering over the better way to share information. The SSGs tended to be the older villagers steeped in tradition that were always right because they've always been right.

"It takes years of learning to send well-crafted smoke signals, they claimed, while any fresh idiot can bang on a log. 'Smoke signals are slow and carcinogenic,' replied the HLGs, and they're useless at night. Hollow logs are 24/7. They're user-friendly and eco-friendly. They're ideal for urgent messaging back and forth between villages. The SSGs covered their ears and hummed, fearing that perhaps the era of the smoke signal was indeed drawing to an end.

"Believing they had little to lose, the SSGs made a suggestion. 'Let us settle this once and for all,' they said to their rivals. 'Let us go together and ask the Great Wise Chief (GWC).' The HLGs agreed, though they had secret worries of their own: throughout the land were rumors of upstart papyrus-writers, yodelers, bell-ringers, horn-blowers, pigeon-trainers, stone-chiselers, and all manner of newfangled messaging platforms.

"That evening, the SSGs and the HLGs entered the GWC's tent just as he was uploading new images to his blog. The GWC folded his laptop and heard both sides of the argument. The smelly smoke this. The noisy logs that. After listening patiently for some time, the GWC spoke. 'I don't care which of you has the better way to send a message,' he said, 'I only wonder if either of you has a message worth sending.'"

Allegiance to the Culture

During the middle of the last century, each of the major collections of talented creative thinkers (e.g., McCann Erickson, Ogilvy & Mather, Ted Bates, J. Walter Thompson) established a unique culture that reflected their personalities, a specific process for selling and producing work, and a secure environment where you or I might like to spend our entire careers with our new cohorts. Unlike teams thrust together in the chaotic creative environment of *Saturday Night Live*'s writing pool, twentieth-century agency cultures meant that partnerships between art directors and writers might last for decades. Even if partners were sometimes to be enticed to leave the nest where they started for other, slightly-more-profitable nests, they stuck together because they learned the craft together the same way. These ways of thinking about advertising and how to approach it were so different that if you were to move from Doyle Dane Bernbach to Lord & Thomas to J. Walter Thompson to any established firm back then, you'd likely experience culture shock: yet another good reason to devote yourself to the place where you cut your teeth and the team you worked and played so hard with.

The cultures within the agencies became critical for allowing everyone to move away from doing the same old thing over and over, the way most of us are trained in school and what most everyone else faces in the workplace. To build a structured business around creativity, you need to not just support, but fuel the different methods people require for mining or harnessing it, whether they are experienced or just starting out with all of the potential in the world.

For when you are young and filled with beans and dreams, you tend to imagine the advertising world as a nonstop party of ideas, hilarity, glamorous travel, and the most interesting people in the world. You think about how sweet it will be to have people pay you to blue-sky fun concepts because, you know, humor sells, although maybe occasionally you'll tell a really emotional story to show you have more than that one side. Plus, not all clients probably have as sharp a sense of humor and you, my friend, are no prima donna; you are flexible. A real team player.

The reality of today's big advertising agency conjures up a scene that is more closely in line with Monty Python's *The Crimson Permanent Assurance* prologue to their feature film, *The Meaning of Life*. The once-proud firm of talented employees shackled to their desks by their new corporate takeover masters, living out their days in weary drudgery, mindlessly attacking each repetitive and uninspiring task with the sole purpose of creating revenue for the dread Board and its coterie of shareholders. Each defeated soul muttering under his or her listless breath either a half-hearted plan of escape to a new career or regret for having cared enough about the work to have caught the attention of the men with the money in the first place.

To be fair to our naïve idealist younger selves, those desired creative agency environments did and *do* exist. They're not all sweat shops and Terry Gilliam-designed corporate takeover pirate ships. If you are lucky enough to come across like-minded professionals that enjoy each other's offbeat sense of humor and playfulness, then you absolutely can enjoy yourself as you help your clients hit their goals. You will be worked hard, but there's a chance you'll have some measure of family or social life.

Back before the industry started on the path it is now confidently sailing down, ad agencies actually thought of their staff and catered to their needs as human beings. People were recognized as valuable resources — the precious product the company was selling for a big mark up — and while it may have been a far cry from the treatment of movie stars, employees were actually factored into the decisions that were made, even when it came to those of the budget. This gave them an identity and fostered an actual, honest-to-goodness relationship between staff and agency that was based on a rare item known as mutual respect.

The most striking aspect of a *genuine* corporate culture is that it cultivates loyalty that is organic in the vein of being drawn to supporting your school or city's sports teams. You are a part of their triumphs and defeats whether you did something tangible or you were simply a part of the whole that defines the agency. If the ethos is sincere, the organization will embody the values it represents and reciprocate via mentorship, helping you grow into the most skilled and useful employee you are capable of becoming. If it is just something they tell you about in your interview, then you will likely be left to sink or swim on your own, if the sharks don't get you while you're busily treading water.

The problems begin to creep in when you are no longer answerable to only each other and your client. As you begin to grow and achieve success by way of reputation, you first become beholden to the needs of a larger staff (many of whom are not hands-on craftspeople, but executive/middle management and support who may or may not care so much about the *work*), and then that need eventually causes you to face a holding company that has now bought the agency with the promise of a much easier life for you and your partners and stability for all of those people who now look to you for their livelihoods and career paths.

And, before you know it, you are all chained in soul-sucking cubicles, taking creative orders from analysts and procurement clerks, spending your days on a production assembly line that you are constantly told to "optimize," as if you're a mechanic trying to tune up an engine instead of someone who wanted a life of solving creative problems for people who might need and appreciate your abilities. You don't even have the benefit of a mindless 9-5 job for two reasons: one) people are expected to get to the office these days for any profession by 8 am at the latest; and two) in advertising, if you work fewer than 80 hours a week, you will be replaced by someone with real commitment to increasing shareholder value — most likely in Bangladesh or Costa Rica.

We need to band together like those imprisoned clerks on *The Crimson Permanent Assurance*; fashion our proportion wheels, X-Acto blades, waxing machines, and markers into weapons; and take our industry back from the number crunchers, before we don't have the energy to make a fifth truly unnecessary revision to a layout, let alone reclaim our craft.

〜

Steve Hall, "Back in the day, when our fathers and grandfathers were getting out of college, they would get a job and they would work for the same company their entire lives. There was dedication and honor and responsibility and it was a two-way street between employer and employee. And when your employee left, the company took care of the employee. Now it's become very fickle and everyone financially is on his or her own. They've got to do what they can do to move ahead and make more money and save more money, and not many companies do pensions anymore. We have 401(k)s and so you've got to invest your own money. You've got to plan ahead for your own retirement. You can't rely on the company taking care of you.

"There used to be a different kind of bond when I put in years of service. I knew the company was going to take care of me and the company even said, 'This person's been working for us for 20 years. We've got to take care of them. They were loyal, responsible, effective contributors to the company.' That's changed. For those leaving in six months, they don't have anything. They don't have a vested interest in anything. They're just working on the project that's on their desk right now and they're working on that project so they can add it to their portfolio and use it and move on to their next job. They don't have the loyalty necessarily to stay at that company. There's no reason because the loyalty is gone in both directions, and it's the shuffling of the chairs on the Titanic. It's kind of messy, if you ask me."

〜

Former Chairman and CEO of Hoffman/Lewis, Bob Hoffman aka The Ad Contrarian, "When I first started in the business, Y&R had the largest share of the advertising market in the US. They had a 1.5 share and controlled 1.5% of the advertising in the US. Now there are four large entities that control over 70% of the advertising in the US (three, now that Omnicom and Publicis have merged). I don't think it's healthy.

"Unfortunately, it's not just the advertising industry. Many industries in the US that once were the domain of craftspeople are now the domain of very large industrialists and financiers who have created a very concentrated ownership of an industry. It's not healthy, it's not good, and I don't like it, but I don't know what we're going to do about it.

"What has happened in the past 15, 20 years is that very large entities run by people who are not crafts people, who're not copywriters and art directors or researchers or account people or planners, but are financial people and are now running these very large craft-based entities. It has created a completely different culture and a completely different way of operating that has resulted in an industry that doesn't know who it is anymore, doesn't know what it's supposed to be doing anymore. The big picture to me is that that's what has happened, and I would love to be able to say that I see that changing in the future, but, frankly, I don't, and if anything, it's getting worse."

⌇

Executive Vice President of Agency Relations & Education at the 4As (American Association of Advertising Agencies), Jennifer Seidel, "One of the reasons I joined the 4As is because I wanted to have a family, and global account management at a big agency was just not conducive to that. Unfortunately, many women leave the business entirely because they don't feel they have a choice or opportunity to balance the 24x7 demands. If I *do* decide to go back to an agency, I would probably choose a small to midsize, entrepreneurial place where I can contribute my expertise and add value but that doesn't demand that I give everything I have just to survive."

⌇

Mike Langton, "What has to happen is that those handful who are starting their own agencies have got to set and maintain standards and stick to their guns, like John Hunt and Reg Lascaris and other great people of that ilk who've said, 'I'm not going to take their business because they're a bunch of barbarians who will bully my staff and colleagues and will never let a decent ad get made for them.' Do not go pitching after that stuff.

"When you are working in a big holding company, you will be told, 'You have to pitch.' You will be compelled to pitch for the next colossal multination shopping their way though the agencies whether you like it or not, whether it's going to be culturally disastrous for the agency or not.

"Intel is a perfect example. Many I know feel going after the Intel business is like taking a radioactive poison because once you've worked on it nobody wants to go anywhere near you in case they get contaminated. Going after the Dell business seems like taking something faster acting. The tech companies have been awful – look how many top agencies Microsoft has worked with and the absolutely abysmal ads they've extracted from some of the greatest minds.

"When you are told you have to go and pitch for some of these things, well, some of the smarter people will run screaming from the building. Bad enough to have to pitch for it and then you have to work on it!? That can be really soul-destroying.

"I landed up in a situation where I was told I had to be in a pre-pitch chemistry meeting with Intel on the 24th of December in Hong Kong. I said, 'Sorry, I'm not going to be there. I'm going to be away on vacation with my wife and children,' and I had my ass torn out for me by headquarters. It's the main reason I left that job. I was told, 'No. You don't have a choice in this matter. You are going to be there.'

"Picture this. I landed home in Singapore back from China to find this cryptic 'You will be in Hong Kong on 24th December' email from HQ. I walked into the house and said to my then wife, Sally, 'I've been told to be in Hong Kong on the 24th of December for a chemistry meeting. I've got to fly up there on the 23rd and I'll fly back to Singapore again after.' She blew up and stormed out of the house with our children incandescent with rage and said, 'That's it. I'm leaving you.'

"I sputtered, 'I haven't even said I'm going.' She replied, 'I don't care. The fact that you haven't told me that you've refused tells me everything I need to know.' I called my illustrious leader and said, 'I'm not going. Scott says he's OK to fly down from Beijing and Ken offered to fly up from Singapore so you'll have two really great people there in my place but that's it. Now I have to find my wife and children, so good night.'

"What the fuck kind of client company management has so little wisdom that they say, 'Well hell, we're going to have ourselves this little chemistry meeting on Christmas Eve.' What are they thinking? Are they fishing for masochistic fools to work on their business?

"What the fuck is the agency management thinking that they breathlessly pant 'Okay'? They must be insane. The industry has to put a stop to that shit. Sadly, I do not think that there's much hope out there. The marketing communications industry has fallen to such a low level that it has burnt itself to ashes and risen in a new form. We're in the era of the media agencies, the AB-tested, sell-it-cheap high-speed trading era, where decisions-makers have no grasp of communication and no understanding of how to brief for and elicit brilliant creative ideas whatsoever. It seems like they don't understand the value of content or how it works or why, at all."

⌒

Tobias Wilson, "We're all consumers. The agencies are getting this feeling of frustration from their clients, that the work isn't creative enough or it's too expensive or it takes too long. That's where the revolution in the ad business is starting to happen.

"Consumers are acting up against brands [by being vocal on social media] and there's no escape from that. It has been said that marketer-led revolutions were the first stage of working with one of the first large agencies, BBDO, Saatchi, Y&R or whatever, but now they're starting to lose their shine for the marketers of today.

"When I started, I had friends in marketing that would tell me how they love working with Ogilvy or relate how, 'Saatchi took us out for lunch.' That was part of the wank of being a big-end marketer. Now it's really starting to come down to results, and what's become common is that marketers are now getting their asses chewed out when campaigns don't work. Suddenly those lunches are becoming less important because they don't really help to achieve anything. I'm pretty sure going out for a nice lunch doesn't increase campaign effectiveness, but I'm definitely sure that if you don't meet your targets for three quarters in a row, it's over.

"The big marketers getting smarter is definitely a trend we're seeing, and what do you attribute that to? Because... they're going to the same schools. They're interning at the same places. They're rising up through the same ranks. It's become a lot more difficult and a lot more scientific to be the Marketing Director these days, and it also is happening to the CEO. The business landscape is certainly changing."

～

Craig Mapleston, Managing Director of iris Singapore, "Those were pretty special days. We had an integrated team before the term had any clichéd meaning. What it meant was fresh territory for everyone in the agency, and we were all willing to give it a go to make things as successful as we could. There were no experiential/digital/PR/social ninjas. No integrated channel planners. Just a bunch of smart people who enjoyed working with each other, were curious enough to research and brave enough to experiment to find the right answers. For me, this was the start of the realization of the ingredients of true integrated marketing.

"This is the main thing that has changed over time. We talk more integration, but we're actually much more siloed. More deep and narrow knowledge on single, sometimes useful areas, but more people deferring to so-called experts rather than trying to understand and find solutions themselves. The advent of deep expertise amongst specialists is seeing the death of the suit, or perhaps more the suicide. They think less and defer more. We need the bravery and curiosity to return to the game or suits will kill themselves off.

"Recruitment and retention have always been challenging in advertising. It's so much more important to have an agency that actually stands for something that people will believe in and unite around. These will be philosophies and beliefs and higher purposes, rather than processes or proposed outcomes.

"At iris, we challenge convention to find better solutions in everything we do. That rings true in the types of work that we produce, but similarly in the way we structure the agency, look for better people practices, approach finances... everything. We're not stuck with processes, approaches, and methodologies. We make them or change them as we see best fit. It can seem a bit chaotic for some, but we need people who believe in positive change for positive results.

"It also creates a unique culture, because we have people who believe in the agency."

～

Bob Gebara, Creative Director at Brazil's Master Comunicação, "Those who state they know where technology is going must also know where humanity is going, because in my opinion, both of them walk together. Technology serves men who interfere, change, and make it evolve, and technology follows those changes, interfering with and changing people.

"The extinction of the borders between the analog and digital world is promoted by brilliant people like Dub FX and his hi-tech toys or maybe by the millions of users who carried their lives into Facebook. If we live in a society, it is natural that the Internet follows. Being social is another of our features that technology has been recently incorporating.

"It's beautiful to see that not everything is used the way it was designed. This shows the amazing ability that the Internet, technology, and people have for adaptation. As in life, only the strong survive. Adapt or die.

"The trying period is almost over, and people are no longer satisfied with something being 'cool.' Now, the questions users have are: *What is it for? What do I gain?* That applies to both sides. Companies and users are going through the same process. Communication does not happen in the obvious format now. A simple advertisement isn't enough to communicate, whether analogical or digital.

"Print, video, digital, offline media, online – everything is the same. It's a matter for those who want to sell their products or services to try to communicate with those who want to buy them. It's the artist trying to show his art and audiences wishing to express their opinions. Many times, turning themselves into artists.

"As Gusteau from the movie *Ratatouille* would say, 'A good cook can come where you least expect it.' The explosion of technology is putting this idea into practice. We can be whomever we want, no matter where we were born, the color of our eyes, what sort of food we like. If you want to survive (including in the Communications industry), you must be creative and adapt. Therefore, the role of the communicator is to make it happen. Good ideas, good texts, beautiful images: all that remains the same. We're just changing the way we do. Changes have always existed. The difference now is how quickly they happen.

"Maybe one day we will exist purely in digital form, as well as our consciousness, friends, consumer goods, and tools of the day to day. Just like the paper clip, one of the greatest inventions of mankind, which has become the digital assistant for Word and also the icon to attach files to email messages. Without adapting, it would have probably been extinct in a world increasingly sustainable and digital. Or vice-versa."

Chapter 3: Contently Creating Content

A funny thing happens when a number of talented personalities are put in a room, given a salary, a bit of structure, and a clearly defined creative problem to solve: where there was once a group of individuals with their own ways of doing things, there is now a team with a standard process. Even if we don't always share the same tastes, we enjoy being around compatible individuals who are possessed of a similar way of looking at the world, the people in it, and the zeitgeist. In other businesses, you might feel like an odd duck or that you are hiding some horrible secret about your true identity, because even if Human Resources likes to make everyone feel creative through company-wide talent shows and mandatory expression on Halloween under pain of knitted HR brows, the fact is most people in offices steel themselves for the day's work and go task to task until quitting time. Sweet, merciful quitting time. They do not spend the day (and night) thinking as we do about client briefs, cultural references, clever turns of phrases, imaginative and powerful ways to tell brand stories, and conceiving of mind-bending visuals that may or may not be able to be brought into the world. How many in other fields have to get used to waking themselves up at 4am to write down a brainstorm that went off in their sleep, or worse, email their team about it?

This is how we have to live our lives. We are obsessed because it's perversely enjoyable to be paid to come up with creative ideas. And back when agencies still took risks and were willing to create new opportunities for their clients and themselves, it was a dream come true for many in the business. They got to experiment and go far beyond headline writing. But when you think back to the ad copy of the 1950s and '60s, you might be inclined to believe it was all "Vim and Vigor!" and "Zing!" attention grabbers as if the writers of the *Batman* TV show reflected the entire period. In fact, that's when men were men and writers were writers. Writers who were highly educated and enjoyed long form to the point of penning print ads that were essays, nearly treatises, just to introduce a new model automobile or to describe the atomic age technology that went into the new deluxe washer and dryer. It started with inserts and advertorials and then grew ever longer and more interesting as television programs from soap operas to game shows were created, written, and produced by advertising agencies and the lucky creatives who were free to push content creation as far as the media channels could stand.

There may not have been razor scooters, foosball tables, and in-office yoga classes back when agencies were becoming established TV, radio, and magazine content developers, but the cultures they formed gave you the opportunity to take time to think, to leave the office, and go to a museum for inspiration or a walk in the woods to help fire up your imagination — and that flexibility was even more useful for conceiving not just "big ideas," but great ones. For those of us who joined the field for all of the right reasons, we want to be free to blithely go about the satisfying business of devising interesting solutions and crafting material for our audiences to enjoy on any number of levels, taking into account how and where people are consuming it these days.

New Fairlane Victoria with
the new 202-h.p. Thunderbird Y-8 engine

It's the new '56 FORD

America's fine car... at half the fine car price

...with new Lifeguard design... new Thunderbird styling... new Thunderbird Y-8 power

With all its exciting beauty and power news for 1956, Ford announces the biggest safety news in car history. It's Lifeguard design—the first comprehensive contribution to driver and passenger safety in accidents.

Two years ago, Ford set out to determine the causes of accident injuries . . . so a safer car could be built. It was found that over half the serious injuries came from occupants being thrown against the steering post, against hard interior surfaces, or from the car. To guard you, Ford developed Lifeguard design—a family of safety features described at the right.

To give your safer new Ford the goingest GO on the road, Ford offers the new 202-h.p. Thunderbird Y-8 engine in Fordomatic Fairlanes and Station Wagons—the mighty 176-h.p. Y-8 in Fordomatic Customline and Mainline models—and the 137-h.p. Six in all models.

But this is only part of the Ford story. When you've seen its brilliant new Thunderbird styling . . . noted its colorful new interiors and careful workmanship . . . you'll know that Ford is truly the *fine* car at half the fine-car price.

Lifeguard Design . . . a Ford first for safety first includes new Lifeguard steering wheel with deep-center construction to act as a cushion in event of accident . . . Lifeguard double-grip door locks designed to give extra protection from doors opening under shock . . . optional Lifeguard padding for instrument panel, and sun visors made of similar impact-absorbing material, to lessen injuries from impact . . . optional Lifeguard seat belts, firmly anchored to the reinforced steel floor, to keep occupants securely in their seats. And you get all these Lifeguard features *only in Ford.*

Typical Ford Motors ad with more copy than images, 1955 by J. Walter Thompson.

Steffan Postaer, Executive Creative Director for gyro in San Francisco and former Chief Creative Officer & Chairman for Euro RSCG Worldwide, "I remember before the Internet we used to spend a whole lot of time not doing our jobs back then either because the creative process likes what it likes. It doesn't respond well to a gun at the head, but maybe taking a walk, going to the museum or a movie, long lunches, or drugs and alcohol.

"All these things were used to stimulate – sometimes stupidly, sometimes brilliantly – the creative process. Now you can sit at your computer and get all that stimulation. You don't have to do anything, and while some might say that sucks, it's just a surrogate for the kind of behavior that's always taking place in creative departments since the turn of the century, whenever modern advertising became an actual vocation.

"In some weird, roundabout way, I'm proving the cliché of the more things change, the more they stay the same. I can look out right now and see guys with headphones on and I know what they're doing. They're looking at videos, they're checking out maybe advertising, probably not, maybe clips, maybe inappropriate material, maybe they're perusing through different retail sites. Back in the day, you'd say, 'Fuck it. I've got to get out of here,' and you'd go to Macy's or something and walk around. Or you'd go see a Bruce Willis movie or something or go to the art museum if you were more erudite or pretentious. You do what you did. Then you'd come back, and we all know there's only an hour or two that are real money hours in the creative department. People argue its 10:30 in the morning. The rest is spent going to dumb meetings, unnecessary meetings.

"Back in the day, you'd get out of your Bachelor of Arts and likely no further than that before you'd jump into an agency hoping to be a copywriter or an art director – speaking from the creative department point of view, those were the two jobs. There weren't many others, if any, to talk about or to interview for or to aspire to. Obviously, that's changed, and there's a bunch of different variations on those jobs as well as the nature of partnerships in general, and that's pretty interesting because it's sort of at the genesis of the creative process, just like with human verse or any verse, really. They're a pair and they create something together. That's changed forever.

"Partnerships are by and large looked at the same way old ideas are looked at. It's considered antiquated, and that's selling it short. When a valid partnership takes shape in an agency between a creative writer and a creative designer or art director, magic can happen, no question, and long-term gains are significant. But now there's a whole subset of designers, and there are designers for the graphic arts, designers for online, web developers, motion graphics, illustrators – and a lot of those different kinds of permutations exist within the Art Director subset. Now there are specialists who write long form, not for long copy, but for web site content. They dive deep into that, or they are obligated to write scripts for films that can be any length for YouTube and other channels as opposed to the 30-second / 60-second paradigm that we grew up with. That takes a lot of effort and a lot of different kinds of writing, and some people are more attuned to it and better at it than others. Some people aspire to one more than the other, and some people are a jack-of-all-trades.

"Now where I'm going with all this is I look at the metaphor of when every kid – at least when I was a kid – got some guppies and they were easy to raise and they were pretty. They were simple. You put them in a bowl, and the cool thing was they always had babies, and that was a thrill to see little baby fish, and you could look at them with pride and wonderment and all that.

"If you look at the classic creative pair as a pair of guppies who have babies, what would happen is the babies would quickly grow up. They would resemble their parents. Then they would start to mate with their brothers and sisters and then any other guppies introduced and, in not too long a time, you couldn't tell who the parents of any given guppy were because they would have acquired the characteristics and traits of many different parents. All that could happen within a very short period of time, and you could see how the hybrid of the original parents was the dominant gene in the guppy bowl and, in some ways, the same exact things happens in the creative department.

"You introduce a new element like a designer or digital strategist or some sort of a planner into the mix, and you'll get crossbreeding that creates new forms that resemble bits of all the parents. I look at the future of our business – from the creative point of view – as being hybrids. All of the people coming into the agency world will be on point or in front of the curve if they have a hybrid sense of the original parent.

"They might, in a general sense, be a writer or an art person, but really they will have multiple skills that can prove their merit to the agency. You'll see titles like interactive designer/art director, creative technologist, and all kinds of variations. I look at those as the natural eventuality of what happens when you introduce new types into the creative department. The hybrid creative is now what is necessary, relevant, modern, and best suited to have a good productive career in our field.

"I grew up as a straight-up copywriter and went all the way up to become the executive creative director of Leo Burnett, at least the front half in a classic narrative. Then I really saw a little of the writing on the wall and began to do the necessary things to become diverse and a hybrid, myself. I can't erase my stripes, and I don't want to pretend I'm 20 years old or anything. You can certainly take your pedigree and your past, the good parts about that and what's useful, and apply them to all of these new hybrid skills that are propagating throughout any given creative department. In some cases, whole agencies are built around very specific hybrids like web development, entertainment, and advertising or just placing brands into shows, be they online or on TV. Just all sorts of niches, and that's neat. I don't have a problem with that, and I don't think that that's indicative of anything wrong per se – and even if I did, that's what's happening. You either roll with it or become irrelevant, and as soon as you are out of touch, you are both perceptually and probably realistically not being of maximum use to your agency or your client. We've taken that way too far. I agree."

⤶

Mike Fromowitz, "Way back in '30s and '40s, copy was king. It wasn't particularly smart copy. It used a lot of puns and mostly just stated the name of the product or service and some long copy explaining a few key features and benefits.

"Things stayed this way until Bill Bernbach came along. Before Bernbach, copywriters and art directors didn't work together on projects. The Copywriter created the ad, wrote the copy, slid it underneath the Art Director's door, and the Art Director put the concept to paper.

"Bernbach had the idea that two heads should be better than one. He created teams of copywriters and art directors, and in so doing, changed the advertising agency business forever. His innovation became the impetus for a creative revolution. He was a heretic."

Steve Hall, "Because the landscape has changed, because the way consumers are now consuming information, and when I say 'information,' I mean content advertising. The way advertising works and the way advertisements are seen are very different.

"Print is sort of dying, the DVR has changed the viewing habits on television, and social media has become a free mechanism for people to share stuff – including sharing advertising. The content itself has to be something that is interesting. Content marketing is yet another buzzword, but it's also grounded in history. Really it's just an advertorial. It's a different word for the same old thing.

"We're slapping new labels on old stuff. Content can also be an ad, but creative people aren't creating content because it's a different skill set. Technically, yes, a copywriter could create an article, but instead usually creates the structure of the marketing. It's somebody else that's creating that content. It's somebody else that's developing that Sweepstakes program that's going to get a million 'likes' on Facebook, not someone in the creative department. By the nature of the changing mechanism of marketing and what actually works, there are different people now involved in the creative process.

"You even have ad networks that automatically create ads from content. There's a company like that called OneSpot, and I'm not saying it's a bad notion. But you've got content marketing where brands produce content, and they hope that it proliferates and they hope that they get sales out of it, and some people are calling it native advertising now.

"But OneSpot, for example, sort of can automatically go out and convert a brand's content into an ad, which is then served across multiple ad networks that they have a deal with. Now, that's great because it enables that content that's been created to be seen, and it sort of combines the best of both worlds, where you have the numerical reach of an ad network for a low cost and then the benefits of well-written content. But today, there's no creativity. It's simply grabbing a screenshot of whatever picture was on the content [something anyone can do].

"We're trying to automate everything. We're trying to make it easy. It's like push button, create an ad. Push button, create a video. It's almost as if creativity is not valued anymore. It's, 'Those cantankerous bitchy creative people think they have the answer to everything.' Even in the day of the creative greats, creative was sort of looked down upon as a bunch of whiny, bitchy people who, if they didn't get their way, would throw a fit.

"On another note, you had these creative gods that are still out there. They're still doing great work, but not so much. They're not worshipped as much as they once were. Of course, 30, 50 years ago, we didn't have the metrics that we have now. Let me whip out the famous Apple example. *1984.* They create this ad. They run it once. Technically, it did run more than once because they had to run it overnight somewhere so they could get it into some awards show. That was a leap of faith and you can tie that to what's going on with the Super Bowl today. What was once a big reveal event has now, thanks to social media, turned into an excuse for marketers to plan teaser lead ups to the game or simply release their ads in advance online.

"More than half of the brands that advertised in the Super Bowl last year released their commercials in advance of the game. It was done for several reasons, of course. They wanted to maximize the reach. They wanted to have the commercial be discussed in social media in advance of the game. But the 'wow' factor is gone, and there is something to be said for the wow factor since we're still talking about Apple's *1984* commercial 30 some odd years after it happened."

⤴

Jim Speelmon, "What I loved about the early days of that business was that people were more open to collaboration. They were not as knowledgeable about the tactics because the Web was a big black box. They were familiar with web sites (or becoming more familiar with web sites), but in regard to the technologies or the features and functions and things like that, they really were not that experienced. Not familiar enough to be prescriptive like they are today. Today, you go into a meeting and it's the latest buzzword and somebody says, 'I really want to do this.' Even if it doesn't make any sense for their business, whereas before you spent a majority of time helping them with opportunity creation.

"It seems to me today that a lot of what you do is damage limitation because people are going around with preconceived notions of what they want to do. It makes it more difficult to figure out how the technology or the trend can be applied in the most useful way to the client's business. We would have something more like a tactical discussion than go through a real strategy. What is it that they're really trying to achieve? We'll get what's available and apply that to solve the problem to get the outcome that they want. But today they start with, 'I have a list of tactics that I want.'"

⤳

George Tannenbaum, "So much of our business is about taking complicated thoughts and making them simple. By not having that perspective, which is inherently burned back in ethos. Take everything out that doesn't belong to the idea. Simplify, simplify, simplify. Strip out everything. We've gone in a decorative path as opposed to the simplified path. We make things that are nuances more important than they need to be and we've, maybe, sacrificed communication.

"These things are cyclical. When I taught school, I used to do this game of looking at car advertising pre-Bernbach and post-Bernbach. What you saw in the '60s era was longer, lower, wider, and flowery language and this that and the other thing. It was a decorative approach. There was a reaction to that, just like there's going to be a reaction to the era we're living in. And the reaction from your Carl Alleys or George Loises was to 'take everything away except what matters.' From the moment things were absolutely pure and clean until today, all the crap has been building up again. And somebody's going to strip it away again, and we'll start afresh. That's how these things go: they go in waves, and you can't buck that much against the wave or if you do, you look like the odd man out.

"Apple has done (I'm sure I'm not the only one who says this) a great job at keeping their storyline very simple. If you look at their spots – many of which don't even get recognition in the award shows – they're simple demonstrations. You show a hand swiping over a screen, it's like, 'Gee whiz, is that really any different from commercials 70 years ago or when women showed how easy it was to open the doors of a refrigerator?' No, not really. They do it artfully. They do it in a contemporary way, but in terms of telling the consumer what to think, what the machine does, it's pretty simple."

⤳

Mike Langton, "Every agency must have a content strategy because marketing communication is about content, not just ads whether they are on-line or off-line. There need to be content strategists in every ad organization, and there need to be content producers – they don't necessarily produce it themselves just as when TV producers working in agencies would reach out to a suitable TV production company with the right sort of director and get them to execute the script, etc. That is fundamentally what we need to do."

⤳

Steve Elrick, "Listen, there were always copywriters with poor spelling. Now there's spellcheck. I love the fantasy that having art directors who can't draw or writers who can't spell will somehow mean they understand target audiences better or make them be able to bring a brand closer to the people. WTF? Nah, it just means they can't draw or spell.

"Whatever the literal physical craft, surely we are looking for skilled communicators? Skilled and talented ideas people. Just because someone has solid knowledge of Adobe Illustrator, George Lois or Mark Reddy they are not. The content creation being democratized doesn't mean that the quality of that content is any better – or even up to scratch."

⤳

John Lambie, Founder of Dextr and former Regional Digital Creative Director for WPP's Enfatico and Bates141 Asia, "Staring us in the face is one of the most amazing brand opportunities, if you think about it. The original soap operas were actually created, produced, and distributed by advertising agencies for their clients. Imagine if you could be the brand who could pro-vide those small chunk-sized bits of people's movies."

⤳

David Sable, "We always did content. We just didn't always call it that. I always say we did all these things; we just weren't smart enough to know what to call it then. Don't forget, agencies created content. Who the hell do you think did the soap operas? We did that. *We* did that. That was *our* business. We lost it. Now everybody's, 'Ah, content…' That's what kills me: it's all bull-shit. It's not new. Get over it."

Part II:
Things Fall Apart

Bob Greenberg, Chairman, Chief Executive, and Global Chief Creative Officer of R/GA, is famous for saying, "Everything is digital." David Sable's supplement to that observation, as we read in Part I is, "...but digital is not everything." Yet, although it is far from being the only culprit, digital is one of the main reasons the whole advertising industry is in a state of turmoil, from agency executives to marketing directors to brand managers.

Every brand is desperately trying to figure out how to be as successful online as the two kings of social media, Wil Wheaton and 77-year-old George Takei — without their advantage of having had a feature role on a *Star Trek* series. Forrester's Research calls this phenomenon "The Great Race," which also sees the above-the-line (ATL) ad agencies continuing to look to hire "digital natives"[3] to add those with true leading-edge skills and insights to their roster. And while they are (finally) trying to be taken credibly in the space, successful digital groups are attempting to break through the unnecessary, artificial divisions of traditional vs. new media (or passive vs. interactive) and convince clients they can do anything the ATL agencies can do, but more authentically and without being fixated on forced integration of media channels.

The reality is that each medium simply presents an opportunity to bring an idea to life and reach people where they want to be and where they are. Each one has their advantages and disadvantages, and it is probably blindly obvious to any outside observer who doesn't have ego invested that they are just tools, not battle lines. Choosing to execute a creative branding message on television does not mean that you are choosing sides. Developing a mobile app in no way sends a signal that you think print is over.

It makes about as much sense as any political argument, but this "us vs. them" mentality has done a great deal of damage to the reputation of our entire industry and, unfortunately, those of us caught up in it. Those who work on the agency side are being battered and beaten by executives giving dodgy directives that seem more like blind stabs in the dark, and the marketing groups aren't sure who to blame for failed efforts or what to do, other than try to regain control themselves. Either by managing a number of specialist vendors or trying to do things themselves (instead of focusing on running their business, as they should be).

---

3 Those who grew up in the age of technology (specifically with the World Wide Web and mobile devices) and therefore didn't have to learn it.

Meanwhile, the work, the people, and the clients' goals continue to suffer as Rome burns and the holding company chiefs fiddle about. Part II is all about where these things began to go horribly wrong in the business and what we can do to reengineer it before it's really too late.

Chapter 4: The Creative Content Assembly Line

One of the greatest pleasures of working for a general advertising agency is the constant movement from one brand challenge to the next across completely different categories. On Monday, you could be working on a hotel chain learning the nuanced features of the travel & tourism vertical market; by Wednesday, working out how to appeal to a CTO looking to hire an IT services company, and by the weekend, setting up a campaign strategy for a retail clothing store. We are paid to research, analyze, and become experts in a number of different fields, learning about the unique differentiators that separate a business from its competition, and what is important to a wide range of people with a plethora of emotional and functional needs. We used to help guide not just product and service strategies, but those for the entire business. Of course, that's back when we were given the time to do all of that.

For the past decade or so, the industry has gone from its previous long-standing welcoming environment—where we were encouraged to practice our crafts; were treated as the prize; were given leeway to explore, think, and experiment; and where everyone recognized our time is as valuable as the entire established process—and turned into more of a soulless production line on a harsh factory floor. We've gone from being respected as having the talent and skills to create and lead efficacious programs to expendable workers akin to seamstresses in a sweat shop or line cooks in a large, busy restaurant. Clients need a product — a mobile app, print ad, web site, billboard, television commercial — and we are told to fill the order as quickly as possible. "Order up! Ding ding."

Without our own differentiators like culture or creative perspective, everything becomes homogenized and commoditized. With digital tools, just like back in the era of desktop publishing (thanks to PageMaker and Photoshop), anyone can now set up a shop and claim to be an expert, just as anyone can set up a web site and call it a real business. Worse, since managers do not possess the knowledge and experience to vet people and are facing tremendous pressure to get warm bodies on the assembly line, "anyone" is being hired. The hiring managers don't know what kind of skills they need, and they don't even know what they don't know. There are many cases of people being hired simply because they told the desperate hirer, "No problem. I can do that." And off they go to fail miserably on a Fortune 500 brand, but at least now they can say they have experience, put it on their LinkedIn profile and in their site's keywords, and get more work.

Lou Dobbs left his cushy position as an expert business reporter on CNN to jump into a dot.com company during the exuberance of the late 1990s online gold rush. Stockbrokers became strategists within marketing groups. Agencies popped up overnight to provide the picks and shovels for the online gold rush of the time, which ended in a spectacular bursting of the bubble. Not much has changed since then other than the clients believing in us less and often not even bringing the more interesting work to the agencies anymore. They ask, "Why should I pay premium for talent when it hasn't been effective? I want it overnight and they're going to be prima donnas and demand a full week." It doesn't help when account managers who haven't bothered to learn anything more than basic terminology agree with the client that it should and will be done overnight or be made to do things that are not possible, certainly not within the stated budget and ridiculous timeframe; setting up false expectations, a great deal of internal frustration, and a sorely disappointed client.

From Crafts to Tasks

Steve Elrick, "The craft and the pride in craft have definitely suffered. Ask the art-based creative directors who now have to tear their hair out seeing how little thought, energy, care, and pride goes into some of the work. That might be a massive generalization because some of the most exciting design, photography, and art creation is going on a digital space, but in general 'advertising' terms, I still feel online is aesthetically appalling a large proportion of the time. But this isn't just about digital. Some of the ad colleges have to take the rap here when people come out of them being neither writer nor art director. They say, 'We're both *concept guys.*'"

"Malcolm Gladwell famously says in his book *Outliers* that it takes about 10,000 hours or 10 years of experience to get really good at something. When agency creatives were focused, that was pretty easy to do. With things fragmented, it's more like 1,000 hours here, 1,000 hours there. Obviously, the craft suffers.

"How can you get 10 years of experience at something that's only 7 years old, like Facebook? Especially considering that the platform that Facebook is today doesn't even resemble what it was like just two or three years ago. Excellence in craft requires specialization, but the industry is now demanding creatives that can do everything."

∽

Paul Kwong, "There is lots of suffering these days. No time to craft. Or comps made so tight, done so fast, that's there's no chance to redesign or explore once something is bought. Drawing a comp is not acceptable. You've got to find the exact photo at the exact angle with the right coloring to put into a comp."

∽

Ignacio Oreamuno, The Art Director's Club Executive Director and President of GiantHydra in NYC, "The thing that is very obvious is that campaigns are no longer campaigns. They used to be held together by art direction. Seven years ago, if you would see the print ad, the banner ad, the product, everything, it would have the same color and it would always have the little tagline. That would hold it together. But now, because the campaign is just sort of like a mechanical grid where when you download the app, you go to read the book on your iPad and then you go to the event, they no longer have to look the same, and they no longer have to have a tagline, and they no longer have to be connected other than in getting you to the next experience. Therefore, you can use five different companies for that."

∽

Steffan Postaer, "The common tropes being bandied about for the last 15 years say that advertising used to be an industry where you could practice your craft and talent and have passion, but has become more about production than ideas. And that drum continues to get louder, I suppose. I fail to disagree with that assessment, and there might be more exceptions than identified, but by and large, that's the way it is. I tend to throw a wet blanket over things. If you want to look at the old way as the right way and use words like branding, awareness, and storytelling, it would appear there *is* a wet blanket over it.

"There are a lot of tangents and a lot of different ways you could break that down, taking either side – and certainly a guy like me remembers the days when it was all about building brands and longer-term relationships, etc. I also have fairly embraced the present tense in every sense of the word. I'm heavy into my blogs. I enjoy a number of social media platforms. I work at a B2B [business to business], below-the-line agency now and create and direct there.

"I don't want to come to work every day thinking that what we do is tactics and that is something I would regret. There's no reason for guys like us to do tactics. You can just get a bunch of 22-year-old Mac jockeys and tell them what to do, and they'll push and pull and make the little levers and widgets and you'll have like a dancing chicken here and some act there and some stupid self-promoting clip."

〜

Tim Leake, LA-based Senior VP of Growth & Innovation for RPA and former Creative Director and Director of Creative Innovation for Saatchi & Saatchi NYC, "Creatives used to focus on about four different media: TV, radio, print, and outdoor (which is really just like print, but seen from far away). Some focused on direct mail, brochures, and point-of-sale, too, but they usually worked at specialty agencies. Now digital has added hundreds of new possibilities to this mix. Obviously, this creates all kinds of problems, especially for full-service agencies that still want to do it all."

〜

Steve Hall, "The big idea in my mind is just gone. And technology has killed it. Back when there was just TV, radio and newspapers, it was much easier to envision how a big idea would play out. Now, for some, it's 'How do I even make this thing that's going to appear on a computer or a phone? I don't even get it.'

"Your average creative person doesn't know how to make a lot of stuff work online, and so who are the heroes? You've got the coders who are creating these amazing applications for phones and obviously creativity goes into that, but your average creative person who is focused specifically on art and went to art school or some design school, were unlikely to have been educated in the technical aspects of how to make stuff work on the Internet.

"Some people get flustered and confused at the prospect of developing something because it's going to take a lot of work. 'I can't just come up with this very cool idea.' Yes, you can, but someone's got to implement it. I feel like the notion of a good creative idea, one which still needs to be in place and can be executed across multiple media, is becoming a lost art."

⤻

Barry Wong, "I've had account management teams go off to clients promising three digital creative concepts delivered in 24 hours. I've had account management teams promise two weeks to build an entire e-commerce site sans information architecture. I've had account management teams agreeing to the clients' demands of creating a series of six viral videos for 10,000RMB (US$1,500) in high-definition within a week.

"There were times when we simply had to tell the account management teams that without first conferring with the creative team and getting an alignment, anything that was promised to the client was void. There were times when the creative team had to blatantly tell the account management teams to deal with it since the creative team never gave their agreement. Over time and multiple push backs, the account management teams learned more about the intricacies of the requirements.

"Did it get better? No, it did not. They understood it perfectly and knew how much time and resources were required to get a project done. So what was the problem? The account management teams weren't able to convince the client. On top of that, in China, the belief is the client is always right. That's a whole new set of problems altogether."

⤻

Group Account Director, Kay Johnson-Suglia, "Clients push farther into production before they'll approve work. It has a detrimental effect when creative and production have been decoupled from an agency standpoint (and often two different agencies are managing each phase)."

⤻

Commercial Launch Planning Director at Microsoft Devices Group and former Director of Product Marketing Planning of Nokia in Finland, Clara

Lee, "The instantaneous nature of digital media has somewhat diminished the process of thought and craft. For example, it's so easy to conduct A/B tests on a piece of communication to see which actually generates a better response that marketers are getting somewhat lazy at perfecting and crafting a piece of communication to make sure they get it right on the first try.

"I feel this has somewhat removed the ownership of producing effective marketing through prior research and intuition from the marketer and placed it in the hands of the consumer at large. The consumers at large, I might say, either don't know what they want or their wants change like the weather on a daily, weekly, or monthly basis. It is scary, in a way, that marketers are studying this data to determine their next move. The cycle is fast and somewhat shallow, which can sometimes lead the marketer down the wrong path.

"A concrete example is this: a series of online tests and surveys we conducted showed that consumers valued some very basic features of a product way above some of the more differentiating features. This information landed in the hands of one of our marketers, who then decided the best way to market his product was to focus on communicating the basic features, thereby neglecting the more differentiating ones. The result was his product didn't stand out from a sea of other products offered by competitors who have the very same features, and he lost a great opportunity."

↜

George Tannenbaum, "At Sears, I worked with a former CMO and I had worked with her on IBM. I was at Digitas at the time, their digital and strategy agency. I remember she said, 'I don't need another creative agency. I need a strategic partner.' There's been a stanza that TV does certain things and traditional agencies do certain things, but they aren't dealing with communications in a holistic way. It says they're very narrow and probably not as thoughtful as they might be. There's been a pitched battle between the two camps, even when they're housed in the same agency: OgilvyOne versus Ogilvy, for instance. Each trying to undercut the efficacy of the other's media.

"Traditional has been the dominant player for so long and in many ways remains the dominant player, at least in terms of span a lot of the proclamations 'TV is dead. Print of course is dead. Radio is dead. Therefore traditional agencies, they're dead,' have come from the digital agencies. I hear it, the difference, and I certainly hear it and, no names mentioned, though *Nike+* is more impactful than Nike TV. At the end of the day and when you have a message that needs to go out to 40 million people in one fell swoop, most clients realize that there's a role for traditional. Because of the high profile of traditional advertising, it's usually the people who do that usually have the seat at the head of the table.

"I can't really think of that many instances where a digital shop has uprooted a traditional one on a major brand like on a MasterCard or something like that. McCann has had the ubiquitous *Priceless* campaign for so long that people are bored by it, and they say it doesn't work anymore. The fact of the matter is, and I hate to be negative about it, I haven't seen, outside of probably *Nike+* and maybe one or two others, a big defining brand idea come from a digital shop. On the order of *A Smaller Planet* or *Priceless*. That sniping doesn't really get anyone anywhere, and it doesn't win any points with the clients. It just aggravates them, to tell you the truth.

"It probably will happen more and more predominantly that the approach is more inclusive and agnostic at the same time. Traditional agencies are upping the ante in terms of their digital ability skills, so the sniping is probably going to be coming in both directions.

"It also seems to me that a lot of the traditional holding company structures have acquired digital shops somewhat willy-nilly rather than having a plan for them. I don't really understand. There's Tribal DDB, there's Proximity, and of course traditional DDB has digital experts under its roof. I don't really understand what a lot of the holding companies are doing. These new tools and platforms do not change storytelling. "

Andy Flemming, "I once heard Jeff Goodby lamenting the death of storytelling. He was saying that the problem is summed up by dinner parties he used to attend where people would say to him, 'What have you done recently?' He'd reply, 'I did that beautiful spot with x.' They'd go, 'Oh yeah, I've seen that. It's great.' He said that nowadays when he gets asked the same question, He'll respond, 'You see that big billboard in Times Square?' They say, 'Yeah, you know, we don't really get it.' He tries to explain, 'You're supposed to go to a Facebook page and play a game and then find some hidden objects and you're participating.' The posters don't really make a lot of sense to these people. They're really asking them to go somewhere and do something. Where he was coming from is that digital is not an idea, it's a vehicle. It's a vehicle that needs an idea – and I agree with that."

༄

Jim Speelmon, "Planners came late to America. You didn't really have them until the early 2000s, and instead of Strategists, the strategy was done by a combination of senior account people and a creative director. We would give estimates in our work authorizations such if you had a $100,000 budget, we would take 10% up front to cover the strategy time.

"Then you would have your development budget, which was more about the creative concepts and things like that. Then you would have the production. Where I came from, you got paid to write the creative brief. Why would I take some of the most expensive people in the agency, put them on solving your problem and coming up with an idea that you may or may not take, when instead we can come up with the brief and then you can decide, 'I don't have enough money to do this.' You can then take our brief and hand it to a different agency.

"I sent a letter to Cisco because we put probably 200 hours' worth of work into a brief and concepts and they told us, 'You can't hit the timeframe.' They just took our work and gave it to a different agency that did. I sent them an email and I said I was surprised to see a company that takes the topic of intellectual property so seriously do that – and so they paid us.

"This is one of the reasons that the larger agencies are in the situation they are in today, which is having clients that say they do not need high-level strategy or, at least, they don't need *really* smart strategy people all of the time. I used to have this conversation with my Intel client where we'd argue. He'd say, 'You need to hire more strategic people.' And I'd counter, 'No, they'd get bored and quit because your business is not that strategic. We do an annual planning. We do quarterly planning, and the rest of the time, it's all production work. You need people who can facilitate flawless production, which is 95% of the work on this account. When I hire really smart strategy people and put them on your business, they end up leaving out of boredom, and then you bitch at me because the turnover is so high.'

"You can get a strategist when you need them once in a while and bill them out at $400 an hour. If WPP were smarter, what they would do is create a strategy group that does nothing but strategy, and sell those people's time through the different agencies – because who needs to have that level of strategy all of the time? Very, very few people. Clients expect you to eat, sleep, and breathe their brand as much as they do, but they're not going to pay for that.

"I would tell my clients, 'You are an expert at what you do. I am an expert at what I do. We don't do the same thing. Your job is to build a chip to power the future. My job is to convince people to buy it. We have different jobs. I don't need to know everything there is to know about your company. That's why you're involved in this conversation.' I have to remind people my job is not to know everything about the company or product. My job is to know everything there is to know about the people whom you want to talk to and how to make what you want to talk about seem interesting to them. That's my job. I was always strict about reminding the clients about that."

Just Because You Were Born in a Car Park Doesn't Mean You Can Drive[4]

Global CEO and President of VML, Jon Cook, "If ad professionals feel they haven't been personally rewarded by digital technology, their career has been stunted by it, or they haven't had a really successful digital campaign, it's because they haven't lived the technology and seen the effect that it has in their lives. Or even opened their eyes to the reality of what effect digital has in their life, right now.

"It would be hard for us to think that it's not affecting them. I think they're not being real. They're not opening their minds to the admission of how much even it has changed their own lives. It's changed the way they consume communication. They haven't opened their minds to that. There's a huge amount of denial. I think of people who still don't totally, completely understand the impact, but that's so much better than complete denial. I hope that's it's a fad, but they are being scared by the thought of, 'Oh shit! This is

---

4 From an interview with Steve Elrick for this book.

not going away.' I have trouble believing everybody doesn't, fundamentally, in their brain, understand the impact."

⌒

George Tannenbaum, "I shot with Errol Morris, the director, a couple of years ago, and he had a phrase that he used which was 'subtlety is for amateurs.' To tell a story, do so in a simple declarative way, and if it's an interesting one, people will watch and pass it along. We look for these crazy things that mean nothing to no-one, and then we have this adaptation phase where we *have to* do something no-one's seen before, that's never been seen and all. It tells us to dig a hole slightly deeper. It comes from both agencies and clients. I think probably more agencies.

"Certainly, since the recession we're in for already seven years, clients have gotten more nervous and less risk-taking. They've gotten more prescriptive, and if we don't do this, we will fail. Any fans of enthusiasm or experimentation are removed from the system. They don't want to trust, and they look for proven breakthrough, if you will. There's no such thing. You put fear into the equation, the expensive cost of the agencies, and how everybody has been seduced by this idea that you can measure everything, which you can't. If they don't see it's working, they react, and so it's a whole lot of things.

"Occasionally, you'll do a pre-test and in *this* shot, the eye-tracking movement goes down, but the thing I always remember... I shot a spot for IBM, honest to goodness, it was the highest-tested spot IBM ever in their history. They ran it as a direct spot, and it ended up costing something like $50,000 dollars per lead. I've always said 'Well, that's what testing does for you.' It proves nothing, but it allows you to have a meeting. It takes a special client to move forward without testing.

"I wouldn't really trust agencies with so much mania going on about winning awards and so little concern about results. It's always been that way, too. It does seem to me that a lot of people have lost the storyline on what business we're supposed to be in."

⌒

Chris Kyme, "Thanks to technology, the possibilities are boundless, and I love it when you see fresh new ways of solving problems popping up from anywhere. However, the industry is under threat from much more than just technology. In the creative world (at least what I see in Asia), the industry has been devalued because of the divide in agencies between 'real-world' work and 'awards-entry' work. Nowadays, the big agencies budget big dollars for winning awards that they underwrite with the goal of keeping up their creative profile, which is fine, and we see great work every year. It's had a knock-on effect, though, and the losers are clients. Because there is no longer any pressure on agencies to sell in great work to clients. They do safe work that makes the client comfortable, and therefore they get paid and meet the budget. Meanwhile, hungry creative people can feed their egos with the work produced just for awards, everyone is happy, yet most of the work we see produced in the public eye is crap."

⤻

SapientNitro NYC's Chief Creative Officer, Alan Schulman, "What happened was ad agency egos grew to such a degree, that as long as their strategy people were holding down the relationship, they always felt that ideas would win. The fact that those ideas were in television and television alone. They left them in a place where they were:

1. making money and so there was no reason to discontinue doing that, and

2. following a self-serving prophecy... what they really liked to do was to go make Super Bowl commercials.

"Frankly, the agencies that were slower to pivot have paid a great price for that. They've now had to very smartly either grow a digital vestige organically or reel in and acquire one. Probably the biggest shop that's done this smartly is Ogilvy. Ogilvy was one of the big agencies that very early embraced interactive in a more holistic sense and a global sense and did a fairly good job at it, but not to the degree of specialization that happened in shops like ours or Razorfish.

"Most big agencies had really good digital people at the very beginning because they were passionate, they were interested in all this technology and how advertising could marry in with it. However, they all basically left the industry because their agencies were either disloyal to them or condescending or wouldn't invite them to the table to come up with the idea. They were relegated to 'integrating' whatever they were given, or the Art Directors of the TV commercials or the print ads would say, 'I'm not putting a call-to-action URL on my poster because it interferes with the integrity of my layout.'

"From the 1990s, the premise has been that in order to protect their nuts – which is the money that can be made from production of TV commercials and global print campaigns and the media commissions that go along with that – the big agencies kept recommending all of the traditional media to clients despite the evidence that it would be good to experiment and to do initiatives that were more than just static corporate sites. They should have been trying things that would have allowed them to get closer to the consumers, provide them with what they wanted, and extend the brand platform towards real people with whom they can have a one-to-one relationship. All that was ignored or thrown away in deference to doing what they've always done.

"The big agencies didn't prove to their clients that they understood this or were even willing to understand this for years, until Facebook exploded and there was no denying that everybody is now obsessively looking for stuff online. I would say that they were forced there. They were forced there against their will. When I was at IPG, I was never privy to a conversation that said 'recommend TV because we make more money on it,' but I can certainly tell you that to buy five million dollars' worth of TV takes one phone call. To buy five million dollars' worth of digital takes about 15 people.

"They feign partnership, but more and more clients are turning us into pairs of hands. What they need is a production mechanism to manage all of their banner ads globally. This thinking is being done either internally or elsewhere, and they're going to use scale to drive price down. They're looking to turn an agency partner into a factory.

"The fundamental premise, which advertising agencies knew for years, is that if you own the strategy, you own the relationship. The strategy is no longer defined as just the brand communication strategy. It's now lots more stuff, including e-commerce and the consumer as controller. Seeing how that definition of owning a strategy has expanded, even if you're BBDO and you still control the strategy around the advertising, the chances are less likely that you're going to be able to control that strategy around other aspects of the customer experience and marketing funnel.

"That's where agencies are losing their relevance because they can't control all the strategy anymore. There are just too many pieces to it. Which is why we [SapientNitro] are so unique. Whether we're selling to a CTO on the e-commerce side, or consulting as a digital AOR [Agency of Record] to the CMO, or dealing with the chief strategy officer of the whole company about an enterprise digital strategy with a five-year outlook on how their enterprise is going to need to be optimized in a digital world around big data, those are all relevant conversations and important ones. We can have all three of those conversations where BBDO can only have one. That's why I'm betting on us, frankly."

⌇

Susan Kim, "The key is in educated and informed clients because that's the only thing that will change the negative direction our business has been heading. We need more informed clients who will say, 'That's great, you got all the back end stuff, and you can optimize, and the front end needs to be better.' That is the key to making this work. Otherwise, it's always going to be theoretical. That's what is going drive it.

"In order for the stand-alone, technology-focused digital advertising agencies, as they are called now, to be able to understand the importance of design and concept and strategy and insights and all that, the clients need to push them. I think a good client would be interested in that.

"I don't know how some of these people got to be the directors of marketing because it is astounding how little they know, and sometimes they are from one side or the other. They are either all about digital or you have more of the old-school thinkers. It's important that that gap is bridged."

⌇

Ignacio Oreamuno, "When you talk to the head of the agency, they do get it. But it's very hard to move a whole agency. Think of it like this: let's say you're a senior art director at BBDO and you've been making TV ads for 10 years. Every year, you won awards, and so you doubled your salary. Then one day comes change, and change basically means that, 'Now I have to create an interactive game for Nike instead of a TV commercial, and I have to create an app, and I have to create a magazine that goes with iPad, and I have an event to create. Their reaction is, 'I don't want to learn to do that new stuff because it means that I'm probably going to screw up.'

"If you take an art director making TV ads for 10 years and you tell him, 'Okay. Now you have to build a game,' they won't even know where to start. They won't know. They will say, 'How do I design a game? What's my involvement with the gaming company? Do I write the game script? Do I design the icons? Do I design the screen or do I just give it up?' They are in denial because if it means that the Art Director does something for you, then next year he will not win an award. It'll take him three years to become really good at making an app or a game or anything new, and he's going to become an ostrich and put his head in the ground and just forget that change is coming.'

"Even if you have a leader who really wants to change his agency – and I get this all the time – they say, 'I'll get a creative director,' and you see the press release. They hire this superstar from like Wieden or wherever, and they put him in this big monster agency, and he's going to be the 'change agent.'

"A year later, that guy retires or quits – or even six months later, it has all failed. Everybody there did not want change. Humans do not like change, period. That is just a fact. Until the agency goes broke or something really bad happens, they are not going to change. There is no better proof of that than when the Internet came to advertising. All that people talked for five years as soon as the Internet really came and hit everything and asked, 'Is the TV 30-second commercial dead? Woo, we're scared. We're scared.'

"I was there at Ogilvy when they started OgilvyInteractive upstairs and we never talked to them. It was as if they were completely separate from us. Different group. It made no sense. How am I doing IBM when I'm not touching IBM digital?"

⤸

Thierry Halbroth, Executive Creative Director Commonwealth//Mc-Cann Bangkok Cluster and Chairman of the Creative Council at McCann Worldgroup Thailand and former Creative Chairman for The Association of Accredited Advertising Agencies of Hong Kong, "If they're not trying to do things the old way, they're trying to adapt, but then the problem we have is everything falls into the mediocrity basket. Everybody is able to adapt. Willingness in adapting is a different story altogether. You can always take brands into new territories. At the end of the day, it really depends on what the client wants. Some brands will remain very traditional, will have a limit to the exposure to digital channels, even though it's more and more difficult to escape them. We've seen that in the luxury category, for example, where they break the taboo and inspired every other brand by putting serious amounts of money into digital because it works so well. Where you don't need digital may be a 100- to 250-year-old whiskey because that's the way they want to operate. I don't know what or where they would advertise.

"The first step going into this is bridging the gap between advertising and communication and after communication is below-the-line direct marketing. That's what I started building my skills around. By the time digital came up, it was a very easy step to embrace because of the nature of the media and the fact that it's very direct."

ꟷ

Steve Elrick, "In a 'trad' agency, if you don't have the people with the tech/production know-how of what it takes and, just as importantly, how much it costs, then you have some very steep K2-like learning curves and even more scary descents. We have had to put in place an awful lot of checks and balances in budgeting for projects, and we are very careful about promising the Earth when all we can deliver is Uranus.

"One of the biggest gripes I have had from friends running the best digital agencies is how the client pretty much expects most digital components to be the cheapest bits in the mix: 'C'mon, my Poodle Stylist has a web site, how much can it be? That Facebook thing's pretty much free isn't it?'"

ꟷ

Bob Hoffman, "The point is, everyone is afraid to be thoughtful. If you're not perceived as being ahead of the curve in the marketing and advertising world, then people start calling you a dinosaur, so you have to pretend that you understand. You have to pretend that you buy into every new thing that comes along, and that's what the advertising and marketing industry has done. Rather than be thoughtful and say, 'Just slow down. Calm down.'

"The first person to even have a web site, nobody even knows who it was. The first person to have a Facebook page, nobody knows who it was. You don't have to be the first to do everything. There's way more risk in trying to be the first than there is to being a fast follower – see what works and then do it. Look at Steve Jobs with the iPod. How many MP3 players were there before he got it right? If you're in the technology business, maybe you have to be first. If you're in the marketing business, there's very little advantage to being first. Who's the first company that had a web site? Do you know? Who's the first company that had a Twitter feed? Who's the first company that had any of these things? Nobody knows. There's very little advantage for a marketer. For a technology company, yes, there's a lot of advantage to being the first one in technology. To a marketer, it's not that much of it. Just once in a while, there is. But usually, there isn't. If you're just smart and you're thoughtful and you wait and you do it right instead of trying to do it fast, there's way more upside for you."

↬

George Tannenbaum, "Bob Hoffman brings up some good points. He's also said in the past that there's a perception within traditional advertising people that those who have fully embraced the digital world are always on. They always have access to being on, but there's something to be said about that. Why don't you turn on the software and just chill? I'm watching, not texting and Instagramming things. TV is always going to be in the mix, because it's an important way to reach masses of people. For the client, it's not all there is. Bob's contrarian, and he's probably too absolute by half, but that's part of his charm."

↬

Jon Cook, "You start counting where you are in your career, and when you're over 30 you begin to do the math and think, 'Can I survive without knowing digital four or five more years?' I've heard people speak out and describe those calculations of how little they have to learn to be able to survive the rest of their career."

↬

Steffan Postaer, "Everybody has a little bit of the fear of God, and you're only as good as your last ad, as they used to say. Now, it's your last act.

Either your last ad or your last act. It's weird because you can't attribute those very old clichés like that one, and the more things change, the more they stay the same. In some ways, if you just stand back and look at the whole big mess, it is exactly the same; just at first, the appearance looks completely different."

⌇

Ignacio Oreamuno, "Because you're getting your ego beaten up all day long by all these groups of people, you become very insecure about yourself. Every time you look at a white piece of paper, you basically have to question yourself, 'Do I suck at this? Is this it? Is this piece of paper the end of my career?' That breaks down your confidence, and when your confidence is broken down and you fear that the floor is moving, you don't want change. You don't want any change. You just want to do your dog-walker ad. You want to do your pro bono ad for the film festival at Vancouver and just win your award and take your salary and get your Canadian dream, your cottage, and that's it. Once you got the cottage, you're done. You don't need to take any more risks. It's the same thing. You just want to get there, and it was so hard to break in, you had to spend eight months doing unpaid internships, all that stuff. By the time you get it, you don't want to change the game. Don't want to change the rules. Don't want to change the media."

⌇

Global CEO of Organic and former President of Wunderman NY, David Shulman, "The generation of employees coming into the workplace today are digital natives. The folks who we're hiring now are coming in as true users of the digital world. They're on Twitter and Instagram and social sites and engaging it as part of their life. I don't think that there's a distinction in the way people think, and whether you go to a pure digital play or a startup within the digital space or a traditional brand agency, you come from a mindset of understanding the digital world that we live in. Do they understand branding, relationship building, and everything that's required to build engaging digital experiences? No one does coming into this space. Even if the person has academic experience, she still needs work experience.

"I do think that for an agency to be successful, they should not only hire great, motivated people who live and appreciate digital, but you have to provide the foundational training, development, hands-on experience, and mentorship. Digital shops who specialize in producing digital tactics really cheaply and effectively won't bring any of that. They're not going to bring that understanding of brands and understanding of engaging users. If you're comparing a unique player like Organic, which I'm partial to, we can bring valuable training and development to staff. In comparing a digital tactical shop to a general agency, the latter can provide training and development around understanding brands and how to do advertising that is actually engaging."

〜

Creative Director and Founder of re:DESIGN and former Creative Director for the McGraw-Hill Companies, Paul Biedermann, "The effect on my career advancement by the sudden shift to digital had a definite negative effect at first, as I was largely known as a print specialist for many years. But one needs to embrace new technologies, platforms, and media shifts to survive in this business.

"The key is being able to integrate all media in order to develop the best all-around, all-encompassing solutions for our clients. I believe that those who have background in traditional media and strategy actually benefit with that experience and can now apply those skills and knowledge to the digital channels, as well. I believe those versed in only digital channels are actually at a disadvantage here."

〜

Paul Kwong, "The folks who don't have that much experience with digital will slowly gain it. The folks with only digital experience will slowly learn how to tell stories, stay on brief, and concept big ideas."

〜

Jennifer Hoe, former Director of Operations for Yahoo! Asia and JWT's digital outfit, RMG Connect, "When I decided to move into digital, the trigger was an overwhelming desire not to end up in the 17th level of Hell posthumous from being in advertising too long. It was the same work, same challenges, on every campaign, and an ever-decreasing sense of integrity and self-worth. With the Internet – ah, anything and everything was (and is) possible. I got to *build* real stuff that real people actually used. And with technology, *anything* was possible (with time and money). It was awesome.

"Over the years, the challenges in working in digital have largely remain unchanged. Non-digital folks in the industry are afraid of technology. They back away from it like it's some disease, or else their brain just shuts down and refuses to open. It's ridiculous and needs to stop. Now."

Neil Leslie, "Obviously, some people have embraced digital more than others. But to be honest, I don't really know anyone who is actively resisting the shift to digital. That doesn't really seem wise at this stage. You can only bury your head in the sand for so long.

"That said, I don't think that the rise of digital renders the creativity and experience of traditional creatives obsolete. It merely adds a new (albeit rather complex) weapon to their arsenal.

"Selling and storytelling through the use of pictures and words is still at the heart of what we do. It's just that there are many new approaches to packaging these stories online with the potential to involve our audiences to a much higher degree."

Susan Kim, "What you do find is everyone fears change, and you would think that some digital people would fear it less, but *everyone* seems to be resistant to change. When I say everyone, I mean everyone. Some people are a little bit less scared than others, but most people do not want to change, so it can get so frustrating, especially if you are not being paid by the hour to be doing something like that. I feel like I am working more as a consultant. What I like about it is if we tell a client, 'Here is why it is important to have A/B testing, here are the tests, here we can set it up if you want to do it," I don't get that vested because I am getting paid no matter what.

"Whether they sit on it for a day or they sit on it for a year, I have found I can sleep better because I am not like so vested in the outcome. Now, sometimes, just to be responsible, I thought, 'Why am I more concerned than the clients are about this?' and thinking, 'Holy crap! Look what a big difference this can make.' I find by being removed from what the outcome is, I can still give that information, but I don't stress about it if they take it or if they don't take it because I'll get paid either way, and so it's, 'You want to dawdle on this? You go ahead and dawdle. The meter is still running.'

"I am not saying one way is more effective than the other. I am saying it's the frustration of trying to get anyone to really change. People who have done this and then tried to be the agents of change got frustrated with it. It's only more effective for me, personally."

∽

Steve Elrick, "I began to get scared when I started seeing great stand-alone digital *creative* work. But that's a natural reaction of creative people when they see any creative work that's brilliant. It scares you 'cause you wish you'd done it. It was the introduction of some of those ideas *not* based on the big ad idea that caused people to sit up and take more notice of it.

"Maybe this is terribly arrogant, but I never felt like I was on a precipice unable to keep up because I was often surrounded by people who knew their shit. In retrospect, perhaps not enough of them and not soon enough, but, hey, that's hindsight again.

"I do remember doing a Hyper Island session through BBH London years back, and the speaker was trying to reassure a very mixed audience with different levels of tech experience: simply asking for a show of hands on who texted, tweeted, was on Facebook, etc., and his conclusion: don't worry, you're all digital natives, we just need to freshen you a little.

"To be honest, was I worried about all of these new creatives who were coming through who grew up in this world? Nah, just because you were born in a car park doesn't mean you can drive."

Experience & Wisdom vs. A Fresh Perspective

To Maurice Sendak from his editor Ursula Nordstrom on August 21, 1961: "Thirty-three is still young for an artist with your potentialities. I mean, you may not do your deepest, fullest, richest work until you are in your forties. You are growing and getting better all the time."

There are countless examples of artists and innovators doing their best work — in some cases, the work that made them world-famous — well into the second or even third act of their lives: Stan Lee and Jack Kirby, Julia Child, Col. (Harlan) Sanders, Tim and Nina

Zagat, Peter Roget, Raymond Chandler all had not achieved success up until their 40s or 60s; even Bill Bernbach didn't make Creative Director until he was 36. And in advertising, if you're approaching 40 you'd better already have a game plan figured out for what you're going to do next no matter your job title.

Your options are to:

1. start your own agency
2. try to move client side,
3. or take that first step on the road to your exciting new second career, whatever that turns out to be.

For some reason, ours is an industry that does not act as if it values decades of experience and insight, even though a lot of what we do and act on is cyclical. Creative leaders are being forced out or leaving because they feel the need to step aside or out of frustration for not being able to do what they've been screaming about for so long. The clients are no longer tolerating creative departments that operate in silos or talent that does not have answers that include smartphones, tablets, Facebook, and other non-traditional channels. The Boards respond with, "Off with their heads!" and "Get me a kid that knows something about this," but good luck finding a kid with the acumen to run a large team of very experienced professionals, usually in several offices, and who can also manage humorless, prickly clients that see their bottom line dropping versus the amount they're spending on media. Hey, good luck finding a kid who even knows about digital and real, honest-to-goodness brand strategy. It's a skill that develops over many years of observing and doing.

The answer these agencies seek is to open the minds of the highly trained and proven creative professionals that are already there in the traditional agencies. Their problem isn't that they're dinosaurs with no place in the new world order. The problem is the agencies haven't invested any serious effort in training them, while the creatives themselves have arrogantly ignored, dismissed, or otherwise been blind to the real way forward. They've paid enough lip service to "integration" to keep Wyeth's ChapStick in business for a few more decades, but they have been absolutely closed-minded when it has come to understanding that they need to change their own mindset and approach to this new, sophisticated audience.

If agencies continue to explore "radical" approaches to replacing the talent that has sustained their half-a-trillion dollar industry for so long, like looking to comedy writers or people from completely irrelevant fields, all they will do is implode. There are many other types of companies rising up to supplant advertising agencies the way typesetters were replaced by technology, and if they are foolish enough to throw away what has made them so effective for so long out of reactive fear, then all of those fears will most assuredly come true. The answer was within all along.

❦

Alan Schulman, "It's like George Lois. He was doing it [creating ads] into his 70s. He was still coming at the market like even if you know what poison gas is and you know what effect that has on people, it's still your job as an idea person to market it.

"I didn't jump to digital because I wanted to get retrained so I could work in the field longer. I did it because I thought as a copywriter who believed writing would change and the way that we told stories would change, and it has. I would say to those who are facing age issues, it's still about ideas, and it's still about doing the same things you did when you put a spec book together, which is making experiences that are compelling and really cool. If you can't do that digitally, then figure out how to use the open-source stuff that's out there, and partner with people who can. Play with people who can allow your ideas to surface digitally, and you might end up where I did.

"I would say don't throw in the towel because you're an old above-the-line advertising person. It's just a matter of using different crayons and a different canvas. If you have the perseverance to do that, the rest comes easy… if you still believe in the power of ideas."

❦

Steve Elrick, "I have also witnessed some of the 'older' people really embrace all the opportunity that the new world has to offer. Smart, creative people realize they now have a lot more toys in the sandbox these days. The ones who were brilliant at creating engaging stories and connections with people through TV spots, print, and radio are now able to extend that story in so many other different ways.

"I see something of an analogy in Hollywood: some of the most respected, edgy, and innovative drama isn't restrained within the format of the 90-minute blockbuster. *The Sopranos, The Wire, Mad Men, Breaking Bad, Boardwalk Empire* are where the best actors, writers, and directors are finding new ways of telling stories that have more freedom to develop more engaging characters and stories."

⤚

Jon Cook, "There's an unspoken responsibility that's inherent in people of a certain age. (I'm 42.) There's this window of years for people in our industry that cross certain barriers where they aren't yet old, but still get why people want things to be the same as they used to be. The people who had enough early exposure to what it was like to have very little technology – just fax machines, no email or barely any email, FedEx – we have a unique understanding of the balance between the discipline of no technology and the freedom of technology. That's probably why we're pretty good at our jobs. We can still relate to enough of the past to make a difference in the future. We know how to operate with a complete mastery of technology with modern-day sophistication, but people older than us don't, and people younger than us don't. Both of those groups have an appreciation for the craft of messaging, but they don't appreciate the medium.

"We can't forget that the cliché of the old guy in an ad agency who refuses to embrace digital has a counterpart, which is the young digital guy who won't embrace advertising. It's an equally threatening progression. Ok, probably not equally, but it gets overlooked since as a digital person, it's not seen as cool to advocate the power of television. I believe the best digital professional is a young person who embraces including the remaining power of broadcast as part of the campaign. That is equally as refreshing to me as the older professional who embraces digital at a time when they don't have to. Because a red-hot digital creative doesn't have to embrace any of it to succeed in their career. If they don't recognize the power of it, they can still make a good career right now, and I can see why they'd want to be 100% digital. So, it's refreshing to see that kind of thinking. And then a guy four years from retirement knows that he's going to make it, and he doesn't have to embrace digital at all. That makes it extra refreshing when they do."

⤚

Maya Mathias, Innovation Coach and Founder of Inventive Links and former Engagement Lead & Senior Consultant for BLUE in Palo Alto, "I did feel disconcerted about my career prospects by the sudden shift to digital for a while, when I hadn't spent enough time learning about the newer technologies like social media. On the surface, it seemed as if the youngsters had a leg up because they've grown up with the technology, and I believed that being effective online would be second nature to them.

"But now I don't believe there is an age limit on being credible as a digital marketer – then again, I've had role models like my 72-year-old business school classmate to draw from, so my opinion might be in the minority. As long as you're able to stay abreast of technology trends and, more importantly, help brands & clients make sense of and capitalize on the technology, then age is not a factor."

↶

Paul Kwong, "I believe that great thinkers will always be needed, no matter how old you are. The threats are that the folks hiring or the human resource departments and headhunters only want to see folks with '*x* years of digital experience.' Also, the threat is that the only way that large agencies can make money these days is to save on staff salaries, and that means younger folks with lower pay expectations will be hired.

"I don't think people are refusing to change. Most creative folks are pretty curious folks by nature and like to expand themselves. That's probably happening. But what's also happening is older employees are getting phased out in general for cheaper, younger folks. The move to digital is delivering people who can't draw or write a headline or even body copy."

↶

Åsk Wäppling, "I've met students straight out of school who are brilliant that I would totally recommend for a job tomorrow. It's not youth, it's gut instinct. It's not even creativity, it's just there's something that people know. Some people will learn it by experience, and some people just know it. A lot of people are saying that the kids coming out of art school today are much better than the 40-something-year-old creatives because they've grown up immersed in digital and they understand it more intimately. It's just bullshit. I keep saying it's bullshit. It's bullshit. It's bullshit. *It's bullshit.* They'll say that because they grew up with this media. At the same time, nobody taught them anything about discipline or propositions or strategy or how to actually create a campaign or how to hold the brand together or what the tone of voice is or what the base idea is or any of that. They taught them how to put a logo on the far right with Photoshop. It's bullshit.

"There're some kids who are very, very smart, but they're the brainy ones, and it's the same as when I went to ad school. There are some people who will seek it out and learn as much as they possibly can and ask everybody they know loads of questions. They will come out as the good kids who you will want to hire. Then there are some kids who just sit there and think they're entitled to stuff. To me, it seems that there are a lot more entitled kids today than there used to be. It's, 'I went to x school, so therefore I should have that job.' And I'm thinking, 'Well… but you suck.'"

$$\backsim$$

David Shulman, "I certainly have had a lot of people in the last two years who come from a general agency approach me for career opportunities. Back in '99 people said, 'I might come from Bronner,[5] but I can be an effective part of what you're trying to develop at Digitas – and with a strong foundation in the core principles of direct marketing most transitioned well to applying their skills to digital. I've had a lot of people in recent days come to me and say, 'I'm at a general agency, but I want to jump into a role at Organic or at another leading digital agency.' It's hard because they might not have had the specific training and practical experience. They may not have the technical background to make that jump.

"When you take a chance on someone, you're betting on their aptitude, you're betting on what insights they bring and what experience they have in general around driving brands – and sometimes people can be a great fit. Sometimes they can make that transition and sometimes they can't. It's not a constant, it might be variable from agency to agency."

$$\backsim$$

Aden Hepburn, Managing Director of VML Australia and former Head of Digital for Y&R Australia, "At VML, we're innovative, growing fast, and the digital spend is shifting towards us. Perhaps traditional creatives are

5 A traditional direct agency that became the integrated/digital agency Digitas.

wondering what the future holds for them. I was thinking about this with one of my planners the other day, and in a couple of years' time, it's going to be really, really interesting.

"A lot of traditional creatives are going to struggle over the next couple of years. Everyone wants someone with digital experience now, so the long and short of it is 80% of traditional creatives just aren't going to be good enough to make the jump because digital is so technical, and a concept isn't just a concept. A concept has to work within frameworks, capabilities, functionality, and technologies. Unless those guys understand that, they're never going to be able to come up with the right kind of concepts. They're never going to deliver the brief and be innovative online.

"There are some who can and who have started to evolve, but for the mainstream of traditional creatives, in two or three years' time, there'll be a massive resurgence, and that resurgence is going to be around content. Traditional creatives are still and always have been the very best storytellers ever. What we'll find in the next one, two, three years, is that content is going to continue to rise. It is going to rise faster and faster and faster, and what we'll find ourselves doing is not making traditional creatives redundant and replacing their jobs with digital people, but traditional creatives will move towards more content-focused roles where they're documenting things, they're creating films and really interesting content and conversation pieces for social channels like YouTube, and all sorts of things for mobile and whatever might be next.

"I'm sure a lot of people will say that traditional creatives will just die out, but I think they will come back over the next couple of years and will be as strong as ever, just in a completely different format. The role of creatives will flip over the next couple of years. Instead of being largely led by traditionally focused creatives, who're leading accounts from a brand perspective, I believe at some point that will flip to be led by digitally focused creatives leading accounts. And that will then be fueled by all the traditional creatives creating all the content that goes back into the digital frameworks.

"It is a really interesting shift in the creative industry that's going to happen no matter what, just because the new digital creatives coming through will understand everything better. At the same time, with the typically traditional guys being such great storytellers, they're always going to have a job, and their job is going to become more and more important to all the digital channels because it's important to be filled with content [that is] more brilliant and better than competitors."

⤸

George Tannenbaum, "Every generation thinks they invented all this stuff, and the older people in the industry (I think at 57, I'm the oldest surviving copywriter) can maybe take a step back and learn a little wisdom, too, but there's a lot of younger people who haven't done it before, and it's just the splendors of self-discovery. They gush about how you now have more forms than ever before to talk about this stuff. There's a self-serving value in proclaiming new discoveries and whatnot because it makes you seem ahead of the curve and smarter and all that.

"If you look at an agency like Goodby, which has enjoyed being a success for almost two decades now, and you deconstruct some of their better-known commercials, basically what they do is take very old forms and update them for the twentieth or twenty-first century. So, they'll do a side-by-side comparison. For instance, if you take *Got Milk?* It's what the world would be like if that product didn't exist. It's not really a new concept. It's a pretty universal thing, and I don't know if it was formalized or happenstance, but they came upon some pretty standard techniques and then executed them brilliantly for this century and enjoyed a great deal of success doing that. What they did, if you really look at it at a plot line level, was never really, 'Holy shit, I've never seen it before,' but still very effective. Really, we've made things very complicated and baroque when they don't really need to be. That has slowed us down and probably frustrated clients to a certain degree."

⤸

Ignacio Oreamuno, "I haven't seen people adapt. What I've seen is people quit. Before, if you were 44 and you were still in the business, you would just end quickly and you could get burned easily and out you go. Now those people go to teaching or something else because it's too hard to catch up when the 15-year-old intern says, 'Hey, here I just built this augmented reality Instagram app with geolocation. What do you think?' It's like, 'Whoa.' I get that a lot because at portfolio night, we get 4,000 juniors coming in every year showing portfolios. Ten years ago, the creative directors would treat the juniors like crap, saying, 'Hey okay, whatever. Your book sucks,' or, 'Okay, you're good. I'll give you a chance.' Now, the juniors are coming in with portfolios that the creative directors don't even understand. That's the way it is."

~~

Steffan Postaer, "If you want to be a real artist, you've got to first learn how to paint still life, and you've got to learn how to do a landscape, but the kids now want to jump right to Cubism or Expressionism. They want to go right to the cool thing that they feel is what it's all about right now, and they don't want to learn how to paint the picture of a person the way Picasso did or to learn how to paint a picture of a landscape the way Renoir did. They don't want to do any of the work and then adapt to their own style. They just want to go right to style, and that's becoming more a problem with all creativity like with the field of photography. If you go to school to learn photography, you'll find that everyone considers themselves a photographer by virtue of having an iPhone and Instagram.

"If you go to the Art Institute to study the craft, the first two years of your classes are going to be about those who came before you and what they did, about black-and-white techniques and how to develop film, even though it's completely not how it's done this day. Because that's how you teach. Now everybody wants to go right to Cubism. Nobody wants to learn how to draw. They want to go right to the app. It's like, 'We don't need to know how to draw because there's an app for that.'

"I say the clients and the agencies that support that attitude are all 40- and 50-year-old CMOs and ECDs who are all afraid that because they don't even have a Twitter follower, they are secretly vulnerable, so they better start fronting and hiring a bunch of kids so that they don't get exposed. I feel that connecting the dots to that deep fear and insecurity is pretty much all you need to do. Ageism and all the *isms* are tough big problems. They've always been around in some form or fashion, and it is tough. I don't have a great answer. I'm in my 50s. I'm old. Would I hire me? That's the question. 'Would I hire me if I were interviewing myself for a job?' It's a great question. I bet you everybody, if they're being honest, wouldn't be so sure. My tendency is to be my own worst critic.

"To answer that fair and square, I don't know. One of the reasons I wouldn't hire me is because I wouldn't want to pay me what I get. I don't know. I've taken significant pay cuts since the salad days. Altoids makes a lot of people a shit ton of money. It was a $500,000 account, and we made $1,500,000,000.00 for it, with Lifesavers getting $700 million and Altoids getting like $1 billion. That's *billions* of dollars – all because of the posters I made, not because the mints were awesome. Those mints were awesome for 250 years, and no one bought them. We made a handful of posters that changed everything. So I made a lot of money because of that.

"Nobody wakes up thinking they're company men anymore. Everyone's a mercenary. I tried to reconcile it with, 'How can I be of maximum use to the place I'm at today?' and that's how I try to keep my old values in line with the philosophy I can live with that's relevant. That's me. That's what I try to do."

⌒

Edelman's Senior Vice President of Digital in Toronto, Dave Fleet, "You can have smart people regardless of what age they are. You can have people who can come up with great ideas, great creative. It doesn't matter if they're 12 or 42. The challenge for the folks on the junior side of the spectrum is getting the experience to know whether your idea is a good one or a bad one; learning often through hard experience what's likely to backfire and how to spot the signs of things beginning to backfire. We're not in a one-way world here anymore. If people don't like something, then what you thought was a very positive piece of content or a very positive campaign could turn out to be highly brand-damaging and in a very short period of time.

"That is a challenge, and what I've seen in a lot of people coming up through the ranks who think after a couple of short years of working on the cumulative end of things that they want to be a strategist now. These people who think, 'I'm young, I'm creative, I get digital, I want to do strategy. I don't want to go work my way up.' That's a massive challenge because until you got that experience, I don't think you can be as an effective counselor. Don't get me wrong here, I have on my team some absolutely brilliant young professionals straight out of school. Our team is better for it. They've got all the qualities that you want from someone that's at that stage of their career, and they do bring the knowledge of social experience from their own personal experience. That's the key differential, but that has to be paired with the experience. I'm so thankful for the four or five years I spent working in traditional PR because it taught me to think about issues management, and it taught me to think about communications strategy, messaging, stakeholders, and all sorts of things that we just wouldn't necessarily naturally think about."

✐

Neil Leslie, "I'm fairly confident that I'll be able to keep up. At least for a while. I'm an Internet addict and techno-geek at heart. Always have been. It's not necessarily going to be easy. It's just a case of doing my best to embrace and sometimes shape the new, which is something that as creatives, we've always tried to do anyway. We're still searching for fresh insights. Fresh ideas. Fresh writing. Fresh visuals. Fresh stories, etc. It's just that now many of these creative skill sets are converging in the digital space and evolving to drive increased interactivity, involvement, and sharing."

✐

Paul Biedermann, "The young, technically proficient crowd has had an arrogance and sense of entitlement that can be frustrating for older, more experienced practitioners in the creative industry to watch. For good reason, the work suffers and, in the end, that isn't good for clients or their businesses, either. If one has real integrity in this business, it is more than just producing fantastic creative, it is also about doing work that is ultimately effective for the clients we serve.

"There has been a preponderance of focusing on the bells and whistles rather than concept and overarching strategy. Industry professionals are just as guilty of this as the clients themselves, so it has been a self-perpetuating problem. I am optimistic that this problem won't last forever, as focusing only on the technical aspects leads to uninspired work that gets really boring really quickly. Just like watching a movie with all the latest special effects, but lacking a truly compelling story will have audiences flocking to the exits."

✐

Steve Hall, "When I was 38, I had a discussion with someone who was 42 at the time about how I don't know too many over-40 creative directors... and now he's off as a marketing director and 10 years later, here I am. I'm doing my own thing, luckily. I couldn't imagine myself at my age being at an ad agency because I'd be looked at like some old school fart who doesn't know a thing. It's like a bias. It's sort of built-in. I don't know what the solution is. It's just a cultural thing. No one respects their elders anymore. There was a day and a time when people would respect their elders. They would look up to their elders, and they would want to hear the stories, and they would want to learn the wisdom of the elder. Now, it's sort of like, 'You're old. You're a jerk. You're clueless. You're not connected. You have no idea what you're talking about. How could I possibly learn something from you?' There's a large degree of disrespect.

"There's the notion of the experienced person and the apprentice, as they used to be known, and you would learn from the experience of the other. The apprentice might come up with these fascinating new wonderful ideas, and that's what younger people do. It's like, 'This is new and this is cool, and maybe we should try this.' They're going to bounce that idea off someone who is more senior and that person is going to say, 'We've done that before and it didn't work.' There's always going to be a push and a pull.

"There should never be a wholesale handing over of the reigns to the new generation. You learn by your mistakes, or you learn by the mistakes of others, and so if you have someone who's been around for a while, who has done tons of campaigns and perhaps along the way has made several mistakes, then you can learn from that person and not make those same mistakes, or you can take the idea, the campaign, the notion, the program that that person did and look at it and say, 'Today we could do that a little bit differently. We could do this. We could do that.'

"You need both the mentor and mentee. You always need the wisdom of experience. Sometimes it comes with the length of time someone's been doing the work; it becomes stale. More experienced creatives can become bored or jaded. They don't think about fresh ideas anymore. They're pushing the pencil. They're just doing what they need to to get through the day. They're bored and they're uninspired. Any time you have new blood come in, there's inspiration, there's eagerness, there's youthful thinking, you're unencumbered by the structure of the agencies, the negative cultural connotations of the agency. Everything's new to younger creatives but we older ones too. The older ones may never learn how to do the 'new stuff,' but they may understand it. Older creatives should at least be able to understand the concepts and constructs of certain ideas. It may not be their bailiwick. It may not be their love and desire, but they should be able to understand the concept."

⤙

Chris Kyme, "I really think it's important to move with the times and be up to speed with what's going on. However, the mistake being made is that technology is now being used to disguise poor ideas. Highly finished layouts are done up to present to clients, and they're impressed by the execution rather than concept. I still encourage people to work up ideas as roughs, not done up on a Mac. It's true that the technology has affected and diluted craft. I would blame the lost art of copywriting on that. It's because the industry in general has become less professional because it's easier for non-professional people to 'have a go.'"

⤙

Dirk Eschenbacher, "The 'older' creatives I work with are all quite open to new things. Many of them now work on stunts that can turn viral. They have ideas for apps. There's a natural adaption and adoption happening across the board. I haven't really met anybody who just focuses on print ads. Even people who are really good with TV aren't just making commercials, but all sorts of video content.

"The older guys have great client relationships and good leadership and management skills. They all understand what's going on. The older guys can always hire the right people, and that's what they are trying to do. That's why I always get requests from older, senior people who want me to try and help them on the digital stuff. As long as they understand that they need help and then try and get the help, then things are all fine. I don't see any fear.

"The older guys can pass on the importance of an idea to younger colleagues. That's the main thing, whereby ideas become much more complex now than just a single-minded idea. There is discussion going on around that, which is quite interesting. Those guys, they can make complex things very simple, where the digital guys can make simple things very complex.

"They can definitely learn some of those things from the older guys about packaging and selling the work and really getting down to the core of what it is you are really doing, because oftentimes the digital guys get lost in too much execution and add too many layers, too many legs, too many arms. There's the focal sharpness and the thoroughness of the older colleagues that helps them to stay focused. The focus thing is something the younger guys don't really have yet."

⌇

Former CEO of Publicis Greater China (2012-2014) and former Chairman of Bates141 Asia Pacific and the Hong Kong 4As (Association of Accredited Advertising Agencies), Jeffrey Yu, "The 45-year-olds and the 50-year-olds are now using Facebook and are into everything. It's not that these people don't understand. It's about bringing all this together. Obviously, the younger guys are much more digital savvy, but at the same time, it is no different from any other industry where you say, 'I've got to mix the best of the young and old.' It is not the old, but the more mature. With the rise in the importance of digital, the traditional media people are not as arrogant as before. It is actually very, very cool to be in digital creative, but even cooler if you are into digital planning and all that. Digital has now been elevated in status, big time.

"It's more open because all the traditional advertising people keep saying, 'I don't understand that. I want to learn about it, but it would be best if done by the digital agency.' That's why I'm putting all of these training teams together so that the digital planner and the brand planner can work together. In the older days, it was about, 'Here is the brand. If you understand, do it. If you don't understand, fuck it, don't bother even trying.'"

⌇

Tobias Wilson, "A lot of the new guys and gals that are coming in are much younger, have all their friends online, and they don't really like spending time outside. They'd rather be inside on their computer. But they lack perspective. They find it really hard to put themselves in somebody else's shoes, and when you are 21 or 25, you tend to think you've done and seen it all, right?

"The older guys who have been there, done that, they understand client servicing back to front. They know humility, as well. You don't get that with the younger guys. Experienced guys might not have the tech savvy, but they certainly know how to run integrated campaigns. They're street smart, which is something you can really only get with experience.

"Think about campaigns that have gone past and how the older suits and creatives would sit around having a drink at the end of the week, talking about old campaigns that we loved and things like that. The younger guys really just don't have the passion for that one line or for that beautiful visual. They are too technical, and so that's why you've got to rely on the older guys to bring class back into the campaign."

⌒

Dr. Neal Burns, Founder and Director of the University of Texas Advertising Department's account planning program, Director of UT's Center for Brand Research, and former Senior Partner and Director of Research and Account Planning at Carmichael Lynch Advertising, "The people who are long in the tooth in their careers are the primary reason the bright young guys who understand the importance of digital creative leave and set up their own shops across the street. That's always been the case in the advertising world. Take, for example, GSD&M, where almost every agency in Austin [Texas] has principals who at one point were employed by that one company.

"Some agencies are really struggling, some are being disrupted, and they're certainly not making the money that they used to – and they're losing their client base in an interesting way. By and large, the people with whom we deal came out of the Procter & Gamble heritage method. That's what they bring to us. Some of those guys are really quite bright, and they realized that they don't want to be held around the throat. They are perfectly capable of having a group of specialists. They can have someone who does their research or copy testing. They can have someone who does their PR. They can have someone who takes them into the world of digital and Internet, etc., and they might still keep the agency that thinks it is the keeper of the brand.

"But product managers and CMOs generally view people in advertising as children, and the risk that you have in your role is that these very cute assholes dressed in black shirts and black jeans, often torn, are going to come up with some idea that they think is brilliant, but that is going to harm your career [because it may be cool, but it doesn't bring results]. So you have to watch them very carefully and look more to these specialist agencies."

↬

Susan Kim, "You have to actually become a user and to not be afraid of the [digital and social] environments if you want to work in this business today. I am not saying you need to learn to code, although find out just a little bit about it. It's not nearly as intimidating as you would think. An example is how a few years ago, AOL bought Bebo. They bought it for $800 million, and while they were in negotiation, this was before Facebook was really big, they could have bought Facebook for $1.1 billion. It was Randy Falco, the former Chairman and CEO of AOL, and another executive that made this decision. They had never been on social networks like Facebook or Bebo, themselves. They had never bothered to use them. To them, they were commodities; all the same thing. As soon as they announced it, I remember when they did, everyone went, 'Ahhh!' You could hear the room just gasp because all of us who had been using Facebook knew that none of us were going to ever go on Bebo. What were they basing this important costly decision on? If my old boss, Randy Falco, hadn't been so afraid of Facebook and just thought, 'I'll check out the digital stuff,' or if he had just been a natural user, he would have seen why that was such a stupid idea. He wouldn't have had to have been a hardcore user, just had to be in the mix and talked to a few other people that were actual users.

"I am not saying we are all Randy Falco, but, that, yeah, we make mistakes. I had to spend a lot of effort to convince a traditional creative friend to get her to experiment a little with digital because she was like, 'I'm going to hold off, I'm going to hold off.' I had to tell her, "I know you're so great at traditional stuff, but you're going to have to just get comfortable with this.' The thing is, once you get in the water, it's not nearly as cold and shark-infested as you thought it was going to be. In fact, you'll like it, but you have got to put a toe in the water.

"Just to be able to have some informed conversations. Once you have just at least dabbled in it so it's not a total foreign language, then you can have the philosophical discussions. I was the digital traditional. You can have it, but without at least dabbling, there is no way you can have the higher-level conversations, and I would say that should be the angle. You are not being asked to code, you are not being asked to tweet like 20 times; you don't even have to tweet at all. Be an observer. You don't even have to watch what is going on in Facebook, but you need to be logged in, and not that it's all digital, but if you are not at least at the airport in order to get to New York, it's hard to even discuss travel.

"The end thing should be like, 'Look, you've been around so long, you have so much knowledge, but in order to really contribute to the big conversation and to be more of a leader and help bridge this gap, you have got to be getting your feet wet.' First of all, say, 'Hey, it's not like anyone has nailed this yet. Anyone that claims they have is wrong,' because the social media thing, there are some best practices, but a lot of them that don't even work.

"The big picture and emotions that grab people, that's what defined good advertising traditionally, and that is what is missing in the more the digital realm. You can bring that, but the only way you can bring that emotional connection and coolness and then the big picture thing is you have got to know where the airport is."

⌒

Andy Greenaway, "Old age and cunning will always out-wit youth and enthusiasm. But seriously, there will be a continuous flow of knowledge between the generations. Older guys like me in their late 40s will learn an awful lot from the younger, more tech-savvy guys. But they will also learn an awful lot from old guys like me. When the younger guys get older, they'll learn something from the next generation and vice versa. This will become a continuous pattern going forward.

"I fundamentally believe the day you stop learning is the day you need to be put out to pasture, no matter how experienced you are. We are now in the era of continuous learning. There will no longer be gurus who have done it all and know it all."

Chapter 5: Fragmentation: Shift Happens

If you are old enough, you may remember — or if you ever happened to look into the past, you may have noticed — that with every generation, there has been a great gold rush of new advertising channels that cause marketers to move or "shift" the dollars in their budgets away from the tried, proven, but stale media that everyone has finally figured out and become expert in after much, much pain. Outdoor advertising lost out to newspapers, newspapers lost out to radio, radio (and even Hollywood) lost out to broadcast television, broadcast to cable. Television was finally beginning to bend at the knees to online display when social and mobile began to eat everyone's lunch, including the remnants of magazines, newspapers, and what is now being dismissively labeled as "traditional digital" (read: banners, e-mails, and microsites).

"That is the sound of inevitability," sneered Agent Smith to Neo in *The Matrix,* and although it will be tougher to pinpoint the telltale noise of the shift in this universe than in their future virtual one, there is no doubt that it has happened here, is happening, and will continue to happen. The only thing as certain as a new medium rising up to attract the bulk of marketing spend is the significant number of years it takes before the large agencies of the day see the writing on the wall. It's not that they are incapable of recognizing it; they simply are too focused on the short term to care. For most companies owned by shareholders of one sort or the other, if there is no immediate financial return, the businesses tend to ignore whatever it is.

Why would advertising agencies that are generating enormous, established, and accepted media commissions and production fees for television commercials and, to a lesser degree, print campaigns, spend all of the time and effort required to learn about digital, mobile, and social? You think to educate and prepare their clients for the future? To have a workforce that is ahead of the curve and capable of adapting to new technologies and tactics? *Are you nuts?*

No, the prevailing line of thought is that low-hanging fruit that you don't pick just rots away, so the prudent thing is to keep planting seeds that are equally easy to pluck until everything has been harvested. What happens after that will undoubtedly be someone else's problem, so why sweat it? The board is happy, the holding company chiefs are happy, the client brand and product managers are happy they hit their short-term goals, the agency staff have jobs they can do, and retirement is not that far off. "It's not *my* problem!" Shift happens to other people. But it's important to understand the factors, beginning in the 1980s up through the advent of digital/social, which had a huge (not positive) effect on agencies and started us down the road that led us to this unhealthy position we find ourselves in today.

Cable TV Created the First Fragmented Markets

When television was in its heyday in the US, very few brands could afford to avail themselves of its reach and effectiveness. There were only three commercial networks plus commercial-free PBS (beginning in 1967) vying for eyeballs, which meant that most people were watching one of them. But how was a smaller brand or local company to get the word out if they could only afford air time during late night shows, featuring actors no one wanted to see during waking hours? It wasn't especially hard to do the media strategy and figure out where and when you should put your spot to grow your brand and get the message out, but it was very competitive and ridiculously expensive because of the massive size of the captured morning, day and, especially, prime-time audiences.

For example, in 1964 when The Beatles were introduced on *The Ed Sullivan Show,* 73 million people were screaming simultaneously at their tiny black-and-white television sets; and on the final episode of *M*A*S*H* nearly 20 years later, more than 125 million people tuned in disbelief solely to CBS to see the Korean War finally end after 11 years. Another decade after that, there were still more than 40 million watchers of the nightly network TV newscasts, and everyone was getting rich off of the ads. But *waitaminute,* as of today, that last stat is down to a mere 6 to 8 million steady viewers. "What happened?!" shouted the executives, with veins popping out of their doughy necks. Oh… right. *Fragmentation.*

Now, cable has been around in America since 1948, 20 years after the first television station made its debut and just seven years after the first television commercial aired. But since the primary purpose for the first 25 years of its existence was to relay the broadcasts of the commercial networks to rural areas of the country, it was much more a signal booster than anything that could be considered competition.

It wasn't until Ted Turner drove into the ground what eventually became known as TBS Superstation — and the first basic cable network — that the earth began to move and broadcast swayed and eventually felt the effect. Soon, early cable channels and new networks came into their own. Some were general and others were highly targeted: USA (1971), HBO (1972), Showtime (1976), Nickelodeon (1977), ESPN (1979), CNN (1980), Cinemax (1980), MTV (1981), Disney Channel (1983), A&E (1984) and what eventually became known as a platform hosting "hundreds of channels with nothing on."

Still, people began to subscribe for the privilege of flipping stations, until watching each for a few seconds became a show in and of itself, and while some cable channels like HBO were as commercial-free as PBS, others provided a major benefit for advertisers that the broadcast channels did not: they were dirt cheap. What you lost in concentrated numbers of people in single viewings could be made up for in frequency, frequency, frequency.

Thus began the war of attrition of viewers of broadcast, along with ad spend allocations. They went arm-in-arm to the vast open spaces and opportunities of cable — at a remarkable rate of about 20% growth each year.

Of course, for the first several years, our brethren in the larger ad agencies eschewed getting involved with cable television commercials since they wouldn't have been able to pull in the same level of money as they could for executing slicker, higher-production value spots for broadcast clients. If you want to know where an agency is going to be, follow the money!

When you have a holding company doing the books for you and the many other agencies they own, they tend to fly up to a 50,000-meter view, level off, and uncover gross inefficiencies that exist across the businesses. They start playing with their slide rules, abaci, supercomputers, and spreadsheets and begin the bewildering process of creating massive wealth from where before there had been nothing but great wealth. This is done by eliminating brand conflict, realizing economies of scale in buying power, automating as much as possible, and creating specialist companies that, on the basis of their focused expertise, can charge a lot more than an agency that just offers *it* as another service. These managing entities realized pretty quickly that various units of a full-service advertising agency could be calved off, float down the currents on their own, and eventually gather more surface area to become major forces within the industry in their own, independent right.

For instance, the media-buying practice used to be a couple of people in the back who would make calls, get the best prices, and help plan out an informed placement strategy. Suddenly, they were in their own office with their own brand name, taking in projects from "sister" above-the-line agencies of all stripes, with clients from across the board. Agencies were no longer in control of media strategy and fees; they were simply aligned with one of a handful of large media agencies owned by the same entity.

Clients now had to pay for the redundant infrastructure and costs, support personnel, the now higher-priced specialists, and also get pitched many different new tactics that were being conceived to help justify the need for a new company, with more people getting bigger salaries. There's suffering from always being experimented upon: "We're innovating!" Then there are the campaign-ownership conflicts between the ATL and media agencies, that, like anyone competing for client face time and the pole position as the key advisor, live for undermining each other and eroding trust all around. It also makes for lovely awkward joint client meetings and ferocious closed-door meetings, sister-to-sister.

Next, the public relations gang had their own Independence Day, followed by event planning, direct (aka below-the-line), and then... there was digital. Over a period of 18 years (so far), digital teams have been forced into a number of organizational structures, over and over, as agency executives tried to figure out what to do with the nerds.

- First, they were an agency sub-unit, then a wholly owned subsidiary, then placed under the below-the-line agencies ("Well, it's *not* above-the-line, so it must be BTL...").
- Then a major integrated piece of the above-the-line strategic team ("The clients are asking for it! Quick!").
- Then an independent shop with a partnership ("We need to show we 'get it' and have them as the Group jewel to bring out").
- Then back as a division of the agency ("Hey, we need their credibility in the main agency!").
- *Now* as part of a Digital rollup of all the "on-the-line" groups ("It's important to show clients and shareholders that we have expertise in *all* of these weird new areas that we were never really interested in before — and we can bring the specialists together for you.").
- And on and on.

Regardless of that game of ping-pong with positioning (and people's lives), one clear result occurred due to this fragmentation: the full-service agency is no longer capable of full service. Oh, sure, they claim to be able to still do everything with or without their holding company partner specialists, but so do the specialists. Direct marketing firms now do video, PR companies handle social media, media companies develop web sites and mobile apps, and "traditional" ATL agencies do it all, too. The blood had been in the water for quite a long time, and existing within the very Darwinian universe of bigger holding companies means that the Powers That Be (PTB) expect their children to eat each other, if it means *more profit*. <insert thunderous echo effect>

At some point in the near future, these now-fragmented but completely related and overlapping areas will need to be put back together or managed by someone who isn't the client and who is looking after the client's revenue goals and not their own. Then the client can get on with his or her regular job and not be involved in the constant vendor drama of trying to undermine the other guy and sell their expanded services.

∽

Senior Research Fellow at the USC Annenberg School Center for the Digital Future, Brad Berens, "I actually don't think that most of what's happened to the ad agencies happened to them because of digital. It happened because of fragmentation. And the mass of fragmentation that we have, we had first with cable television, which had an extraordinary hockey stick of growth that's only continued to grow. And then added a bunch of gasoline to the fire when the Internet was thrown on top of it.

"The craft of advertising has gotten more complicated, and the business of advertising has gotten worse. It is a worse business to be in if you are a media property that is ad supported because both the advertising and your media have become aggressively commoditized. If you're in the ad business, the problem is it's no longer a competition about who's going to do the best idea. It's, 'I can do that idea cheaper.' It's a really rough business to be in when your product is being aggressively commoditized from the top end and from the bottom. I look at Borders (books and music) in the face of Amazon and with the exception of Amazon and Google, I don't really see a lot of digital companies becoming as big as their analog ancestors. Instead, what I see is the Internet as a great leveling force that takes value from some centralized place like the classified ads in the newspaper and grinds it up and puts it to the wood chipper and then spreads that value over a much, much wider area than previously it was taken. There is very hopeful story buried inside of this, which is we might see the rise of an artistic class. We might see a world in which people who work for ad agencies in a distributed way might have lots of little independent companies that combine together in order to serve brands almost the way that Hollywood approaches production. Where they don't have a lot of people on staff 100% of the time; they have people who come in on a project basis or gaffers with musicians who are on tour. Who might be on tour for six months of the year and then doing other things the rest of the time."

⤶

Alan Schulman, "One of the major factors that led to the devaluation of advertising agencies was when the holding companies began unbundling media from creative and combining their media services for the purposes of buying clout. When they unbundled the media shops from their creative brethren, they really did a disservice to the agency business. They promised that buying clout would drive the marketer's media price down in the name of value creation, but what it also did was prevented us from collaborating in ways that let great creative ideas and great contextual ideas work together.

"As a result, today our media brethren and we are really missing opportunities to truly function as teams. We're just these large entities who are forced together at a tabletop. We're asked to collaborate, but most of the time it's more just co-existence. I would say the accountability for co-existing rather than collaborating, in part, resides on the marketer side. This is due in large part because they ask us to compete with each other first, to win their business, and then suddenly, they ask us to collaborate. They foster a spirit of competition between us to win their affection, but soon after, they expect us to put down our pencils and swords and collaborate like business partners. In my view, that just goes against the competitive nature of business.

"As a result of this very separate dynamic that now exists between creative and media, we now have media service agencies that have moved well past their media-centric planning and buying functions and begun offering integrated creative services. The premise is 'Hey, if we understand the media placement opportunities and strategies best, well, why wouldn't we also be suited for creating the messages that are supposed to be contextually appropriate for that?'

"Other factors hurt the traditional agency model as well – it wasn't just the unbundling of media, it was direct marketing agencies and dozens of new little digital agencies who enabled the holding companies to maximize their revenue opportunities and reduce conflicts within the traditional agency roster so they could still go after the business. That was the beginning of the end of momentum for the major agency brands. They spent all those decades building up this mighty ship that could handle all of these things in one complete holding company offering.

"The theory was we can bring all the marketing disciplines together to deliver the best value to the client, the brand, and the media savings, and internally, they turned us into competitors. Even within the same holding company, we were competing from the same pool of dollars. I was part and parcel to that – having to compete for intercorridor dollars. It was not a setup for delivering the best client results.

"The cracks we're beginning to see in this are when media budgets and automation begin moving marketer side. Now that we have programmatic buying, demand-side platforms (DSPs) and trading desks where you can allo-cate and buy digital media on a software platform, you're going to see clients starting to bring that in-house and not using the big media service companies. I believe that will be a tipping point where the last fundamental leverage media agencies have is going to begin to erode – and that's likely going to be your first tree falling in the woods.

"Automation is going to happen on the media side before it happens on the creative side. Because the truth is, creatives are in the daily business of generating ideas – be they visual, interactive, or copy-based ideas – and algo-rithms don't feel, people do – so automated headline writing from algorithms might be possible in the future… but will they make anyone feel something?

"It will be a long time before we start to see clients bringing the cre-ative side of the agency business in-house. I do, however, think that the media side is coming, and that will un-entrench the current model. As a result, hold-ing companies will have to determine where they're going to get value and growth. Is it going to come from consulting? If it's not going to come from media dollars, it better come from somewhere else, and the only place it can come from is e-commerce, consulting or technology. That's where it all has to pivot towards once media dollars start to move client side."

⌣

Jon Cook, "We think a lot about the new millennial workforce. Frag-mentation is one of the two big factors that lead to a laziness or lessening of the work ethic, and too much of it breeds 'that's not my job' syndrome, which in turn creates a 'start and end to my job' type of thinking. I don't know if laziness is too strong a word. It's not everybody who is lazy, but it leads to a culture of entitlements. I'm being paid for eight hours a day: I do that job and nothing else.

"But there is still total strength in fragmentation. You have a specializa-tion of a specific skill set, not just in our industry, but any. It's coming across in ours, which is a dilution of the work ethic and a potential for 'that's not my job' attitude. I'm saying all this as one of the biggest advocates of big visual agencies and of technology – personally, as an enthusiast – and it couldn't be more part of my life.

"Not like a grandfather saying, 'I wish it were like the old days,' but as with the idea of when you had to FedEx something to get it to someone. We needed to FedEx a layout, and we were driven by very published and stated and immovable deadlines. The work ethic was more intense then because of that, and I don't want to go back to the era when there was a FedEx deadline at 10 o'clock and you had to get to the airport or you'd blow the project.

"The drive and the closure then was that I would do anything I could and everything it took to get great work by that deadline, I knew every way to do it, and I would prioritize. I would be the one person at the agency to prioritize accordingly, multitask accordingly, who had the discipline.

"If we could capture the technology available to us today and the portability of deadline and collaboration with the sort of discipline of nontechnical deadlines and nontechnical structure to how we produce work, we would be really strong. There is not for every disadvantage a major advantage to technology, but it can make you lazy. It can take away the discipline of the deadline, of how you collaborate to get somewhere."

～

Asia Pacific Managing Director of HootSuite, Chairman Emeritus of the Internet Advertising Bureau (IAB) SE Asia, and former Regional VP of Yahoo! and Salesforce, Ken Mandel, "There has been immense fragmentation in the digital industry in terms of services, and this will likely continue. However, there also continues to be consolidation, so this balances the pressure on client base erosion.

"Good agencies can find the higher-dollar opportunities. What is key is that the barriers to entry – such as staging environments, servers, and equipment and hosting – have all but disappeared, thanks to l'cloud. You do get many little agencies ankle-biting away, though.

"Being digital today is quite different than what it was years ago. Today, you must be able to think through the lines of ATL, BTL, etc. Digital is much more pervasive today, and what was traditional media a few years back is now also digital. For example, TV has become online video and is no longer consumed in a linear fashion. Outdoor ads use Bluetooth or mobile to activate them and are no longer static. There are print ads with QR codes. We're now reading magazines on a tablet.

"The digitization of all media (or most of it) means that digital skills are much more widely required. Agencies that can think digital at the core, but still apply cross-media strategy and execution, have huge an advantage over the single-medium agencies. These tend to be the smaller agencies (Crispin Porter, or, one closer to home, Arcade in Singapore) where everyone works on one floor and are not siloed physically or monetarily. The death knell for any agency is when there are internal pie fights for revenue between different departments."

⮌

CEO of Victors & Spoils, Havas Chief Innovation Officer, and former Executive Director of Strategy and Innovation for Crispin, Porter + Bogusky, John Winsor, "Agencies lag behind due to this business of exploiting. It's easy to make money and exploit a million-dollar project. It's super hard to figure out how to create a new model or to invent a new revenue stream. I'm in love with the old adage of analog dollars, digital dimes. But when I was talking to somebody at this Digiday conference, they added 'mobile pennies.' If you are an agency, why the hell would we spend any time on mobile? It might be something fun. You can do a chart a few hours off, but if you are making pennies when you used to make dollars, it's really hard to make a business grow."

⮌

Angeli Beltran, "It used to be the age where everything was fragmented. There were specialists even under one agency's roof: there was a unit for this, a unit for that. A unit for PR, a unit for direct, a unit for events, and each one had its own P&L. What the structure did was instead of the agency focusing on what the right solution is for the client, it became an internal fight for a budget.

"Remember that the purpose of the agency is to help find the best solution for the client to deliver their results; we need to study structurally how we're able to do that. If it's all about focusing on internal struggles in order to get more budget, or 'How am I going to get more budget than this guy,' then everything is upside down.

"It's like left pocket, right pocket. Some agencies were quite integrated to begin with. Some agencies that had split up into disciplines in the past are now struggling to work closely together or bring things back together. As the saying goes, it's like trying to put the toothpaste back into the tube.

"I'll give one example of an ad agency that we met when I moved to Client side and called for a pitch. We wrote to them and said, 'You were recommended, and we want to see you because this is what we need…' After writing to agency A, someone from agency B within the same agency group wrote us to say, 'Hi, we are from the same holding company, and we'd like to meet you as well,' and then agency A came back and said, 'We're bringing in agency C because they're a specialist in digital.' And we looked at each other and said 'Wait, then who's agency B?'

"Agency A had no awareness that agency B wrote us. It's a demonstration of how siloed things were within that holding company group. We were super turned off because what we *needed* was an integrated campaign. How do we expect them to be able to work together when they're already trying to grab business from each other, and we haven't even met the original agency?

"Agency structure really does follow the client that you have and their budget. For example, because the Unilevers and P&Gs of this world have huge budgets, the agencies can afford to have specialists in-house. Of course, there are smaller agencies such as BRIQ, which has an alliance with Dentsu. Their model is to have all of the brains in house. BRIQ has project managers, but they have a whole network of partners who they can use anytime, depending on the client need. That approach allows BRIQ to be a lot more nimble in the way they operate. It's a very interesting agency model because they don't have a big team, maybe about twenty.

"A lot of the work they are doing is with select partners who they have at arm's length relationships with, and whenever the client needs something, they bring the combination together and are able to deliver. Everyone wins."

⌒

Jim Speelmon, "There is this severe fragmentation of media in Australia, and the challenge now is that you've got media agencies who still work on relationships and volume and rates. They say they can give to you the best rate and you reply, 'Yeah, but you can't get me the media that I need. You can give me an excellent price, but you can't tell me if that's the best media for what I want done.' That is why you see a move now away from the major media and creative agencies to more of the smaller consultancies, where you now have a [specialist] shop you go to for SEO. You have a [specialist] shop you go to for SEM. You have a [specialist] shop you go to for social media.

"It's a self-perpetuating cycle, and it is on a downward spin, in my opinion. I don't think it's going to re-aggregate [within the traditional agencies] anywhere near where it was before. When you look at things like Twitter, for example, which is very instant, very now, and very short, it's like marketers are training people to have a very, very, very limited attention span. Where everything is on demand, when you want it and how you want it, it will become increasingly difficult, if not impossible, for brands to build and maintain a long-term, ongoing relationship with customers. They just don't have the attention span, and the brands have now trained them to expect tiny, mouth-sized bites. There's really no reason for you to invest anything in this kind of relationship. That's where I see it going.

"You're going to see the same players fighting over the same amount of money every time something new comes in, and you're going to just have more and more churn. If the environment doesn't work for you, then you should create a new culture to stimulate a fresh one. This is an environment for smart people who can rise above the fray and craft the larger story, write the script for the players, and then assist the client in auditioning the actors for the play, if you will.

"It could even be somebody like me when I went over to UniQlick, which is more of a client-side thing. We build software that media agencies use, and we *will* eventually replace media agencies. I quit looking for a job in the industry because I couldn't sit through another interview and listen to somebody say, 'At our agency, digital is the center of everything.' It's just that it has been at the center of everything since the *1990s*."

"When you then consider the current dynamic of the industry, the fragmentation of media with all the social media, it becomes more difficult to find the consumer insights. One way that an agency could become more relevant, or for a person to re-ignite their career, is to shift what we mean when we say we need 'insights.'

"The role of the strategist is to figure out how to create the opportunity for an insight, as opposed to going out and looking to see what are people doing. You have to work harder about it – or harder than you did before. You need to be able to look at where someone is today. Where do you want them to be? How are you going to facilitate the creation of an opportunity where what your client wants to talk about is going to be meaningful? I tend to think of it as just paying more attention to the way that people think and behave. Whereas before, you're looking at a group of people and a certain situation that defines what the thing is that really turns them on.

"There's a much higher level of risk involved with immediate publication of social media. In general, I would say that creatives and planners and clients are very focused on the insights. The insights are pretty much done in isolation of the real world, in my opinion. CMOs are now doing the whole of managing the integration of all the different players because *somebody* has to be in control of this. The agencies are not good at it. From a strategy perspective, it's the same thing.

"If somebody needs to be in control of the total strategy, I don't think it should be a case of 'I'm going to go out and see what people are doing and find an insight to match to my message.' It should be, 'I'm going to go out and look at people to see what they're doing, where are they doing it, how they're talking about it so I can find what the most appropriate place is for me to start planning the message.' Rather than it being the insight = message, it should be behavior leads to an opportunity where you create a journey that you'd like the customer or the recipient to go on with you. It will cross all of the channels, but it's planned that they all work together.

"One of the challenges is that the CMO was taking on that coordination integration role because it needed to be done. He didn't, and they still don't, trust that the agencies will be able to pull it off. The agencies are trying to be everything to everybody [by becoming 'specialists' in every niche area], which means that they are five miles wide and just a few molecules deep.

"People in the industry see a lot of disillusionment with how things have come to be; primarily because they have such a tiny little piece. If you're a strategist or a planner, you're at the end of the food chain where all of the media investment decisions have already been made. The master strategies have been put in to place. You are really put into a small executional budget. You're trying to create a project strategy to fit into a master strategy that you probably weren't involved with. It creates a self-fulfilling prophecy where the client thinks, 'I don't really have much use for advertising because it either is too confusing or the agencies don't understand my business.'

"Part of that is true because of the way the agencies have positioned themselves to be everything for everybody instead of having some areas of deep expertise. That creates the problem on the client's side, but it creates yet another problem on the agency side because how do you come up with a really fantastic strategy to achieve the client's objective if you are stuck in a little box?"

~

Craig Mapleston, "Fragmented to integrated to fragmented is a cycle in our industry. Clients want specific skills but generally would still prefer to have to deal with one agency to deliver. There is more than enough business to go around."

~

Joe Zandstra, APAC Regional Creative Director of Vertic and former Chief Creative Officer of VML Qais, "People are understanding digital agency capabilities more. We're able to be much more strategic. I found that my role and the role of others with whom I'm working in digital agencies have become primarily a strategy role that happens to use digital as a channel. Whereas, in some cases it used to be we were just the fireworks that were stuck onto someone else's work. I think this is primarily because when we do web sites or digital campaigns we have so much data available to us – we have inspired creatives on-hand, sure, but what they do is based on something real and considered. You end up getting into a de facto business consultancy role and while that's a side effect, more and more, that strategic element of what we're doing is actually being seen as an accepted and chargeable aspect of what a digital agency is expected to do."

~

General Manager of Ogilvy & Mather Africa, Harish Vasudevan, "The respect the agencies get from marketers has declined over time, and it's due to the siloization of the business and the talent being driven away. That is a catch-22 because when the clients don't respect the agency, the talent leaves, and because the talent leaves, the clients don't respect the agency.

"We are also seeing something else happening, which is the big guys like McKinsey and the other management consultancies that had been doomed to the outer borders of marketing now getting into the area of brand. And for some reason, they come with greater credibility than agencies, so we're seeing some business going off that way.

"I suppose agencies are no longer considered able to provide solutions to the clients' problems, so we're seeing a rise of boutique agencies. Guys leaving big agencies starting their own shop; one or two guys staying focused on creating campaigns. The clients are finding that going to these guys is getting them better work at a lower price and greater pace of turnaround. The classic, 'You cannot get it fast, cheap and good' thing. Well, the small guy is able to prove that he can optimize on all three and deliver solutions that the clients believe are working for them.

"We're seeing budgets from clients going into other different areas, just as the McKinseys are getting the brand consulting work. Those hot shops are getting 'Let's do a campaign!' type work with digital agencies on the other side, so they are growing because they attract the better quality of digital talent, and then they are able to come up with better solutions.

"The holding companies are ending up being like the middle class in a country where they've got the mass and they've got the average talent, but they're not the guys the clients are turning to help them with their real marketing problems. Instead, they are the guys who help campaigns get rolled out or the guys who can do the everyday work.

"If I really need something that is going to transform my business, I am more likely to go to one of these other guys than to a large holding company agency. There will always be a need for them, though, because as you build global businesses, you need groups with global reach and that can create global networks. So you can either feed stuff out of the network or get stuff from the network into your business.

"I had been talking to WPP for a while before asking if anything was going on in Africa or Russia or places like that, which seemed to be next frontier after China. Out of the blue, I got a call saying 'Are you interested in going to Nairobi to run a business?' The thing I didn't want to do was run an office.

I wanted to run an account and do some real work, but I got this call with a voice asking, 'Are you interested running this telco in Africa for Ogilvy?' So I came here and liked what I saw and thought, 'This is good. This is almost exactly what I want to do.' Even though… it was in Africa for a telco that I'd never even heard of before."

Chapter 6: Acquisitions, Bean Counters, and Holding Companies, Oh My

In the '80s and '90s, behemoth holding companies were formed by combining global advertising networks, including Saatchi & Saatchi, Ted Bates, Ogilvy & Mather, J. Walter Thompson, BBDO, Chiat/Day, Doyle Dane Bernbach, and Needham Harper. These agencies became subsumed into WPP, Omnicom, Dentsu, and Cordiant — holding companies formed by businessmen such as Martin Sorrell and Bruce Crawford and their dense mountains of cash. The owners and shareholders of these agency groups and specialist shops must have certainly felt like they were riding a rocket into space. Their remuneration went through the stratosphere, but, unfortunately, their reasons for being in the field in the first place were no longer part of the mission. When the agencies sold themselves to financiers, they began to stop being about places to practice crafts in creative services and became commodities. Ads went from concise, creative pieces of branded communications in the form of emotionally powerful or illuminating stories to widgets that one can perform a cost-benefit analysis on to determine if they are providing optimal value and are being executed as efficiently as possible in order to maximize shareholder value in each quarter.

RJR Nabisco's chairman said of the formation of Omnicom in 1986, "I see disruption, but little value. With very few exceptions, the wave of mergers has benefitted the shareholders and managers of the agencies [but not the clients]." He promptly pulled his business from BBDO (and therefore Omnicom) to punctuate his feelings on the matter.

The holding company chiefs have never created an ad, established a brand from the ground up, conceived a brand strategy, designed a corporate identity, spent hours searching for the perfect photo or perfecting a layout, kerning type, or building complex layered Photoshop files. They haven't collaborated with incredibly smart, creative, hard-working, and hilarious colleagues to translate a client's very specific goals into something exciting, entertaining, and effectively on point. They may be proud to riff off the awards and accomplishments of the people employed by the creative entities they own, but they have no passion for what it is the people they are so quick and casual to RIF live for. We may as well be making fishing poles, aircraft engines, or salad dressing instead of building brands, architecting ad campaigns, developing loyalty programs, and creating mobile apps because they are unashamedly in the business to do one thing: make money and lots of it.

When your sole focus is to get wealthy, and then once you're rich to become even more filthy rich so you can buy more places to put your growing wealth, then it's quite likely that your attention on the businesses you run is going to be on squeezing the costs down in order to put even more room in the profit margin. It's not going to be on a far-sighted plan for making sure you're staffed with loyal, well-trained employees who are looking after the best interests of the clients they partner with and the future wellbeing of the agency. It's going to be on keeping salaries and benefits low, reducing the number of full-time staff you have to carry and invest in, cutting down the frills that establish a corporate culture, turning bonuses into rare occurrences, reducing the time for each task, eliminating business class travel and private offices in lieu of depressing rows of cubicles and maddeningly noisy open floor plans, eliminating overtime and holiday pay, cutting back on supplies, implementing policies that require employee monitoring, micromanaging, and playing people against each other. Basically removing the joy from life.

If there's one thing that's going to get creative people to turn out gold, it's putting increased pressure on them to perform while making their lives less comfortable and enjoyable. Isn't that common sense? For it's unlikely that these leaders care anything about what is being produced so long as it is being purchased for a lot of money. Pride probably is not invited to their fancy dinner parties because it can't be relied on to pick up the tab, so they turn to good old reliable Profit instead. Profit at all costs for as long as they can churn it out in a $500+ billion above-the-line advertising industry.

⤻

Åsk Wäppling, "A big shift happened in the mid '80s to early '90s. The holding companies started buying the ad agencies. This actually had a massive effect on how ad agencies operate and is what's really steering them today. I don't want to be one of those creatives who keeps blaming the bean counters. But honestly… *it's the bean counters' fault!*

"We can't take risks in the same way that we used to. We can't bet everything on a dark horse anymore. You could do that before, and brilliant people who had vision could actually follow through on their brilliant visions and that would change companies and perceptions all around the world. We cannot do this anymore because we have to answer to a bean counter about it. This is a problem because essentially creatives are all poker players."

⤻

Steffan Postaer, "The [focus on] quarterly earnings was the beginning of the end in terms of going from one way of doing things, having long-term relationships, the freedom to make mistakes and being able to take a chance and not fear for your job. As soon as you couldn't ever make less money tomorrow than you did yesterday, it became paralyzing – and it is unfortunate.

"I had a client meeting yesterday where the guy was like, 'Yeah. I agree with you on everything you guys have told us, but can you guarantee me I'll make my number tomorrow, because if you can't, I don't have the confidence to buy any of this.' Talk about a wet blanket comment. No one can guarantee you're going to make any money tomorrow because there's no such thing as ROI. I don't care what anybody says. There's no such thing as being able to guarantee ROI. So digital has this fault. This is where I get unreal and I yell and rant.

"This whole idea that just because you can count clicks or say, 'See how many people *like* me?' has no basis in marketplace reality. You try something and you'll know soon enough whether it worked or not. More or less, that's exactly how it will always be, and to the degree that you could measure where a dollar was being spent and who spent it and all the data analytics, you still can't guarantee what that person's going to do tomorrow with any certainty, and no piece of creative comes with that magnet attached to it.

"Agencies all go to meetings and tell that same white lie. Sometimes, it's a lot darker lie than that such as, 'Because of our savoir-faire and data analytics, we can tell you how much you're going to make quarter per quarter if you run with our programs.' Big agencies are trying to parlay all that sort of mumbo jumbo, and I think it's bullshit."

⌒

Oliver Woods, former Arc Worldwide Social Media Planner and Digital Strategist for George Patterson in Melbourne, "Say what you will about independent agencies being more creative and nimble, holding companies have one killer advantage: capital. Setting up agencies that can meet the complex demands of clients, often in different markets, requires far more investment than those of us in the industry often acknowledge. Having switched agencies a lot in my early career, I came to quickly understand that – for all their faults – holding companies add a base level of discipline and focus to the political madness of daily agency life.

"Hiring the best talent, buying computers and furniture and renting office space across entire regions isn't difficult for the WPPs of the world.

That competitive advantage creates what economists call 'path dependency': clients would much rather work with agencies that have a track record of rapidly scaling up to meet their needs, and thus the behemoths become even more entrenched.

"Which is why I'm betting that the failure of the Publicis-Omnicom merger may not be permanent and isn't really a big deal: the industry is evolving to become more intertwined, more oligopolistic. Perhaps we will see a greater diversity of mechanisms for alliances between advertising and marketing firms: more partnerships and joint ventures as opposed to mergers."

↬

Bob Hoffman, "The large, global, monstrosity agencies are successful because they can promise clients the whole package within one framework. Whether they can actually deliver on it and whether it's any good is another thing. But they can promise it, and for a CMO who's lazy and doesn't want to have to manage all these entities, why do they do global advertising? It makes no sense. Why would anyone run the same advertising in the US that they're running in Zimbabwe or Ulan Bator? It makes no sense. The cultures are so different. But it's easier to do one global campaign; something so bland and so general that it's completely nonspecific. If you're lazy, it's way easier to do that than to have 14 or 15 different campaigns running in different parts of the world. That's a pain in the ass. But it's the right way to do it."

↬

Andy Greenaway, "There seems to be a gap in brand strategy and idea generation. The new generation is too focused on technology for technology's sake instead of understanding how technology can create better human connections.

"There will be a big role for training and mentoring in the future. Ogilvy and JWT used to be known as the universities of advertising, but since they've been taken over by essentially banks, their training budgets have been slashed to almost nothing. The agencies that invest in training will rise above the others. At this moment in time, I can only see the independents doing this. They're not shackled by the stormtrooping money monkeys."

∾

Mike Langton, "The problem with the holding companies is that they're run by people who don't understand the business. I'm absolutely dead serious about this: accountants, lawyers and finance people run them. Martin Sorrell is not an accountant. He studied finance. They are run by people who have never in their entire career made an ad. They don't understand the process. They like looking at ads. They think ads are pretty cool and they go, 'Whoa! Look at the ads that one of my companies made.' But they have not made ads. There's a huge shortcoming in that because they don't understand the process. Their view is purely, 'This is a money-making business, and it has to be run accordingly.'

"There are all sorts of structures and strictures that they put into place, which are fine in a process-type business, but are not in an invention-type business, in a creativity-type business. The biggest issue that has settled on the advertising industry is the inability to retain profits and invest in the agency you are running. Most agency heads in a multinational network find that the funds that the profits that you are generating can't be reinvested in improving the people that you have by giving them wider exposure to training and to stimulus like cultural events and similar experiences.

"By giving them deeper training, by sending them on assignment in New York for three months to get even sharper and brighter at what they do. And all the companies that say that they do this? I've been a managing director since 1992, and I was on agency boards since 1989. In all that time, I've seen one staff swap. One. *One*! All the companies say, 'We swapped staff. We sent somebody from New York to this place.' I've personally seen it happen in all the companies that I've been involved in, just that once. You've got, what, 175,000 people in WPP. If you look at the training budgets divided among the people, you can work out pretty quickly that what they're really getting is fuck all. What training are any of them really doing now? How are they building communication skills?

"If you want to look at an agency that was always great on training, the university of the ad industry in most markets has been Ogilvy. David Ogilvy enforced that. It was a rigor in the company. Training was regular. Training was in modules called 'Magic Lanterns,' which were designed to shed light on a new subject and give you this magical ingredient to be really great at what you did. One of the things that happened when Ogilvy was being acquired by WPP was that David Ogilvy went off his block and he reportedly said words to the effect of, 'Nothing would cause me greater disgust than having to work with that odious little shit.' Later it was reported as 'odious little jerk.' He was referring to Martin Sorrell[6] who (as referenced in Wikipedia) put the initials OLJ after his signature on the WPP annual report that year.

"The thing that really worried Ogilvy was they had all this wonderful training and education culture internally, and he was terrified that that was going to get stripped out because it was a cost. You know what? He was right! It's the first thing that Sorrell and the accountants went after, to try and to cut that off. All the management in Ogilvy went, 'You touch this, you destroy the culture, and the company is not worth half the money that you paid for it. You have got to leave it alone.'

"Now, years later, it has been watered down a bit but what happened back then was the Ogilvy management was so strong and so vigorously opposed to anything being messed with that you still find that Ogilvy has very good quality internal training, staff support mechanisms, etc. One, because they had the critical mass they built themselves to that level. Two, they managed to sustain that critical mass because they were making really good advertising with the well-trained people they had, and they also tended to have very good local connections.

"The global Chief Creative Officer of Ogilvy for several years and, prior to that, CEO of Ogilvy South Africa, was Robyn Putter out of Rightford Searle-Tripp and Makin, which merged with Ogilvy in South Africa in the mid-'80s. He died of a heart attack a few years ago on the job. Robyn was one of those decent, really grounded, deep thinkers that weighed everything up carefully. They were the thinking men's agency in South Africa. They really were. Ogilvy said right at the start, 'We have to be gentlemen with brains,' and 'women as well, for that matter,' he added later. They wanted intellectual people, deep thinkers, so they invested money in research. He was research-ing their own ads at their own cost from day one. This is what all agencies should've been doing. When you see the really great agencies of any mar-

---

6   "WPP's leader admitted the Financial Times had watered-down Ogilvy's remarks about him being an 'odious little jerk,' saying 'it was actually odious little shit.'" http://www.campaignlive.co.uk/news/1133996/

ket like the Campaign Palace in Australia, which is now defunct, it was the company that hired great people at great expense, put a lot of time, effort, and money into thinking and planning strategically. No knee-jerk campaigns came out. They would tell the client when they could review the creative. Not agencies let their clients get away with saying, 'Here's the brief. Now, I want to see the ads in two weeks,' which is what Colgate and Procter & Gamble and marketers like that are like now.

"The management at Rightford Searle-Trip & Makin which took over Ogilvy in South Africa would not work with clients who behaved like that. They said, 'This is how we work, and if you don't like that, don't come to us.' The Colgates and people like that would say, 'You have to work like this.' They'd say, 'No, you're not listening carefully. We don't work that way. We won't work that way. We don't want your business.'

"I interviewed Reg Lascaris of Hunt Lascaris TBWA in South Africa for my MBA thesis. When I was interviewing Reg, I said, 'What's your new business process like?' He said, 'Well, it's pretty extraordinary now.' He said 'Everybody knows who we are, and we have a queue.' I said, 'You what?' He said, 'We have a queue. At the moment, we have four large clients who want to work with us, but we don't have the right people on board yet so we told them they'll have to wait and we'll let them know when we have the right people in place.'

"Can you imagine that coming out of the mouth of any agency on Earth today. What he did basically was he said, 'Look, until I can do great work on your business, I won't take your business. To do great work on your business, I have to hire the right people, and they're not always available immediately. It may take six months to get them, but when I have them, I'll let you know. On the basis that I'm going to do that and you're committing to give me your business. I'm not pitching for it.' And clients would do it. They would give Hunt Lascaris their business without a pitch because they saw this incredible portfolio of brilliant advertising that came out of that organization and they would say, 'Sure, we'll hand you the business.' There were lots of occasions when there would just be a press announcement that this-and-that business had moved to Hunt Lascaris in a closed-door pitch. 'Closed-door pitch' means there was no fucking pitch.

"That means you sat down, you discussed the credentials, you had a look at all the ads they have made for other marketers and they said, 'We'd love to have advertising like that for our brands. Can you do it?' Reg and John would say, 'Yup, we believe we can, and here's the deal.' These guys had never cut their cost. They never dropped their pants to get business, and few great agencies ever did, generally. Because they said, 'Look. No. We need that money to invest in great people to make the great advertising that you're looking for. If you want to get cheap crap, go down the road and you're sure to find someone who would love to give you the cheap crap you are looking for.'

"Fundamentally, if you can invest in finding great people and invest in keeping them great, which means they've got to be stimulated and positive; they've got to be in an environment they love, there have got to be all the cultural components that make them feel happy and motivated. If you can give them enough time to think to do great work, then you will find you start to produce great work. But when you allow a chivvying, cost-cutting, bitchy culture, and a lot of staff turn-over, you end up with a breakdown of the culture of the agency that could have enabled it to do great work to start with. You're no better than the guy down the road – and that's the problem.

"The thing that sort of hit me even back then when I landed up working on Colgate Palmolive and some of the other big accounts was that the issue of globalization was becoming very serious. People on the marketing side were saying, 'Wait. Instead of having a different product in every market, why don't we streamline? We don't need a thousand brands in the portfolio. Why don't we slim it down?'

"Unilever, more than Procter & Gamble at that point, had lots of dots on the map. Everywhere the British Empire had been, Unilever had a pin, and they were strong in every pin in the map. India, Syria, freaking Nigeria, you name it. They were there. It was really interesting. What I was seeing at that point was the marketers saying, 'We want to streamline, and we want more efficiency,' and the agencies were ignoring them and saying, 'Yeah, sure, blah blah blah, whatever. Hey, let's have a drink.'

"Very soon, the big marketers wanted the big agency networks to be giving them standardized services and reduced rates around the world. Coca-Cola was with McCann. They had been there for donkey's years and you had Marlboro in Leo Burnett, likewise. The Colgate Palmolives and Procter &

Gambles, etc. all had a bunch of agencies here and there, and then suddenly in the early '80s all this talk about global advertising, global marketing, which Saatchi & Saatchi was riding heavily on, was getting very loud. Y&R became the global agency for Colgate Palmolive, having worked on Procter & Gamble as one of their multiple agencies around the world, and then they landed a big chunk of Colgate.

"What seemed to happen simultaneously was media started to fragment progressively and make that a more complicated part of the business, while clients were trying to take cost out of things. They were all listed companies in the US or the UK, and they were all trying to make more money, be more profitable, and create towering edifices of power. There was a confluence of forces.

"There was globalization. There was fragmentation. There was the idea that if you consolidated all your business with one agency, they would let you pay them less because they'd be so delighted to have a business all around the world. The idea that you could squeeze agencies on their charges started to take root and the agency management went with it like lambs to the proverbial slaughter instead of investing in their craft.

"All of those trends have continued their runs, and the increasing competitiveness of major players in marketing around the world has intensified dramatically, but so has the education of consumers and users. People are not easily bamboozled anymore. They are quite aware that there are active ingredients in detergents, the levels vary, but that they're all pretty much the same. The products were parroting each other, and the consumers were no longer fooled. They used to be. They used to react with, 'Oh wow... an ad!' These days, it's, 'An ad? Who gives a crap?'

"The other part of the consumer side of things was increasing consumer education, which predated the Web. To quite a large degree, consumer choice magazines had popped up left, right, and center. There was a whole movement towards consumer awareness, the original consumerism. 'The consumer is king' but needs protection. Not consumerism, the way the word is misused in Asia – they think 'consumerism' means 'buy everything in sight!' No, that's 'consumption,' guys.

"All of these forces started to converge during the '80s, probably during the '70s, but we only really started noticing them during the '80s. By the end of that decade, we had far more awareness of the international networks of advertising agencies, global alignments of advertising accounts and, as a result of a number of forces during the '80s, that there were more and more holding company entities arising. You had Saatchi & Saatchi as an original holding company, and then you had Martin Sorrell jump out of that and set up WPP, where he originally was purely focused on below-the-line.

"After that, J. Walter Thompson landed in financial trouble and Sorrell really did his due diligence, which was an unheard-of concept in the advertising industry up to that point. What he apparently discovered was that JWT had a property asset on the books in Japan for something like $20 million, but its market value was more like $200 million. He put in a bid that required him to take on huge debt, but he knew that he was buying assets he could sell on the open market. Remember how high the property and stock markets were in Japan in the late '80s?

"Once he could liquidate that property, he was able to retire the debt. He just had to market it carefully, and he knew that in Japan, it takes a long time to get things moving and get things done. Ultimately, he nearly went bust with the JWT acquisition, but managed to flip the property, and then he went off after Ogilvy.

"At the same time, you had what is now Omnicom getting put together by the various heads of BBDO, DDB, and Needham Harper, with TBWA following seven years later. They said, 'This whole consolidation move, this is a good thing, we should do this.' They were not acquiring each other. They were just putting their businesses together in one place, and the rest went on a 'Let's copy Martin Sorrell' spree. One agency group ended up owning go-kart tracks that came out of some acquisition's books. They went really mad on doing as many acquisitions as possible as fast as possible, and by the time we got to 2000 everything collapsed in a festering heap.

"The trouble was that all of these businesses – which had been traditionally a blend of art, sociology, research, and local culture – became parts of global holding companies focused on efficiency and streamlining just like the marketers: taking an idea from one place and running it around the world. Not doing 10 sets of creatives for the different cultural regions of the planet, but doing one, which many organizations proved can't be done well.

"You lose a lot of the local touch, the local content, the local understanding, the local awareness, and the local connection to community. As a result, a lot of the local relevance goes out of the advertising. If you look at advertising, what are the things that you really need to do fundamentally? It's got to entertain, enlighten or educate or people will go, 'I'm not interested. I'll go and have a pee.' It's got to improve their life in some way or other or you don't deserve the public's attention. Otherwise, fundamentally, if it does not add value to one's life, why would you bother with it? If something is informative, it makes you go, 'Wow, I didn't know that. Could be useful,' or, 'I'll be careful about that. If I take some while driving, it could be a problem,' or 'Ha, ha, ha, that was bloody hilarious. That's absolutely fantastic. I love that thing. It makes me feel good when I see that ad.' Good ads do things like that or you get very little engagement with people, Most of the magic comes from local touch, local content, local culture, local understanding. It's local relevance that is important. That's where you find the consumer insights that make people looking at or hearing an ad say 'This is for me!' Generic consumer insights only appeal to a non-existent generic consumer. In the '80s in South Africa, there was an agency that nailed that brilliantly. They were Rightford Searle-Tripp and Makin. People used to laugh in the beginning when it started up and called it, 'right foot, left foot, trip and fall over,' but they never did fall over.

"They created some of the best advertising around the place. For Volkswagen, they ignored everything that was being done overseas for the brand and created highly relevant local advertising. It was brilliant and won buckets of awards and helped sell hundreds of thousands of vehicles. Eventually Volkswagen overseas were asking them to give advice in other countries. They replied, 'No, we're going to focus on this place, thanks.' They then were acquired by Ogilvy, which turned out to be culturally a reverse takeover. Ogilvy South Africa turned into a giant Rightford Searle-tripp and Makin South Africa. They were producing really brilliant local content, and they were the number one agency in town by any measure. Hunt Lascaris TBWA, started by Reg Lascaris and John Hunt, started up in the mid-'80s, and they took a very similar path. It was local relevance, high quality creative, really top creative people."

⌒

Aden Hepburn, "It's not like the advertising industry is making a shit-load of cash anymore. Holding companies want 20-25% margin. If you look at a legal firm, I don't know the exact margin those guys are taking, but they are in a similar situation. You've got seriously smart and talented people in there. They're charging out three, four, five hundred bucks an hour or more. They bill you for every second that they talk to you. No one debates it, ever. You just pay it. That's what you have to do because they're a specific professional service offered, and advertising, I'm afraid, is very much the same thing for me."

～

Jeffrey Yu, "Holding companies can talk about lofty goals, but at the end of the day of every quarter, in every annual, in every budget meeting, Martin [Sorrell] talks about written expectations of the shareholders. That means that everybody is there squeezing money from everybody as much as possible. They are only forced to put a team together because the client asked for it, not because they want it.

"They are now trying their very best to embrace digital, but in the same breath, we are looking at short-term profit. Every day, we have to deliver. Even today, digital doesn't have to mean low profit. Actually, it means higher margins than what normal agencies are used to.

"Big executives are so lopsided. It's so easy to fool our holding company bosses when you can just tell them something and they will start salivating. It's, 'Oh my god. This is a big opportunity.' It's all crazy. I've seen how fancy ideas can turn into billion-dollar-losing fiascos for them. At Bates Advertising, we were the guys who set up the first digital agencies, like XM, in the earliest days. We were instrumental in driving the new media industry forward even though, at that time, I admit, I didn't know shit about digital at all, but I could see the value of building and supporting specialist agencies. Then our WPP owners stole XM away from Bates and passed it on to J. Walter Thompson. Big guys are very good at killing digital agencies. We don't understand them or how to nurture their growth.

"The issue is either we do not understand or we send people in who don't understand. At the same time, we don't have the foresight to develop and to nurture these new media channels and ventures, and we end up running everything like an advertising agency. We still do that. In my group, I'm running a digital agency and an activation agency, and we still like to apply the agency model to everything since we see the agency model works.

"The agency model is this: I am selling you a creative product. But we don't have agency media commission anymore. We work on a very stable scope of work and based on that, I'll get you a retainer from the client, and that's about it. We are trying to be entrepreneurial and say there are projects where we started to get into incentive schemes and all that stuff, but this is not really happening or happening in a very, very small way. The agency model is still very conservative. It is all about either a commission-based model or a retainer-based model. It is all short-term income because every year we have to deliver to that income level. When it comes to other business models, we are not very adventurous in trying.

"In the 1990s, we were still working with the agency commission model. That was a very rich one whereby the more the client spent, the more money we got. The agencies were living a very, *very* nice life. At that time, people didn't look at margins. People looked at, 'Hey! I get 50% agency commission,' which is a lot of money. We also charged clients for creative development and miscellaneous fees. Even on a gross margin basis, we are talking about over 20%. The debt was subjected to how fast your client grew and how much they spent. It could go up to 30%.

"Agencies at that time were totally oblivious to how cash rich we were, and all that led to the situation of Martin Sorrell buying up agencies and realizing how much cash was being chucked at advertising agencies. He is the guy who actually saw that. Even though the money didn't belong to us, there was a lot of cash flow within advertising agencies, and he saw that the stupid advertising people didn't know how to use that cash flow.

"We were paid a standard 15% media commission, even though towards the late '90s, it started to drop, and eventually, the agency commission model broke down because everybody was fighting and trying to keep a piece of the business. Eventually, it dropped down to 8%, 7%, 5%, 3%... it kept on dropping. As a result of that, Martin Sorrell developed the separate media companies and became the maestro of the old agency model.

"He is starting to regret it. Recently, every agency is now talking about re-grouping into a 360 model because of the benefits. If you remember the early days, a client could talk to us as one company, and then we were able to address all media and become the all-solution focal point. The one advisor for all issues of advertising and marketing. We were able to grow people who understood everything.

"As a result of the last 10 to 15 years, we have become weary, isolated specialists, with the client controlling the whole picture. Now we do not control our destiny at all. We are only told, 'Jeffrey is in charge of a creative campaign for us, and he gets half a million Hong Kong dollars,' or whatever. That's what we live on.

"Separately, there are the Group Ms of this world. They are told, 'Buy this media for us,' and none of us have the big picture. Neither do the digital companies, as they are told to only do the digital part. How does it fit within the whole framework? We all try to play 360 specialists, but the power returns to the client. The client is saying, 'Oh my god. My job is so bloody hard nowadays because I have to orchestrate all you little bastards.' Because what they have to do is do the job that *we* used to do.

"We used to be together and also, to be fair to other marketing agencies and the media companies, they were previously considered as a secondary, non-important partner of the communications mix. Do you remember that everybody else besides advertising was considered second class? Hence, we proud advertising people sort of imposed our standard onto everybody and told them how to work. Digital was not making enough money back then because advertising at that time was still very popular. The good thing about the admirers of the advertising agency is that we allowed the different disciplines to come up to the front stage.

"If we didn't break up the creative agencies, it might be that the media or digital specialists would never have seen the light of day. The good part is it frees up all this talent who are able to surface, take a breath, and then prosper and do well. That's the good part of the breaking up.

"The bad part is that now the control has been lost forever. Now the holding company is trying very hard to regain that position. For example, I saw that Colgate and Ford and many other clients are now rebuilding a full-service agency with all the different components into a single structure. The clients demanding it is key when they ask, 'How can I be talking to 12 different people on 12 different teams with 12 different strategies? I am the poor bastard who has to consolidate everything and make sense of it.' The client's job has become very hard."

⌒

Greg Paull, Founder of R3 and former Asia Pacific CEO of Draft Worldwide, "There are a lot of factors involved, but I would suggest the holding company model is one of the biggest factors. I think the issue is that the mindset of change from making our clients profitable to making the agencies profitable as just the nature of business. But if you look at all the other sectors that service companies, whether it's lawyers or business consultants, they're also independent product companies. You can become a partner in McKinsey and then get equity, but that's not so you can do it in public. The rest of the service sectors haven't done that, and also all the other service sectors don't do stupid things like reveal their profit margin to a company. A McKinsey doesn't tell you how much profit they're going to make on a project; they just give you a fee and get on with it. Agencies will tell you, 'I'm making a 15% margin or a 12% margin' or whatever there is, and that broke down the transparency between the relationship. It was too much transparency.

"Charging at 15% media commission and production: those days are, fortunately, pretty much gone now. But the problem with the fee-based system is it's based on hours. What sort of business works when it's 'the slower I work, the more you pay me'? 'The more mistakes I make and the more I have to redo things, the more I'm going to be able to charge you.' The whole concept is crazy, but that's the nature of the fee basis from those traditional agencies now.

"No one's come along with a better idea, including wonderful consultants like us, but obviously, you have to move to some sort of value-based compensation. Coke has tried that in the last couple of years, but ultimately you have to have compensation based on the results, which are a combination of sales and brand equity and other KPIs, or you have to come up with another model that says 'Look, I'm TBWA. I've generated this intrinsic idea for Apple and for Absolut Vodka. I should be getting a part of their business results and profit.' It's a very difficult area for the industry to work through.

"If you look at the fringes of the industry, you already have actors and photographers and all of these people charging licensing fees. If you shoot a

photo in America and you want to use it in China, you have to pay the photographer a royalty. These guys all figured it out. It's just that the ad agencies
have yet to figure out a model like that."

⌒

Steve Hall, "The holding companies definitely played a role in the ho-
mogenizing of all of the agencies' distinctive cultures and the disintegration of
company-employee loyalty because it has become the biggest creative industry in the world. Hollywood is run by bean counters now as well. Everything's
run by the bean counters when you get down to it.

"There used to be a day (and there still is) when there were plenty of
agencies starting up that were run by creative people with the mandate to
be creative. But it's awfully hard to say 'no' when someone comes knocking
on your door and then they give you a billion dollars for your company and
you're set for life. It's hard for people to say, 'No, I'm going to maintain my
creative vision. I'm going to stay small, and I'm going to continue working on
my client base.' It's hard to say no to that gigantic paycheck and, like in all
businesses, there's bigger is better, or so that is the belief, and that's the case
in advertising, too.

"Now you have holding companies talking to other holding companies
about buying each other. Theoretically, there could be just two ad agencies
left in the world in a very short period of time: two holding companies that
own everybody.

"In a sense, that gives scale and allows you to go after larger clients,
but, at some point, there's really diminishing return because you've got a
nightmare of conflicts and all that stuff, and it does become more about what
you can do to get bigger and less about the creativity. The standard belief is
that as long as you're not shackled to a holding company, you can do more
of what you want, and when you can do more of what you want, you can be
more creative. It doesn't necessarily mean the creative is going to be good,
but you have freer rein to do what you want, unrestricted by or not having to
answer to anyone.

"It's absolutely about the numbers now, which I feel terrible about, but
it's difficult to argue against it. It's, 'We've got to make x number of dollars to
pay for our expenses. If we can't do that, we've got to cut something.'

"Now it's rare for companies to make a leap of faith. In the past, it was easier to make a leap of faith because we didn't have the ability to analyze things to death. Now we do and that's led to a sort of analysis paralysis that often leads to lowest-common-denominator, risk-free solutions.

"And you have creative by committee because everyone wants to have their say. It's stupid for non-creatives to get into the actual aspects of creativity, which is why we have the now familiar phrase, 'Make the logo bigger.' Non-creative should just trust the experts."

∽

Richard Bleasdale, Director of the Taipan Partnership and Asia Pacific Regional Managing Partner of Roth Observatory International, "Generally what happens is that the independent is subsumed into the larger holding company organization. The spark disappears relatively quickly because there's a whole new range of demands and ways of working and for people who are very, very used to having independence, just suddenly at some level, having a boss again and someone to report to changes their outlook on the world substantially. In very few cases do the original partners hang around for a great deal of time because while they have financially succeeded out of the transaction, personally and motivationally, chances are that it has been not a great thing for them."

∽

John Winsor, "I think every agency-holding company is going to face the same thing: their time is over. They're done. But until then, people are going to fight to the death to hold up the old model. I don't think they've gone astray. You don't become conservative until you have something to conserve, and I think that the whole existence of a holding company is to exploit the current paradigm. So, if your reason for being is to make efficient the old paradigm, then there's no way that you can risk inventing a new one.

"I just think about this in the old paradigm when I had the magazine business back in '96 in the days of 28.8 Kbps modem speeds. We had an early web site that had inline skating how-to videos, and I was trying to digitize the videos and put them up online for dial-up. The reality was that I could go spend a shitload of time and a shitload of energy and money trying to figure out how to do all that crap, or I could choose the alternative. I could actually expand a headline in our article and sell a remnant full page ad and make $5,000.

"Where would you put your time? Of course you put your time against selling that extra page because that's what makes everything else possible. I think this whole idea of companies innovating their way out of the status quo is total bullshit. I don't think it's possible. I think that – and I know I'm in the minority – but I think that the only way to change is to have visionary leaders who are willing to risk a lot. And secondly, to be able to go to your core most profitable processes and really blow them up and transform them from the inside out. You have to do that. You can't hire a company or an expert or have a chief innovation officer change these because every fiber in the organization is about exploiting the old model – and so it just doesn't work."

⌐

Chester Tan, Lead for CRM / Digital / Social Media for Friesland-Campina, "The holding agency structure pits each agency against each other. Working on Project da Vinci, the predecessor of Enfatico [the WPP-created global agency to singularly service the Dell account], was one of the most eye-opening experiences of my life: having probably about five different WPP agencies sit together in a massive conference room trying to decide the future of how they would handle the Dell account. It became painfully and plainly obvious that the traditional agencies still do not allocate the same level of respect to their digital counterparts that a digital agency gives to them. The holding company structure that has each agency working solely for themselves, each agency network responsible for their own bottom line, etc. Doesn't exactly motivate these agencies to work together. Because, in the end, why would a traditional agency want to allocate more budget to digital when it has a negative effect on their own revenue performance?

"That was the premise of WPP Digital. To have a network of digital agencies that does not fall in and report to a traditional agency network, but could carve out a new plan and new territories unto themselves. I think a lot of big, pure-play digital agencies have found out it's hard to do that without the backing of a holding company because the 'big idea' still resides within the brand agencies. I think that is the problem because once they come up with a baked idea, it is generally considered for brilliant above-the-line execution, but not so well thought out for digital and below-the-line."

༈

Dave Whittle, "Look at the stock prices of any of the big holding companies and you'll see they're doing okay. That must mean that when it all nets out, they're doing pretty well. But the agencies that are within holding companies are having a difficult time. They're obviously not taking advantage of the agent that's representing them.

"It's no different to being a model or an actor or having any other representation. The agent will take their commission for introduction and management. Once you're in that machine, you're a slave to the group, and that's okay because those groups are producing good creative work. They're winning big global clients and they're growing. Look at Aegis, for example. Aegis's stock price has gone up, has doubled in the last half, after having doubled over the last four years. That's a pretty good return. Dentsu acquired them a few months ago and that's pretty good going, I reckon.

"In the last three years, Omnicom and WPP have doubled as well. So these groups are doing pretty well. They must be doing something right."

༈

Ryan Lim, Executive Council Member of the Institute of Advertising Singapore and Founder of social media marketing agency Blugrapes, "If you're trying to do everything, you're going to undermine your proposition, and I know for a fact that WPP is trying to do all and be a one-stop shop for everything, and if you've read the recent market news, you see they are buying up a lot of the big specialists like AQKA.

"They are going to be the one-stop shop. They're no longer just a PR company. Almost every PR company seems to now be digital, creative, and advertising. They're feeling the pressure, and everyone wants to be everything. I don't think you can get one agency that can do everything. The clients that we've spoken to don't believe it either. The best analogy that they've given us so far is when you go to your generalist primary-care physician. He's supposed to be able to diagnose and do every darn thing, yet you still want to see a specialist because you want a deeper opinion in specific areas and, for a doctor, it depends on what their areas of focus are. You can't focus on everything. You've always got limited budgets and resources.

"In the case of the holding companies and agency networks, it's great on paper. The reality is that the expertise that they have is actually not there, and even with all the different entities together, they are like a very loose conglomerate of sorts. Take, for example, the biggest one that we know like Ogilvy. Even internally, they're still trying to integrate all the different parts of the business together. They've got Ogilvy Public Relations, OgilvyAction, Neo, OgilvyOne, OgilvyInteractive, etc. They've got great groups, and a couple of them all mesh up together. They've got so many, but when you actually listen to them, you'll find that they are not as integrated as you think they are. They're not just one big happy family. Everyone is still worrying about their own business and they are all siloed, even though from the outside it looks like one cohesive group."

⤿

Managing Partner of SKYLABS and former Vice President, Group Director of Business Development and Marketing for Digitas, Adam Trisk, "Selling an ad agency to a holding company destroys the business, and unfortunately, the business of marketing and advertising, however one wants to phrase it, is *not* a commodity industry.

"What inevitably happens is a bad marriage. You meet this person who wants to acquire your business, they wine and dine you, they think you're an amazing agency, talk about how great your work is, they don't want to change your culture, they want you to be just the way you are, they just want to help you do it in a bigger scale. And then… they acquire you.

"About a year later, they start to say, 'Hey, look, your systems aren't right, and we'd like to change them.' Because they're the ones holding all the purse strings, you've become beholden to what they say you need to do.

"The first year, they *almost* leave you alone, let you do what you do while they assess your business. The second year, they roll in systems integration and start to remove benefits and say, 'Let's optimize the business.' In the third year, they start to look at all of your financials and demand more out of you than they ever had before.

"For me, Digitas was truly one of the most amazing agencies I'd ever set foot in. Those six months prior to the Publicis acquisition, not only did we operate incredibly well as a company, but also there was a culture that was unique and very supportive. Over the subsequent five and a half years, I watched that culture disappear. I watched management become ineffective as they took a lot of the decision making power away from them. Bonus and compensation structures started to change to where all the things that had been good no longer were good."

༄

Andy Flemming, "I haven't had the greatest experiences with holding companies. I'm lucky to now work in M&C Saatchi and just be independent. We have no holding company. Those guys always say, 'Let me come in with an axe,' and they come in with a fucking chainsaw. Scores are settled and profits are made by going, 'Well, fuck it, let's just cut the work force down to a third, and everyone else can work fucking harder.'

"Who knows? Maybe I'm giving them a bad rap, and maybe I had a bad experience with a bad apple. What does come with a holding company is that you get access to global business, which is fucking awesome. Where your agency in Manhattan is working on Coke, you can get the brief here, or, for instance, DDB is doing work on VW right now that may absolutely come to us – and I'd like to see them do some worldwide work. The double-edged sword of that is when you lose Coke in Manhattan, you lose Coke worldwide.

"I've been out of agencies that have had a holding company for five or six years. I can't really remember any influence they had. At M&C Saatchi we are, to use the cliché, masters of our own destiny. You just are. You have an agency that has built up clients that you have gone out and found, that you have nurtured, that you won, that if you lose, it's down to you here. It's your responsibility to do the best possible ad you can. You're not only just handed the account flat, it's something you fought for.

"I feel that it's probably a different culture in an agency like that than an agency that is ready made with 10 very big clients that the Americans have got, the British have got, the Germans have got. We didn't earn them. We didn't win a pitch. We were just given the account. You act in a different way when that thing happens. I am making very big generalizations, and I have to say that this comes from not having experience with a holding company for many, many years, and there are some very good ones out there. I just haven't been fortunate enough to have worked for them."

⌒

Diane McKinnon, "There are still clients out there that want holding companies in some form or fashion. Their presumption is that a holding company pitch now means, 'I get advertising, I get digital, I get social, I get mobile,' because the holding companies – particularly WPP, but the others as well – have diversified their holdings beyond traditional agencies.

"If you've listened to Martin Sorrell over the last few years, the two things that he talks about the most are digital and emerging markets, particularly Asia. He knows where the money is. He's thinking in those terms. He's not saying traditional agencies are going to go away or anything like that, but this is the guy who owns and runs one of the largest advertising and marketing network in the world and where is his focus? Digital and Asia. That tells you a lot right there.

"The traditional agency model and structure has to evolve. It's a scale thing. They have to evolve or they have to scale down. That means scaling down traditional advertising talent and infrastructure around the media companies... or the media companies having different kinds of buying services and doing less television and things like that. The evolution is both in function and scale. I just don't think in 10 years' time, you're going to see traditional ad agencies that have three, four, five, six hundred people. It doesn't make sense. But it's very hard to see the client budget shifting from them. These are big organizations. These are entrenched companies, the Y&Rs, the O&Ms, the whomevers. Shifting their business models is like turning a battleship.

"It's always going to be a reactive approach. Until the big agencies see wholesale losses of business to the AKQAs, or the VMLs, of the world, which you *are* starting to see in places, there's a belief that the pendulum will swing back. Because it does swing back and forth a little bit. Go to media-only agencies. Then integrate media back in. We have seen some of this. Go to the specialists. Then go back to the big agencies. Move away from the big agencies and go to the boutique shops. Then they realize they don't have enough reach. You're still seeing a lot of movement, and I'm sure there are some in the big agency world that figure the pendulum will swing back, but it's ultimately going to be the pocketbooks that will make change.

"A lot of big agency management feels like this is still the same old thing. When, in fact, it's a much more seismic shift. The companies that are emerging now as powerful brands are companies that have grown up in the digital era. Working with Campbell's versus working with Google are two very different things. What are the emergent brands and companies that are coming up, and how are their models? The agencies still are using adjuncts: pull in a digital agency, pull a social agency, pull in whatever. They just don't think their model is going to have to change, and they're probably wrong. There's this idea of an elitism around the New York, Chicago, San Francisco agencies to some extent. It's as if, 'No, we know better.' We've had to deal with that attitude about our business for a long time. It's partly because we don't have the scale of some of these guys, but it's going to take pain to ultimately drive change."

⤻

Laurent Stanevich, VP of Operations at Fluency Media of Ann Arbor, Michigan and former Group Director of Strategy for Big Fuel Communications, "What happens within an agency that I think is really true is that you get to where the level of personal interconnecting within the organization starts to decrease exponentially with size. As that starts to happen, you see a lot of the companies that have successfully grown that way or have been able to stay on task because what it is they are there to do inherently organizes them.

"In terms of focus, one of the things I think is true is they're necessarily great when they're big, but they don't fall apart if they get that cultural infighting that ad agencies tend to get. There's not enough of that, and so you just end up with a lot of distantly connected people who're all competing for what they all feel is very clearly some gain."

⤻

Dirk Eschenbacher, "The big holding companies acquire one agency after the other and one specialist after the other, adding to their portfolio and covering different needs left and right, from analytics to research to digital production to content to social media. It's all there. The leadership in the agencies is open, visionary, and sees the need for bringing in the right people.

"That doesn't always mean having to build huge departments, but in the end, the big stuff always gets done by 20% of the people doing 80% of the work. It is always the case in every agency, but as long as that 20% are smart people and the right people, it's all good. Normally, in the bigger agencies, the big pitches tend to always be won by the same team of 5 to 10 people. As long as they're quite savvy and know what's going on and can bring in the right people and go away and get it done, then agencies will be fine, actually."

～

Paolo Formenti, Online Marketing Director at GN Netcom A/S, Jabra in Denmark and former PeopleGroup Account Director, "TBWA had this culture and methodology called *Disruption*. I was really inspired by it. It was a good thing, and it created an awesome positive vibe around the agency. I was really proud to be part of TBWA at that stage.

"Unfortunately, I felt we began to lose the spirit of what the agency was before it became part of Omnicom, and that I think was mainly due to having leadership who perhaps would send a group email around every three months or so, telling us how good the business was doing, rather than focusing on perhaps telling us how awesome some of the campaigns were or just showing up in that manner and being part of the vibe of the agency.

"I saw that firsthand at TBWA, but then I saw it many years later with my agency being bought by another large holding company. It was interesting because I got the notification that we've been bought by this big holding company and told how they would create a bigger network for us giving us better routes to more clients. How we would be able to tap into different resources and specialists. It's almost a case of trying to avoid cannibalism within those big companies, because everyone tends to safeguard their own client base and safeguard their own methods of doing things.

"I haven't really experienced massive success from these big holding companies coming over and buying six or seven different agencies in three or four years and saying that the main benefits would be that these agencies can share resources and share their client base. At the end of the day, every managing director of each particular agency will safeguard their own and only really open up when absolutely necessary or forced."

∽

CEO and Managing Partner of BBH India, Subhash Kamath, "Holding companies are all driven by that fact that they're publicly listed and therefore, they need to report their financials every quarter. Whether it's Publicis Group or WPP or Omnicom, they're responsible to their shareholders. The business monitoring, if I may use the term, is far tighter on a quarterly basis than it would be when, say, BBH was independent. It's a good thing, though, because it makes the managers more fucking responsible about the commitments they're making. It's a pain to deal with, I understand. Ultimately, I don't think the heads of these holding companies ask their own questions such as, 'Are you going to achieve what you set out to do? If you're going to achieve that, we're willing to allow you to spend the money. If you tell me you're not going to achieve what you set out to do, then we can't let you spend so much money.'"

∽

Bob Hoffman, "I see the big agencies growing bigger, and I see the big clients going away from independent agencies to the big agencies. Maybe I'm misreading it. I hope I am. I hope they are starting to be dissatisfied with those people and are looking elsewhere. But that hasn't been my perception."

∽

Jeffrey Dachis, Chief Evangelist of Sprinklr and Co-founder and former CEO/Chairman of Razorfish, "Marketers don't see advertising agencies as the go-to groups for strategies like they used to because you're dealing with a confluence, a variety of elements that have shifted the way marketers market and brands get built. That has, by necessity, created a different dynamic for what used to be the big agencies that were created out of the *Mad Men* era and then aggregated via the consolidation of the advertising agency holding company. If you think about the *Mad Men* era of post-World War II, people coming back from the war, the consumerism that occurred, and the way in which brands sold soap and every other possible product – the advertising agency was born of that.

"The big idea, the hook, the catch phrase, that type of advertising as it was known was based on trying to help products stand out from other products and get people to think about them in the pre-purchase consideration phase. Subsequently, in the '70s and '80s, you ended up with a highly fragmented advertising agency landscape, and the consolidation of that landscape started to occur because of the economies of scale you could generate by buying media at scale.

"The success of the agency holding companies came about because they were able to put in place a better financial model for servicing the large clients like Procter & Gamble or Coca-Cola or whoever the big consumer product companies were. Because you could offer them a suite of agency-like services, both above-the-line and below-the-line across a wide variety of shops, you could garner more of the market share of a Coca-Cola ad dollar if you could offer them PR, advertising of many flavors, trade marketing, direct marketing, circular buys, etc.

"The agency holding companies were born: WPP, Omnicom, and Interpublic, and then Publicis ended up aggregating the world's marketing services firms into these supermarkets for marketing services both above-the-line and below-the-line.

"The big agencies kept a lot of the media-buying business, and then creative started to take a little bit of a back seat because, in essence, most of the money was made on the media-buying side of that equation. The 15% or whatever the fee structures were at the time. Then, gradually, as that world evolved, you started to see an effect, the unbundling of the facets of these large agency-service types.

"The media used to be all held at, let's say, J. Walter Thompson, and then in the J. Walter Thomson media-buying department, and then creative was done there, and then you had J. Walter Thompson Direct, J. Walter Thompson Street Marketing, J. Walter Thompson Circular Buys, and then gradually, agency holding companies started to see that they could unbundle those facets and offer clients different mixes of their services.

"So the advertising world has gone through a remarkable transformation from the advent of the big-idea agency of post-World War II to where we are today, and all of that has nothing to do with digital or social or any of that stuff. That landscape, the relevance of that type of service buy has shifted dramatically all on its own, having nothing to do with the revolution of digital."

Chapter 7: Marketers Losing Faith; Clients No Longer Believe in Agencies

In Jackie Merri Meyer's *Mad Ave*, Ed McCabe opines, "Advertising has evolved into a business driven by megalomaniacs who know a lot about making money, but little or nothing about making advertising. In some respects, it's also being driven by 'creatives,' who have it wrong to the opposite extreme. They believe the ad or commercial is everything and that winning awards is something. They've lost sight of the fact that advertising, in and of itself, isn't anything. Advertising's sole purpose is to be the cause of something else. To cause a sales increase. To cause a shift in perception. To cause the creation of an edifice of imagery that allows a product or service to be something. But advertising itself is nothing. Nothing but a means to an end. Only fools believe the means is as important or significant as the end."

⌐

David Sable, "A couple things have changed. One is that we were once, as an industry, our clients' best partners. There was a time when the ad agency sat with the CEO in the most important meetings. You were privy to everything that went on. This myth that all you do is 30-second spots is bullshit because in those days, in fact, that was leading edge. We did what was leading edge. If you follow the industry, if you follow even Young & Rubicam, we were huge innovators. We were the first people to do a commercial in color. We were the first people to buy any time on cable because we saw that as becoming new and important, while others were deriding it. We made the jump from print to radio, from radio to TV, etc. It wasn't just us. The industry always was at the leading edge, and it wasn't just that we did advertising. What we did was marketing. We helped our clients. We were involved in product design, we were involved in testing products, we were involved in everything that they did around their business. That was what our job was, and then along comes this thing called 'digital' and, foolishly, most agencies abdicated. In fact, I'd say all did because they didn't get it.

"I see it as opportunity for us, and that's what's building our business back up: be your clients' best partner. Get back in and be their best partner. The goods to deliver are pretty simple: you just have to come back in with great stuff. You have to show the client that you understand their business, that you can talk serious business strategy, that you're not hooked to any one thing. You get that they have customers who are doing lots of stuff and reading lots of things and involved in lots of channels.

"How do you make sense of it, and how do you not put one channel over the other, and how do you bring in the right people and bring in the right ideas and understand that the game is always the same: drive their business. Not just drive digital numbers. This is as old as the hills: you put up a banner that says 'free sex,' you get more clicks than anything else in the world. It's always been the case. That's just good direct marketing.

"You have to go back and bring in people with passion about the business who believe in the business who aren't either Luddites or digital bullshitters, both of which are the bane of my existence. You just have to have people who walk in and can talk to it. You talk to them in 10 minutes, you can tell. We've made some great hires here. Some other agencies have too. People learned. It just took them a while."

✎

Chief Digital Officer for the American Association of Advertising Agencies (4As), Chick Foxgrover, "One of the things that we talked a lot about at creative technologies conferences is that the business world itself is obsessed with creativity and innovation these days. But marketers don't think they are going to find it in the advertising world. Where they're going to find it is in the technology companies and in design firms. There's this amazing focus on the equivalence between what's considered innovative and what's considered design thinking. This is very far away from the way advertising agencies think. Though for those plum assignments where design and innovation firms are becoming partners with the advertisers and large enterprises, advertisers don't necessarily think of an advertising agency as being up to that level of work.

"Ad agencies are good when you have some campaign work to do. But if you want to go deeper into service design and a very holistic look at the business, well then you're going to go to a consultant or you're going to go a famous design firm or product design firm like a Frog or an IDEO or somebody like that."

✎

Twitter's International Marketing Director and former CMO Lead for Microsoft Asia Pacific, Frederique Covington Corbett, "The agency model is broken. When I made partner at my agency, I tried to instigate change from within. I really tried. I tried to make it happen from the ground up at the local office level. And I tried to make it happen at the senior level across the network. People just weren't interested, especially the creatives. I even fired everyone and tried to rebuild it with people that did get it. I put in social media and analytics teams, hired digital creatives. But it was such a struggle – an uphill battle. The ingrained culture was just so hard to change from within.

"It was then that I made a deliberate choice to go client side. The moment my life changed was at Cannes. I'd never been to Cannes. It was crazy. In some ways, it was exactly like being back at Madison Avenue. All these 40-, 50-, 60-something agency guys looking and talking exactly like they did when I first started. All saying the same old things they'd been saying for years, 'You know it's all about the big idea. Gotta have the big idea.' But the other thing at Cannes was that there were all these clients there. They were the ones giving the interesting presentations and having all the exciting conversations. They had all these visions for the future, but those visions didn't involve their agencies, except maybe to help them execute their vision. But the vision wasn't coming from the agency. The only agency that had anything inspiring to say was R/GA. But mostly it was the clients – I remember the Microsoft Xbox presentation, specifically. I remember thinking, 'Wow.'

"These clients really knew what they wanted to do. They seemed to really understand their customers, how they used all this new media and all the opportunities it presented. The clients also had the money. And the power to make real plans and effective strategies. They made all the real decisions, not the agencies. That's where I realized that that's the only way to make real change. The only way to make the agencies change is to force them to change. And that means being on the client side."

‿

Jeff Perlman, CEO of OneSaas and former Director of Strategic Innovations for Visa Asia Pacific, "At the end of the day, I was told by my CFO in Euro RSCG to just stop worrying about the client's business and just manage the agency job the way it supposed to be. Let the chief financial guy worry about the other stuff. He told me that my job as an agency general manager was to keep the clients happy and maximize the number of hours we can bill and push up the retainers. When you're on the client side, when you're not in an agency, it's everybody's job to worry about the bottom line, all the time.

"That pervasiveness of worrying about the bottom line is missing from the agencies, and that's why people are interchangeable and disposable there. That's why it's so easy just to retrench people and use the client because you have a bunch of people who are engaged in the culture of the agency, but not engaged in the business of the agency. There are places where it's changing. There are places where it's getting better. There are agencies that have always been exceptions or have little areas within the agency that understand and get it differently. My experience has been predominantly negative and the reason why I believe the agency, the traditional agency model should die. Why it continues to survive continues to confuse me. But the traditional agency should die."

⌒

Ignacio Oreamuno, "Since I left the agency world at Ogilvy where I was an art director, I started traveling over the world, and I had the privilege to go in every single major agency: bigs, smalls, digital, non-digital. I get to meet the companies that create technology that's used by brands. I get to talk to event companies, experiential companies, viral companies, app companies, everything. And what was clear is that the people doing interesting types of media, for example a flash mob at an event company or something like that, used to be hired by agencies, and now they're being hired by clients. They handle the ideation and the creativity themselves. It's the same thing for everything. If you do interactive screens, you're going to have a client come directly to you and not through an ad agency.

"It's too hard to think that a copywriter and an art director at one agency are going to know how to do every single type of execution because campaigns *used* to be very simple. It used to be a print ad, a web site, a TV ad, a banner and that's it. Now, you scan a QR code on a poster, and then you download an app, and then you play a game where if you win, you can then go to an event where you can download another thing and scan another thing that connects your toaster, updates your Facebook, etc. Now, it's so much more complex that no longer can that be done by two people or one person. You'd really need 10 people, so it's dramatically changed. That's just the reality of how things are."

⤻

Mike Fromowitz, "Marketers are looking for agency leaders who view customers as much more than opportunities for manipulation and exploitation. Marketers need agencies that know the consumer better. Unfortunately, many of them believe that ad agencies are losing their grip on the very people that advertising is directed to, because agencies are no longer doing enough to understand them. When media planning and buying moved out of the ad agency and set themselves up as independent brands, agencies became further removed from understanding the consumer.

"Over the years, agencies have squandered their biggest proprietary advantage, the insights into what drives people. If ad agencies can get back to basics, back to understanding their audience better than their clients think they themselves do, they will have regenerated themselves and be seen as critical partners to their clients.

"Why can't agencies just carry on doing what they're supposed to do? Create big ideas. Make wonderful, memorable ads that convince consumers to purchase brands. Maybe, if they followed that simple path, they'd have no need for re-engineering, and maybe, just maybe, their clients would be happier with their ad agencies. Surely, there is no better way to regenerate an ad agency than through the creation of wonderful advertising ideas that build client brands. Or is there? It's a case of all things to all people. It doesn't work. Rather than regenerate themselves, many agencies are trying to be all things to all people and getting a lot of it wrong. Agencies are brands in their own right, and brands have personalities. Who in this world wants to deal with multiple personalities? Agencies are so busy trying to re-invent themselves that they've lost sight of who and what they are. There's no focus. They have lost sight of their own brand, so how can they possibly promote the brands of their clients?

"Research of this last decade indicates that not many agencies command the loyalty of their clients solely through insight into the brand. Many clients no longer see much, if any, value in how well the agency understands the marketing strategy. They prefer them to basically manufacture and place ads. Many clients no longer see agencies as brilliant planners and strategists that can help them succeed. This has happened because agencies have permitted it to happen. They've allowed clients to believe that they themselves have better people, better consumer insights, and better ideas. That's why so many clients are dictating what the ads should say and how they should say it.

"I recently saw a research report that revealed a number of weaknesses in the armor of advertising agencies. The main points of the study showed:

- ad agencies are relatively weak on enhancing client thinking and instead, just replicate it
- ad agencies are not seen to have independent and unbiased views of the client business goals
- ad agencies are more focused on keeping the business as opposed to doing what's right for the business
- ad agencies' strategic planning abilities and innovation are rated only average

"Let's face it, most ad agencies have thrown out their senior and knowledgeable people and replaced them with 20 year olds who don't know what branding is. If I were to write an ad for a digital agency today it would read: 'We're looking for a 20-25-year-old digital expert with at least 10 years' experience.'

"Reading between the lines, ad agencies are being slighted and designated incompetents, being criticized for their unwillingness to learn, modernize, and change old formulas. Perhaps, there is no better time than now for ad agencies to take a reality check. The industry is being read the riot act by client marketers and being hauled over the coals.

"The quick-fix solutions some ad agencies have undertaken – reengineering, downsizing, restructuring, staff cuts, outsourcing, and more – will not do the trick. Agencies that blame the economic crises for their weakening positions have the wrong outlook. They are simply talking themselves into an advertising depression.

"In economics, one talks about investor confidence. In advertising, it's client confidence that is eroding. At the industry's current levels of angst, it is not another answer we need, but the right questions. The incessant stream of answers so far tabled by the industry has not been able to heal the maladies.

"We do not need research to tell us that agencies that take the initiative within relationships are rated highly by clients. However, merely responding to client requests will not improve the relationship. Termination can occur, despite close working relationships, expressed client satisfaction, and the agency's confidence in its own performance. The more highly valued relationships are those with higher degrees of agency involvement in the client's business.

"In response to marketer demands, agencies large and small are seeking to position themselves as strategic partners with clients. Some are also rejecting the 'advertising agency' tag, aiming to reposition themselves instead as 'ideas companies' or 'solutions providers.' A number of them are embracing 'brand initiatives,' in which agencies become 'business partners' with their clients, not just advertising agents to their clients.

"Does this not suggest the need for agencies to be more entrepreneurial in their relationships or at the very least, help clients crystallize their thinking?

"Proactivity is central to the entrepreneurial approach. Proactive behavior requires the agency to expand the opportunity horizon beyond that dictated by its clients. Such an approach involves identifying and exploiting new opportunities, leveraging resources, and creating new sources of value. In the context of agency-client relationships, being entrepreneurial and proactive would involve actively shaping the relationship to develop new opportunities, and being predisposed to anticipating and acting on the future needs of a client, including suggesting new directions to advance the relationship.

"God, it infuriates me! I see this as a time when ad agencies are squandering their biggest proprietary advantage."

Digby Richards, Founder and Managing Director of AJF Partnership Sydney and former CEO, Asia Pacific for Bates 141, "Agencies have to be bastions of confidence for clients. A security blanket as they go out into spending their millions of dollars. I want to know a definitive plan. I don't want to know anything more experimental these days. For example, when developing a participation platform I want to know much more around the numbers we'll hit across the campaign – whether that's via social media engagement, foot/call or Web traffic – and how does all this convert into some type of commercial win for the company. What do we actually do is sort of hit these numbers, whether it's social media engagement metrics or how can we convert that type of talking conversation back into some sort of commercial win for the company."

⌒

CEO of Dentsu Digital India, Glen Ireland, "In the advertising business in general, the pressure is on margins. This is perhaps true even at a global level. Often the situation is such that one is taking on a business knowing fully well that it's not going to be profitable in the long run, but just to ensure that the business doesn't go elsewhere you go and say yes – hoping that the tide will change. Which unfortunately, doesn't. The pressure comes from being stacked up on fixed costs, so you're saying, 'Let's get started for now and we'll make things work later.' This is possibly more reflective of smaller agencies though that need to survive and don't have deep pockets to invest ahead.

"The position of agencies in the overall ecosystem seems to have moved from strategic communication partners to being vendors. We're aren't necessarily seen as adding strategic value to the overall marketing process anymore. And therefore, a lot of work in the digital space ends up being just executional and tactical. Agencies in general were respected for what they brought to the table a decade ago. A marketing person would say 'You guys know your stuff. It's your domain – you are the experts. There was certain level of trust and respect, so the 15% commission made sense and life was okay. That sentiment seems to have changed. There are many reasons for that change such as the marketing department continues to invest in training and skill development while agencies, on the other hand, haven't kept pace. Training is often seen as a cost and therefore a waste of money.

"I can say that from my personal experience of running digital marketing boot camps in my previous avatar as founder of a digital training academy that 95% of all attendees were from marketing & communication and the rest from the ad world. That says a whole bunch. The whole training thing is lacking in agencies, and it has a huge impact because people then tend to be left behind the curve. Possibly why agencies are getting relegated to doing just tactical, executional work.

"There are very few agencies that can walk up to a client and say 'I'm sorry. We don't want your business because a) It's not profitable, or b) You don't respect us for the value we bring, or c) We don't agree with your strategy or ideas."

～

Co-founder of The Art of New Business, Karla Morales-Lee, "There aren't that many great agencies anymore. Even if you ask a client, 'Can you name me ten top digital agencies?' most of them can't get past four. They'll probably name AKQA, mainly because agencies like theirs have got to the point where they've achieved market resonance. Everyone else is kind of picking up whatever work they can, and that's not really a new business strategy. That's just like going to bed and sort of crossing your fingers and hoping for the best.

"I also personally believe that there really aren't that many agencies that can really do everything [digital, above-the-line, social]. The people who start them generally come from a particular background that they focus on [and understand best]. For instance, I come from a design background and have experience working with disruptive agencies. Naturally, when I'm looking for new agency clients, I tend to look for companies that are creatively challenging the status quo."

～

Sarah Bradley, the other Co-founder of The Art of New Business, "What's also happening now is we're getting reports of marketers not answering their desk phones anymore because agencies bombard them with introductions so frequently. The people that legitimately need to get in touch with the [CMO or Marketing Director] have to use different methods to get ahold of them. These marketing directors delete all external e-mails that are from someone they don't recognize, and some are even now considering closing their LinkedIn accounts. We believe that agencies are running a very real risk of alienating the clients that they're trying to impress.

"We're not fighting against cold calling. We're encouraging agencies to really think about the market they're communicating with before they pick up the phone and try to prospect. There's normally massive debate around the technique because cold callers point to apparent success stories and say things like, 'If you ask clients, they'll say they don't like receiving cold calls, but they still hired us.' For example, an agency in Mexico said that clients will not accept cold approaches anymore, so agencies don't even attempt it since they know their prospective clients will completely shut down. Even when you're invited to a pitch, apparently, the client will not give out their contact details because they're so scared of being bombarded by agencies.

"I think the answer is that you need to find whatever channel is the least saturated and use that to communicate with your clients. At the moment, there aren't many agencies that are really, truly demonstrating their abilities through their marketing. Whenever I ask clients to give an example of an agency that really is practicing what they preach, they always talk about HubSpot – and HubSpot's not even an agency. Why they've suddenly got a perception in clients' minds as being an agency when they're a software provider is probably because of the content they produce. HubSpot writes an awful lot of blog posts. They write e-books. They have video content they produce. They have an event as well, I think called Inbound. They're very active on social media. They're really good at building an awareness of themselves internationally."

⤸

Senior Regional Vice President of dmg APAC (ad:tech and iMedia), Paul Beckley, "Brands are not as trusting of agencies as they used to be. They worry about the cost of production, and they're not actually buying the space from the publishers or any other sort of social medium that they might be using. The biggest issue in Asia is that it's just not got the skill set to get a lot of this stuff done, and when I talk about brand loyalty to agencies, it unfortunately turns out the talent is not as loyal as it used to be back in the day.

"What you've got are people swapping jobs very often, and the reliance on the brand marketer to the person with whom they were dealing in said agency is now off somewhere else. There's a lack of consistency with people and talent in the agencies, and somewhat on the marketing side as well. That's one of the crazy scenarios of who's where? Who's doing what? That's where the lack of trust is getting worse."

⤸

Neil Leslie, "While I'd say that digital has been beneficial to the industry overall, we are still in a bit of a no-man's land. Clients are starting to see the value in shifting the majority of their budgets into the medium. But in many cases, they still seem to see digital more as a means of reducing cost, rather than enhancing results or building brand. Or they still like to craft their messages in a distinctly ATL way. This results in tired traditional television commercials that are considered 'viral' by the mere fact they have been posted on YouTube and tagged incorrectly.

"Many clients I've worked are still trying to maintain complete control of their brand, but now, much of that control lies in the public domain. Anyone can now make an ad for any brand online. Just ask Shell, for whom Greenpeace built a fake pro-arctic drilling web site, filled with sarcastic headlines and comments from supposedly irate customers.

"I think that technology isn't necessarily making the daily lives of creatives any easier. Sure, it's ridiculously easy to conduct research, manipulate images, change layouts and all that, but it has certain unpleasant drawbacks. Tighter deadlines. Quicker turnarounds. Homogenized inspiration and references. And worst of all, it has made the client an active member of the creative team, now able to art direct and write copy down to the tiniest detail. Repeatedly. And in the case of digital, change the work after it has already gone live to suit their every concern or whim.

"It seems we spend a lot more time following routes we already know are wrong, just to prove they are wrong to our clients. That is a pretty big waste of everyone's time."

ᔕ

Jim Speelmon, "When you are a CMO within an organization, you think about the marketing strategy 24 / 7. You have access to so much information that your customers do not and would not even want to know. That affects the kinds of things that you come up with, the strategies that you create, the tactics that you put together, the media selection that you make, because you are coming at this with so much information that you are prone to over-thinking this. The reality is the majority of people that you are trying to communicate with probably aren't thinking of you, probably don't think whatever you're talking about is that interesting.

"Having access to all the information in the world doesn't make you any more insightful into what they're thinking about or what they're doing or why this. As a CMO, you tend to see the world through a kaleidoscope, where you don't really see that the agencies having any strategic value. Because you end up in a position where they may as well work at your company since they are not adding anything. They are not bringing in an independent third-party perspective, which is why agencies used to be hired. If they are just going to tell you what you can get from your staff, then why do you need them?"

~

Steve Hall, "Sometimes there's so much pre-testing done that it waters an idea down so much no one wants to take a risk anymore because they think that there is so much data available to concretely prove stuff before anyone actually has to take a risk. That's probably the case in a lot of industries. There has been this giant shift to agencies being treated as vendors rather than true business partners. That's partially because agencies in their current state aren't really prepared to answer the important questions that the boardroom and the CEO have, such as, 'I spend $2.5 million on marketing. How did that directly relate to my revenue, positively or negatively?'

"There're a lot of metrics out there right now that can determine how many people saw an ad, what happened when we ran this campaign. But there's not so much that ties it back to what's important to the people running the company like the CEO. A lot of CEOs don't think that CMOs understand the financial metrics that are important in running a company from the boardroom [and therefore incorrectly brief agencies]. There's a lot of good and there's a lot of bad going on. The trouble is, in the ideal world, you'd have great data and great creatives, and they would support one another. But for some reason, it seems like there's so much over reliance on the data that creativity almost doesn't matter anymore [and neither do creative agencies].

"When a new CMO comes in and they want their dent, they want to make their mark, the easiest way to do it is to hold an agency review. That whole thing just causes all agencies to run scared. A new CMO comes in and it's like, 'Oh my god, we're going to lose this account!' [There is no loyalty to the agency of record.] Then on a continuous pitch cycle trying to bring in new business rather than trying to make the work they do for their current client better. There's something to be said for a long-lasting, trusting relationship, but I don't see that as much anymore. That's affecting the work because it's like a constant new business pitch.

"Now some people argue that that's a great thing, that you should constantly be pitching the business as if it were a new piece of business. But if you're always trying to come up with some idea that's going to seem super fancy and impress the client rather that actually do what really needs to be done like increase sales. Put your heads together and try to do something that works. It's a bad place for both parties to be."

❧

John Winsor, "We have tried to attack the most profitable weakness, and that's big television creativity and big traditional creativity. I certainly think there're lots and lots of opportunity there, but it's so foreign to most of the agencies, this whole analytics stuff. As people like to say, 'If the CEO of a big company wants a duck in their ad, then the best thing for the CMO to do for longevity of his career is to put a duck in the ad.' That's the way it works. Nobody goes to a dinner party – if your CEO actually goes to a dinner party – and talks about how great and effective their analytics are."

❧

Former Chief Strategy Officer for Digitas India, Manish Sinha, "Today there is a need in every ad agency for a chief storyteller running the campaigns not some control-freak brand guardian. To clients I say, 'It's your fucking brand. You need to understand and tell your brand's story the best. If you are unable to do that, maybe you're not fit for the job.' See traditionally, at least in India, the way it works is the client always used to outsource his thinking and brand story to the agencies. It worked because there were smart people in the agency, and it worked because it was only an assignment of three months, at best six months. It is not possible for an external agency or a vendor to understand your brand story in the digital age. One guy has to be that central brand storyteller in real time, and it indubitably has to be from the client side. The sheer randomness of the conversations, the shifting context and the always on audience leave no other choice."

Craig Mapleston, "Because technology can be so integral to the delivery of an idea, often clients know more than their agencies. Traditionally, clients choose agencies to deliver insightful creative communications solutions through the right channel to motivate the desired response. Now, they are constantly challenging the channels and the technology to bring ideas to life. Again, that's a good thing for the industry, because we need to challenge ourselves to be better and to constantly be looking for innovative solutions."

Richard Bleasdale, "We are often introduced into situations by agencies because they are struggling with a client relationship. The agencies will always struggle to be able to tell the client the truth because they're so paranoid about losing the client. In some cases, they're much happier to suck it up rather than try to make any fundamental changes. We've been working with one of the big Singapore telcos for the last 18 months, with them and their three primary agencies, which are a creative agency, a media agency, and a social agency. It is getting to the point where all those agencies play nicely together and focus on what they're good at and stop trying to eat each other's lunch and get focused on helping the client rather than competing with each other. But we're also working with the client group to upskill them and develop their abilities in-house and their processes and that sort of stuff to work more effectively with their agency roster. We've probably made more change in a shorter space of time in that organization than we could with a global organization because some of the globals have set ways of working. We have to work within a certain framework, whereas with some of the locals, you can effect change more easily."

Ringmasters

Alex Bodman, Group Creative Director of Razorfish NYC, "On a big account, you can have a minimum of five to six agencies that are brought in, from the people coordinating their events to the ones handling their PR to the specialist handling their digital to the agency doing the above-the-line work. Then there's the media company, which will be split up. It means that they have these interagency teams that come together on an account and work as partners. Occasionally, if we are talking about sort of the beginning of the process, we try working with the above the-line-agency from the beginning. The upstream, as we call it.

"The challenge for the client is that it becomes really expensive. It's something everyone disagrees with in principle, and I've heard a lot of really valid arguments that getting it right the first time saves money long-term. But for the client who is used to going to one agency and paying them for coming up with the big idea, then getting other agencies to activate it, it's very hard to convince them that they should be paying for two full-service agencies. Let alone to start on that at the beginning, especially since neither of them are promising they're going to a) come up with a better idea or b) agree on everything. We would all agree that, ideally, the idea already should have the seed of digital in it. You should already have an idea of the goal, of what's the engagement component and everything else. But if you have a powerful idea, it can work the other way. The fact that it can work is the reason why clients still see inefficiencies preparing for it.

"I don't think it's about clients trying to eat someone's lunch. I don't think it's about them being short-sighted enough, and I'm talking a bit more generally. That much is true in the other ad agencies about wanting that particular line item of revenue or income. What does happen, though, is creative people or even planners or whatever will have ideas that they fall in love with or will have a different view about what will be right. I do think what will happen is if you have people that own the idea that has started from there. They have already got an idea of what they think would be effective; everyone knows it's hard to talk a creative out of their idea.

"Increasingly, above-the-line creatives and suits are thinking of themselves as generalists. They're thinking of themselves now as digital natives, themselves, who are able to think within that area and perhaps resent having somebody who works at a digital specialist place with the power to dismiss their digital idea. Of course, the lines of ownership have blurred.

"Gamification and mobile are two areas where digital agencies have such an absolute edge. If they're doing their job properly, they shouldn't have to worry about their lunch being eaten there. That's one place where the above-the-line agencies and social agencies are happy to back off because they accept that they don't have that level of skill. Digital agencies that are thinking about it cleverly would double down in those areas because it's a lot easier to win that fight if you're performing than it is to win when it comes to, say, online video content.

"Your PR agency, your event agency, everyone is going to say that they have a good idea for online video content; and your media agency is going to jump in and say that they've got a media partner that already has a whole audience built in so they'll throw in creative for half the price of the digital or above-the-line agency. That's where things get really blurry – there and social. In social, you'll have a PR agency who maybe has ownership over the brand's voice. A lot of people think that it's not necessarily rocket science to come up with a promotion or a play that works within the social sphere. Those are the areas, particularly social, and particularly the world of online content, that are becoming increasingly blurred. With digital agencies, you need to have a record of great work and a great relationship with the client, or they can expect their lunch to be eaten."

⤚

Ignacio Oreamuno, "Somebody was telling me the other day about a major financial institution that works with like four different agencies. Why would you need four different agencies? Shouldn't one do the trick? No, it's just one's really good at one thing. One's really good at the other thing. One's really good at another. One's well known for this part – and out you go. Those companies now do essentially creative management. They're the Creative Director for all the creative directors of the agency that you work with."

⤚

Karla Morales-Lee, "I recently spoke to the head of Diageo's Advertising and Agency Services Group. Globally, they have nearly 500 agencies on their roster. It's crazy. For example, they have a CMO for one brand who's got 20 agencies across lots of specialties to manage by himself – yet that brand also has an agency of record. They've got digital agencies. They've got POS [point of sale] agencies. They've got e-mail marketing specialists. They've got all of these different people and all of these agencies vying for their time and saying, 'Hey, we've got an idea,' and this CMO is trying to police and manage them.

"When clients are on the look-out for new agencies, they follow the people. They're not so bothered really about the agency itself. It's the people they work with on the account [that are important]. What an agency stands for and all of that is good because it's about stating your position in the market, owning some ground, but I completely think that people buy people [not agencies] by building rapport and demonstrating credibility. The days of saying on your web site, 'We're the best fucking agency you'll ever meet,' and giving a presentation saying, 'You know, we've done some work in your sector. We'd love to work with you,' are completely over. What people want to know is what you think about them and why that's relevant, and what they care about is whether like and can trust you."

ᔥ

George Tannenbaum, "What we've seen is this huge increase on the client's side, there's a huge desire for complete client control. Along with that, communications complexity has gone up accordingly. It's just the clients' need to be in control. But of more shit than they need to be in control of and they simply can't handle it. Trust is so eroded. The old, 'I'm not going to put a URL up on my end frame,' because trust is so eroded. That was the success of Ogilvy on IBM. We were IBM's marketing department. They said, 'This is really complex.' And we responded, 'Sure, but you don't have to do it. We'll do it.' I worked on HP after I worked on IBM, and everybody there wanted to be Apple, but nobody wanted to make decisions like Apple's had to. Simplicity and clarity of purpose are so important, and so few people actually do it."

ᔥ

Professor Jerry (Yoram) Wind, Academic Director of The Wharton Fellows Program and Director of the SEI Center for Advanced Studies in Management at the University of Pennsylvania, "If the holding companies were built as marketing organizations and not as a Wall Street play, you would expect them to play the role of what I'm calling the network orchestrator. If we're trying to reach all type frequencies, which are all touch points – and all touch points include old media and new media, sales, call centers, PR or packages on product design, store design, etc. – then you're dealing with the need to bridge those internal silos because each one of these is a silo within the organization. One has to have the ability to reach across the open industry because each one of these silos has got an industry behind it. And to try do it, you need a new role, which is someone who can orchestrate all these different silos effectively and lead to an integrated message. That's a position that does not exist today, but is needed.

"The big question is, who should play it? Is this the CMO? Is this the agency? Is this a new type of agency that's going to emerge? This is the big role. Once you have this role, then the question becomes, do you still need people to perform the other functions? The challenge is how do they perform without becoming silos? You don't want the dilettante generalist who doesn't know anything about any of the areas. You want to be able to get the depth that you have in each one of the kind of functional areas but the ability to bridge across them."

⌒

Digby Richards, "On one hand, clients are becoming the 360 stewards themselves. The good marketing directors have multi-agency departments. They have a media agency, they might have a search agency, they might have a creative agency, possibly a digital creative agency, a PR agency, and maybe a few other bits and pieces as well as even a social medial agency. So, they might have six or seven agencies. A lot of agencies have found themselves just being a master of their wedge of that pie and not really being seen as a close partner to the Marketing Director. The Marketing Director is really at the center of that, and he or she is supposed to moderate and orchestrate a brand through that path to purchase and through that range of arbiters and specialists. How do you divide a budget? How do you attribute where an idea starts and where it finishes and how do you bring people on board? How do you manage that? It essentially puts a lot pressure back onto clients to have that knowledge base, to have that people management skill, because there are largely emotional people on the other side in terms of the partners they're dealing with.

"It's a pretty big gig when you think about it. To quote a client the other day, 'My life has just got a lot harder. It's got a lot more interesting, but has got a lot harder.' I've got to create some work, go to the media agency and say, 'Let's run it on *x, y,* and *z*.' I feel pretty good about that and got to go to lunch. That doesn't happen anymore. The good clients really are very pithy and robust about understanding their path to closures, which allows them to line up their suppliers. The area of tension that you find is really who leads the discussion and who does the client trust to be at the head of the table next to them versus this committee of suppliers, everyone fighting for their turf. That's the issue clients have. That's Clientland."

⌐⊃

Åsk Wäppling, "Ad agencies have to take a step up because media never comes before the idea. It never did, it never should, it never will. It used to in the '90s, which was a problem. I remember the day when creatives actually could dictate where stuff would go. That's where genius ideas were at work. Because you start at the far end of the problem and maybe you move over to the client side and look at it from their point of view. This is what ad agencies used to do. They used to partner with their clients, and they used to figure this stuff out together. They anticipated where the client needed to go and showed them what they should do next. Now it's the clients that come up with stuff, they demand things, and that's not going to help us.

"Another problem is that clients will have not just one agency, they'll have twenty-five. They have the PR agency, the digital agency, the social media agency, the Web agency, the *whatever* agency. They'll have agencies everywhere. Only one of them is agency of record, and that's usually Grey. How are we going to make all of these agencies march to the same tune? Because you can't you can't have them all speak in the same language. There are 25 different agencies on this one brand.

"The Marketing Director has to play orchestra leader suddenly instead of the person who is engaged in the conversation of strategy and what to do with their issues. Like the conductor from a Bugs Bunny movie. Because it's wrong. You can't have a marketing director or brand director or product manager managing 25 agencies who are all trying to undermine each other by getting bigger pieces of the pie and telling the client 'Hey, you know, we can do this part. Why do you need those guys? They don't seem to understand this at all. Let us do it.' That's not sustainable. It would be lovely if we could still have one-stop shopping so the marketing group could partner with an agency. When we have holding companies that usually own half of the world, it doesn't seem that difficult for them to orchestrate putting this digital agency with that traditional agency. You can all have meetings together, but it doesn't work that way."

～

Andy Flemming, "We are lucky that we are the conductors of the campaign, to be honest. Half of the cynical part of me would say it doesn't do the client any favors to have five companies. Basically, not only are we competing against each other, but also it doesn't mean we work well together. I don't think it helps if the originators of the campaign can't choose the very best people they want to actually take that campaign on and move it forward as the orchestrators. If you've got a client in the middle who says, 'I want agency one to do above-the-line, agency two to do experiential, and agency three to do digital,' what you might find is that suddenly, that orchestra stops playing a tune together and it starts in-fighting. You sit in these fractured meetings where you put up an idea, and agency two goes, 'Well, I don't think that's very good,' because it's point scoring. Then ultimately, that agency would like to grow and get the part of the business that's yours. It doesn't help anyone when you put people in direct competition. I think the only way you get a good result is when people are working together honestly.

"If you look at the 20 plus years that I have been doing this, we have been lucky here to have marketing directors that we've dealt with for a very long time. What that means is that we've gained a level of trust. We understand how they think. We understand the kind of campaigns that are not going to work. When we present something, it is trusted. I don't believe a brand is about constant repetition of a message or changing that message every 6 months or every 12 months because a whole bunch of people leave and a new guy comes in, and the first thing he wants to do is to mark his territory. Being a marketing director is very tough because you're in between the devil and the deep blue sea. If you decide to keep the campaign that your predecessor did and it is successful, then all the success will be attributed to him or her. If you go off and do something new and it's successful, it will be attributed to you, and that is good for your career. Sometimes people makes decisions that they know are not necessarily the right ones, but that are based on that. If everyone loves it, then everyone is going to always go back to you since you are the guy who came up with it. Five years ago, it was John the Marketing Director who was the man.

"The guys that survive and the guys that are in charge of the best campaigns are the ones that realize that their brand is doing well and so they don't change it. They keep it. Because if you suddenly go, 'Right, well I'm young and I'll change it,' it may work out and you may survive, but it is important to stay on message, to stay on the brand, and the best brands have done that."

⤻

Peter Moss, "This is the killer: Whichever came first, the chicken or the egg, I don't really know, but agencies have replicated their clients... or the other way around. Therefore, it is not uncommon within a big company like P&G or Unilever to have a marketing department that is broken down by its media and PR, advertising, direct, digital, social and, if it's going to completely fragment, mobile, as well. Because they are shaped and structured in that way, we tend to mirror it or they mirror us. Either way, it's not the way.

"The problem I am facing increasingly is if you give a solution to the business problem – everything that it needs to do to start making them a lot more money from much more engaged customers – they can't buy it because you've got three or four fiefdoms that need to unite to understand and see the solution for what it is, which is a customer-centric solution, not a discipline-centric solution. Therefore, internally, they're thinking, 'Well, I've got my advertising budget, I've got my digital budget, and I've got my direct budget.' It's, 'Guys, let's think of something that brings everything together, which your customers will love – then it will make sense.'"

⤻

David Shulman, "The model of orchestration forced our talks about what agencies offer clients these days, and we've been talking quite a bit. One thing all ad agencies do really well or can do very well for our clients [rather than having them try to do it internally] is to orchestrate the other vendors, partners, and internal stakeholders within a client to help drive great customer solutions and great consumer engagement. And that's a different type of value that is substantial, meaningful, and valuable to clients. It depends on where we are in the engagement, but many times when we're coming in with the solution, there could be areas of expertise that we bring in from partners across Omnicom. They could also be external partners, from an established external partner (i.e., Google or Facebook) to an unexpected startup that we think is appealing to bring forward as part of the solution. It's not that I have to do everything within Organic, but I certainly want to bring forward collaboration for areas that fall outside of our core expertise.

"It's a shared responsibility of the core agency (or agencies) and the clients to clarify scope and the swim lanes. The best relationships are those where you're putting your energy into driving client solutions and not protecting your turf. I've experienced that firsthand with some obnoxious clients that think that they're getting more value because they're playing games with agencies and keeping everyone on their toes. While it's certainly the client's job to ensure agencies are always bringing their best, it's not effective when energy is focused on protecting turf rather than generating big ideas. The best environment is one where an agency feels comfortable and is encouraged to bring in partners in the spirit of driving the best solutions for the client, yet secure in their responsibility, scope, and swim lanes. There's no ambiguity, and there's no gaming. That's a great engagement. I spent half of my career on the client side, and I know the responsibility of the client is to drive a healthy environment where agencies are clear on their responsibilities and confident that when they bring in partners, they will be encouraged to do so. We're lucky because that's the case with almost all of our engagements now, and that's a smarter place for us all to be.

"It's still down to client by client, by relationship. What I've seen in my experience is that agencies have to truly add value. That's measured in many ways. But the value has to be based on an honest assessment of what they can and can't do. When it comes to a general agency, they can't just get by on trying to drive dollars towards the obvious places that are in their DNA."

↜

Diane McKinnon, "In some cases, it's absolutely true that the clients are well ahead of the agencies, and that's where you see the clients starting to fracture their agency relationships. You see big agencies that have been entrenched a long time losing some key pieces of the account – although they might not lose the whole account at once.

"The other 'Aha!' about all of this is that it's not necessarily that the big agencies are going to lose all their business, but it's going to fragment their business in a much different way. The AOR [Agency of Record] relationship is going to change. Even if they're still called AOR, there're 20 other agencies that are doing other pieces, parts that they won't or can't do. We certainly see that with Y&R and we're going to Y&R, 'You know those pieces and parts you don't want? We want them and we are in your network. Try to get them to us, as opposed to other little agencies that are nibbling around the outside of your client's door. Those are the good parts to us.'

"There's going to be a real fragmenting of the agencies' business. When a big client goes from $100 million piece of business to a $15 million piece of business, then their agency will have to go out and get another $15 million piece and then another. It is going to change their model when they need to have more accounts in order to make the same money. That is what is going to drive a model shift because you can't sustain the large retained structured teams. That's what forces you to try things more like our integrated marketing models. If large pieces of the budget are shifting, if the budget is $100 million and the marketer has shifted $50 million of that to something else – social, digital, mobile, or whatever – then the agency has got to find a way to make up that $50 million. Does that mean they can get another client for that much? Do they have to get two more clients for $25 million each? That shift is going to drive change over time, but not that quickly. I don't think the large-scale traditional advertising agencies will go away, but they will scale down dramatically.

"Everybody is a specialist within the big agency. It's not about the channel; it's about the relationship between the consumer and the brand. That's going back to the core of what this business is supposed to be about: the relationship between the consumer and the brand. If the big agencies don't focus on that, then they just focus on what they do, TV, or whatever their channel is, then they've lost the plot. I'm not sure that they're not capable of doing it. It will be slow, and some will go by the wayside, and some will succeed just like in anything. For some, it will be too late, but not for all of them.

"There's a lot of white labeling of specialty agencies as part of the traditional agency of record going on. If I were a big agency, that's how I would handle it. I talked to a new business guy for a boutique agency that does couponing and promotional stuff. That's all this agency does, retail promotions. They white label for several big agencies. In some cases, they have a direct relationship with the retailer, but often times, they don't, and they don't care. They really don't care if Y&R or DDB or whoever uses them to develop these programs because they're making money. The smarter and the best of the big agencies use adjunct partners to deliver the services."

↩

Jim Speelmon, "We're seeing a combination of two things. One is more fragmentation, and the other is people trying to pull that fragmentation back. If you think of what an advertising agency was in the old days, it was everything. A one-stop shop. There were two different kinds of strategy: a creed of insights-driven strategy, which is ideal for a campaign, and which I am not very good at. Then there is a more of a business strategy, the kind of outcome are you trying to drive. That is your math for how you put things together to get your outcome, and that's what more what I'm into. That is sorely lacking in the agencies. They have people who don't know how to do it or don't even know how to begin the conversation of how we could contribute to this; and that leads to everything being fragmented. The whole split of pulling the media functions out of the agency and setting them up as a standalone group was all done to take advantage of the volume. I can get better rates because I've got a bigger span. That worked very well until digital came along.

"Basically, there's an orchestra. I don't need to be an expert at playing the bassoon in order to be the conductor of an orchestra. Because my job isn't to play the bassoon. That's the opportunity for Sir Martin after years and years and years and years and years of buying up all of this stuff. Now, you need to pay attention to the experts because it's not the one who has the most stuff that is going to win."

↩

Ryan Lim, "The client doesn't have to manage the agency. He can be just like a captain of a warship. A warship is extremely complex machinery with different specialists sitting together in one big huge command and control tower to drive and steer the ship and then function like it is one huge organism. So that is possible. The brand needs to invest as the captain and, as the captain, he need not know all of the details. He needs to know, strategically, where he wants to go, what he wants to do, and have an appreciation of what the different leading team specialists sitting around you arguing. There are not just three or four guys, we're talking about the captain of the ship having multiple components ranging from engine, radar, intelligence, machinery, weaponry, and everything else. If you can envision that as the model, it works. The military is one of those environments that is very complex yet functions in a very well-orchestrated manner."

⌒

Jeffrey Yu, "There is weakness with a consultancy model, because they do not, at least from my limited perspective, deliver the product. At one point, we were so scared of all these McKinseys. I said, 'Oh my god. McKinsey is going to overtake the agency.' But McKinsey has never been able to attract the creative or been able to retain the creative types who turn the strategies into actions. The consultant model is still about very big business strategies.

"I heard all the Sir Martins of this world talking about management consultants and all that, but, now, there is still a big gap between the management consultant and what they consult on and, eventually, what it boils downward to is actually doing communications. There is a huge gap between them and the communications part. Of course, we are the communications consultants, but we are also responsible for delivering the results. Someone has to put everything together.

"We are given very open briefs. There are the margin objectives and all that, but as to how we want to achieve it and how digital and every other component works together is now up to us. We can say, 'We are a traditional advertising agency. We only take the advertising brief.' Then the poor client has to consolidate. He or she has to put together a digital brief and brief everything separately. But for us, now, because we have all they offerings, we are able to say, 'Give us a total brief, and then let us put it together for you.'"

Bringing it In-House

Greg Paull, "Nobody's quite cracked the right model yet for a one-stop full-service agency. Part of the issue is that they're part of big, ugly holding companies that have different revenue streams and investment areas. That's been part of it. There are a lot of clients that like to have multiple agencies. It's this idea of keeping agencies on their toes. McDonald's always works with DDB, but they also work with TBWA because they don't want to have one agency all the way. Some of it is client-driven, but a lot of it is funding-driven. If you need to invest in digital, you probably won't give the money to BBDO, you'll give it to Organic or one of the other Omnicom specialists. It's also to give you that whole nature of it, because you can get more revenue for breaking things up than you can for putting them together, which is tough to argue against.

"We did something pretty cool with Coca-Cola during the Beijing Olympics. We staffed a pop-up agency for them in Shanghai. They employed 60 people in a sideline office that was wholly owned by Coke. They hired people from Leo Burnett, Starcom, Momentum, Edelman Digital, etc. They ended up with a full-service agency for Coke with a 100% focus on Coke. For two years, they were fantastic. They were developing complete solutions for Coke for the Olympics, and then we took that down to South Africa and did that again for them for the World Cup in 2010. It's more of an old-fashioned way of working, but a much more integrated model where everyone is under one roof."

❦

Jeffrey Yu, "Coca-Cola tried the internal agency model. I don't think it works. I still believe that there is a role for an external advisor. Otherwise, Coca-Cola would not have kept all of these agencies partners it has. I have seen a lot of people going to the client side, and I have seen people become very successful, as well. I still remember those guys from Bates going client side at Mars where they became very good marketing directors, but I still believe that there is a role for agencies. I know that everybody tries to put Apple on their client list, but every one of them is actually an executional agency, while Steve Jobs was the real creative director of everything. But that only works with highly charismatic clients. Does Michael Dell have charisma? No, I'm sorry. I don't think so.

"If you look closer to Asia, Samsung tried True Communications. Even though they started with a very big client, they still had to look beyond Samsung to grow because it's very difficult to keep people that work on one single brand every day and night. Especially if you have any ambition, because you will feel trapped. If you have internal clients, then it is very difficult to motivate these people unless you're Steve Jobs, because Steve Jobs was such a taskmaster. The reason why we are agency people is that we enjoy working on multiple brands."

↬

Alan Schulman, "Some marketers have added a Chief Content Officer that works on the client side. Some marketers have adopted entire creative excellence teams internally. These creative directors work on their brands all over the world and are responsible for creative excellence and for working with their partner agencies to maintain creative excellence. Those types of organizational cues are things that the marketplace needs to move towards more systematically – Apple has shown us that even product companies can be highly creative."

"This means that certain 'enlightened and desirable brand' organizations are able to finally attract talent internally. They're seeing companies like Google and others creating an infrastructure across the organization that fosters a very improvisational, innovative culture. To allow this to exist organically, puts them on an accelerated curve well beyond that of the agencies – which makes many agencies less desirable for younger people to work.

"It's a Yin and Yang thing. On the Yin side, there are always marketing side people who want to learn, who profess that they're not experts and are very willing to say, 'Come, teach us. Do a digital immersion day. Come out and conduct a lunch 'n' learn.' What I have observed is that 50% of the people go back to their cubicle and do things just as they always have and find the material 'interesting' but really don't change anything. The other 50% get really inspired and want to become change agents within those marketing organizations, if not at some level of scale, at least on a brand-by-brand basis.

"On the Yang side of it are the marketers who are frequently encumbered by procurement. Once the procurement people get involved, you're not sure whether they see the marketing function as a cost center, or truly as a growth engine.

"If you read many of the CMO studies, you'll find that amongst a hundred CMOs, roughly 50% of them say they are seen in the C-suite as a cost center, because they're buying 17 things from 17 agencies. Because the cost of that is so enormous, procurement has their eyes all over marketing as a measure of keeping operational cost down. On the other side of that equation, you've got a minority of CMOs who truly are considered the growth engine of the company. They're the ones who are organizing differently, taking more risks, looking at what their consumer experience is going to look like three years from now instead of having a conversation with their board of directors about agency selection or a campaign or a Super Bowl commercial. They are having conversations with their board about evolving their customer experience both physically and digitally.

"In the future, that's the smart C-Suite conversation to have, not an ad campaign or an agency conversation. I think we still see way too many brand managers resting on their laurels by holding up a Walmart sales chart while saying, 'See, here's where I started my TV flight and my sales went up. As long as my case shipment sales go up, I'm going to continue focusing on my television advertising.' But I would say to that marketer, 'What is the opportunity cost of maintaining that attitude as we move towards one to one marketing at scale through Big Data?'"

⤳

David Shulman, "As I took the reins here at Organic, I went out and immediately met with my clients, engaged with them and their teams, making talent my top priority. The one thing that became really clear is that 10 years ago, people like us were considered magic men. We could walk into a client meeting and we knew something that they didn't know. We had a language that only we spoke. We had expertise and insights, and we had a little bit of magic dust that we could sprinkle on stuff to wow people. We were considered magicians. Back then, you had clients that were sophisticated, intelligent individuals that knew they had to understand this, and they wanted to know the value of it. They said, 'Come show your magic!' and we would wave our wands and do all kinds of digital stuff.

"In today's landscape, what I'm seeing as I meet the clients who hire Organics that they, themselves, have brought in digital resources on their own teams. In some cases, client teams are impressive in training and development to bring in new talent because they're investing internally. They're much more savvy about the digital world. They have expertise that is far beyond where we were, say, a decade ago. And it raises the question now: what does a digital agency have to do in today's world to add value? In the past, we showed up with our wands and we were magicians. We contained a lot of value because we added a capability that wasn't part of the client organization. Today, you have a level of intelligent savvy that's pushing us as an agency, and an industry, to ask ourselves, 'Where do we add the value? Where do we contribute and raise the bar way beyond where the client teams might be, and how do we live in a world where our clients are a lot sharper than they ever were?'"

↬

Ignacio Oreamuno, "To use Apple as an example of a great client marketing organization is actually not good because there is an Apple and yes, there's a Nike and there's a Red Bull. That's like 0.00001% of brands. Most of the stuff that we work on, if we're creative, is not the cool stuff. When you turn the TV on, most of the stuff that gets shown is just garbage. It's fair to assume that 99.99% of clients are not inefficient. It's a fact. We should not even consider the few organized, slick client companies out there."

↬

Harish Vasudevan, "It's an interesting dynamic, I suppose, which is that there are marketers such as P&G that are saying our business is marketing and not, say, HR or IT or finances, and they handed over those functions to specialists. IBM does all of P&G's HR and IT, and P&G employs agencies only to do marketing. Coke has a similar model. They have some guys do the bottling, and some guys do the marketing, and so they can focus on their core. If a company says the core is purely marketing and not any the other stuff associated with it, then marketing is defining the brand and the marketing strategy and then handing it off to somebody else to implement. Maybe a model that they're not inclined to take on the operation side of the business, but there are clients who may concentrate it in-house. However, the more you take staff in-house, the more you have a whole set of other issues around HR and cost and things like that.

"It's easier to give it out to a third-party operation and keep pressure on them to deliver the results-based compensation. The more you take it in-house, the more you lose track of the amount of money you are spending and the ability to optimize. By giving it to a third party, you are able to manage it better than doing it in-house. They could do it if they wanted to, but I am not sure that they would find the same efficiencies. I don't know if the marketers want to get involved in the operations of stuff themselves and not hand it out to somebody, as it could be even be a safer method by saying to them, 'You better make it happen.' Accountability tends to be better when it's pointed outside than when it's turned inside."

⤳

Andy Flemming, "If you get 20 people around the table and tell them, 'We need to find a piece of music. Let's go around the table and come up with some sort of happy medium.' One might go, 'I love classical; I might love trance.' Another girl might love hip-hop. Generally, if all of those opinions are taken into consideration, the only thing people can agree with is something like Simon & Garfunkel. A committee will always come up with something that has been done before, something that's quite safe and definitely not as groundbreaking as Steve Jobs and Lee Clow sitting and writing, 'Here's to the crazy ones.' It was just two men working very closely together, coming up with something that everyone looks at and says, 'Jesus fucking Christ! That's what that company stands for.'"

⤳

Åsk Wäppling, "When it comes to certain aspects of social media, clients will take a lot of it in-house. This would be the clients that aren't large enough to be able to employ a large enough agency for it. It would be wise of them to do that because it's closely tied to their own PR. Somebody in-house that knows their PR would probably be a faster responder on certain things.

This depends all on the client because social media can be used in so many different ways.

"An example [of a brand being able to organize and move faster than their agency could have... having to seek permission and find the right internal corporate resources] from right after Hurricane Sandy is when Duracell placed trucks out in New York City where you could recharge your batteries and buy batteries and recharge your cell phones and do all of that shit. Duracell is out helping people, and the only way they could mount that they were doing this was via Facebook and Twitter. That's all they did. They just said, 'This is where the truck is going to be. Now, we're going to be over here on this street, over there at so and so an hour.' You can't talk about the covert op after that because its social media is only used for that moment in time. I don't know if that was an agency or an in-house, but it was brilliant.

"Look at the Best Buy's Twitter help thing, Twelpforce. Best Buy came up with that on their own [because they understand their business drivers and how to help their customers much better than an outsider]. I hope you realize that because it won a Titanium Grand Prix Lion at Cannes in 2010 with Crispin Porter's name on it, but it had nothing really to do with the agency. It was Best Buy who was doing it. They had the blue-shirt people running out on social, helping people that they saw were asking questions about stuff that they bought at Best Buy, which is exactly what should be done in house."

⤵

Naked Communications' Head of Strategy, Brett Rolfe, "I think that advertising was a beautifully engineered gravy train for many years and that gravy train has derailed. We've been forecasting the death of 30-second spot for more years than I care to count. It's not dead, and that's all okay. In terms of the amount of money that's available for that advertising, yes, it's diminishing. Large organizations that are in the advertising and marketing space, the pure advertisers, are either disappearing or starting to spread out in terms of footing a whole bunch of different marketing comms, even business-y type camps, to avoid that disappearance.

"The first thing that's happening is the pure advertisers are becoming marketers or business service companies in the broader sense. How much of the stuff your marketers do can you outsource to an agency? Outsourcing printing, outsourcing digital, outsourcing all of this different stuff. There's really this balance between the company itself and the marketing agency or agencies that they're going to employ, and it's really about what's being done where. The same amount of work is probably going to happen around brands and products. It's not going to be in the form of advertising, as we currently know it. It's going to be in the form of a bunch of other stuff that's often messier, more complicated, more fragmented. Things like management of social personas online, which very few people are doing well now because… it's messy. It's really close to the brand. It's hard to make good revenue off of it.

"Maybe marketing and advertising is better done within the company than within the agency. Those kinds of things that, compared to going and doing a two-million-dollar shoot in the Bahamas, are a lot less fun. We're seeing that move to marketing becoming more fragmented and problematic and then the company going, 'Hmm, should that be done internally or by a marketing agency?' The whole thing is a zero-sum game.

"We might have marketers now that don't advertise anymore. Advertisers are going to take more and more internally, and really, which ones are going to continue to follow an outsource model? That's going to be driven by larger business issues rather than, specifically, the advertising space. For marketers, the nature of their relationship with their clients then becomes very interesting because rather than being the specialist advertising agency, it becomes the broader outsourced offering that's going to start to be more balanced. As a large multinational-type traditional agency, you're now really going to want a client that you are doing 10 or 12 different things for – and that creates a very, very different relationship.

"I think that there will continue to be an increase in the number of specialist production agencies. There always have been TV production agencies, and so on. But now we've got the mobile guys. We've got theme development guys. The fragmentation of technology will continue to mean that the actual doers will become increasingly specialized. So, potentially, what we'll get is more of that middle layer linking together the bigger-picture stuff with those specialists. This is postmodernism at large. The world is becoming more bits and pieces that you sort of bring in together rather than doing the whole thing yourself."

John Stephens, Director of Digital Marketing at Dolby Laboratories, and former Marketing Director for Dell's in house digital agency, "It's not in an agency's interest to come up with campaigns that are not going to make that money for themselves. They are in business, too, in competing with the boutiques or the brands bringing stuff in house. Certainly, at least with Dell, as an example, bringing stuff in house relates to the fact that they are an e-commerce site, and so the experience is on the site, and how that relates to outside campaigns is a gap.

"The reason that Global Site Design (GSD) exists within Dell is because no one outside of Dell can really appreciate or understand how it's all supposed to work. You can't expect an agency to necessarily understand the ins and outs and metrics and the gearing and how all that stuff works since it's a jigsaw puzzle. So it does make sense, especially when it comes to the experience on an e-commerce site. It does actually make a ton of sense for the site owners as long as they're connected with the mar-com folks to see a way that they can hold it together. That investment makes way more sense than trying to plow through agencies every 18 months to make your site 'cool'. They might get some agency work that pushes the envelope, only to realize that it would take years for IT to implement it. Then it becomes the agency's fault, so they go away, and then you get a new one in. That's, unfortunately, a cycle.

"It's one thing to have bodies in house to do this work. But not every company is going to have the luxury of having a talent pool like we have in Austin or San Francisco or New York or Chicago or Toronto. There's still that issue of how to bring the right type of talent in from either a design or UX or strategic standpoint to really do the work that's required for the site. But you also want folks who aren't just homegrown, who've only worked with some small place, locally, and then decide to come to Dell. Can the talent, the real talent that can really drive innovation, only come from the coasts?"

⌣

Tobias Wilson, "We lost two of our senior marketers at our two major clients last year. One of them had been there about 18 months and one of them has been here for a year. Now, I think a brand can do a great campaign themselves, but if the internal processes aren't set up to manage it, it isn't going to happen. Too many politics, not to mention the 'forest for the trees' effect.

"The marketers are the ones that know what their boss wants with the delivery inside and out, and they're the ones that are trained and are experienced in pleasing the company's hopes, wants, desires, and dreams. They need to guide the agency so they can create a message that engages the consumer enough to fulfill those hopes, wants, desires, and dreams. Especially if we're talking from a bought-media perspective, that's really only one part, we're seeing a huge shift in that as well as social, mobile, and digital."

⤸

Current Chief Marketing Officer for Cloudwords in San Francisco and former VP of International Marketing for Polycom, Autonomy and Interwoven, Heidi Lorenzen, "In more recent years, my experience has been that the agencies themselves are so fragmented in trying to figure themselves out that they really need some adult supervision. All I used to have to do is sit down with my agency and be really clear on what my goals are: basic goals, objectives, key parameters to keep in mind, etc., and then let them do their thing. They came back with some magic, and I would just choose which one I thought was the most magical wand. More recently, I've felt like I have had to be so much more hands on and almost to the point of thinking, 'Why am I even bothering with this?' It's so much heavy lifting. One of the reasons that I've seen is there being a dichotomy within agencies between the creative and the metrics driven. I think agencies, in order to sell business, are always touting how focused they are on driving demand and revenue, and other tangible business metrics. They need to be both. Some of them have gotten extremely good at metrics, but have lost sight and probably talent on the creative side. I've had things shown to me that are just really uninspired and, maybe they'll accomplish some goals, but they're not going to break through, they're not going to be the breakout campaign that will stand out and drive exceptional response. It may look okay, it may be brand compliant, but there's no big idea behind it, or it's certainly nothing that's going to capture the attention of *Ad Age*, let alone the audiences I'm pursuing.

"I've often felt like, 'This is something my internal team could have put together, and the reason I go to agencies is because I want to raise the bar.' I like bringing outside experts to help bring my team along and show them how great things can be done. That's been lacking. Great marketing today needs both great art and science."

How Can Marketers Be Won Back?

Ignacio Oreamuno, "What's changed is quite simple. I run two award shows and I have a club and yet, I have an ad blocker on my browser. I don't have a TV, so I don't watch television and therefore no TV ads. I don't subscribe to physical magazines anymore. And I'm a typical consumer. To reach me, you really got to get in front of my face and do something crazy, and a lot of people are like that now.

"I know I would say as Director of the Art Director Club, maybe two-thirds of our members don't have television and so, when people are much harder to reach, then clients have to do more interesting things. That's why you have brands like Adidas and Nike creating museums and art projects and basically saying, 'Hey, here we're going to take this shoe, and we're going to give it to 10 graffiti artists, and they're going to design an amazing art piece around this product.'

"There's an agency in Amsterdam called Achtung! and they did a very interesting thing for Volkswagen where they were trying to sell a new Polo model to a young demographic. Instead of making it about the car, they make it about what kids care about: sneakers. They hired a famous sneaker designer to create a shoe to match the new VW Polo they were launching, and it was just crazy that they made it all backwards. They said, 'Buy this sneaker, and it comes with a Polo.' You don't buy the car and get a cool sneaker, you buy this really expensive sneaker and you get a car [which sold a lot of shoes]. As a brand, you've just got to go out and just do crazy stuff."

꙳

Digby Richards, "With regard to marketers wanting to try new approaches [that involves other creative sources] a campaign we did for Sony comes to mind. It involved tapping into a co-creation network across the globe where we gave them a simple brief – 'What does the Sony power button mean to you?' From a supposed pool of 70,000 creators we received a ton of submissions. Unfortunately they were all crap. And it was only until the last week, that we received six videos that were okay and just usable. Clearly some preferred reliables came into the mix late. I thought the experience was a good strategic one, but a poor creative one. Great content needs to be crafted – albeit in more nimble way these days – but it still needs to entertain, inform and be valued for it to be shared with purpose among a person's community.

"This is why I always worry about user-generated content. We picked up the RAMS Home Loans business, which is now becoming an online bank in Australia for the Westpac Group. They have a ram as their icon. There's a whole range of things that they were discussing with the client about how much we should give RAMS over to the people and how much do we contain to try to control and not incite too much participation or disruption or abuse or conflict with the brand. That's a whole area that clients get excited about, especially old-fashioned clients. They get excited about any sort of co-creation idea. You've got to be really careful with them. For example, if we were developing a product and we co-created it around its strategic importance and stuff like that, and then represented it to the people and said, 'Ta-dah! There's a product that you helped design.' I think that's okay. But when it comes to co-creating campaigns [with the client and/or the crowdsourcing masses] and interpreting brand icons or brand stories, I'm not a big fan of it at this stage.

"Just having TV, [which generally requires an ad agency] regardless of effectiveness, from a marketing point of view, sends the signal that you're serious about your brand to those other audiences, which, you can argue, are nearly more important than the consumer. There's that whole dynamic in this particular product category of FMCG [fast-moving consumer goods, aka consumer packaged goods] and, probably, the alcohol category. It's saying to them it's visible. Visible action on a campaign is still TV, whether we like it or not. It is still seen by clients as important, when it comes to the final decision on that media plan, where and how you carve up that 20%. It's still seen as a really important part of it, something they can push play on, 30 seconds that sums up the campaign. It sums up what the brand stands for, and that's what they like.

"I do think it's definitely getting to a point where [the expense of] TV is being questioned a lot, even though the ratings are strong for something like *The Voice*, and what's the switch-off factor?[7] How much is this work really making an impression, really? It's very traditional with research, too, TV ratings. Is it really making an impact? How engaging is it? What are they doing? Digital TV obviously helped put measures around that, but that's going to be the interesting thing. In a couple of years, I'm sure that it'll shift the other way completely. What's happening in the world is that you need to be on more. Your message needs to be on. It needs to be fluid. It needs to be able to adjust. You can't just do it by sitting and forgetting work like you used to be able to do. There's a listening role, and there's a responding role.

"I reckon, just a bit of crystal balling, that the ad business will do a complete turnaround. If you think about TV commercials years ago, it was that there was a ceiling on the average TV commercial. Then it went nuts. This was probably in the day of Dire Straits' *Money for Nothing* and MTV and all this sort of stuff. Similarly the Super Bowl and all those. Some of the people were spending millions and millions, and I wouldn't be surprised if digital goes through a similar thing, where someone like a Nike or an Apple or a Microsoft spends a shitload of money on a range of digital assets, as well as, obviously, media and shoots, everything there. It's a bit of a tipping point. You just need a need a couple of big marketers to do it."

Dirk Eschenbacher, "The breakthrough for me working with clients [in new media] was in 2006, when I partnered with North Kingdom on a project for Motorola. That was the kick-off to a series of projects with those guys for the brand. Motorola was one of the first clients that really understood that putting a bit of money down on a good production could do something, and it worked. It got a lot of views, a lot of hits, and we developed a lot of marketing around it. I went to the client and said, 'We can do it in house and it's going to cost you this much, and it will be pretty good, but will it be world-class standard? Or you can pay this much more and go with the guys who just did the Vodafone web site and some stuff for Absolut Vodka.' I showed it to them and they loved it. They went with it. It wasn't cheap at that time: they had to pay

---

7   When an ad is seen too many times and the viewer grows weary of it, such that it becomes ineffective.

over $100,000, which was a big thing. They were the first client that did that, but it turned out to be really worth it. It had a really big upside.

"[Producing brave and effective work] always starts with a good relationship with the client. I always tell them, 'It's up to me and you to push for the importance of the idea.' If you really believe in it, you can make an argument for it. I met the guys in North Kingdom a few times when they were at the height of their success. Now everything has changed a little bit. Everyone is going through very tough times in Europe, and everyone is going to less expensive, smaller, boutique agencies. Just two weeks ago, I did a training program for Ogilvy Asia, and I got a guy in called Mark Chalmers who's D&AD digital president. He runs Perfect Fools, a digital production shop in Amsterdam that does amazing things and has won quite a lot of awards and stuff. I know a few of those production studios, and they're great; they do it. They make things. They don't work like digital agencies [and clients appreciate the focus].

"I had a long talk with Mark, and he says it's definitely very challenging to maintain a 40-person studio. You really gotta find the jobs nowadays. It's not that easy any more. They all specialize. For instance, North Kingdom is great with video, but maybe in my opinion not so good with Facebook and social media. Others are better with social media. Perfect Fools did *The Super Mega Rainbow Updater Machine* for Skittles. Everybody has carved out a niche, and they all have their direct relationships with agencies, and they operate like mini agencies. If they're smart, they'll try to go to clients directly and act as the agency.

"Especially in China, the brief always comes with a very clear idea of objectives: you figure out what you need to do, then comes the idea, then you execute it, and then people on the client side tend to beef things up rather than cut things down. They add things left and right. That's an experience that I have that doesn't necessarily makes things better, just more complicated. [And makes the idea of them bringing the work in house, conceiving of the strategy and creative ideas, and managing the executions hard to imagine.] The simple stuff prevails. The big issue still is that in digital, everybody thinks you can just add a lot of stuff to it. Nobody really understands that adding to it will actually make less of an experience. That's a big issue on the client side.

"On the agency side, the trouble is that they are not really good enough at managing client expectations [and that has had negative implications for the client-agency relationship]. They have to be very clear about what needs to be done and why it needs to be done and why we're not going to do more than that.

"I worked on a campaign where I collaborated with a graphic novel writer from Marvel Comics. It turned a really cool story that played out in a magazine, a booklet, and on all different kinds of computer screens: computers, tablets, and mobile-phone screens. An interactive story was really nicely done and very nicely produced. [There's no limit to what you can do with today's technology, a sharp understanding of the brand and an imagination.]"

Kingdom of Night, 2011 by DDB Guoan Beijing for Volkswagen to launch their Scirocco brand in China using an interactive graphic novella. Creative and art direction by Dirk Eschenbacher with writing by Andy Diggle and artwork by Jock (a famous DC/Marvel comics team).

Dave Whittle, "The change on client side [to move away from advertising agencies for anything more than media buys and production] has been driven by Boards and CEOs. The businesses that are more innovative or more advanced in this space [of advertising] are the ones that have been seeding the need for innovation at the Board or CEO level. Go back and look at fantastic dot.com success stories in Australia. With most of those businesses, their success was largely due to their leadership 'getting it.' Their leadership understood what was happening and got their timing right. You can pay that to the relative failure of their competitors, even though everybody had the same talent to use. They have the same ideas. The failure of execution is not because of the people doing the work. It's the leadership."

᠆

Jim Speelmon, "Even the spoof Shell campaign when people thought it was really Shell and it wasn't [it was environmentally-minded members of the public chastising the brand for what they considered to be severe failures of corporate responsibility], the company was slow to respond. This is a sign of an internal strategic failure because, just like when you write a business strategy, you don't write your strategy under the assumption that everything is going to go your way. Why would you write a communications or an advertising strategy on the assumption that every single person you come in contact with is going to demonstrate the behavior that you most want? A strategist has to be much more these days, a risk manager and contingency planner as well as being someone that can just draw boxes and arrows, and it's no longer a linear path. [Agencies know this, but do corporations?] One of the issues for digital has always been that the mainstream agency or the Creative Director comes up with the concept and you are handed it. And now you have to render that into whatever your digital is going to be. *Nobody* ever liked that. People that really knew what was going on from the very beginning disagreed with that approach.

"This is just a continuation of thinking you still have to operate at a tactical execution level. If these people are just implementing your tactics, then you have zero input on what the opportunities are either to expand something or to grow it or to do risk mitigation. This goes back to when I look at myself, just for example. My responsibility [as a Director of Strategy] is not to be the know-it-all, but to know what it's like to be a Microsoft customer. I'm supposed to know about the consumer, how they consume media, what they do, how they think. That's the value that I bring. If I'm at the end of the food chain, I have my ability to really add value to the business seriously impaired.

It is this bizarre dichotomy. Whereas, in order for the client to get what they need, they feel that they have to do all of this upfront work.

"The by-product of that is you're going to limit the contribution of your partners and the value they bring at the other end. For someone to re-invigorate their career and for an agency to become more relevant, to be more realistic about what truly needs to be done and what shouldn't change. Don't try to change things, and don't beat your head against the wall for things that simply are just not going to change. For people who are really into this or looking for a new opportunity or a new challenge to re-invigorate their intellectual fire, step back and look at how you can become a change agent for the clients that have an opportunity or have an issue. Or how do you create the opportunity? Because if you're really good at what you're doing, you should be able to do that."

⌐

Subhash Kamath, "There are clients and then there are clients who have already moved to being far more cutting edge, like my Red Bull client, for example. He lives in the digital world. In the experiential world. He doesn't live in the traditional advertising world at all [and may soon no longer want or need a traditional agency partner]. If I look at clients like Airtel, India's biggest telecom operator, they are fabulously there in the traditional world, as well as fabulously there in the digital world. At BBH, we have interesting terminology for this thinking; it's called 'Super Bowl' and 'Super Social.' It's a combination. It's not either/or. It's about cracking a brand idea that straddles both Super Bowl and Super Social. It's 'and' thinking.

"There are clients who have done that and very well, and then there are clients who're the laggards who are still waiting and watching to see what will happen. There are clients who still say, 'We want to go digital. Can you build a web site for us?' Or there are clients who have said, 'We are very digital. We have created this Facebook page which has 15,000 likes.' Then you ask them, 'Okay. What are you going to do with those 15,000 people who have liked your page?' 'What do you mean? They liked our page!' they shout. I say, 'That's not digital. A student could put up a Facebook page and he would get many likes, but that's not digital.'

"...one thing that is certain, is that a lot of people are asking questions. A lot of traditional clients are asking questions [and learning more than some of their agency counterparts]. 'What do I do? I want to be in the digital world, but I don't know how. Could you tell me what I should be doing?' I believe we have come to a stage where people are asking those kinds of questions. The sad part is a lot of these so-called digital specialist agencies, themselves, don't know how to take the brand somewhere. Many of these so-called shops are only selling a set of services. They don't quite know what to do with the brand and what the next step is. 'No, we will set up a Facebook page for you, and we will monitor conversations, and we will put up these regular updates, and we'll send you a report by the end of every week,' and yeah.

"I had a client who actually called me up and said, 'Listen. My digital agency is putting up these updates. But that tone they use brings us further from the brand. They're not getting it, man. Could you write it for them?' I said, 'I can't write fucking updates in a day. They have to learn.' Then we conducted a workshop for their digital agency writers, young kids on what a tone of voice of the brand is and why is it important to have that tongue-in-cheek style, that wit. Why the same thing can be said with a bit of sarcasm and not straightforward, why there needs to be a twist in everything you say. They wrote it and sent it to my creative director whose reaction was tough. It was tough, because many of these digital agencies are happy to do things not knowing where they're going. It's like what Paul Simon sang. 'I don't know where I'm going, but I'm on my way.'

"It's that solution, which is okay for certain clients who want to experiment. Many traditional clients worry these kinds of solutions coming from these small shops, because they're even more scared now to invest money since nobody's going to tell them how they should do things. That's an area that is now upcoming, but hasn't been there. There's the whole business of analytics. Analytics has got a very strong future, and we're watching this gap of not just 'What do I do?' but 'How do I measure it?' How do I keep improving upon it?'

"There are quite a few analytics businesses being set up, and there was a similar trend when the direct marketing world opened up and clients were asking, 'When I send direct message to your client, then to my people, how many should I send? How many will redeem the coupon, and how many will respond?' There are various people saying, 'If you get a 5% discount, you should be happy. Blah, blah, blah.' Clients would be happier with better measurability of what they do versus a bunch of creative guys just telling them, 'Do this. It'll be fun. It'll be very nice for your brand and fun for your brand. Just put it out there and see what happens.' That's the gap that we can help bridge because we can come out with these exciting ideas, but we're always rooted in strong strategy. It has to be at the confluence of intelligence and magic. It's called transforming intelligence into magic. It's about creative excellence, no doubt. Creativity and excellence, based on strategic relevance. That sweet spot is not easy to come by. That sweet spot is the most difficult thing to get, and that's equally true of the digital world."

↜

Google's Managing Director, Head of Global Agency Sales and Services, former Global CEO of WPP's Enfatico and former President of Digitas Boston, Torrence Boone, "I see clients becoming much less risk averse than 5 to 10 years ago. There's now an openness to experimentation and agility in how they think about marketing campaigns. I attribute this shift to the powerful role social media now plays in the marketing mix, as well as the fragmentation of media in general that makes consumer engagement more distributed and less predictable. Advertisers recognize that they're no longer fully in control of their brands, but that there is strength in a well-managed, well-orchestrated dialogue. They understand things can go terribly wrong very quickly, but that they can recover by engaging and being authentic."

↜

Mike Fromowitz, "There's a big shift underway because of digital. Ideas are no longer just intellectual property, they're emotional capital. Your brand means nothing unless it's activated and wired in a meaningful way for your target audience to respond to it. When it's wired, it's a network capable of brand building and delivering a message, a motivation, and an idea.

"What underlies all this however, is the sense that something is shifting in the foundation of our belief about how communication works. We are, today, experiencing a fundamental shift from persuasion to permission-based communication, the slow death of mass advertising, and the rise of the Internet, the ultimate tool of empowerment for a new age.

"Someone once said, 'Advertising is the engine of commerce. Oil it, and it will serve you well.' Indeed, advertising has been an amazing and powerful tool in building brands. But ad agencies have dropped the ball and given up ownership of the consumer. Agencies used to know more about the consumer than their clients did. I don't think this is the case any longer.

"Advertising agencies need to become vital to their clients' marketing efforts once again. Ad agencies, for the most part, have been comfortable with their traditional roles for years. Everything seems to fit neatly into a predictable box: make more ads, buy more media, and win a few awards, which is no longer sustainable in a fragmenting marketplace.

"Ad land is experiencing a crisis of confidence, living in a time-warp of its own making. It seems that advertising has allowed itself to get left behind, to the point where there is now a gap between what clients want and what advertising delivers. Advertising agencies have become separated from the end result. What's also making things difficult for ad agencies is that many of their personnel lack the entrepreneurial skill sets required for business planning and strategic focus, existing instead in splendid isolation, like an exclusive club.

"Integration has also been an agency buzzword. But 'real' integration has proved an elusive beast because in most big ad agencies, their areas of discipline are set up in silos. Certainly a large-scale bundling up of services does not necessarily add any value; quite often, it delivers the opposite.

"Furthermore, in spite of the proliferation of new thinking around marketing and communications, much of what we do is still based on outmoded, awareness-based, mass market thinking. The shift requires us to move from an awareness model to a new model based on influence. If we don't, all we will get is a continuing diminishing return on marketing investment.

"The reason why TV advertising remains a lead medium in most campaigns is that advertising is the best means of creating rapid, large-scale awareness. The problems with awareness-based thinking are becoming more and more numerous. Not only are the mass media increasingly becoming fragmented, but the audience increasingly rejects those messages that are perceived to be 'mass-market,' preferring personalized and customized communication.

"I don't know about you, but I do know that consumers don't behave like they use to. I'm one of those consumers.

"The Internet is making niche marketing more viable. The Internet has transformed our ability to find information on any conceivable topic. The availability of instant information expands thanks to the Internet, but trust in companies and brands declines.

"Thanks in large part to Google, we've become experts in cutting through trivia to get to the facts. We've also become experts in finding sources of reliable information through friends, family, and the Internet. Consumers trust all three more than advertising. We want to see samples, we want to know the benefits, and we want to reduce the risk of making the wrong choice. Because reducing risk in brand choice is a major force shaping customer behavior.

"More and more, I wonder though, whether we are forgetting the basics when we try to create integrated marketing and advertising campaigns. The basics lay in the insight of how and why consumers make purchasing decisions, and of what and who are the best sources of information and influence to reassure and inspire consumers to try and buy."

Chapter 8: Reengineering the Agency Model

It's not easy to contemplate rebuilding the agency model. Thinking about the amount of effort it will take to transform what has worked so well for so long into something that will continue to do so for the foreseeable future takes the wind out of most people's sails. Every agency structure is pretty much the same, whether you're mixing things up by having standing-only or walking meetings, open floor plans, flat structures, agile methodologies, team pods, or deploying other tactics gleaned from the latest hyped business book or an episode of *The West Wing*.

Despite the stylistic differences, you can go from any global agency brand to practically any mid-size shop, and nearly all of them will still have the traditional silos of: new business, account management, creative, project management, production studio staff, and maybe a couple of developers or a media department and a strategy group. Projects are pitched and won, briefs come in, strategies and concepts are conceived, presented, dismissed by the client, redone, and eventually executed and placed. Everyone knows their role in the process, and most even know when they are supposed to add their expertise into the mix. It is a tried and proven methodology that has become an assembly line for the talent and skilled labor — and a cash cow for the owners.

Fortunately, there are those who have already begun walking down the path, clearing the way, and showing the possibilities for creating something much more efficient that can flex and scale without forcing team members into becoming self-interested mercenaries, as has been the norm in the ad business for too long now. As Subhash Kamath says in this chapter, "The idea is to infect the agency, the main team itself, with people that can be carriers of the digital virus." These days, it's easier than you think to spread that infection throughout your organization and adapt your structure and offering into something your employees and clients will intuitively understand and appreciate. They're certainly not thrilled with the status quo, whether they're smiling at you through clenched jaws during performance reviews or nodding their head in agreement about the problems with the kids in the business today, on the inside (and, more often than not these days, right to your face), they know there needs to be change… and soon.

But so do the major agencies that employ the bulk of the industry's professionals, and they are trying everything from hiring comedy writers to replace creative directors in the hopes of cracking the secret to viral video success, to placing the digital experts in charge of their entire agency network, including TV, radio, and print. It's great that they're finally coming around to the idea that things can't continue as they have been and are trying new things. Now they need to take a deep breath and think very seriously as to whether their current revenue sources are sustainable for the long term, if they are still going to be able to attract the people they need in order to keep the clients happy, and how radical the changes within will really need to be. Deck chairs being rearranged on the Titanic, anyone?

⌒

David Shulman, "As an example of how traditional agencies are trying to move with the times and reinvent themselves from within, look at Y&R's appointment of David Sable, who is as credible a digital leader as anyone in this space. That's how you change it: you change it from the top. You don't add a social specialist in the mix and put them in the corner and say, 'Sit at this desk and make us all social,' or 'Bring flashy social ideas,' or 'Bring me a mobile idea.' That's the *wrong* way of doing it. You start by embedding knowledgeable senior leaders, whether it's a David Sable or an Andrew Robertson [President & CEO of BBDO]. Andrew, no doubt, is able to talk the talk and really bring value in the dialogue that goes beyond traditional channels. You get people like Andrew Robertson, David Sable, and you put these people in positions of power that allow them to continue to evolve their organization's skills and thought leadership. That's the *right* way of doing it. The agencies that just stick in the token leaders or the token experts are the ones that are going to fail.

"You need to be a leader that drives change and inspires leadership that can cascade throughout the organization. Being able to run a digital agency doesn't give you the automatic creds to run or to create an integrated – if you want to use that word – agency, or to take on the challenge of reinventing a general agency. It starts with being a great leader and having the ability to motivate and drive people, and to select and retain the best talent that does amazing, results- driven work for our clients. That drives the bottom line for the agency.

"I took my executive team off site for the purpose of stepping back to talk about what we are about and what we are doing as an agency. What emerged – especially around the 'why' of what we're doing – is this really interesting notion of human connection.

"Human connection is the most powerful force in the world. Don't think of that just from a marketing context, but also around the ones you've made in your own life and how you engage with them. Digital, in a marketing context, is not about removing the human element but about nurturing the human connection. I shared this with Andrew Robertson about a week after we started to go down this path. He said, 'Well David, isn't that what Facebook positions itself as? A human connection?' I thought about it for a minute and I said, 'Well, okay Andrew. There's a two-by-two chart out there, and in the top right quadrant are Facebook and Organic.' I'm okay with that.

"If I think about how we get things done within the organization, we are finding, creating, and amplifying how people connect to brands and to each other. Our heritage is largely around technology, and in today's world it's data and technology that inform and enable the experiences we create. We're deeply into customer intelligence, not just analyzing and optimizing what we've done, but really creating a sophisticated and predictive marketing intelligence capability that tells us what to do, when to do it, and how to engage people with it. We are finding those connections. We are finding those deep insights. We are creating powerful ways to connect brands and people and then we are amplifying that, obviously, in social and digital spaces.

"At Organic, we create connected and captivating experiences. That word, 'captivating,' is critical to us because there is so much noise out there. As a user, as a consumer, there is so much. We're so bombarded by messages, by marketing, by advertising. The thing that breaks through has to be powerful, engaging, exciting, and relevant, in order to connect brands and consumers. What we'll hopefully find interesting out of that is that the word 'digital' doesn't really jump out at you there. We start with the premise that we, with our expertise in this digital world, not only have permission but also a need to drive those human connections.

"My background as a psychology major influences the way I view the world along with the people I've recently assembled at Organic. This was a natural articulation of what, to me, is a view of the space, but I still believe that so many people who are the so-called digital natives come at it from a channel perspective. The industry created and reinforced a notion of digital as tactics, channels, projects, and execution. But people don't behave that way, and agencies that are from the past are oftentimes still briefing from a traditional standpoint, just tacking on digital execution. As long as that's happening, no one's going to step back and look at this idea of human connection, and see the power of what we can do. It is so obvious but people miss it.

"This is the core of what drives people to go online and browse and do all this stuff. They want to make connections to the things they engage with every day, that they spend their money on, and that they spend their time with. This is what the agency of the future should be spending its time on, as opposed to channel tactics and media placements."

∽

David Winterbourne, President of the Global Talent Management Agency Winterbourne Recruitment, "The late Gil Scott Heron was right when he said, 'The revolution will not be televised.'

"The new dawn for marketing communications is already here. The advertising agencies' role is to help brands engage with existing consumers and to entice new ones by creating seamless integrated advertising campaigns initiated from a great creative idea. This hasn't changed. What has is consumers now have the power to influence brands and choose how, when, and where to interact with them. Because of this, brands and their agencies are changing, too. Agencies need to orchestrate the creation of a media neutral 'Big Idea' utilizing all the data available to them, including data gained from interactions in the social and digital space (aka 'Big Data') to create and deliver specifically targeted and relevant communications and entertainment. This richer brand experience is required to entice the target audience to commence the consumer journey, follow the brand, and/or engage with it in the future. This is the revolution.

"It requires all of us to re-align how we think, what we do, and how we do it. We must now work together in a more honest, empathic, intuitive, integrated, collaborative, agile, professional, and strategically creative way; creating a new breed of ad people and agency model organically that I believe should be embraced and celebrated."

∽

Dave Whittle, "Usually, by starting small and making sure that clients are not threatened or by empowering them, we can help get them through the move to digital. A new technique or new method or new idea and they have ownership. In turn, helping them take their boss on the journey of change or transition in the organization, encouraging them to take risk, and proving it with results."

⌒

Nimal Gunewardena, "I've been the Chief Marketing Officer in addition to being the Chief Strategist and CEO of the agency. In my career in marketing, I have worked in new product development and as a lecturer. I try to take the lead in learning new things so that I can share them with others, to generate new thinking in the team and take everyone else along. It has been a challenge I've been happy to take on. I don't expect to be able to do the things my team is doing or know all the technicalities, but I try to learn as much about the nature and value of things so that I can sell their potential and applications to overall brand communications."

⌒

Peter Moss, "As an industry, we've got to look at not the headaches that all of this tech and all of this change is causing us, but what it can do for us. I don't think a twenty-first century agency is just a few hip talented people who have a little company together, which is very cool and does things probably better, maybe a little bit quicker, and a little bit cheaper than an agency. We bigger agencies should be looking at what we could be delivering as services, which were unimaginable prior to all of this technology."

⌒

CIO for The Tombras Group in Knoxville, Keith Casey, "I see big agencies wanting to become production companies and production companies wanting to become big agencies. There's a layer on those things that they're missing on both sides. I knew of a production company that wanted to become an agency, but they did not understand what an account service layer's function is for. They said, 'We'll just hire executive producers instead,' and they couldn't get their heads around what account service meant from an agency standpoint. I've also seen ad agencies do the same thing in reverse. (I'm living in that world right now.) Someone wants to start a video department, but they don't want to hire an executive producer because they don't understand how a video production house *works*.[8]"

Building Flexible New Structures

Jim Speelmon, "Going back to regional and global footprints is really starting to be quite irrelevant. Your ability to say, 'We've got the smartest, most creative people for this.' Whether it be an audience, a country or category, that's where you will kick ass. The losers are going to be the people like Martin Sorrell. Well, actually it won't be because he will still own a whole bunch of these little subunits.

"The agency model, as we know it today, is definitely on its way out. What can they do to survive? Specialize. I would shed. You can't be an expert in everything. You really can't. If you are going to be the expert in everything, then you are going to be the strategic consultancy or the data consultancy. If you can take data and analytics and match that up with strategy, that's going to be a big thing. Because you're going to need to have people who understand how you set up and manage analytics as well as how you interpret the information. The people who do that generally are not really very good at how you would take the insights and apply that to something else.

"They should be building up the data side. The Accentures are better placed than anyone in the agency world to do that thing, but they are a little weak on the human aspect. Data will tell you a lot, but when I went to college as an undergrad we were asked, 'If *this* is where people are, and *this* is where you want them to be, how do you manufacture the steps that you would need to go through?'

"Data gives you an excellent opportunity; as the data analytics say, 'Here is where we are today. This is how we think, how we feel. This is what the data is telling us.' The data is good for keeping you on the road, but the data and the analytics, they can't create your strategy. You still need to have somebody who can help you figure out if *this* is where you are, and *this* is where you want to be, then there are multiple ways you can get there. Which one of those ways is going to be most advantageous? The customer journey isn't happening at the campaign level. It should be at the relationship level.

---

8 Josh Sklar, "They need to take the time to learn from people who have been hands on – and not simply assume these specific disciplines all fall under the same process and structure."

"If I were Martin Sorrell, I would clean house before I bought new stuff. You have to do this slowly because you've got a lot of very big personalities that you're going to have to deal with. I would turn my Ogilvy, my JWT, my Y&R back into specialist tactical groups.

"Right now there's Ogilvy. There's OgilvyOne. There's OgilvyAction and there's Neo@Ogilvy. There's social at Ogilvy. I would scale them down so it's very clear in people's minds why you would go to an Ogilvy in the first place. For people who work there, as well as the people who hired the services. Then in the process of cleaning up this very broad but not very deep mess that I've got, I would then take my units and say, 'HSBC, you need advertising, and we've got JWT. You need media, we've got Mindshare. You need social? Well, here's a WPP social agency.' It's not rolled into one of the big agencies.

"People are always bundling stuff together, but you reach a point of diminishing returns, and the networks have surpassed that point. Where adding further to your operating brand is not gaining you any value, it's actually diminishing your opportunity because it doesn't help people pick best breed. Instead, you have a severe duplication of resources with limited opportunities for you to charge the price that you would need to charge to make that financially feasible.

"They need to clean up what they've got. Sharpen the focus of the things that they're going to keep. Take out the trash, just like they pulled media out of the traditional agencies. Pull these other things out. I see absolutely nothing wrong with the digital pure play. As long as you're going to keep it as a tactical service provider, which is the role that you're playing anyway because CMOs don't believe that they have the ability to deliver on the strategic end. It's not like they're going to be fighting their clients to make a move that they don't already think should happen.

"If you want to win the alternates and keep companies like Accenture from coming in, you're going to have to develop a group. Operationally, it will depend on your clients and what skills you have, but you need to have your strategy team, which could potentially be just standalone groups like management consultants. You could pull people out of the different groups to be assigned to an account. There are a number of different ways that that could be rolled out.

"The alternative is that the companies like Accenture *are* going to come in. They are going to do the high-level business management. They have it all figured out. They are investing heavily in data and analytics. Someone from Accenture can go work at a large client, go through this entire scenario, turn around and say, 'Okay, well, we need this from this agency.' It's already starting to happen.

"The new model for agencies will probably end up being some strategic consultancy type of thing where everything else is freelance. That's where I see it going, as the CMOs who are now trying to play that role realize that they need to have a broader perspective. I don't think they will go down the road to delegating that responsibility far down the hierarchy.

"The big losers are going to be the big agencies that are trying to be everything. Because even today, you see it is very important that you have either a global or a regional footprint to facilitate the work. With the advent of things like social media, it's far more important for you to be reflecting local insights and local tastes. Having a large footprint is not a benefit. It needs to be best of breed in each geographic location.

"Who needs an Ogilvy if you're not going to be doing that 'one-size-fits-all' global-, regional-, or national-style campaign? When you are instead able to take a very solid strategy that reflects local taste, at the local level, because it was designed by somebody who understands that strategy and implementation are not the same thing?

"You can have a consistent single strategy that is executed in different ways depending on what the local requirements are, and an excellent local provider could fulfill those. I would guess Martin Sorrell's biggest mistake was that he bought everything he thought would possibly make money in digital, and he basically recreated the chaos of the Internet within WPP. They don't work together. They don't leverage each other. It's the same mess that you have in the broader interactive world. In my opinion, the future for an Ogilvy is being a subunit inside of an Accenture."

↩

Mike Fromowitz, "Do we need to forge new strategic partnerships or create a new model agency? Perhaps. Up until very recently, the spearhead for brand development and expression was the advertising agency. Keeping communication 'on message' and 'on brand' was relatively straightforward, given the dominance of the advertising medium.

"Today, a new agency model calls for a mix of specialists, collaborating and working together to create the right blend of influences for the brand. Ensuring that all these collaborators march to the beat of the same brand identity will be a challenging task, but one well worth it. It's a pity that most digital shops today are getting it all wrong! I still believe in best-of-breed specialists. They stand a far greater chance of creating effective communications than do agency 'generalists.'

"The new model is really a new mindset. It requires us to think differently about planning and implementing communications – to develop a mindset based on finding interconnections between the various communication elements. The model calls for cooperation, teamwork, and a willingness to blur the distinctions between the disciplines of traditional and digital advertising, public relations, retail, promotions, event marketing, and more.

"The real challenge is for both agency and client to bring fresh ideas to the party, to inspire new thinking, and discard outdated models and ways of thinking. Although change is uncomfortable, spending less and achieving more should be an attractive motivator. After all, the idea is not to outspend your competition, but to outsmart them."

⌒

Rob Martin Murphy, "When someone asks, 'Is the copywriter/art director team sacrosanct?' It is as long as the legacy structure of the client-agency relationship remains like it is. That's a creation of the '60s and there are still a hell of a lot of agencies that work in a linear way because that is the nature of their process and output, 'We get a client brief, the strategy gets written. The brief gets done. The team works on it.'

"Now there are cases when, yes, that team expands and includes a technology person. A lot of times, it is down to things like agency culture and agency size, how incumbent is the financial arrangement that the agency has with their client, the way they have to work. If their whole deal is billing clients on head hours, they structure themselves accordingly.

"That's the interesting thing, and the agencies that get it right are the ones trying to break that mold and go, 'If you could start from scratch, what would you start with?' If you're hiring from the start, I'd hire creative people, but they wouldn't necessarily be purely writers and art directors. Because I just think that's limiting your chances of creating great work in a myriad of ways with the media and technology platforms we have at our disposal.

"It'd be silly if you started own agency today and didn't hire technology people. There are agencies that do those things individually really well. It'd be nice to have this sort of hybrid where you could pool that skill and talent together. We talk about hiring T-shaped people, they've got one deep core skill, but they've got a sort of breadth of other skills that, when combined with others, makes the team stronger. You also can't dismiss the chemistry of teams. You've got to work with people that get you energized. You're hired into a company and you're forced to work with people. Sometimes you go, 'Wow, why do I feel so drained of energy after I've dealt with that person?' If that is the case, and you can't change who you're working with because of the system you're working in, find a way to get out. Fast."

⤶

Aden Hepburn, "At VML, we don't have any teams. We have copywriters who write across a couple of different art directors and creative guys, and we pull them in and out depending on what we need, probably because we have such a varied technology base. It's really hard to build teams who can just work on stuff because what we're doing at VML here in Sydney is experiential installations.

"One of the things that I preach a lot is digital convergence, the fusion of online and offline coming together to create tangible digital experiences. What that means is we need people who can conceptualize brand experiences using technology, whether it be RFID[9] or Microsoft .NET and big screens and distance sensors, weight sensors, and all sorts of things like that, which can build real-time experiences. All based off the interactions with the brand and with its digital experience.

"Just putting a copywriter or an art director together simply doesn't work anymore. There's no point in pairing them up. We definitely have an expanded creative team, and I see our technology, our programming team, as

---

9 Radio-frequency identification. A wireless device and system for transferring data, usually used for helping tag and identify objects (and, these days, even people).

being just as creative as our creative department. They need to feed off each other to create the very best work. So there is no division, there are no silos.

"We bring a technical director and varying levels of programmers into creative brainstorms. We bring in the digital producer, we bring in the digital planner, we bring in the digital creatives, and we have the user-experience guy coming as well. We craft solutions with a much, much wider skill set, which I believe definitely gives us an advantage. 'What if we could do this? What if we could do that?' The tech guy jumps in and goes, 'That's cool, but it can't work that way because they just released this API [application programming interface] that allows it to do this.' Then the creative guy responds with, 'Ah. Holy shit. I didn't know that was possible. I'd love to do this if we can get that data out over here, and can we push it into Google Maps over here,' and the tech guys will give feedback or the music-experience guy goes, 'Yeah, but that's really disjointed, if we can pull it together into this kind of framework instead…' Suddenly, you walk out of these meetings with these intense, richly shaped ideas that give us such a great advantage over our traditional agency when talking to businesses."

⌒

Greg Paull, "I wish I could say 'Oh, you should look up to R/GA or AKQA, or this is who you should look up to,' but I don't think anyone's completely cracked it in terms of relationships and structure and everything else. I mean, I just got back from San Francisco and did pitches with a lot of very cool digital-centric ad agencies. But there's no one with the right model just yet. Honestly, the best agency in the world, in my opinion, is still Dentsu because you brief them and they will manage everything for you in Japan from TV content to digital to mobile to sponsorship. The way they work in Japan is incredible, but they haven't scaled that to other countries."

⌒

Diane McKinnon, "I appreciate a less hierarchical model. It's obviously why I am drawn to what I do, which is a little bit different from a traditional agency. That's why I'm not in favor of the traditional constant of art director/ writer pairs. It can create great work, but I like the synergies of different people being pushed to work together to push ideas around to bring new thinking in people from more traditional backgrounds. With people who have more digital experience, that are younger, that are older. If you allow it, you can get great mentorship and connections by letting people talk to each other and work together and bring ideas to the table, rather than creating a formal structure of, 'Okay, you two pair off, and you two pair off, and everybody come back in, and we'll do a tissue session and put it up on the wall.' I like organized chaos better than some people.

"We have the challenges, the friction of the millennials versus the boomers and Gen Xers. They all have different expectations and senses of entitlement and some of those challenges that you read about in the HR world in multigenerational workplaces. The core is to be open on both ends of the equation. The younger people have to be open to learning and being mentored, which some are and some are not. The older generation has to be open to not only being a mentor, but also being a mentee about technology and what it is like to have grown up in a digital world. We just have to make sure that whatever the structure is, that there's openness and willingness on all sides of the equation to learn from each other."

↬

Jeff Cheong, "We have various teams set up. At the basic level, to handle pure digital assignments, it will be a copywriter and an art director partner. For integrated accounts, it will be a copywriter, an ATL art director, and a digital art director. We have also included a technologist to partner the various teams to brainstorm for ideas. I have a team of 35 technologists who cover all aspects of our work. From social to mobile to installation to backend, these guys are the hottest property of the agency.

"Specialist talents fall into new service offerings from agencies. Each division will have their set of goals and KPIs. When we hire, we inspire our talent to lift the game in their area of focus. It's very clear when a team member performs."

↬

Dave Whittle, "Local insight is so critical to producing effective creative work. Local insight is ultimately the motivating factor to draw the line between offshoring and onshoring.

"Sure, we're up against a global network, but you look at it objectively, and while I think they do have some advantages over us, we have won global business in the past. Our business has had global wins for almost 20 years. That demonstrates that the local or domestic business can absolutely be successful without global buying power.

"A really important part of our strategy over the last five or six years, in particular, is building a portfolio of specialist teams. At the end of 2011 we acquired a PR agency called Bang, but beyond this all of our local businesses have been grown organically. In fairness to the giant holding companies, we obviously don't have the complete complement, but we've got all of the core components. Now, we haven't gone so far down the chain to acquiring printing companies, email distribution businesses, and ad serving businesses, but the core components we do in house."

∽

Scott Morrison, "Our inspiration [at The Bauhub] to create a new creative collective agency structure takes more than just a Rolodex. It takes a proper concerted effort to sort out how it operates and to create tools that will help it operate effectively. In nature, we see this in an anthill. Every ant understands what they're supposed to do, and they all work together as a collective to produce a result that benefits all of them. That's why the ants will work in such a way where they just do their thing, because they know that the rest of the collective is taking care of them. That's what we're trying to recreate. All these people are milling about, not quite knowing what to do with themselves. We want to harness that and make it the greatest workforce that the world has ever seen.

"It's like we're sitting in the middle of this and we've got the bricks and mortar on one side, we've got the 99designs on the other, and I don't think any of them have got it right because, 99designs, maybe that's a great idea if you have a restaurant and you've only got $300 to spend on your logo because you can't afford to do more than that. I'm not going after that project. I couldn't afford to do that. I'd lose too much money.

"Then there's the billion-dollar marketing budgets for Microsoft. We also can't chase those. Those are too big. They need the big agencies for that kind of thing, but there's a ton of work right in the middle that would never consider 99designs because they wouldn't get the proper attention or the integrated support and all the other elements and they don't want to pay the big agency invoices.

"eYeka. That is the first crowdsourcing platform I've seen that I need to really take a close look at because there's something interesting to this that I haven't seen before. There's lots of money to go around. There's lots of work to go around, and some companies will respond to Victors & Spoils. Awesome, good for them. Some people respond to The Bauhub collective. Some people will respond to traditional businesses. Good. I do think that the only group that has to seriously consider their position in the market is the bricks-and-mortar businesses. Because they have employees and they have people on staff and they have to downsize if the sales go down. If I have a slow month, I use a bit of my savings to cover a bit of what's going on. I don't have a huge problem on my hands. I don't have tons of overhead to feed, and I can fire clients because I don't like them, and I go and find other work.

"There's space in the market for everyone. I'm not supportive of the competitive design space at all. It's unethical. It is further degrading the industry in the same manner that it's been degrading for years. I hope that the Bauhub's approach proves to be the one that provides the best integrity for the industry, the best working environment for the people who participate and the best value for the end clients that work with Bauhub members. That's what I hope."

⌣

Rafe Ring, Global Director of Strategic Alliances for eYeka, CMO of the Global Insights Group, and Innovations Columnist for *Campaign* magazine, "The crowdsourcing agency, Victors & Spoils, and my company, eYeka, are two completely different, but very new models. EYeka's model is not agency-based, it's consumer-based. What you're getting out of the Victors & Spoils model in this world are agency people. You're still getting the agency mindset being applied to particular problems. What eYeka does is it actually allows consumers to interpret the brand in whatever way they like. You may get a very poor execution, but you may also get a brilliant idea or brilliant interpretation of the brand in a way that an agency with its traditionally structured way of thinking and their approach to solving problems could never do.

"What a lot of our work is being used for is generating insights that can be given to focus groups to then say, '*This* idea appeals to me. *That* idea appeals to me. *That* idea doesn't appeal to me.' Oreo is a good example. Mini Oreos was launched on the birthday last year of the traditional Oreo. They were launching this new version, and they wanted to know how to position it vis-à-vis the original mother Oreo. The brief was with agencies and focus groups for quite some time, and they couldn't really get a handle on what the optimal position should be. They came to us, and we got 515 entries in three weeks from 80-90 countries.

"What came back in that short period of time was an amazing array of different ideas. We took some of them that were executed well. Most of them were executed at a very high quality level, which was quite surprising. We took the entries and did symbiotic analysis on it and clustered them into seven key territories. Here's how consumers around the world are viewing Mini Oreo. Here are the key territories. They then took those territories and found that one particular one was, globally, much stronger the others. Then they tested this territory and a couple of others in a focus group and found that it was it was absolutely spot on. They gave that to their agency and said, '*Here* is the positioning that we want, and *here* are 150 examples of consumers' ways of interpreting that positioning. These are the stimuli for our needs.'"

"The opportunity for agencies is to become curators of ideas from the global brain. Curate them and help fine-tune them, refine them, and evolve them in a way that gives them a legitimate strategic role within the client-agency relationship. But do not discount the crowd and say, '*We* own creativity. They couldn't possibly crack anything,' because the reality is, the public is pretty damn smart."

⌐

John Winsor, "[How I started Victors & Spoils.] I was very much into cycling, and this guy by the name of Alex Bogusky had just moved to Boulder. He was hanging out and called me and said, 'Hey, I want to ride bikes,' and so we went riding.

"He had broken off from his agency, Crispin Porter + Bogusky, and brought a few people to Boulder to be a creative hot house. While I was telling Alex how frustrated I was with WPP, he was like, 'Well, we haven't had to pitch in five years. Why don't you guys come in and be our planning and strategy department?" I wasn't that thrilled and said, 'I hate advertising agencies,' and then he laughed at me and said, 'So do I! This will be awesome. We'll blow things up.'

"So he sold me, and I went off to Crispin with all 12 of us from Radar Communications, the strategy and research company I owned. We became the planning department and while I was there, I was one of the first people to say we have co-creation in marketing way back in 2003, with my book called *Beyond the Brand*. It's what I truly believe in, and so we put co-creation at the center of the strategy at Crispin. And we got pretty darn good. The CP+B Boulder office went from about 50 people to 650 people in two years – and we won like 18 pitches in a row.

"We definitely went on a rage, Alex and I, and kept very busy. We wrote a book together called *Baked In* about creating businesses and products that market themselves. Then, we were screwing around with one of our small clients called Brammo, which is an electric motorcycle company. One of the things that happened was we didn't have any creative resources in the house, so we thought, 'We should try this thing called *crowdsourcing*,' and in a week, for $1,000 incentive, we got *700* corporate identities for Brammo.

"It was crazy. Alex looked at me and said, 'Holy shit! This whole thing is over.' It's like this whole agency-propped-up, place-based organization – there are just too many people with digital tools around the world that are creative directors – or they're art directors or copywriters – that have the same tools everybody else does. In a free world, it's going to be a meritocracy, and it's going to be a scary thing. So we talked about starting a company. We went to MDC [an advertising agency holding company], but they decided that they didn't really want to be involved because it's too disruptive, and so we went off.

"I quit after my earn-out at Crispin and started Victors & Spoils with one other person from there. It was off to the races, and we had a good time. The whole idea was around this new world where we have less fixed-cost-based and more variable-cost-based, where you can have a small crew of creative directors, but a bigger crew of variable costs and the people that participate more on meritocracy. Whether it's assembling a team off five free-lancers or putting a brief up to several thousand people. That was the idea.

We called ourselves the first agency based on crowdsourcing principles, but it was more the idea that we had a digitally connected community that we leveraged for brands.

"So that's gone really well. We were off to the races, and in a couple of years we won a bunch of business with Harley-Davidson and some other major brands. We won Suave and on one of our first projects, we worked with General Mills on Tortino's. We got Dish Network and about 15 or 20 others. It was cranking along and then I met this guy, David Jones, who is the CEO of Havas [another holding company]. He's this pretty visionary guy, and his point to me was, "I know you're shaking out the industry and throwing rocks at the glasshouses of holding companies. Instead of throwing rocks, why don't you come inside and help me reinvent one?"

"That seemed intriguing. So a year ago, we did this deal to kind of reinvent what Havas is. Man, it's interesting, for sure. The most gratifying thing is how it has been super tricky to understand how this big, old legacy company is working – so now schools are doing an 18-month longitudinal study on how our relationship is going. There is a guy at Harvard by the name of Michael Tushman. He's done all this amazing research on innovation the way old, established companies like Kodak did it. Because of the way they did things, like putting chemicals on pieces of plastic, they realized they couldn't do anything more in that area, so they reinvented themselves. They invented a new category, digital imaging, and didn't look back."

⌇

Brian Tiong, Managing Director of b-side marketing consultancy, "We have the reverse agency model. Let's say there's a print ad or whatnot. You have your creative director, your art director, and a few designers in your agency. I assume they are good. But how does it compare when people come up to us and ask us to do the same job? We can do it for half the price, and we have 30-40 creatives that we can activate at any one point at a time at a different price. Our model is the reverse of the old one.

"If there was one thing about our company that is very different from any other company, it's our network. We have a huge network of people that we can work with, collaborate with, or activate. So when brands come to us and say, 'I need this video produced for content variations,' then we have 10 options ranging from a $500 to a $50,000 video, depending on what their budget is. This model has the flexibility to create anything, while an agency will want to do the work themselves, though their abilities are limited to their knowledge and experience.

"If you wanted to do a project in Shanghai tomorrow, we can activate bloggers there; creative people that you can collaborate with and event people that you can produce with. And do it very quickly. Some agencies actually use us for that. We spent a lot of time and effort building our network through media sites. We are able to share the content our members are contributing to us all the time, so that we know what's happening in any city, even beyond the pulse of that city. A lot of agencies don't invest enough and party all the time. They should really showcase their understanding instead."

⌁

Angeli Beltran, "Is it better for agencies to have everything in house? This will be dictated by the client need and budget, but there is an opportunity for new services and innovations to be made in partnership with clients. This is what Dentsu has done well. The relationship with clients is so close that the client co-funded new innovation or agency service areas. Dentsu has earned the trust and relationships with clients long term, such that they are able to invest in new services together. It's truly a partnership, and this is how agencies and clients should come together: how they can help both businesses prosper.

"The digital field is becoming more and more fragmented, to the point that I really do wonder if everything under one roof is feasible. The benefit of working with partners is that they focus their business on specific digital areas (e.g. mobile application development, technology solutions, etc.) such that they invest in service improvements and innovation. The challenge is how to work with partners so that they feel part of the agency organization. I've seen this done by having some partner teams within the agency premises or by having a consortium of strategic alliances – all bound by service and commercial agreements. Again, the model will be driven by client need, but there also has to be a balance in pushing boundaries so clients can try new things.

"I appreciate the clients that set aside a portion of their marketing budget for innovation – this allows the agencies and partners to invest in new ideas that push boundaries and find new ways of delivering the brand experience. It's always a win-win situation, even if the experiment fails, as there is always something to learn."

∽

Subhash Kamath, "We still are in the initial stages of actually incubating our digital team. We just have a few people right now, all specialists, but at least we got to create a digital arm. We want to create a digital soul for the agency, which means that we don't want a separate division for digital. We want our main, top-line thinking to begin around the new world. We hired a digital special strategist, an additional creative from Tribal DDB who spent time in the digital world and a creative technologist guy, and we made them sit as part of the main team.

"Suddenly, we found that our 'normal' account management people and our 'normal' creative people were having conversations with them about what we can do and things like that. The idea is to infect the agency, the main team itself, with people that can be carriers of the digital virus. Rather than create a separate cell or a separate division – we don't want to do that. We want to create an ecosystem of partners, collaborators, and suppliers for the execution part of it.

"We brought in somebody who does a lot of work in social media to amplify what we were already doing. We got in somebody to help us with technology, to execute it. We brought in somebody who sets up apps and things like that faster than we ever could. We've brought in various people based on their kind of thinking. However, the base thinking, the ideation, the creativity, all come from the core BBH team. We started with wanting to focus on just creating the soul. Now as we go forward, I would be quite open to even acquiring some of those partners as part of the group.

"But the thinking and the strategy will always be part of BBH because one of the things that the digital companies don't have, that I've seen, is they're not very good at understanding brands and thinking strategy for brands. They've got a lot of good ideas. They've got a lot of tech guys, but they don't have the brand thinking. Many of them are from different working backgrounds, and they found that they've got the technology skills to do these things, so they all come together while advertising guys have traditionally grown up thinking brand. They just have not done enough work in the digital to understand what it takes to execute things.

"It's the same thing I've seen in design. There are some fantastic designers out there, but very few of them in India are thinking about brands. For example, why shouldn't a design agency have some red-hot, kick-ass planners? They've never even done planning. They should."

⤿

Craig Mapleston, "Our reasonably successful approach, so far, has been to ensure we have deeply skilled production capabilities. That means experiential producers that know how to put on an event, big or small. A/V [audio-visual] producers who are equally adept at managing a multi-million-dollar TVC [television commercial] shoot and a campaign wrap-up film at a fraction of the budget. Equally, it means having digital developers and producers who can realize a vision where creative meets technology. You can't compromise on these guys.

"We have successfully found hybrids in the worlds of strategic/brand and campaign planning across multiple channels. Similarly with creatives. If you start with a strong idea, you can integrate the most appropriate technology to deliver through the most appropriate channel.

"As we grow and are recommending more complex solutions that marry creative and technology, the role of creative technologist becomes more and more important. Not just a tech guy who says what can and can't be done, but someone who works between the creative and technology teams, who understands the creative intent and can find the best way to use technology to deliver that. These guys are very sought after, as they have unique knowledge and can move between the emotional creative ideation and the more rational technological delivery of that."

⤿

Erin Iwata, VP of Digital Marketing at Denver's Heinrich Marketing, "I've been at the small shop I'm with now since I've been immersed in digital. We have a small senior team made up of creative, biz dev, account planning/direction, and me. We work cohesively because our clients are demanding results-based, integrated campaigns and solutions. I do have to fight with everyone often on process – establishing, following, supporting. The lack of understanding makes complete support difficult to secure. On the other hand, I'm lucky because we've built chemistry that works, and I don't see these things as permanent impediments. They are looking to me to set the pace and drive the digital aspects of our offering.

"I will say this, though. Being a woman in a digital position that isn't social media has been difficult at best. I have had to work very hard to be taken seriously by partners and colleagues because there just aren't very many women in my position, at least not in my market."

⌒

Thierry Halbroth, "There are two forces to this. It's very variable. If I need to ask my traditional teams to think digitally, then I need to ask my digital people to understand what storytelling is and what form that will be in the real world. Basically, there are things that need to be done. I'm trying to find the right balance. That they all understand each other and they can get moving. But they *all* have to be digital, end of story. Everybody has to. There's no, 'Oh, it's digital, that's not my realm.' Sorry, you cannot. If you are in the position of account management, you need to understand your business. If you don't understand your business and you have limitations in what you understand, you're just an account service person.

"Digital is a huge part of being creative. If you don't have that thirst for knowledge, in a way, and I'm not saying technical knowledge, because everybody is scared about that. They are all scared about this technical beast and how long it will take before they finally understand it. The knowledge, as in, 'I want to know. I want to know how these things work. I don't want to go into the details, I just want to do the work. Give me the top lines.' If you don't have that today, then you're off to a really bad start or you're in the wrong field – so that's the first thing.

"The second thing, for example, at McCann, we have training: we have an entire site and modules that lead you to building skills with web seminars that you can attend, classes that you can take over certain weeks, and things like that. We encourage lots of self-learning. We do have tools in place to do that. But unless you make it mandatory, nobody takes the time to actually do it. You can't rely on people to do it in their free time because, frankly,

I don't believe it's right to ask them. It should be part of a training program from the company, and everybody should have a proper training program in place where there are certain dedicated hours during the workweek that visibly focus on learning new skills or getting up to date with new technology.

"The third thing you can do is driven by management, who should be trying to inspire, as much as possible, the people that they have employed. Discussing case studies, talking about their experiences. For example, what was judged in an award show, why did it win? Basically sharing knowledge. To show things that are happening and say, 'Wow! That kicks ass! I want to do something like this. I want to understand more.' It helps, and I've seen it happen in agencies. Some agencies are very good at doing this. Some are not that good.

"The problem is we are caught in the reality of our business, our work-load, and so education is just adding another layer of things that needs to be done. I don't think it can be done with everybody. It should be a rite of passage when you start at the associate creative director level. Obviously, you should already be very good at facilitating it by that point. That's the bigger thing we need now from the early stages or period. We need it to happen when we recruit. You're seeing it still today, recruiting people who are straight out of polytechnic or university and they still don't have a grasp on digital. If you look at Hong Kong, *one* of the courses in Design and Advertising at Poly U [Hong Kong Polytechnic University] is digitally focused. If you fail that course, you do not graduate. It's a glorified image that the industry is having. It's all about TV and print ads. People don't even understand storytelling or what an idea is. They come up with these illusions that they have got to be doing that and this. It should change, but it's still taking too long."

Tearing Down the Silos

Gareth Kay, former Chief Strategy Officer and Associate Partner of Goodby, Silverstein & Partners, "I'll be contentious. I will say the reason at Goodby Silverstein we are able to avoid silos, unlike many of our competitors, is due to our obsession with making sure our work is not only really good, but is relevant to people and the world today.

"It's stuff that people care about, want to use, and it is seen as being a good thing in their lives, rather than a spammy annoyance. Because we have a focus on the work, we just want to bring people in to make the work better. You just don't have that desire that exists in some other agencies, where they want to have new separate divisions so they can go and talk to their clients about selling in a new skill set and a new service and use them as a way to go and drive more revenue."

～

Heidi Lorenzen, "What I've seen in the bigger agencies is that there have been these silos. While they may have great creative and great digital genius and great performance marketing gurus, they're not one and the same; they are all thinking in their silos, and it's not all being assembled together. I, as the in-house, client marketing person, need to be making sure that those teams are bringing the best. It can ultimately come together."

～

Principal Analyst of the Altimeter Group and author of *What's the Future of Business (WTF)*, Brian Solis, "Today, advertising does not work with marketing, marketing does not work with public relations, public relations does not work with digital, digital does not work with customer service and customer service does not work with product development or customer strategy – and now you have, by default, a broken journey. I think that the future of advertising and the future of marketing all have to think about this customer journey, how it needs to play out vs. how it plays out and the role that they want to play in its evolution. How they can take the friction out and put in not just storytelling, but experiences and customer journey management counts for everything. It's more than just clicks. If I see something on television, what do you want me to do next? If I see something online, what happens next? Everything has to be integrated, not just one landing page for everything that scales to whatever screen you're using but also the context of my state of mind and my aspiration or intention. I'm talking about a dedicated experience that is native to the environment."

～

David Shulman, "The industry created this idea of digital which created more reasons for employees to engage and organizations to support this behavior. Look at what Jonathan Nelson created 20 years ago when he founded Organic [the first digital agency in the world]. Organic was all about creating authentic connections between people, and that couldn't be more true today. I'm not positioning Organic going forward as 'digital'. It brings to mind Simon Sinek's notion of why vs what: 'Digital is what we do. It's not why we do it.'"

"A general agency environment with a chief digital officer and a set of specialists further reinforces the idea of a siloed approach, and you have talent that becomes frustrated by the briefing process. It starts with the so-called 'big idea,' which is really a TV or campaign idea that isn't necessarily driven by marketing intelligence and digital insights.

"So digital becomes about executing across the channels, which means we need a banner campaign, search, landing pages, or a web site – and that gets very frustrating for the talent. It's not ingrained in the organization. It's not embedded in the culture. It's a siloed approach."

↜

Jeffrey Yu, "From what I have seen, Ogilvy is all about silos. It's all about individual profit centers. During the days when I was working for Bates (which was by then part of the Ogilvy bigger structure), Ogilvy would try to take from Bates, and OgilvyOne would try to take from OgilvyAction, and OgilvyAction would try to take from OgilvyInteractive. I'm not defending my new employer, Publicis, but because they are a late entrant to the whole thing, they are much more open as to how a holding company works and how all the components should be working together. In WPP, I saw there are very traditional walls already built up, and I found them very difficult to break down."

↜

Chief Marketing Officer of Pernod Ricard Group, Martin Riley, "One of the key challenges for agencies today is to seamlessly integrate different media, including digital, around *one key brand idea*. In my experience, advertising agencies recognize this need, but are so unsure of how to proceed that they have not yet managed to put in a structure or model that will allow for it.

"The acquisition of specialized digital agencies by traditional advertising agencies does not automatically mean that digital expertise and the ability to execute them will be integrated properly or at all. This is a management and, often, cultural challenge that should not be underestimated. It also has caused the traditional agencies to not yet come to terms with what crowdsourcing can do for them in terms of the role they can play curating and developing ideas and concepts that have been submitted by people around the world (who have less information and involvement in the brand than the agency itself). This presents an opportunity for the agency to reconsider its role, model, and cost base and to leverage the potential of crowdsourcing for initial ideas, which it can refine and develop.

"The same is true for strategic planning research and crowdsourcing of groups of people to research lifestyles, preferences, behavior, and reaction to new concepts in products and communication. Fast, frequent reactions using digital can reduce the time required to develop marketing initiatives, and speed becomes a key element for achieving competitive advantage.

"In recognizing how consumers obtain information and how they use their mobile devices to seek comparative data on pricing information, for example, it is also important to remember that content itself is essential. In other words, we must balance the quantitative benefits and speed that digital brings with the qualitative aspects of content. Marketers must not sacrifice the quality of an idea because it is the idea and what the brand represents that is the enduring and attractive aspect of a brand: this is what differentiates it from other brands. The ability to entertain, involve, and create content that can be shared by consumers is essential in building brand loyalty and advocacy, which remains the key objective for marketers. As Lee Clow, the legendary creative genius behind the Apple campaigns at TBWA\Chiat\Day, said in Cannes earlier this year, 'When photography came along, we learned to use it, but we did not abandon the paint brush. The same is true for digital, but I don't think we have learned how to use the medium of digital to best creative effect yet.'"

⌐

Subhash Kamath, "It's a beginning stage for us at BBH India. Ours is an agency born in 2009, and therefore we have to do things very differently from the agency born 30 years ago. BBH London has to transform itself as a big elephant turning around, and they've done that very well. We are just toddlers. We can decide to grow the way we want to grow. We have never tried to copy BBH London or BBH New York. What we said was, there is a certain set of values that BBH will always stand for. We will retain those values, but we will create a BBH India born in 2009, which will be far more future-focused.

"We broke the hierarchies of account management and planning. We call them all brand partners. We seat them all together. We don't have divisional or department or silos. It's a complete open office system, and so forth. The difficulty was that right from the beginning, when we started, you needed a few founder clients to help jumpstart the business, and most of those founder clients were traditional clients – hopefully, because of the reputation of the partners or the trust they had in the partners. While BBH is a well-known brand globally and it's a well-known brand within the advertising circles, amongst the marketers, BBH is not well known in India.

"You have to unlearn a lot of the past from when we worked in big agencies, to be able to be part of a startup; especially if you're going to work at it from a partnership perspective versus a hierarchal way of working that you're all used to in the past. We struggled. We struggled on our creative product, big time. We had to change our creative leadership twice. For four years, it didn't work out. There was difficulty in aligning with our first partner; it didn't work and so she left. Another guy came in who was culturally not compatible. We had to remove him within eight months. Now we're settled into the kind of people we want."

꙳

Andy Flemming, "We always were one of the most unified agencies in the country, and that still stands, because we work with the digital guys so often and because they're geographically so close. The idea that there's an above-the-line department, a below-the-line department, a digital department, and never the twain shall meet is all over. It's gone. All of us have worked on, been exposed to enough digital campaigns or been in meetings with enough digital people to actually be able to add a fairly advanced digital component to the work that we do, as a matter of course. Obviously, the digital guys have a level of expertise that's greater than ours, but we work so closely together there is a real merger. If we've got a question about a page takeover or we want to make a crazy app or something, then they can help answer and give advice.

"We can come up with a pretty decent and well-thought-out idea, most of us, that is not going to be something that is a pie-in-the-sky, million-dollars-to-make kind of thing. Then, obviously, we can use the digi guys who sit meters away from us to go, 'Yeah, that's possible. It will take this much time and take this much money. Have you thought about doing this?' So, actually, we work really closely with them.

"Where I am right now, I've got the digital creative director sitting next to me, and to my right, I've got a digital production system that I can ask to put together a demo that might help me with something. We don't have to go through a resource person to have permission to actually talk to them like some agencies do. We just wander over and chat.

"It's absolutely logical. I'm not entirely sure how every other agency does it since I've been here for a while, but here the departments are change and mutate the skills that they need to work with different mediums. We've always had a very high level of devotion. Lucky, in fact, that we have scaled in size and can attract some fairly big hitters when it comes to digital. We've imported some guys out of the UK. They're very experienced digital professionals that are causing not only our digital team to think bigger, but also they make sure that we're exposed to the ideas that they think are cutting edge. Almost daily, they tell me that I've got go and check this out; this is a pretty amazing concept, or this amazing execution from Brazil that's on Unity or something.

"I prefer it that we actually have guys sitting a few meters away that can put together very high end. Of course, we can outsource if we need to do something that we either don't have time or resources to do."

∽

Digby Richards, "Digital is the new norm. We don't think in an offline-online way at all, anymore. We really think through-the-line. We won the Wild Turkey business and it was during the pitch that we challenged ourselves by constantly asking – is it digitally complete? And the end solution that we presented didn't have one mainstream component and we're talking a multi-million dollar budget."

⤺

Åsk Wäppling, "I want to respect all of the copywriters I worked with who were big poster guys and came up with awesome five-word headlines all of the time. It's a craft, and every single aspect of advertising is a craft, and dumb people can be really, really good at their one part of it. There are people who are genius at radio – and I'm not knocking them. I don't think every creative can do every media ever. I just think that the big base idea has to be an idea that's so well thought out, it can function in all different media. Everybody else who is good at their different parts of it should be on the same team. We should be at the same agency. We should all go, 'Yes, we're working for this client on *this* idea.' We can't have different agencies that are sort of fighting for different pieces of the pie. It just creates problems.

"Even the biggest agencies section out the digital areas. That's what I mean about being in DM [direct marketing] or pixel-pushing hell. I mean, you're suddenly not allowed to talk to the other people. Like in the '90s, I was on some brief that required me to use Photoshop, which art directors apparently were not allowed to use at BBDO at the time, which I still don't understand. They expected you to send really large files to the printer, and then the printer would stall for 20 minutes, and it's, 'I'm an art director, not an idiot. Can I *please* have Photoshop.'

"They finally gave me the red-hot computer that I wanted, and by having that and Photoshop, I was relegated to the studio. I was the only art director sitting in the studio where the studio personnel were sitting. Therefore, the copywriters in the creative department treated me like I belonged in the studio. *Everything* was siloed. It was ridiculous. To me, digital has always been another palette of tools, but I can see by the output that a lot of the creative execution has suffered over the years. It's not necessarily due to the change of media that we use. It's due to the change of the audience. The audience today and the way we're all interacting and talking to each other is very fast paced, and it's sort of like we've all got amnesia. People forget what they were doing yesterday."

⤺

Jim Speelmon, "Whereas, two people can run a $10 million traditional media account, there's a lot more work involved in digital. You're tagging, you're reporting, you have all of those things, and they are all very administratively focused. That requires a lot of people. For a lot of agencies, digital remains a loss maker, which is amazing. But it was interesting being on the media side. You can't think about your client's business unless you know how much money they're going to spend, which is a very old-school media approach. I won't consider TV if you don't have enough money for TV. From a standalone digital agency perspective, like at XM, we used to get told what the clients have got to spend.

"The first one to get a grab at the budget was the media agency who then said, 'This is how it's going to be apportioned,' and next was the traditional agency who said, 'Okay, here is what we are going to do for TV, this is what we are going to for print, and this is what we have left over.' In digital, we often felt that perhaps there was some collusion between media and traditional because we just got the crumbs from the table, supply-side advertising, if you like. When I went to work with George Patterson Bates down in Sydney, much of the digital group was definitely a little appendage within the agency. The above-the-line guys would say to us, 'We'll tell you what media we bought, and you will come up with something to fit that media.' I also note that when talking with the media folks, they sometimes said, 'You might think that we're at the start of the food chain, but we're not.'

"Media and traditional and then the crumbs went to digital and we were just sort of seen mostly as production taking the fragments and trying to turn them into at least a digital strategy. Then it would come back to media, and then it would all be a revised budget in terms of, 'This is going to cost this much to make this ad, oh, we can't afford this much in media as we thought we could.' You ended up with a little bit of a of a merry-go-round, which was everyone playing next-door neighbor and saying, 'I want this piece of the pie.' The response is, 'You can't have it.'

"When I worked on HP when I was at XM, we pitched an idea and worked with the client starting with technically available markets. 'What sort of penetration do you have in Korea?' 'What's the replacement cycle?' We went through all of these exercises to end up with what we could afford to spend. She had a number of units that she needed to move, and we were able to factor out how much we could spend per unit; factored out the whole thing of how much money overall would be available. Then it gets divvied into,

'This will be set aside for media, and this will be for this, and this will be for this, this will be for this.' That process happens when they're working with an agency; it only happens in very general buckets.

"At HP, your marketing budget is based off of your previous year's sales efforts. If your sales were really good, you get more money, which is ridiculous because you think you would want to spend more money in marketing when the sales weren't so good. In other companies, it might be driven by market share, brand awareness, or whatever, but, generally, the clients come in hand and they will pre-allocate. They all have a spend, and they will do a pre-allocation. The media agency might be the first group that gets brought in, but there has been an allocation done before they got there. What I always thought was amazing is the opportunity for the media agency being involved in the first-pass allocation.

"If these are your business objectives for the year, then this is about what it's going to cost, and instead of waiting for the client to come and tell you what the budget is so you can start thinking about how you want to spend that money, you should be more involved in their business to help them know how much money you should spend overall – and give them some options. 'If you want to do heavy TV, you might go this way.' Or you say, 'Do you want heavy digital with light TV.' 'It could be this way, and here's the cost difference. Here's what you could expect to come out the other end.' That's what I was expecting of any agency.

"My assumption was that somebody was guiding the client on baseline allocation. Now, as it turns out, not really. When it does happen, it happens at a high level. They just say, 'We know we're going to do these things.' You have a very high-level business strategy, and you have a very high-level marketing allocation. By the time you bring in partners to figure out what you're going to do, it's not a case of 'is this enough money,' it's a case of 'how do we spend it as mine?'"

꙳

Chester Tan, "If their clients are more relaxed or a bit more behind the curve, then I think they have between five to six years to get their act together. But the traditional agencies always said, 'We've got an integrated guy, and we're an integrated agency, and we have the integrated approach, and we have digital specialists.' Unless maybe they have the balls to put a digital agency head as the head of a traditional agency and make some of the department heads people from digital agencies, things won't change."

⌒

Susan Kim, "It's amazing how it still is a little bit of the red-headed stepchild for digital professionals because among big agencies, there is so little interaction sometimes between the two groups. I still can't believe the silos are as big as they are. It's not just their fault. It *used* to be totally their fault, I would say, for not breaking it down because, for one, there is resistance to anything new. It's like maybe this is a fad, and when you don't personally know about it and aren't in it, of course, it's not happening. It was their fault before. I will say now it is some of the digital folks, it's partially their fault for not reaching across the abyss because they don't have a concept or know what a concept even is.

"It almost seems too touchy-feely, or they act as if a concept is not important at all. It's all about technique, it's all about technology, it's all about, 'Let's just find a good picture or something, and then we'll trick it out with all this stuff.' Part of it now is the digital folks are helping to create the silos by almost not acknowledging that creativity is important, and you can't confuse technique with creativity.

"There still is not that much crossover. Either you've grown up digital and that's the way it is, or you understand traditional, but in your own way, you are still looking down at the digital stuff. It's like that's not the real sexy stuff. It's going to persist for a while. I thought it would be completely gone by now, but those silos are still pretty distinct.

"Just because you have the technology to do something, I don't think means that you have to use all of the technology. I am thinking QR codes. I see so many ads that think, 'Hey, we're really cool and we're doing something really hip because we have this QR code.' I was reading the Southwest Airlines in-flight magazine and they have one, but how is this QR code even helping? Plus, I'm in a plane and I can't use my phone anyway.

"On several different levels, it was their tactic of QR code and confusing it with, 'We've got a great concept going here because we're bridging the gap between print and digital with this QR code.' I don't think anyone had a clue. There is a good example of technique for technique's sake. The technology exists. You can put it in, but I have yet to see QR codes used really well, and this doesn't make it cool. This is not a concept. Try, but it should have a reason. A lot of times, all it does is send me to their web site. Well, that didn't help. I did just use one recently on a bus shelter because it said, 'We will give you 10% off this triathlon.' They are madly expensive. If you scan the code, it will give you the password.

"Even Macy's. My gosh, they were using it so much, and I scanned it at the beginning just to see what would happen and to make sure my QR code reader was working, and it took me to the web site. It just took me to Macys. com and they tracked to see if someone did it. But I didn't get any reward for doing it, I didn't get any additional discount or points just, 'We're having a sale every weekend.' No additional information that I didn't get off that print ad, so I do think though sometimes people think, 'We've concepted a great thing to bridge digital and print just by having it,' but that needs to be more involved. There has to be a reason for the QR code, and it has to make sense."

Some traditional agencies do not quite understand how to implement new tactics. A QR code for United dangles 20 feet up in the air far beyond the reach of humans that can fit into their seats. Source: http://wtfqrcodes.com

Former Head of Digital for American Express Singapore and Founder of Foodmento, Jeffrey Woo, "Being in Singapore for a few years and having talked to many global and local agencies, I've found that great digital thinking resides in individuals. When these individuals leave, the quality of work from that agency is compromised. I've also found that when given strategic reign, many agencies fall short of advising a really great program. My belief is that it's a brand's responsibility to hire the best team of digital marketers and drive the strategic conversations to ensure successful programs. Some agencies are motivated by awards rather than their client's objectives."

～

Joe Zandstra, "The big agencies keep saying, 'We need some digital awards and we need to be innovative, so let's get somebody in,' and then they'll bring in a digital guy and try to pitch digital ideas to their existing traditional clients and it goes horribly wrong. It's not supported and doesn't make any sense and it's tacked on to the traditional work. There are no KPIs being met, so it fizzles and dies. Budgets are slowly slipping our way, but it's a slow creep. I do think, however, that more and more, clients are trusting pure-play digital agencies to properly handle their marketing investments. It's not like an avalanche towards digital. Yet.

"When digital ideas get presented to a client within traditional agencies, it's all too often not the digital people presenting it directly to the clients. The digital people don't get the brief from the clients. The digital people don't get to interact with the clients. They don't get the mindshare and the information about the client to really get the right solution across.

"I think that in some cases there's a feeling that digital people are nerdy and probably shouldn't be interacting with the client. Accounts people will ask for some digital sparkle and present it to the client as an addendum at the end of their meeting and see what they think about it, and invariably that solution doesn't answer any brief.

"There's a belief that the practitioners of digital are perhaps making stuff up as they go along, whereas ATL is an old tradition. 18 years experience or not, you're still a neophyte if you're digital.

"I'd say that all of us do still value the tangibility of print. We still value the power of the big, bright thing that comes into the living room, unbidden. There's something magical about it, still. Even for us in digital, you get digital agencies that have their own traditional communications. Sometimes they print out nice little booklets and send them around, because there is something solid and pristine about print. An agency I worked at in New York produced their own flipbook animation and I think that got more attention than some web sites we did. So print is not dead, for sure. We have show-reels and shit because that kind of packaged video and MTV-feel is attractive. There is still a genuine reason to be attracted to established media and there is a power behind that. The neat, polished perfection of traditional media has some gravitas behind it, as does the size of the companies involved. Most digital agencies are very small by comparison. We're always trying to do wacky things to outdo each other in craziness. I'd grudgingly say there's perhaps some substance behind digital's credibility issue. So yes, it's not cut and dried, but no one can deny the trend, just as no one can deny that there is power in established media (and I think that will be the case for a long time.)

"It's important to look at how media consumption has changed. Traditional advertising is still moving too slowly away from the water cooler days when we would all get together and talk about having seen the premier of this show or the last episode of whatever – the days of limited choices and captive audiences. But interestingly, when you look at digital media there are actually more people watching the same thing in the same general space of time than there are watching scheduled TV blockbusters now. Within the same week, I could talk to friends about having seen the honey badger YouTube clip, the *MasterChef* finale (all of us watched it on Hulu), or Netflix's *House of Cards* – all non-scheduled digital programming, but still a shared experience like the old days – except that I talked about different experiences with very different groups of friends. I think we're still all about the big shared experiences, but unlike the old days there are many many more possible experiences with digital and we're recognizing more societal sub-groups.

"I think this fragmentation is where the rift is. It's not controllable. It's scary. It's messy. It's dirty. I, myself, have had to move on from the paradigm of microsites and owned spaces where we market – we create a microsite, we create a URL, we market from our own space – to creating experiences on Facebook and Twitter. That was hard for me, because social media is such a chaotic space. I can't control the whole of the experience, I have to adopt a totally different mindset to be successful. So in that sense I'm almost experiencing what the traditional folks are experiencing moving from traditional to digital, except that for a digital person, this accommodation of change is business as usual. Painful, yes, but them's the breaks."

⌐

Peter Moss, "Hopefully, the word 'integration' in our industry will disappear very soon. First of all, it's a hangover from the advertising days. It just makes people feel like they are tackling the problem properly. I like solutions. Integration, to me, has always been about bringing together whatever needs to be there to successfully reach, communicate, and engage with the individual you're after.

"A good way to figure out what a platform looks like is to imagine the customer journey. Really get the persona right. Figure out who it is, and none of your usual rubbish like, 'Oh, we're targeting expats,' or 'We're targeting blokes who used to have a bad leg on a Tuesday.' Don't go after groups or demographics. Look at *real* people. What a day looks like for most people is actually not too dissimilar. You can do a customer journey and, by that, I mean looking from where people are thinking right now all the way to where you want them to be thinking. What are we going to have to do to convince them that this is, indeed, the case? Look at their lives, look at their devices and places that they move around in, and then create points of opportunity – touch points – whatever you want to call them.

"Integration is quite literally understanding what the reality is and then figuring out all those things you are going to have to do to cover those bases. Arguably, then, that could be, 'We're going to have to do something on mobile, we might have an iPad ad, it might need some TV, certainly, or there is a lot of movement around bus shelters and whatever.' It's not a question of all these things coming together because they can – and they all seem to fit nicely together. It's all these things have come together because that's how that person is, and that's our best shot of getting that person.

"It's pretty much everyone's responsibility to have that understanding now. Linear thinking is legacy thinking. If you look at any newer businesses, big or small, that have started up in the last 5 to 10 years, they have a much more all-in, all-the-way approach: that huddle mentality and that collaboration. That is, why would you leave the head of technology out until it got to the build? While we are talking about the people that we need to capture, then it makes a lot more sense for him to be there in the room working out that strategy with planners and the account team than to sit in with the creative team.

"The big problem is that creative teams have been patronized, but only through their own making over the years. They've been treated like children. You have wacky little creatives: don't give them any financial responsibility, don't give them any budget, don't put them in front of clients too often, don't even show them a spreadsheet or business plan, because it would interfere with their ability to draw pictures. This isn't some insidious scheme. This is well brought on by their own desire not to be involved in anything. That's why you quite often get something coming out of the creative department which is creatively brilliant... but as a solution, you just want to go and cut your head off.

"One thing I've seen work brilliantly, if you really want to do the best work, knowing full well it's going to be right and quicker, is you organize yourself around the client. You have a client team. And when it doesn't work brilliantly, it's due to generally the people and not the process or the setup. Now, the backlash to this is, if you put creatives on the same piece of business, day in day out, they're just going to walk... This is about certain kinds of people who are perfect for this kind of role.

"Believe me, I have met people who have been working specifically on one client, and when the distance and the time it takes for information and ideas to spread from A to B is reduced to zero, amazing things do happen. Really. If they just spent a little bit more time to understand why the client didn't buy their idea, then they would think differently about it. That's the problem: creatives are very dependent on a brilliant planner right now. They should be more dependent on themselves and on their understanding of the business they are in. Then, believe me, if you spend more time with the client, they will let you do a lot more for them.

"I left Ogilvy Hong Kong at the end of 2000 and went to London for a couple of years. I immediately started to look at the departments differently because I did a brief spell at a little boutique agency in London called TidalWave. They were the masters of the interactive eDM [electronic direct marketing, aka an email] and lots of very rich-media banner stuff, as much as you could do at that point in time. But I noticed something really weird: they had a creative department that almost felt like two separate departments. One was full of coders, and the other was full of the people you'd expect. I asked the ECD, 'Why have you got these guys split up?' He said, 'Well, they're more like the people who do it.' He treated these coder guys like the studio. I was more receptive because, as an ex-programmer, I was fascinated looking at the tools and what they had to play with now in terms of 3D modeling and virtual worlds. I was always asking, 'How'd you do this?' I got in with those guys to the point where I just moved in with them. I thought, 'How refreshing this is?' Not only from a point of view where I was looking at ideas through a different lens, but also how many ideas these guys came up with.

"We would spend way too much time trying to think our way out of a brief, when this programmer would say, 'Oh, have you seen this?' and he pops something in front of me that I play with for 20 minutes, and I realize if it had said 'Kit Kat' on it, it would have been the best ad of all time. It was just something really interesting that would *never* come out of a brief.

"We created a 'blow banner' for *The Economist*. It said, 'This is the competition, blow it.' You blew on it, and it would blow away by having Flash listen to the microphone. That came completely out of the techies coming in, saying, 'Look at this little bit of technology, can we do anything with this?'

"That was when I moved to Singapore the first time around. After the spell in London, I thought, 'Well, this is a much better way of working.' I completely disbanded the whole setup of teams of art directors and copywriters. I mean, loosely it was there, but I stopped hiring art directors and I started hiring interesting people who were mad about tech and really good at design. They had a refreshingly different attitude.

"I've always hated – and I know that's a strong word, but it's true – this mystique around ideation and the way in which it's used almost as a weapon by people. It is very dismissive to others. It's very exclusive. Actually, I consider myself quite a good ideas person and know how easily they come. There's a lot of contention around this, but my point is really simple. I didn't just want people in the creative department that would have come up with the idea for *Jaws*. I wanted someone who was big enough and cool enough and excited enough to take the book and make the film. It's the Spielbergs rather than the Benchleys. Spielberg took a good book and made one of the greatest films of all time. I don't think for one second he was pissed off because it wasn't his idea.

"What I found with a lot of these younger, savvy designers and very happy-go-lucky newbies was they didn't have this hiccup with it not being their idea. We could get ideas in really quick. I could have a company that was launching a new product with eight massively brilliant features. You just pass one of your guys and say, 'I'm thinking *octopus*. Do some stuff!' You come back later and what they've done with that word, I could never have thought of.

"It wasn't completely random, but we also didn't go through this mental heartache of sitting in a room trying to come up with the next *1984* spot. One of the reasons is that everything had to be done quicker. It was an expectation on two fronts. One depended on the billing model. If you're charging by the man-hours per job by discipline, then the longer you're on it, the more it's going to cost you, but not necessarily the more the client's going to pay. It was a bit of a balancing act not to sacrifice creativity, but to be really honest with yourself and realistically figure out how long it takes to do whatever the task is. The second comes back to the point about expectations, as in where we are now is quite a sad place. The expectation is that technology has speeded things up, not allowed us to take the same time to make something completely amazing. That's a constant battle we still have today."

꘍

Steve Elrick, "Silos are something that all good (and bad) agencies, digital or traditional, have struggled with and experimented with – and kept experimenting with – even if the results aren't good. Yes, the traditional agencies have had (by definition) more of the old practices to shake off, and we have done it, sometimes, kicking and screaming. If someone had said they had cracked the foolproof new system or process on how to create amazing campaigns *every time,* then they are almost as delusional as the people who say it can be done the old way.

"In this circus now, you don't only have more performers to manage, but every individual member of the audience, too. Internally, you simply have to get the best people and have total confidence that they can also see their contribution in service of the bigger picture. Cracks happen when individual experts start to have their own siloed agendas."

↜

Andy Greenaway, "Ogilvy has always had a direct/digital operation. They never had to go outside for help. Everything was done internally. I always worked closely with OgilvyOne, even when I was running the Ogilvy advertising agency. I always believed that the two entities should work in a more integrated way (a view that wasn't shared by most of the ad guys).

"When I joined Saatchi, we didn't have a digital operation and didn't do any digital work. It wasn't until around 2007 that the agency started taking digital seriously, despite my efforts to get them into that space earlier."

↜

Neil Leslie, "Unfortunately, we're often faced with resistance from the money people when it comes to breaking down the barriers between the ATL and digital teams. So, on a day-to-day basis, we still have a stable of flexible copywriter/art director teams largely focused on print, TV, ambient, etc. And a digital team that operates independently, updating web sites and translating largely ATL-driven ideas to the Web. Certain projects do offer the potential for all of us to work together in a fully integrated manner. This is definitely the way I'd prefer things to operate and hopefully the way the industry is going. Albeit a little too slowly for my liking.

"If we're doing our jobs properly, almost every project we take on should feature an element or two that none of us have tried before. As such, I need to have complete faith in my technical people. If they say they can or can't achieve something with the time and resources available, I can only take that at face value, as my own programming experience is limited to basic CSS. I can only hope that they are as passionate as I am about creating something special and that their advice is genuine."

↜

Jeff Cheong, "Integration has been on the lips of many people since day one. I've seen various permutations and even within my own agency (and previous ones) we've tried. True integration can only be grasped by a small elite. They understand the complexity of transmedia storytelling[10] and have great managerial skills to bring different people together. They are the play-makers and not politicians. I am glad to be working alongside a strong team of creatively integrated leaders in my current agency now."

⌒

CEO of Vocanic Social Media Marketing, Ian D. McKee, "Certainly, from our point of view here in Asia, we don't really see any agency having managed to find the right structure, the right integration so that their digital teams and the traditional teams work in a cooperative seamless way to deliver the best result. Typically, they have structural issues, which are having their own different P&Ls, which creates an internal fight for budget that results in suboptimal things coming out of the agency. Also culturally, often the client servicing is being run by the old ATL guys who feel exposed when they're presenting some of the newer things. This is both cultural and structural aspects.

"There's one final part we think is very important, which is that instead of using the definition of traditional ATL and digital, we use a differentiation that describes it as interruption marketing and relationship marketing. The traditional ATL agencies are very experienced and crammed full of very bright people who have a good understanding of all the techniques to make interruption marketing work as well as it possibly can. All of their knowledge and their gut feel that makes them successful at that is actually counterproductive in relationship marketing. But in a relationship, you don't want to be continually interrupted. The more relationship-oriented sides of digital marketing, such as CRM and social, the guys coming from the traditional point of view are having an extremely hard time adjusting. Sure, they can Facebook a campaign and get their digital arm to develop a little Facebook game to feed on it, but really understanding social strategy for the brand, I've yet to see it."

⌒

Richard Bleasdale, "In all of my experience, the most successful way for agency progression happening is actually organically, rather than acqui-

---

10 Telling stories across different media and channels (e.g., The TV show *Heroes* also being told through physical and digital comic books, online videos, interactive games, etc.)

sition. It's organic on the basis of the bringing in culturally right superstars. That's the most effective way of making it happen quickly and to help to change the digital culture of the agency. I'm talking about individuals, as agencies are unbelievably resistant to change no matter what specialism they are in. Too much change, too quickly, in agencies tends not to go well.

"Bringing in someone who is highly respected in their field, but is a good cultural fit with the agency that they're coming into, is the most effective way to make change happen relatively quickly. Because if they have respect, they will be able to build trust, and if they can build trust in the agency group that they're working with, then the change will always happen faster."

Rebooting the Agency Process

Torrence Boone, "We're encouraging our agency and advertiser partners to embrace the tenets of agile software development in how they create and manage campaigns: embrace a more holistic approach to collaboration and ideation, be prolific, launch and iterate, fail fast."

⌒

Jon Cook, "We do that day-in-the-life planning of the consumer journey, all those good things such as if I were the consumer, a typical scenario might be my father, my daughter, and I going to a Royals baseball game. Thinking about how our conversations and interactions there are not born out of academia, they're born out of living life. We'll look at the way the three of us are all sitting in a baseball game together. What happened there? In what ways did we interact at this game, before, during and after?

"We are not talking about Royals and baseball or marketing, we're talking about life. And we have a really interesting conversation about this day in the life, to just be opened up to the real world of how people think about things. For example, at the game, I get up to get a Coke and while I'm in line, I text my father and daughter to ask if they want anything. The Royal's ticket has a QR code on it that I scan. We are using wireless in the stadium to check Facebook. After the game, my dad texted a picture he put it up on his Facebook, which I 'liked,' etc. All of the day-in-the-life stuff that shows us where the opportunities are for providing consumers with branded tools, information, or entertainment.

"We create the journey against a very specific event, not just a random day in a life, although that can be effective, too. But we think approaching it from a start of an action, a decision to consume and figuring how the person got to that point is a very helpful exercise. The day-in-the-life approach also works just as well for the digital person that has not embraced traditional enough. The same thing is going to happen when they walk through the exercise. It is not just for teaching the old the new, it's for teaching the new the old. Because you are going to find out how powerful other things can be besides the digital. If your eyes are open wide enough to consider them, then you are facilitating it a little bit agnostically, which is going to help the people you are trying to think more broadly."

⌐

Alex Bodman, "Crowdsourcing is not greatly different to what a lot of great agencies have done and continue to do with their internship programs. You throw a brief to 10 passionate, hungry people, and a few ideas that you can polish up come back. That can end up being amazing, it's just a bit more formalized. If I talk to somebody in the agency about doing that, then they start to say, 'How long until the client just cuts us out altogether, if we said that that's a valid way to get creative?' But, would that be better?

"From an intellectual point of view, it is interesting. The proof will be in the pudding since we have yet to see great campaigns come out of this type of approach. When some really game-changing pieces of creatives come out of it, then people will take notice."

⌐

Dirk Eschenbacher, "I personally think that e-commerce is really cool. Of course, I have to say that because I own an e-commerce start-up. The way that shopping works – and advertising is a big part of that – is completely changing right now. If it's a cool shopping experience, you don't even needs ads for it anymore. My thing is probably experience design. Experience design is a big area for me, at least sorting it out across mobile devices, and how to create great experiences on mobile devices that are not necessarily just stories, but tools or functional the way e-commerce sites are.

"That's a very interesting area that I certainly want to keep on looking more into. How to craft experience design based on narratives, how to improve it, how to involve consumers in the experience, and how to make it a social experience. It's a huge field just opening up and should not just be limited to web sites, but really considered a holistic consumer experience. That's the easiest touch point between a brand and a consumer experience.

"I don't think I ever sell complicated ideas. I always try to sell the ideas very simply and try to hide the complexity. Most of the time, you're not really aware of the complexities until you start working on it. It always just starts with a very simple idea. In the case of the graphic novel, I literally put on the wall a print ad, three panels of the graphic novel, and a QR code and said, 'Wouldn't it be great if you could connect the three via your mobile and get people on the subway to read the graphic novel on their devices?' Everybody was like, 'Ah, that's a great idea, let's just do that.' I didn't have a story yet; I didn't have a writer yet. I didn't know what to do yet. The complexity all comes later with the execution. You start with something very simple, ideally, a story."

~

Paul Kwong, "I'm currently working at a small shop, so everyone needs to be very diverse in their expertise. Creative folks need to be able to think in traditional media as well as digital. As a designer-cum-art director, you've got to be able to concept TV spots, Web films, banners, billboards, packaging, point-of-purchase. All these media are just media; creatives still rely on the same skill sets as before."

"Working with so many different folks is just the same. I try not to be too prescriptive at the start of solving a problem. Just make sure you can articulate the problem and what you want to get accomplished. Let the other person figure a way to get to the solution."

~

Sean Lam, Founder of Plate Interactive and Co-founder and former Creative Director of Kinetic Singapore, "I prepare all of my presentations digitally. It's usually a casual affair, and if it's a big meeting room, I'll just hook up my laptop to the overhead projector. In terms of mock-ups, I always believe in presenting a very convincing-looking model. Not one with extra bells and whistles, but, rather, a very close reference to what the actual finished product will look like. If it's a Flash-based site, some of the animations and interactivity will be working and showcased. In HTML sites, a sequence of very finished-looking templates and designs will be shared. It is important to me that the client understands what the end product will eventually look like. I do not like to leave clients to their imagination, and by doing a detailed mock-up, expectations are immediately managed.

"I have no issues or choice (being a small outfit) presenting the work myself. In fact, I much prefer it this way. Who else better to present the creative than the creatives themselves? Being the conceiver of the idea, I'm in the best position to push for and/or defend my proposal. This, coupled with a finished-looking mock-up, usually seals the deal. In fact, quite a number of my clients have told me that they prefer to work directly with the creatives."

⤺

Neil Leslie, "We try to apply the same approach we always have when it comes to presenting ideas to a client. Simple line drawings and storyboards. And for the same reason. To keep them focused on the idea itself, instead of the execution. Depending on the situation or client, we may also create additional mood boards or present videos depicting the proposed technology in use. These help the client understand our approach and gives them a little more faith in our ability to deliver what we say we can.

"In terms of who actually presents the work, I'll often present the broad idea, rationale, and approach, before taking a back seat and letting the specialists elaborate on their own areas of expertise. I don't pretend to understand the finer points of every aspect of every project. I wish I did, but there aren't enough hours in the day."

⤺

Scott Morrison, "We're in the process of building a system called Pivot. Building that system that will help our members do five things. The first one is find work. The second is get work. The third is do work. The fourth is manage work and ultimately, the fifth, build that work. What that entails is getting your profile up, finding the opportunities, or having them find you.

"Getting the work is about estimating and coordinating joint estimates with other individuals to land those projects, the whole proposal process. The doing of the work is the management of your own activities. The timekeeping, the scheduling. Managing work is managing the other team members or groups of teams that are working on the project with you and, ultimately, billing the work is the part where you go to the end.

"There's one other factor that The Bauhub is doing. We are working to collect data about self-employment so we can start providing feedback to the members, because that is really critical. The biggest problem with the tools on the market right now is they're all disparate. You have to use six or seven different pieces of software to do what I just described. We want to do it in one platform, and that's under development right now. When it's ready, what it will do is allow us to also collect business intelligence that you wouldn't be able to see otherwise.

"For example, if you want to make $150,000 this year, and you've said you want to work Monday to Friday and you can only bill maybe five hours a day, what would your hourly rate need to be set at and then, on a day-by-day basis, are you above or below your trend? Nobody has time to track that where their business is financially day-by-day. It's very difficult. If you have a few people in your company, it's extraordinarily hard to stay on top of. We want a tool that will let you open your dashboard and you can enter a new project and it can instantly tell you, up to the minute, 'Okay, your workload is overloaded two weeks from now. You're open the following week so maybe you should shift it around. Your billing rates aren't going very well. You're 5% above your schedule for this point in year. Why don't you take a vacation in June?'"

Bringing in New Talent

"The artists of new media will materialize," said Lee Clow at the 2013 Cannes Lions Festival. "Right now it's a little bit blurry, a little bit vague. You've got some interesting companies out there. You've got David Droga and some others poking around, trying to figure out what it's going to be. But it's still in its infancy. When the artists truly take over the new media as well as the old, then those names will materialize."

George Lois, also at Cannes, was heard to add, "The name of the game isn't technology. The name of the game is creativity. Guys come to me and say, 'It must have been great back then, when clients would accept good work.' And I say, 'What the fuck are you talking about?' Do great work, and have the courage to sell it. Force it to be sold."

⌐

Barry Wong, "People I've wanted to hire included hackers and other people who weren't from the advertising industry, like bloggers and fine artists who had no experience in advertising. Was I successful? No. I would always get the 'Oh, but they have no advertising experience.' I was prepared to make that radical change and break industry norms with the hope of an even more interesting creative product. My plans were never endorsed because the management would always be in resentment of my overly radical plans to break the silos and what's termed as normal and typical."

⌐

Jon Cook, "I recommend taking an internship with a digital agency or the digital part of [an] agency. I actually use internship as a sort of descriptor for being open, putting yourself out there, just giving all of yourself in terms of your work and your ability to learn, to be a sponge. But in action, not lip service. I also say it because it's not just semantics. It needs to be a literal internship. Where, you can call it that in your mind and you go somewhere, you put aside your ego and you ask to be educated by doing the work.

"In our network, when people say they'd love to have an internship at VML, they're usually met by others with, 'Oh, that's funny. Yeah, you're the successful leader of this agency, and you want to be an intern.' It's the best way to learn. Go ahead, take an internship appropriate to your situation with as much as your time can allow. Take the definition of an internship to the utmost, let yourself go and do it. Do it, and don't do feel like you'll be there for three months, just do it for a couple of weeks.

"I cannot believe how much impact it has had on people, but in an internship you think about what you're doing. What an internship is, in addition to learning, in addition to doing, you are making contacts and networking. You are trying to gain access to the mentors that you have for that short time period. You're an intern: nobody cares about what you don't know, so you can make mistakes and ask stupid questions. In the framework of internship, you get to be naïve.

"There is nothing disrespectful about being an intern. I've seen it work; I've seen it be great. I've seen people who either had no demonstrative ability to understand being digital be selfless enough to say, 'I don't know this stuff, but I might put aside my pride and learn through an internship. I'm going to participate in it.' If it's the utopian learning experience, why wouldn't everybody do it? It's because it takes somebody pretty big to say, 'I'm a successful ad executive and I'm still going to be an intern.' If you're in our network, why wouldn't you go work at VML for three weeks?

"If you're at an independent company, why wouldn't you go work down the street and do a trade with somebody? All I know is that we are so flattered and impressed when a person does it. We become more open to do it, and it can even be a staunch competitor of ours, from an advertising standpoint. It is so flattering to us if they want to do it with us, in our industry."

〜

Executive Search Consultant Anne Ross, "I ask questions about senior roles, such as, 'Can you articulate what success will look like?' I get a lot of requisitions and specifications that say we want a person who looks like *this*. When I ask 'Why? What are you trying to accomplish? What will it look like? What will your company's bottom line look like if this job is filled successfully?' I very rarely get an answer.

"Recruiting on the agency side is seen as a cost control center. They usually report into operations, maybe, and finance, for sure. It's a way to control the cost of getting people into the organization that can fill slots. The Internet has, starting with monster.com, commoditized people and positions and actually commoditized holding company agencies. Because they used to say, 'We need a person who can build this culture.' But now they don't. Not anymore.

"It used to be I could talk to an AE and say, 'You must be at Thompson,' because they could articulate the core values of the organization and supervisors or directors. I can't do that anymore. The first question I get from a prospective director or senior VP these days is, 'What's the money?'"

╰┈╮

Andy Greenaway, "I don't think anyone is good at everything. I've always talked about creative gardening. You need to hire different people with different strengths and capabilities. The individual is only part of the overall team. If you look at what the team needs to look like, then you can work out the types of individuals you need to hire."

╰┈╮

Dave Whittle, "We look for people who're passionate about simplicity, because that's what we care about. That's who we are. We look for people that will go above and beyond to add value, in order to achieve what might have otherwise seemed absolutely impossible.

"We attract people from all kinds of backgrounds. We've got bankers and lawyers and artists and actors and all kinds of people from different industries. Increasingly, a lot of technicians are joining the agency. Whether you're a technician in video or in film or code or recording or photography or whatever."

╰┈╮

Craig Mapleston, "You hire and empower the right people to satisfy the right needs. In terms of structuring the organization, it's just an extension of what an agency had 20 years ago. Where the difference lies is that an integrated agency, like iris, now has a lot more analytical thinkers than it ever did before. These tend to be your project managers and developers. They are driven by rational thought, rather than the emotional motivation of many creatives or even the amiable suits or the driven management.

"HR now plays an even more important role because we have a different make-up of staff. We've done a lot of work internally on running workshops that enable people to better understand their own personality profiles and that of their colleagues. Then work up strategies to get the best out of each other.

"While the personality profiles now differ greatly, we are careful to make sure that all our hires share the values of the agency: collaborative, caring, ambitious, curious, brave, and proactive. These are agnostic to any personality type."

↬

Peter Moss, "I'm a big fan of an expression we used to peddle within the walls of Ogilvy New York: perpetual beta. I love that expression. They stopped using it because they thought it made people too worried and nervous. It was absolutely spot-on for the mindset. If you can feel comfortable in perpetual beta, you are well suited to the task at hand.

"If you were to ask, 'What will an agency look like in 2017?' The reason you would ask that question is because of perpetual beta. Because we are all conscious of the fact that things are not going be the same tomorrow. That is exactly the point. You have to embrace change as a given. People who get excited about change are the people I really, really, *really* want to work with and those are the people I look to hire."

↬

Chris Kyme "In our current setup, we don't have that many people. When I look to hire, good digital experience is essential (if anything, to counter my own shortcomings). In terms of structuring, in the past I've experimented with having no divisions – the creative department as the central ideas hub – only when it got into execution did we let individual executional skill sets come into play. Not much different than a writer and art director working on ideas together, then going off to do their respective jobs at the executional stage."

↬

Subhash Kamath, "Qualitatively, from a character perspective, BBH has a very simple way of identifying people. We call it *good and nice.* You've got to be extremely good at what you do, and you've got to be an extremely nice human being, as simple as that. One thing we do is all the three partners interview every candidate regardless of what the supplement is. Because we are small, we can afford to do that. Even after we grow bigger, typically a candidate will go through at least three to four interviews before we decide because apart from skills and experience one of the things that is foremost in our minds is, does this person fit into our culture? That's one thing we have done.

"From a skills perspective, we have tried to bring in as many people, even at the junior-most levels, who have a digital bent of mind because while they may not have worked on specifically digital projects, are they in social media? What do they do? How are they interested? How much time will they spend on it? Are they inquisitive? Are they reading about what's happening in the new media world? Those are the kinds of things we always look out for, and I must admit that it's not been easy to find the kind of people we want because a large amount of people are very good, but they're still in a very traditional mindset. We have taken a few of them because certain traditional businesses need them to run. In many cases, we have found people who are very digitally savvy.

"There's an account manager I hired who's all of three to four years in the business, but one of his hobbies is to work with an engineering friend of his to create apps. He's an account manager, but his hobby is creating mobile apps. There's somebody else whose hobby is to create ringtones. I've always looked for mavericks in my life. I like the sense of chaos that mavericks bring. I have always looked for people who have an interest outside of work. You could be a musician. I hired an account manager, very bright young kid, two years' experience, not for anything that he learned in advertising, but because he spent his summer holidays working for the Mumbai Indians in the IPL [Indian Premier League] on weekends as a photographer. I said, 'Show me a photograph.' I took one look at his portfolio photography and I said, 'I want you in, man.'

"I like people who have something else in life to live for rather than just getting inspiration from the Cannes reel or the Black Book. The average age at BBH India is 30 or below. It's a young team, extremely talented, extremely hardworking, full of zest and vigor, and we've given them a lot of space. We've put in a very flat structure where the youngest of the guys can interact with me on a particular job without the hierarchy blocking him.

"I have a copywriter who is absolutely non-digital. He's very, very non-digital in his lifestyle. He hates the cellphone. He hates intrusion in his life. But he writes fucking brilliant television scripts. I want him because you create a team. As long as you're very good at what you do, you'll always have a good career path ahead of you."

⌐

Neil Leslie, "When it comes to hiring digital people, I try to maintain a diverse mix of different skill sets. Everyone from creative, artistic, storytelling types that can crack a big idea, to passionate technical people and developers willing to be creative in their own right, to bring these ideas to life often in ways that surprise the original ideators.

"Of course, every project has different requirements, and there are times when the ideal resources are not available. A typical team for a project might consist of: me, a senior above-the-line creative team, two art-based digital creatives, a digital producer, and one or two developers, depending on the project budget and scope. If the team gets too big, it often slows the entire process to a crawl, as gaining a general consensus takes longer.

"If the campaign idea requires specialist expertise or more resources than we can spare, we'll usually consider the possibility of engaging a third-party developer to take on some or all production."

⌐

Alex Bodman, "One of the first questions I ask someone I'm interviewing is, 'What kind of work do you like right now?' You'd be amazed as to how many people get tripped up on that. I always like when they mention one that did not win the Cannes Grand Prix, and it is always helpful if it is something that is very current, if it is something where they actually had a particular reason why they liked it, then instantly, I would be quite interested. More often than not, it is just about the work. Of course, their attitude and everything else is also really important, but doing great digital is a lot easier when you have already done great digital or if you've done a lot of digital, you sort of know what works and what doesn't, you've seen production processes from beginning to end.

"There is always a role for juniors and people getting into it with strong books and knowledge. Often, the people who are coming in with the strong junior books from ad schools, most of their concepts will fail if you actually try to execute them. This has always been true of students' books, but even more so in digital. Yeah, they usually have two or three fatal flaws that would never get them past the beginning of the production period. As exciting as it is to see that work, I am much more excited about stuff that people actually engaged with, that got out there, that got made, that had a life and did something for the client, hopefully. I like that the most when I talk to a candidate.

"The other thing I look for a lot is craft, because the craft in digital is getting lost really quickly. An interactive art director probably understands that because they started as an interactive designer. Probably, at some stage, they were coding. Now you have someone who is an interactive art director because they're good at concepts. They're a little bit more visual than they are a writer, and they think digital is really cool. I am always very impressed if this person can get hands on, if they really care about the craft of the work. Same with copy, even more so with copy, because obviously that is my passion.

"Hopefully, they know how to execute and work their craft for differ-ent media. An above-the-line copywriter should know really well how to work with a director and see that treatment through or work with the photographer. They're going to be doing a lot more of that, even though it is now falling into the realm of an interactive writer. And that's a challenge, actually, for a lot of digital writers because very often they are being thrown into areas where they are not necessarily as skilled. That is great to help build other skills, but that's what I would expect an above-the-line writer to have.

"A digital writer, traditionally, would have the skills such as knowing how to be incredibly good in banners and knowing how to form an eDM. That is moving away a little bit more. The people who think of themselves as sexy digital writers should know how to execute, produce, and then work with the different set of people. How to work with tech people. How to work with an interactive producer. They should know backwards how a program would actually run on a platform like Facebook or YouTube, instead of running into all of the problems of execution that above-the-line writers typically do when they finally jump in and give it a go.

"It's about being specialized in that area and knowing a lot of more about it. I'd like to think that if you throw both types of writers in a room, when you give them a brief to come up with a headline, that they could both kill it. I don't think that they have innately different skill sets.

"Kids coming out of ad school today want to be what people are afraid of, a generalist. They want to think that they're media neutral. That it is about the big idea. For them, and I'm speculating here, but based on talking to them, the ultimate would be everyone's ultimate agency, Wieden. They all want to say themselves that that's one example of a great generalist shop that is doing some of the most interesting interactive work and some of the most interesting above-the-line work. When it works, it seems to work really well. I think that that is where they'd like to see themselves. The work a lot of them really want to share from their book is digital because they see that it's the exciting area. I mean, you have the Titanium category in Cannes.

"These days, everyone is just as happy to get a Grand Prix in the digital as they are in film. All those barriers have gone away. Nonetheless, they do see the excitement that could come from the exposure of a 30-second spot or from a nationwide campaign carrying their big idea. A lot of them are understandably hesitant to restrain themselves to what they might see as the digital-only agency, long-term. All of them straight out of school would take it for a year or two because they see the huge advantage that comes with executing and making digital work to their career. I do not know if they see that as their lifetime goal."

⌒

Diane McKinnon, "One of the biggest challenges I see with some of the younger folks coming out of portfolio schools is a lack in ability to articulate how they got to an idea and how to sell their ideas. We need to focus some of these digital creatives a lot more on writing. That's a real skill set; not that there aren't copywriters, I don't mean that. It's the ability to really communicate and articulate your ideas and connect the dots between a brief and how you got to a solution. I see challenges there.

"The default position with a lot of kids coming out of school, now, is you give them the problem and they go straight to the computer. Instead of thinking, they start designing or Googling or whatever. I might be looking for different skill sets, but the kinds of people we are looking for ultimately are great communicators. Being a whiz at PHP or Drupal isn't enough. They need to understand how to work in a team and communicate what they need and understand communications back to them on what's needed for the client.

"Not everybody is going to be client facing out of the gate, but being able to communicate why you're making creative and design decisions is really important to me. I'm not saying I don't care that people have won awards, but I've never asked that question in an interview, ever. The global creative director at Y&R is focused on winning Cannes Lions Awards. That is a measure of success by which he is judged, so he has to be."

〜

Paul Kwong, "The shift for a creative director is that you're in charge of a bigger group these days. Or at least communicating with a bigger team. It used to be just your creative teams coming up with TV spots, outdoor, print, and radio. Now, the teams are expanded to the PR agency, the events agency, the packaging agency, the Web content or social media agency, the gaming agency, along with all the clients who handle these partners. You've got to be the person who leads these people to the same finish line. The term is brand stewardship."

〜

Joe Zandstra, "I had a small digital team within a bigger agency and I needed to get it up and running. My focus was to look for people who's skill set and abilities went beyond the standard core digital skill sets – I didn't want coders – I wanted Creative Technologists, I didn't just want designers, I wanted designers who understood UX design and had a feel for what motivates users and how they think. Essentially I wanted people who cared deeply and passionately about the 'why' of what they were doing, not just the nuts and bolts of the job.

"If they can show some kind of evidence that they care about these things, I'll hire them. I want to pull in people who start out maybe as designer, but who become art director and then creative director. The only people who can graduate from a basic craftsman to Creative Director are those who already have the ability from the get go, an understanding of psychology, a fascination for how things work, logically, interpersonally."

〜

Scott Morrison, "Out of all the freelancers polled, 61% of them said they were much happier as a freelancer, and 28% moderately agreed. You have almost 87% of the people polled who feel, in varying degrees of agreement, that they are happier as a freelancer than they were as an employee. They polled people from less than a year up to 10 years. As you go from one year to 10 years, you can see that the percentage of 'strongly agree' goes up and 'moderately agree' goes down. More people are strongly agreeing with enjoying the freelance lifestyle, the more experience they get. I'm going to assume or infer from that that most of them have been jaded by the business, itself.

"What we're doing at The Bauhub is working to reinvent the way that the creative industry works so that people who've chosen self-employment can gain access to the projects that they used to work on at the bigger agencies, while maintaining the lifestyle that they enjoy in the self-employed space. At the same time, we're providing a viable alternative for big businesses to get the talent they want that is perfectly tailored to their project, on demand, without paying for the wasteful overhead of a traditional office space and all the things that go along with having tons and tons of employees."

Richard Bleasdale, "The industry's always going to need really creative people because it's the ability to think creatively that actually differentiates. And there are creative ways of executing in digital channels. I don't think it really matters. You still need to be able to think creatively, to be able to be distinctive, and that's why someone like a traditionally trained creative like Andy Greenaway has gone to SapientNitro."

Åsk Wäppling, "It's like everybody has to move to tech. The people who started in the digital realm of advertising and did very creative things that pleased many, many clients and sold lots of stuff, well, they're now moving on to Google and the like. Because they can't get anything done; they can't run on anything up the cycle of a dinosaur agency that's owned by a conglomerate. I think that's very sad."

Rob Martin Murphy, "You go to work in co-working spaces, you tend to be dealing with a whole bunch of interesting people, tech guys and engineers, doing all manner of crazy, intelligent stuff. It's going to be hard for agencies to attract them because they're thinking, 'Am I really going to be able to do some cool things with brands?' There'll be some who'll go there, but it might be based on whether it is a place that is just starting or has started the right way. That might be the only way to attract that talent.

"These guys are coming out, they've got amazing skills and they're going, 'I'd rather go and give my idea to Y Combinator where I can be a developer and founder, or I can be a developer as part of a team that's founding their own startup.' But, what's the dream? The dream is it could be huge. These guys tend to go from, 'Well, I did that. It either worked or didn't work. Time to move onto the next thing.' They're much more entrepreneurial in their career outlook. That's my perception. They're much more interested in the power and freedom of doing your own thing, because the tech guys who are mega successful, we all look up to them. It's not just us in advertising, it's, like, everybody. Everyone is going, 'If Reid Hoffman did that, and Jack Dorsey did that, and Zuckerberg did this, and like they're sort of household names, maybe I can.' They're the next level on from Jobs and Gates and that crew."

Overhauling Compensation

Gareth Kay, "I think we get paid unfairly. We don't get our fair return for the ideas that really do work. But unless the industry changes, it's going to be really hard for one or two agencies to change the industry, because there's always going to be someone who'll go, 'We'll do this for you this way. It'll be cheaper.'

"My hope for the industry rests on some interesting startups out there. They're not even really startups, these are seven- to eight-year old anomalies. They are beginning to change their conversation and attract really good senior proper clients and big multinational brands to work with them in new ways and get paid in new ways. It's difficult for existing agencies to change the way they get paid because they've got existing arrangements with clients.

"My hope is that there are going to be a bunch of younger agencies and a bunch of specialist agencies that, perhaps, can begin to turn this supertanker of an industry around. Otherwise I fear it's going to be a really horrible end. I fear that we'll sink. It's easy to talk about it, but we need to do it as an industry. That's the reality."

↜

Oliver Woods, "The industry's margins have gone down in the last 50 years. There's been a gradual erosion of value even if, on paper, all the holding companies have grown in terms of numbers of employees over the years. A lot of the holding companies have tried to introduce economies of scale. Media is a good example, where holding groups outsource as much as they can to one central group like Group M for search and social. They've been trying this, and I was part of the attempt to outsource social out of all the ends to try and save money, which didn't work very well. We probably cost them more than they took in.

"The pricing models for things like TV and traditional marketing now are balanced out. TV and print are normally not undercharged, and I think there are now a lot of norms and accepted culture for how you present TV ideas. For instance, you don't go out and shoot the TVC before you've signed the deal to do it. Whereas with digital, I think we're now well past the point of the early stages, but we're shooting ourselves in the foot by developing whole web sites before we've even got the business.

"I'm getting quite worried about this erroneous idea that's entering the industry where people in advertising agencies are trying to copy how Facebook works, which is the whole move-fast-and-break things/create-products-very-rapidly approach. Our clients don't understand how that works and, say, they ask us to build them a social app. Often the client will say, 'I want to see all the strategy and thinking before I even sign up for this.'

"What we really should say as disciplined marketers is, 'No. We'll tell you what it's going to do. We'll give you an idea. We can charge you half upfront for the prototype view and then charge you half upon delivery.' Those norms haven't been established in the relationship between agencies and clients. In terms of digital, the agency-client relationships are stunted, wasting tremendous amounts of effort circling around on strategy and execution."

↜

Scott Morrison, "The inspiration for The Bauhub came from the fact that there's a fundamental breakdown in the relationship between agency and client. It goes both ways. The agencies are responsible because they allowed things like spec creative.[11] They allowed themselves to not be treated in the same way other professional organizations are, for example, lawyers or doctors. You don't get to go to your lawyer and say, 'We're going to put out this proposal for a $30,000 project, we're going to have 10 people respond to it, we're going to want to see a little bit of creative, and then we're only going to pay one of you for it.' Yet the industry, itself, for competitive reasons, allows itself to be put through these kinds of practices that other professional industries would never consider.

"We allowed ourselves to be doing things that were unprofessional and therefore broke the trust. It's our fault. We allowed it to go there. I'm not going to sit here and try and blame clients, because it's not the case. If we had, as an industry, treated clients with more respect and had more of a professional relationship and weren't so fixated on the creative side and instead more on how can we really help them, it would've stayed collaborative.

"I've been through so many experiences where you say to a client, 'It's going to cost $50,000 to do that.' The response is, 'I only have $38,000 in the budget.' Lawyers don't do that. Accountants don't do that. Advertising is viewed as a service. I'm not really sure that people are clear that it's a professional service, sometimes. Not all the time. There are excellent examples of big agencies doing great stuff. There are excellent examples of great clients out there. I'm not trying to hound on it.

"On the whole, it seems fundamentally broken, and when an agency is pressed to try and land a whole bunch of business, what happens is, of course, you pitch a bunch of different things, you invest a bunch of time and money, none of which is recoverable even once you have the contract. And then, once you're into the relationship, you're constantly just trying to make your money. You're just trying to stop them from cutting budgets. You're trying to get them to pay attention to what you're doing and be respectful of your recommendations. It's a very hard slug, and agencies get really frustrated with clients, and

---

11 Speculative work whereby an agency will essentially produce the way an ad will be written and how it will look for the pitch before they have been selected for the job.

clients get very frustrated with agencies and so, fundamentally, how do you make that balance? They're both right and both wrong simultaneously."

❧

Dave Whittle, "One of the fundamental things that has changed is that the really big enterprise-size clients are buying creativity like they buy any other commodity. They're buying it like they're procuring soft drinks and staplers and property. A procurement person will often walk out of a meeting buying creativity from an agency and then look in to the next meeting where they'll be buying stationery; it's tough that creativity has been commoditized. That's really depressing. It's sad, because creativity really shouldn't be commoditized. Big, brilliant ideas are invaluable.

"Gone are the days of agencies making 20% to 30% profit. Single digit profits are now the norm. The industry has matured and, therefore, so have the margins. Creativity has been commoditized, commissions from third-party suppliers have disappeared, and the ability to shift work into lower-value economies has all impacted the economics of advertising services."

❧

Susan Kim, "Some of these boondoggle shoots that I remember going on, like this shoot for a major airline brand. The client paid $500,000, and it definitely could have been done a lot cheaper. We didn't need to send 10 people over. There was so much stuff shot that wasn't ever going to be used. There was so much doing all this extra stuff with the client. I can't see spending that much on a TV commercial to make it any more special.

"The airline was just such a dull and boring company that it wasn't even like a blow-your-mind-away TV commercial. That was just for the production stuff. Three months were spent. A zillion concepts produced, when all it ultimately was going to be was shots of the plane and a pilot, a super with whatever the fares are, and then we fly off to Tokyo.

"The agency was very good about saying, 'You leave all of it to us. We are the experts. Don't worry your pretty little heads,' and, 'Don't get too much into what's going on the sausage-making.' It's like only they could do it and yes, everyone else was in on it. All the others were doing it that way. This is the way. Where it started breaking down more was when media agencies started coming in. They said to the client, 'Hey, instead of only paying a lot less for your media, let us do the creative, too, and instead of charging you a 15% media commission, we'll knock it down to 5%. We will give you 10% back.' So that was the biggest thing that hurt ad agencies.

"Someone who was doing media figured out, 'I can still get a big chunk of this, and I don't even have to do any of the creative or anything. Just have someone else do it, and I know I'm going to make it bad for all the agencies, but if I get in first, I'll be in there.' Can you imagine what figures you're paying as a client? Five million to $10 million is how much they're spending on media, and because the agency gives it to the TV stations, they get $1.5 million in commission.

"If the client had bought it on their own, they'd still have to pay $10 million. It seems like it's a win-win for everyone. If you say, 'Hey, I'm going to incorporate myself as an agency,' and you go and tell the client, 'I'll give you half of this. I'll take 7½%, but I'll give you 7½%,' it's pretty easy to do. You don't need that agency anymore, and you'll be getting more money and the same amount of media. Now are they going to get the same level of creative work? I don't know, but that was where it started where you could look and see how the sausage was being made.

"Then some account people would go over to the other side and say, 'You wouldn't believe what goes on in the ad agency.' They would make the agencies behave more, and there were media buyers who did it that way who would say, 'Yes, this makes sense.' Agency people ended up going to the other side and forcing more transparency."

⌒

Jeffrey Dachis, "If you talk about digital and the $60-$70 billion pie in 2012, $55 billion of that is in paid search. Almost 50 of that is on Google. The balance of which is, in its entirety, in the purchase of display ads online that have conversion association to them and then ad tech: cookie tracking, attribution tracking, or commerce conversion. Digital has largely become a commerce-conversion medium. There is a lot of science around it, and it's really good at doing that. It's great at doing that, and if you're good at it, you can be a revenue marketer and have this beautiful closed-loop awesomeness, where you're running lead-gen campaigns and those lead-gen clicks are converting into leads, which are converting into opportunities and finally converting into sales.

"If you do enough of the top-of-the-funnel work in this business, you can generate a lot of bottom-of-the-funnel conversion. The folks who are good at it generate a lot of money, and it's a beautiful system. I don't begrudge the revenue marketers, and I don't begrudge the techniques they use to do revenue marketing. But I don't believe that brand building happens in digital that way.

"Despite the advent of digital over the last nearly 20 years, despite the growth of digital into a $70 billion business – by the way, that's on top of what is a $600 billion global measured-media market – the brands spend $600 billion building brands traditional ways. Digital is still only a $70 billion marketplace and largely search-based. I don't believe brands get built in digital. But here's the next phase of that discussion: social is the Holy Grail for brand builders in digital."

⤳

Åsk Wäppling, "I've always seen it as a problem that advertising agencies don't actually charge for what they do, which is coming up with the idea. There are some campaign ideas that run for 40 years. This should be our intellectual property. This is what we should charge for, but we're not, which turns us into media companies. This is the problem, and this is what's going to kill the dinosaur. If you look around the Web today, it's like nobody owns anything. Ideas are for everybody. IP [intellectual property] is a sucky thing, and copyright should go to hell. This is going to kill not just advertising agencies, but eventually everybody's work in the future. Because it's not like our children are going to be working in factories actually making shoes or jeans or work on farms or something, like we used to do.

"Our kids are going to be making digital apps and coming up with ideas and perhaps writing books or working on bits and bobs on screenplays and whatever else that they can produce that are non-tangible objects and based on copyright and patents. If we just release this, we have nothing. We don't produce tangible things anymore. We should protect the ideas. Since ideas are not tangible, people think, 'That's just something we can copy digitally. It's only ones and zeroes.' This is a really, really wrong mindset.

"It's not the fact that they're not keeping the talent, it's that they're not keeping what the talent is producing. The talent is producing an idea. Now, we can't own an idea. I get that, but somehow, somewhere, when you have a legal department that takes over half of the agency, fucking make sure that the client signs off on the fact that you own the fucking idea. Because that's what going to happen, you come up with something that can last for 30 years. That's what the agency should be paid for 30 years. You shouldn't be able to fire the creative team after two weeks for that idea. That's where the disrespect comes from. I don't think anybody cares about the people who have ideas, and I think that's the big problem."

⌒

Aden Hepburn, "We are never given bonuses for hitting targets, and we would love for there to come a time in the future where everything does revolve around metrics and when you hit the targets and when you exceed them, you get a bonus; and when you don't, you surrender some of that money that you said you were going to hit. As long as those KPIs and targets are mutually agreed upon and the right people in the right rooms are discussing them and setting them together as to what they believe is the right investment. Metrics are a brilliant thing."

R&D and Owning the Ideas

Dirk Eschenbacher, "Creating a start-up company is definitely something I am doing here [at Ogilvy China]. Creating tools and trying to make the experience great while creating brands based in social media. In the advertising world, it is not that simple. It's always based on a marketing calendar and a marketing budget and a checklist to achieve, so you're not tasked with creating more than what is needed at the present moment. Getting a holistic brief for making a company more functional… I've never had that brief yet, to be honest, and the clients that I operate on, like Volkswagen and Motorola, they're so complex internally that they have industrial design companies and in-store design firms lead all of the brand experience projects.

"'Start-up' means you have intellectual property (IP) and a business idea. Unless you offer to take a share of the business, it's very difficult to commit to it, so I see an agency environment as much different from a start-up environment. It's very different, and it's very difficult to fit a start-up environment into an agency. An agency is just not a start-up. You can maybe start one up within an agency, but you have to really treat it very differently. You can't just integrate it into a big agency. It won't work. I can totally understand that every [agency] person believes an agency can make it work, but it's a completely different experience, as I have learned."

⌒

Ignacio Oreamuno, "I've seen a lot of agencies begin to develop apps and content. Seven years ago, Anomaly was one of the first agencies that starting making their own products, but it was more of a PR thing. They were making money off the products, maybe not a lot. Nowadays, it's more of a forced thing because the agencies need other revenue sources.

"I know an agency in Montreal called CloudRaker. They launched an iPhone app that was originally called Nabit, then they changed it to something else, and it was like stop-motion for sports photography, where you take a photo of somebody jumping on a snowboard. It took all the shots and it made one combined photo where it shows all the moves of the jump. It was very cool, and it became one of the number-one apps in the world very quickly. It was free. There was no client, and that was a perfect example of an agency trying to find something else to monetize [through in-app purchases], as it had no client and no relation to anything else."

⌒

Joe Zandstra, "At the end of the day, we're all very reactive because budgets are tight we all spend a lot of time pitching. Often you have a situation where a client is dangling a carrot in front of you, teasing you with, 'Well, you're likely to win this pitch if you have a bunch of PHP developers.' Sometimes you've got to be reactive, because maybe that's how you grow and maybe you look for opportunities with clients that are going to stretch you, but the specialist skill sets needed for different digital projects mean you can end up staffing up around a specific client requirement, which is dangerous territory.

"I was talking with someone today about labs and innovation groups within agencies, specifically about a former company I'd worked at where we were creating custom hardware as a solution that we could own as I.P. It was, as I recall, a combination of Infrared and RF technology – something for a huge crowd of people at an event. We were going to prototype and then manufacture 10,000 of these units. I was like, 'This is fucking awesome. I'm in heaven here, geek heaven' and this wasn't some innovation lab – it was real paid work. I think that you have to struggle to get this stuff done with existing clients – but it's worth it. And that's the right way to go. Labs just create innovation ghettos and usually end up failing.

"If you want to be ahead of the curve with R&D, you've got to be looking to create products that you can white label [rebrand] for companies, as opposed to crazy things that you can show off. That way you can get something exciting done for a client – maybe make a bit of an investment on it – then sell a remix of the solution again to recoup costs and make money."

⌐

John Winsor, "We are certainly experimenting and playing, but I would say all these kinds of new things, including ourselves, do not have scale yet. It is still super early days. I think anybody that's saying that they are cranking it out and they got all this amazing momentum is totally smoking crack. I just do not think it has happened, yet.

"Agencies do not even understand what the playing field is. As I wrote in a *Harvard Business Review* article, the best examples of crowdsourced companies are open companies. Open-donation companies are Facebook and Twitter because they built some software and have some privacy rules. That essentially says, 'The network creates the content. We own the content, and we can resell it for advertising.' That's a killer model. It's like everybody else in the world, a billion people, create the content. We can know exactly what they want and then we sell advertising against it. In that context, there is no room for agencies.

"Victors & Spoils is great for people to throw out ideas, be they insights and inspiration or simple ideas, but it is really hard for somebody without the context of the brand to build campaigns for it. And they think about things like, 'How do we keep that going? How do we make sure it is on brand and on brief and all those things?' It is the classic strategic and creative direction, but the execution of ideas, the stuff where agencies really make their money because of legions of strategists and legions of account people and legions of creatives. It is just not there anymore.

"You can get ideas from anywhere. You can get insights from any-where. It is the cost, and I do not think it is just agencies. I think the whole consumer insight business and aggregate crowds are happening so fast. When we started V&S, it was all about aggregating a community of advertising pro-fessionals. Now we're morphing into, 'How do we take our crowd or our crew of creatives and strategists and help your crowd – if Coke has 20 million fans on Facebook – how do we help them use their crowd to come up with ideas for their brand and we just help curate? That's the risk involved that agencies can play a part in."

꙳

Rob Martin Murphy, "The social good thing for us, it may or may not take off. We may end up sort of doing something else. We might be making our own products, manufacturing something tangible. The reason why we started our own thing was to give ourselves that space and flexibility. In an agency job, you would not necessarily have the time or perhaps the inclina-tion or have the desire to experiment with different things, either.

"Google says to employees, 'We'll give you 20% of your time to devel-op your own passion projects.' Though it was supposed to be Google-related. Essentially, Gmail was formed from that. Google Wave was formed from that. You've got to take the good with the bad. Google Plus, I imagine was probably spawned by that as well. If you look at Google, it does some incredible things, and I just think that they don't get enough credit for street-mapping the world. It's a phenomenal company. They have amazing people working for them.

"If I'm a young guy coming up with skills, where would I rather work? Go to another agency? Or Google's offer? I'd go to Google, too, wouldn't you? Wouldn't that be an interesting place to work rather than just sort of go to with another agency? They're the company that's attracting a massive amount of talent.

"Good companies who've got it right have that sort of culture built in where they have people really sort of self-motivated to do their own stuff. And encourage it, actively encourage it. It's the difference between saying how you spend 20% of your time or saying, 'No, you actually have to do this because we don't want you here on a Friday.' You're developing a mobile gaming app or whatever. Just to do it. Because you've got to do stuff. Agencies are creating ads, but I'd rather look at people's stuff and see actually a product that they've made and launched and run. For me, that's just worth so much more."

⌒

Aden Hepburn, "One of the best things we've done here, and that we're actively doing, is a thing we've called VML Labs. What we ask for is 10% of people's free time. We give them 10% of paid business time to work on collaborative projects across the business, and those projects become our products or installations or new technology. Things that they otherwise would never have got to play with. What I love about it not being the 20% Google model is that the person has to invest 10% of their personal time into it. The people that we've seen getting involved with that, doing that, they are the passionate guys and that 10%, well, they probably would've gone home and worked on a side project by themselves that maybe would never see the light of day. Instead, they donate that 10% of their time to our agency to work with a bunch of their mates that they love hanging out with every day. To do something that is probably going to get in front of a client because we're going to build a prototype, and it will go into market a hundred times quicker than they could've done it on their own. It's building products, services, technology and even products like physical, tangible products and be able to sell them."

⌒

Subhash Kamath, "There's a sense of entrepreneurism and optimism and therefore a lot of the younger people today, younger than me certainly, are not scared of starting their own stuff and seeing where it can go. It's the ideas economy now, driven by the youth, fueled by the youth. As long as you have an idea, which has even the barest resemblance of a business behind it, they are willing to try it out. If it doesn't work, they'll try something else."

⌒

Dave Whittle, "Ultimately, the current business model is selling time and materials. Agencies are making margin on people, which is what we do at the moment. That's likely to change. Selling an idea as a whole, irrespective of the amount of time contributed, must grow. Building products and trying to monetize them across the network. That will absolutely happen. There are lots of different models. I don't think that there's any revolution in any of this.

"Smaller and more dynamic teams working together, prototyping ideas, and having more of a product manufacturing-based approach is how they come up with ideas and execute them. I think the big media agencies are going to get bigger and integrate with the creative agencies. But none of that's any new news.

"We've developed products internally that were used for other clients. We've built quite a sophisticated resource management tool that we are rolling out across the rest of the group, and it's being used into other markets as well. We've been approached by other agencies to license that product. We've refused. Creative businesses come up with proprietary ideas like that, and it's just an example of creativity improving operations. But if a creative agency wants to be in the business of inventing products to commercialize beyond their own clients, then they require an operating model to support this."

Moving From Full Service to Full Experience

Alan Schulman, "The crayons that we have to color with are different, and the tools we have to mix with the crayons to get the crayons to do different things are more advanced. Our work with clients transcends the pure brand communications objectives and pushes further down into the transactional experiences – both physical and digital. In some categories like financial services, 75% of your customer interactions are all digital. That doesn't include ATMs.

"Creating both physical and digital experiences is very different from your standard job at an ad agency where you're just wondering, 'What's the next big idea that I can come up with to pitch this piece of advertising business?' and once I win that, 'What's my opportunity to get a commercial on the Super Bowl?' If that's the extent to which you are in your client's business, you're not really deeply in your client's business. You're just dealing with an aspect of your client's business that involves either paid media or generating some cultural currency around either a joke at the end of a commercial or some kind of organizing principle that you attach to a campaign, which hopefully will have more than five minutes of cultural currency.

"The definition of what a digital agency does in partnership or, hopefully, in collaboration with an above-the-line agency has been traditionally creating a halo of digital stuff and activity that extends the life of a TV flight. The difference on the digital agency side is that we've moved past that flight-to-flight campaign mindset, and we've moved to more of a brand of channel or content creator mindset. As we build out this big digital ecosystem with programs.

"More and more, the smarter brand marketers are realizing they're not in a campaign business, they're in a content-platform business. If you look at IBM or GE or Liberty Mutual, all those advertisers have an organizing idea that they're storyscaping around. They're not just storytelling, they're actually creating worlds, not ads. There's a plethora of content where digital agencies are doing more components of that storytelling. The trouble is that they get typecast by their above-the-line partners as not being storytellers but builders.

"Above-the-line, below-the-line, whose line is it, anyway? It's the client's line. Digital agencies have a different definition of what success looks like to a brand marketer. If they're a TV-flight-by-TV-flight advertiser that just wants you to create a digital halo around the TV campaign of the above-the-line agency, then they're really not getting the full muscle of the digital shop."

〜

Dave Whittle, "Look at the economy of creativity across various industries. If you're an artist, painter, filmmaker, software developer, architect, choreographer, or an actor, very few of them are procured based on an hourly rate. They're procured on a fixed rate that motivates the team to think about the products and the outcome rather than the amount of hours that they're required to spend to create anything. In a funny way, I'm sure you've heard the phrase before, a task will always take precisely the amount of time one has to complete a task. That's a real enemy to the creative industries, to creative advertising. That can be the enemy to a creative team where they've got 146 hours to work on a brief. That's not very conducive to great creative thinking.

"In many instances, the quality of the creative work would be improved by an alternative approach. Many big clients end up retaining a team, and that's one way to reduce the amount of pencil pushing and admin around watching the clock, which isn't particularly inspiring or motivating. That's why retainers work quite well for these clients."

Part III: Digital Takes Over

It took much too long for digital to have its day since it was considered nothing more than a fun but perfectly irrelevant experimental environment—from the time it was introduced until 2007 when Facebook relaxed its elite membership requirements and exploded on the scene, convincing everyone that there might just be something to all of this. Hey, you assemble over a billion active people in one place, and even the most conservative business executives are going to put down their brandy snifters and start paying attention.

Part III discusses the long difficult road, the resistance and roadblocks faced by those fascinated by the possibilities, the bottomless potential presented by the addictive and obsessive nature of mobile devices, the power of Big Data to finally help us understand our audiences, and thoughts about the new age agencies that are opening up intriguing avenues for all of us.

Chapter 9: The Digital Evolution

Digital had an especially tough introduction to the agency world because it began as a secretarial tool and was given about that level of respect. The first digital boxes that entered the scene in the mid-1980s were used for typing up meeting notes and collating research data, not for setting type or creating new means of communication. Briefs were still being filled out on typewriters because no one knew a better way. It took several more years before WordStar on an IBM XT was replaced in studios, with much trepidation and disdain by Aldus PageMaker on a beige Mac IIfx.

The idea of letting two-dimensional representations of what type should look like guide the creation of physical output was maddening to those who had devoted their entire careers to the craft of typesetting. Computers were seen as the enemy of quality work by enabling lazy behavior and cheapening the entire process with schlocky output devoid of soul and lacking finesse. "Good work worth doing takes a lot of effort!" was a common strangled cry directed at anyone indicating interest in the machines. Never mind that a human without aid of a pretty good loupe could not distinguish the quality between relatively quick imagesetter-produced type on slick bromide paper and those layouts set traditionally and painfully slowly by hand.

Of course, these same tools did bring upon us the blight of the Desktop Publishing revolution, the precursor to the Web 1.0 and User Generated Content revolutions, where anyone who had ever been told by a parent, teacher, buddy, or crazy person in the street that they were creative was able to put out a shingle and declare themselves a *graphics* (sic) designer and ad "guru."

So, maybe those traditional-minded typesetters had a point, after all. An inordinate amount of bad work was produced by dabblers and people just kidding themselves (and any client they could likewise fool). Everything was being set in Copperplate and Futura Extra Bold around clip art. But, no, no, we can't blame the tools just because they made things easy enough for anyone without training to pretend they could do the work of a professional. We can, however, still not like or trust them and opt to fall back on what came before and what has always worked. And that's the way it was for years, until typesetters lost the war of attrition as QuarkXpress, Illustrator, FreeHand, Photoshop, and even Microsoft Office took hold and became the staples and new standards of the industry, no matter the opinion an art director might have about the process, artistry, or quality that was lost (or gained).

Then entered bulletin board systems (BBSes) for (slowly) transmitting large project files to color separators and other pre-press services instead of walking down removable media like SyQuest cartridges, and soon after, the public Internet transformed computers into invaluable communication tools, thanks to email. Now, everyone in the agency from account management to the producers to the creatives to vendors *to the clients* began using it to first send quick notes to each other. Then they realized they could start to transmit files directly to individuals and entire teams, set up meetings, even give written approval on a piece so things could quickly move ahead. Instead of trying to chase down people (this was before the ubiquitous mobile phone) and waste hours or days sending something by courier, items could be sent "electronically" over email or FTP. It took a lot to get people used to these new systems, but the benefits could not be denied. Unlike typesetting, there was nothing subjective about it. It was efficient and it left a (digital) paper trail.

While figuring out how and why ad agencies missed the boat on digital (and social and mobile) and lost the massive credibility with clients that is a big part of why marketers feel the need to turn to specialists and boutiques, it's important to understand how reluctant integration of technology into daily life influenced agencies' flippant dismissal of anything connected to the Internet as a worthy channel. My erstwhile creative partner, John Lambie, went through the whole long affair with me as we transitioned from old to new media in the mid-'90s and in this chapter he helps guide us through the sordid tale.

☙

John Lambie, "The year is now 1993, and while the Internet has already been around for a long time (connecting mostly academic, research and defense institutions), it was mostly the domain of an underground of geeks. They inhabited a netherworld of chat rooms, bulletin board systems, newsgroups, email, gophers, FTP directories, and listservs. Each had its own communication protocol. Each required some degree of technical geekery to understand, set-up, and utilize.

"The World Wide Web changed all that. Now anyone with a PC (or a Mac, even), a telephone line, and a cheap gizmo called a modem could connect to the Internet and share information via a simple, robust communication platform."

"Initially, the web was this dodgy, hard-to-use communications tool

• Then it became a catalog (web sites)
• Then a business directory (Yahoo!)
• Then a glorified print ad (banners)
• Then a direct marketing tool (CRM)
• Then a shop front (e-commerce)
• Then it all crashed.

"If we all weren't so busy checking our stock prices and believing the hype, we should have seen it coming. There were too many sites promising too much. And they were dogged by slow speeds, patchy adoption, a clunky user experience (UX), distrust of technology, poor delivery, and – like dogs chasing their own tails – reliance on advertising alone to monetize one's site. And that left all the naysayers with pretty smug looks on their faces.

"But even as the digital world was crashing in a heap, it was already evolving into something entirely new:

• Google introduced active, intelligent search
• Flash brought a new level of interactive engagement and enjoyment
• YouTube: on demand video
• Facebook: social intercourse
• Twitter: instant trending info
• 3G + Mobile: go anywhere access
• GPS: locational awareness

These technologies were all game changers. Some (like Flash) are already superseded but their disruptions will reverberate for years to come."

⤺

It certainly caused a buzz. In 1994, *Time* magazine declared it *The Strange New World of the Internet*. The cover article begins with a recounting of the *Green Card Incident*, which is about a couple from Arizona who began to advertise legal services for helping people get green cards. They used a program they wrote called Masspost to put their ad automatically on over 5,500 message boards on the Internet. They pissed off the early users around the world so much with their crass commercialism that they forced the couple's internet service provider to close their account via their emailed "flames." That's how welcome business, let alone advertising, was first received in this brave new world. The postscript to the story is these married lawyers declared their effort a success, claiming to have produced over $100,000 in revenue due to spamming those sites.

⤺

John Lambie, "Perhaps the first interactive interloper was email. It allowed instantaneous communication between anyone with an email address and was a godsend for speeding internal communications. Who can't recall the expectant thrill as the little MIDI-tootle announced, 'You've got mail' for the first time... or even the first few hundred times? Even unsolicited spam would be opened with a heady mix of glee and curiosity.

"Yet email retained a very workaday format: a simple string of ASCII text, with no attachments over 10kb, thank you very much. It was not seen as a serious tool for advertising or mass communications."

⤺

Peter Moss, "The Internet was already here in '93/'94, but nobody was taking it particularly seriously. In America, they dabbled a little bit more than we did, but there was certainly not much going on in Asia. It seemed like that for the longest time. One of the reasons Andy Greenaway hired me was because he knew something was coming, and he wanted someone who at least understood what a PC was.

"We started this considered move from direct mail, which was already labeled 'junk mail' by '94. What we were looking at initially was the dot.com stuff: it was just web sites and 'your company should perhaps have one.' It mainly fell on OgilvyOne or Ogilvy & Mather Direct because we saw the Web as a direct channel. Plus the advertising guys wouldn't want to go anywhere near that, anyway. It just didn't seem as a sexy as a shoot in the Bahamas. We took it on board, and as we started to get into it, I remembered everything was very cookie cutter. This was pre-Flash, so everything was pretty static.

"We didn't have the systems that could manage response very well on an individual basis. Direct email is mass mailing, albeit customized or personalized, but handling response was slightly different. There were a lot of infrastructure and personnel changes to make inside the building, but also writing the software, which could manage all of it properly. Because email was there, you didn't have that additional system to manage it. We had a data consultant, and we were building a campaign management system.

"It took a lot of years in the making, and it was really smart, but it was just too advanced. On the back of that effort, we had all the real players come in. They were beginning to develop CRM platforms.

"The first issue was ubiquity: At what point do we have enough computers in homes or in front of people? We had to wait for that to happen. Then we adopted more and sold more in CRM at that time, which was a combination of the software plus a lot of smart thinking around it. One of the reasons that CRM is still a little bit of a dirty abbreviation today is that people just bought the software, but didn't really know what they were doing with it.

"A lot of what we were doing was writing DM packs. I believe, direct mail is going to make a resurgence as a premium channel purely because all the junk is now in the virtual inbox. So before someone makes the fantastic decision to not have letterboxes in doors anymore, maybe we can see a really smart role for direct mail in the future.

"Anyway, with DM moving away, we'd begun to feel more comfortable about what a digital presence was all about. Not only for corporate sites, but also at the same time, mobile was becoming something very, very important. At this point in time, there was mobile, you had a desktop in every home, but then we started to get the third thing in place, which was the speed of receiving the data. It held us back for a long time."

‿

John Lambie, "The biggest buzz in advertising circles would be reserved for the web site. Wow! You mean I can hang my shingle online and anyone can visit?

"Those working on the web in the mid-'90s will recall the constant refrain: 'Can you put my brochure online?' It seemed the obvious thing to do at the time.

"Most corporate web sites comprised folksy prose, often lifted word-for-word from a sales brochure. In many cases, a corporate web site was little more than product catalogue – complete with SKU numbers.

"With so few people online, and search engines little more than manually compiled directories, web sites were seen as a nice-to-have addition to the corporate communications armory – as opposed to an essential go-to information arsenal for all and sundry."

↩

Chick Foxgrover, "One of the funny things about this industry – having been in and out of it a number of times – is that it likes to portray itself as very creative and forward thinking, but it's actually a very, very conservative industry."

↩

Jim Speelmon, "Back in the late 1990s, there were very low expectations about what contribution digital would have. If things went poorly, it wasn't that big of a deal. Whereas, now, you might spend tens of millions of dollars on media across TV, print, outdoor, and digital. You might have a quite junior planner whose area of expertise is social media that makes one mistake. Or does very poor contingency planning on one free thing that runs on Twitter or Facebook or something that turns the entire media investment into a massive disaster."

↩

David Anders, Managing Director and VP of Client Service for Javelin West and former Microsoft Global Client Services Director for Wunderman, "I worked for a direct and digital marketing agency in the early 2000s, and I can still remember when the edict came down. One of our clients, a vice-president of marketing, issued a mandate that every single campaign would have its own dedicated landing page with a vanity URL.

"The notion of a brand having content and channel strategies was so nascent at the time that many online experiences were nothing more than digital brochureware. Direct mail pieces included calls-to-action that drove people to a landing page. Landing pages featured nearly the exact same content as the direct mail, and because corporate web sites were often outside of marketing influence, the digital experience was usually disjointed and a dead end. So, naturally, we'd have the landing page drive people back to an 800 number.

"Looking back, the experience we created for people was horrible, but we didn't know better. The novelty of digital overwhelmed reason. I often think about what consumer experiences we're creating today that we'll look back on down the road and wish for a do-over."

⮑

Larry Goode, "I first became aware of the concept of the Internet around 1993. I was art directing a photo shoot, and between shots there was a guy talking to the photographer about this network that would enable anyone to talk and share information around the globe. He said it was going to be 'big.' I don't think the word 'Internet' was used. I was intrigued, but then cautious because I figured he was selling something I didn't want. I didn't have an idea how it would change my business. At the time, I was just starting to transition from doing design to a large amount of illustration work.

"In 1993, the process went as such:

- The client would call me with the assignment.
- If I accepted, they would fax me the story, usually unfinished and unedited, but enough to get the idea.
- Then I would sketch some ideas and fax them back.
- The client would choose one with revisions and fax that to me.
- I would make the revisions and fax that back.
- If all went well, it would be approved, and finally I would start on the final art.
- When finished, I would put it on a CD and FedEx it to the client.

"There usually was no time for the client to check the final before it went to press because the writer was working until the drop-dead date. I was working with the Art Director on a matter of faith, and I would have anxious nights while the Federal Express package made its way to the client. In the morning, if it all went well, I wouldn't hear a thing because the client was too busy to call.

"No call equaled a good job. God forbid if the client didn't like the illustration, then they were stuck with it because there was no time to make the changes and then Federal Express a disk back. For this reason, art directors were reluctant to hire illustrators they had not worked with in the past. We were a known quantity, and the client's trust was a very important aspect of the business. As email and file transfer options evolved, I was able to provide proofs of the final with time to make revisions.

"In the late 1990s, I noticed a drop off in my business and many others. Suddenly, art directors were able to choose from literally thousands of illustrators. That, combined with failing magazines, the bread and butter of illustrators, made it become a very tough market.

"I found the Internet to be a double-edged sword. While it was a great marketing tool, it was a great marketing tool for every illustrator and designer on the planet. The creative individual going from getting noticed with traditional marketing materials (print), to getting noticed using digital meant competing with literally thousands of competitors. Like I said, a tough market to crack."

Seek and Ye Shall Find: The First Search Engines

John Lambie, "As more web sites began popping up and more people began migrating online, so did the demand for some sort of order from this burgeoning chaos. This heralded the rise of the Internet directory and the first search engines.

"Initially, these were little more than glorified business listings. They were assembled and updated manually by ever larger teams of compilers and taxonomists. They included the W3Catalog, Allweb, WebCrawler, Lycos, Yahoo!, AltaVista, Excite, Magellan, and Dogpile. If you wanted to be listed, you needed to manually submit your site for their careful consideration and possible inclusion.

"Rather than scouring the entire Web, they merely searched within their own limited directories – a walled garden of arbitrarily assembled content. The problem was, even the largest army of compilers couldn't keep up. This situation began to unravel in the late '90s, and smart programmers began to develop automated 'spiders' that crawled and trawled the Web for new pages and sites to add to their listings. The battle was on for the biggest, most comprehensive, robust, and up-to-date directory.

"The larger directories became known as 'portals' – your 'jumping-in' point for the wonders of the Web and a logical choice for a personal home page. The big portals attracted legions of hopeful Web surfers in search of 'What's New' and 'What's Hot.' They began offering the latest news, sports, weather, gossip, and other up-to-the-minute content to stay fresh and relevant. Maintenance and upkeep costs were high, requiring much time and effort to stay populated and updated.

"Like the newspapers, classifieds, and yellow pages that served as their traditional business model, advertising was an obvious way to monetize them. Users were looking for content to surf. In double-quick time, banner ads on these portals became the fast track to online visibility for brands and businesses.

Click Here

"Like the newspapers, classified ads, and yellow pages that served as their traditional business model, advertising was an obvious way to monetize portals. In double-quick time, banner ads on these portals became the longed-for path to online visibility for millions of brands and businesses trying to stand out amidst the clutter.

"The banner ad was the perfect shortcut. With a single click could bypass the directory drill-down and take your customer straight to your site. And an early innovation in a simple graphic format, called the GIF (graphic in-line format), allowed basic animations and simple multi-panel storytelling. Five, ten, or fifteen seconds of simple problem-solution-response narrative.

World's first web banner, October 1994 by Craig Kanarick of Razorfish and Otto Timmons of Tangent Design on behalf of Joe McCambley of Modem Media for AT&T and placed on Hot-Wired.com.

"By necessity, file sizes had to be minuscule (10kb was considered excessive), so these ad units were limited to a tiny fraction of the page. Unlike print ads, which could dominate an entire page (or even a double-page spread) in a glossy magazine, banner ads were relegated to narrow side-columns or even narrower rows between chunks of content of a page.

"It wasn't much, but at the time it seemed like a revolution. In those early, what's-this-shiny-new-thing days, click-through rates (CTRs) of 10% or even 20% were not unheard of. Believe it or not, banner ads had novelty value. Like miners to a gold rush, brands flocked to this medium, chasing those curious and happy-go-lucky clickers.

"Alas, high CTRs didn't stay high for long. And as they dropped, so did creative standards. With few brand guardians giving them much more than a sideward glance, banner builders upped the 'look-at-me' factor. Grandiose promises, misleading calls to action and a flood of new formats appeared: pop-ups, pop-unders, drop-downs, interstitials, superstitials, expanding banners, page-takeovers… you name it. Many featured auto-playing audio, even video, so that the only click they got was on the 'X' in the top right corner (which some unscrupulous advertisers also rigged to take you to their page).

First Name, Last Name, Email, Submit

"Having divined a way to distract and divert Web surfers, the question remained, 'Now that they're here, what the hell do we do with them all?' Users could click around your site and maybe even 'favorite' it if they were impressed. This all seemed rather hit and miss.

"Smart marketers, many of whom had come from a background in direct marketing, knew exactly what to do: capture data. Specifically, name and contact information.

"By creating a database of potential customers, brands could keep this for future marketing campaigns.

"This saw the advent of the 'landing page' and the 'microsite.' A promotional banner would offer some sort of reward for clicking (play game, win contest, get freebie, etc.). The pay-off was a user's vitals.

"This, in turn, led to larger-scale email marketing campaigns, built on this newly acquired data. It was quickly followed by huge investments in customer relationship management (CRM) teams, tools, and software.

"This permitted campaigns to live beyond the initial click-thru and interaction. Users who missed out on the big prize could be rewarded with coupons and other goodies, which could be redeemed at physical retail outlets.

"Campaigns could extend their reach by incentivizing users to 'tell-a-friend' to convert a new cohort of suspects to the prospect database.

"Buy Now!"

"Converting virtual contestants to paying, physical customers did not always provide the promised rivers of gold. Driving traffic to web sites is a lot easier than customers driving themselves across town to your store.

"The real money, obviously, lay in converting that cash online – then and there. E-commerce was ripe for the plucking.

"E-commerce existed – albeit in a crude form – from the very earliest days of the Web. A number of technological planets needed to align before it could become a large-scale, profitable concern:

- Secure and encrypted credit card transactions
- Instantaneous payment gateways
- Verified vendor credentials
- A back-end inventory tracking and order-processing system
- A physical fulfillment and distribution system

"Many customers were understandably wary of offering up details relating to their bank accounts and home addresses. Actual anecdotes and urban legends of scams and rip-offs abounded. Such tales were enough to scare the wallets back into the pockets of even the bravest early adopters.

"Online retailers (or eTailers as they were quaintly called) had often spent vast sums putting these complex e-commerce systems in place. But what was lacking was the reassuring social proof of trust – something that could only come from previously satisfied customers. A real chicken and egg dilemma.

Assume the Crash Position

"It had to happen. And by 1999, just five short, frenetic years after the Web burst onto the scene, the first cracks started appearing.

"Like every bubble, crazy numbers, insane profits, and preposterous IPOs were announced with such frenetic frequency as to become almost banal. The NASDAQ was going stratospheric. Share prices, salaries, and bonuses inflated out of control, but effusive expectations kept them buoyant. This boom was different to all the others, the thinking went. The old models of supply and demand no longer applied, they claimed. This would be the boom to rewrite the rules of business, finance, and economics once and for all. The only way was up, baby.

"Every barren patch of dirt contained the mother lode. All you had to do was stake a claim (i.e., buy a domain name), and start digging. In many cases, however, the miners didn't even bother to dig. They had found another revenue stream – not based on sales but on something just as certain to deliver revenue: advertising dollars.

"The excess of the dot.com boom was fueled by a massive Ponzi scheme built on advertising. Nearly every dodgy revenue model had ad dollars as the rubber bands and paperclips holding it together. The rationale was this:

- If I advertise, I'll drive traffic to my site.
- If I own a high-traffic site, I can sell advertising on it.
- I can use that money to drive more traffic to my site.
- I can charge even more for advertising on my site.

"The road from rags to riches to rags was well worn and littered with roadkill:

- Quit job on Wall Street selling junk bonds
- Raise cash (investor discretion optional)
- Hire a team (enthusiasm required, experience optional)
- Build a basic web site (target audience optional)

- Advertise the bejesus out of it (to drive large, unsustainable volumes of traffic)
- Raise more money using inflated traffic metrics (as validation of your proof of concept)
- Fit out a swanky office and buy founders matching Lamborghinis (wealth attracts wealth, doesn't it?).
- Delay launch (but hit up investors for more cash – this thing is gonna be bigger than we ever imagined!)
- Sell advertising space on half-built web site (even if we don't generate a single sale, advertising revenue will rocket us into the black)
- Hire Mariah Carey and MC Hammer for global launch party on Adnan
- Kashogghi's super-yacht off the coast of St. Tropez.
- Spend remaining cash of Super Bowl advertisement to boost flagging traffic numbers.
- Hire 21-year-old usability expert to tweak site
- Visit bank manager for 'Come to Jesus' discussion
- Rather than trim revenue, tell staff they will now be working for stock options only and that this is just a minor blip.
- Endure six months of negative revenue. Smile a lot and reassure exhausted staff that it's more than a minor blip, but by no means a major blip.
- 19-year-old Chief Financial Officer resigns after Lamborghini is repossessed.
- Bank manager admitted to palliative care.
- Buy one-way ticket to Latvia.
- Announce, through unpaid attorney that due to 'unforeseen circumstances, completely outside of company's control, etc.,' company will be ceasing North American operations.
- Liquidators called in.
- Furniture and computers repossessed from under noses of staff who still think they will be receiving stock options 'today, if not tomorrow.'
- Lie low in Latvia for 6 months.
- Get job on Wall Street selling derivatives.

"If this was the digital gold rush, it was fools' gold. The lucky ones cashed out early. They took their money and ran.

"What these dot.com buccaneers failed to account for was that:

1. Everyone else had the same business model
2. Every ad on your own site represents an exit point from your site
3. While you might be making money, you're also losing traffic
4. The solution was to advertise on everyone else's site in one big advertising-go-round

"There were four major flaws with this model:

1. There were still not enough people online to justify volumes of traffic that were being touted
2. CTRs on banner ads were dropping like a stone, thanks to:
   - Oversupply (even more sites, with even more ad space to sell)
   - Under-delivery (customers were getting wary of grandiose claims and weary of disappointing experiences)
3. Banner prices remained grossly overvalued due to:
   - Questionable accounting techniques
   - Lack of consistency and transparency in ad unit rates across sites and vendors
   - Questionable CTR and conversion statistics
4. The very people who could have provided the advertising nous and know-how to run this circus properly – advertising agencies – were nowhere in sight.

"The result was what economists call 'beggar-thy-neighbor.' Based on the less-than-zero sum logic that:

- If I play the system to the detriment of a business partner (i.e. an affiliated web site) – by plundering their web site traffic to attract it to mine, then I win, they lose, and that's OK.
- But if I take so much of their traffic, so that they can no longer operate, then I lose a valuable source of customers. And we both lose.
- And finally, if everyone is operating on the same principle, the whole house of cards collapses. Then we all lose.

What Goes Up...

"The dot.com boom was built on the same faulty premise as the recent global financial crisis – that prices and values will keep rising. Forever.

"It's never happened in the past. And it will never happen in the future. It's a vain hope built firstly on greed, and secondly on hubris.

"It was not just greed and hubris – that's just what caused the massive and rapid overheating. It was also due to underlying fragility within the system – a system built on a rickety infrastructure that could not possibly support it.

"Those signs of fragility were not always plain to see, but they were there nevertheless:

1. **Slower than expected adoption of technology:**
   People were not flocking online in sustainable volumes. The cost of the average PC was around USD$1,000, and the average laptop was USD$2,000. Consumers were slow to upgrade to better, faster models, and the high entry cost was slowing potential new customers from joining the rush.

   Even on the consumer side of the equation, a PC in the home was often a shared device, squabbled over by several family members. And on the business side of the equation, many office PCs were kept offline or had restricted access – due to HR concerns of lost productivity from staff Web-surfing or engaging in private email/chat conversations.

2. **Dogged by slow speeds:**
   We all remember the familiar scratch-scratch-ping! refrain as our 14, 28, or 56K modems sought and found a connection. The pipes were narrow, and with each additional user connecting – either at home or in the office – the slower and more congested those connections got. Peak traffic times could slow an entire city to a halt – just like rush hour on the physical highways in and out of town.

   More users meant page-load times, that could be measured in minutes rather than micro-seconds. Most of the online population was connecting via the choked arteries of a system that couldn't scale. Yet every online business model was founded on fast speeds and infinite scalability.

3. **Patchy adoption:**

Not everyone was connecting. There were a couple of interesting gaps in the market and a few surprising lumps. For instance, the very wealthy were notoriously late adopters – they had much better things to do with their precious time. Stay-at-home mums, on the other hand, flocked to the Internet in much higher-than-expected numbers. And globally, some countries were notorious laggards – with the US as one such country. South Korea was a streets-ahead leader.

4. **The god-awful user experience (UX):**

These was the early days of the Internet. Whatever usability rules existed were still being tested and validated. Many derived from the Web's distant cousin, the CD-ROM.

Anyone with half a design diploma hung out a shingle as a web designer. Anyone who could cut and paste JavaScript, a developer. And many dispensed with this luxury altogether – leaving the vital UX/UI task to the same programmers who were developing the back-end. Interface design was a dog's breakfast confused and kerfuffled by hidden navigation, site maps that looked like org charts, and wild experiments with Flash, Java, and other plugins that crashed browsers or failed to load.

5. **Distrust of technology:**

Consumers were wary of e-commerce. Not only were credit-card scams abounding (or at least wretched stories about them), but poorly configured payment gateways often meant users got stranded mid-transaction, not knowing whether they'd successfully completed the process or just blown their hard-earned cash into cyberspace.

6. **Lack of standards:**

The dot.com boom was like World War III:

*   *Browser wars*
    (Netscape Navigator vs. Internet Explorer vs. Mosaic)
*   *Platform wars*
    (Java vs. C/C++ vs. PHP vs. Perl vs. ColdFusion)

- *Operating System wars*
  (Windows vs. MacOS vs. Unix vs. Linux)
- *Database wars*
  (Oracle vs. SAP vs. Microsoft)

and other tech squabbling, meant everyone was on the losing side of at least one battle somewhere. It was just as easy to back the wrong side as the right one, and the battlefield kept on shifting month by month. This often meant uneasy alliances with every side, requiring multiple versions for every possible system or configuration out there – an expensive and costly procedure.

A classic case of the how advertising agencies got it so wrong: Most outdoor / TV / print ads were produced by agencies that were designed on Macs that ran Netscape. Whenever they produced an ad featuring a sexy screen grab of a brand's home page – the artwork was based on the rounder, juicier visual language produced on that platform. This disoriented and disillusioned 95% of their audience, whose eyes were accustomed to the flatter, grayer, boxier visual language of PCs/Windows/Internet Explorer. Disconnect. Fail.

7. **Poor delivery:**
   Even when a brand could create a simple, usable online payments system, they often lacked the physical resources or robust fulfillment mechanism to ensure a paid-for product could ship within the promised time. For two Christmases in a row, Toys-R-Us.com failed to have their back-end shipment system functioning, delivering virtual lumps of coal to their disgruntled customers.

8. **Advertising as only revenue source.**
   In the real world, only the fittest media properties survive. TV and radio have always relied on a governmentally restricted supply of broadcasting licenses, as well as a geographic oligopoly. Magazines and newspapers less so, but even the best-stocked newsstand only carries at most a few dozen titles. In publishing, it only pays to go big or go niche.

"By 1999, competing portals and larger-scale ad-driven web sites numbered in the tens of thousands. All competing for a smaller, more fickle audience than the big four of TV, radio, print, and outdoor. "Not every web site can rely on advertising. You need volume to attract advertisers, and if you need to advertise to get that volume, then your business model is going to eat itself."

Chapter 10: The Rise of the Device

One in five people reach for their phone as a twenty-first century replacement of the post-coital cigarette, according to a recent report from mobile security company LookOut.

One in 10 people check their phones during religious services, another LookOut survey says. "People don't even tend to think about any of this as a breach of etiquette anymore," says Chris Young, executive director of The Protocol School of Washington. "They see their phones as an extension of themselves."

Most of us are, in a word, obsessed. Even those of us in the agency world where Luddites ruled for so long, where creative directors and chief executives had their assistants print out their emails and respond via dictation, now *everyone* is a techno-consumer. Grandmothers, two-year-olds, jaded account managers, clients, and targeted audiences alike have all taken to the screens as if they have always been wirelessly connected to them.

It was a slow ramp up, a bit of a false start in the late 1990s, and then steadily the promise of the 21st century began to be fulfilled as consumer electronic innovators like Apple, Samsung, Sony, Nokia, and even Microsoft gave rise to a host of other ingenious brands developing the social tools and platforms to lead us away from the old ways of content consumption to this strange new world of anytime, anywhere, personalized, and customized. These devices were not ahead of their time; they were precisely the right ones at the right moment. The dot.com days (daze) did not live up to their hype, but they did prepare people for the near future.

Today, not even the stodgiest of ad agency executives can ignore what is literally staring them in the face, as they, too, find their hands constantly fumbling to check their Internet-enabled device for the latest *out there*. But are they fumbling too late? While they were willfully disregarding the entire area of new media and the relative pennies it was bringing in (compared to above-the-line: television, radio, print), creating token digital groups to keep up appearances with the Ogilvys and the DDBs, consumers were defying the account directors' predictions by turning what was thought to be a fad among early adopters into the mainstream norm.

If unadventurous agencies weren't going to respond to the opportunities presented by these new and relatively unexplored channels, that wasn't going to be a problem for the less conservative brands. They saw where the people were and what they were enamored of; they just couldn't get a handle on how to capitalize on it. They certainly had no sentimentality about having to keep the work with their advertising partner, so they started hiring their own full-time experts with a network of specialists to help them form a project team they could directly manage, while the agency of record, traditional agency continued to pitch

30-second spots on CBS's *NCIS* and work on style guides; even as platforms like Netflix, Amazon, Hulu, and Google produce their own original, award-winning programming to bring in the eyeballs (and clicks) the way agencies used to with soap operas and game shows.

It was easy for agency executives to ignore technology when the core demographics they deal with most hadn't even heard of whatever it was the digital geeks were up to. But when everyone went on Facebook and LinkedIn and then began monkeying with Twitter and Instagram, there was no overlooking it, and the ad execs had two choices: one) to continue to be nonplussed by these areas in which they had no experience or two) embrace them.

↬

Steffan Postaer, "If you look at the kids and their opinions that they look at TV commercials with scorn and ridicule and they want to make apps, I would argue that the paradigm shift happened already. I don't think anybody says TV is king anymore. When strategies all feel like tactics instead of being driven by one big idea, and then when people tell me that one big idea's an old-fashioned construct, that bugs me and I don't have a ton of patience mostly because my strongest skill is coming up with big dumb ideas like *Curiously Strong Mints*. I don't want to think the job isn't about a big idea and that it can be manifested in all these other channels. I don't want to think that.

"It's been a while since I heard attitude like, 'I'm a TV guy, and TV is what matters.' If you go to BBDO, you might get some serious pockets of that sort of mindset. But, in general, if you're making films, it's a thrill whether they appear on some microsite or YouTube or TV or some kind of link off a QR code. However you receive it. Making the film is as joyful an experience as ever.

"The arrogance is thinking, 'My commercial's going to be seen by millions.' I still think copywriters and art directors go into every film they make just believing it had a chance to go viral and therefore achieve the same kind notoriety as a TV commercial. In some ways, I don't think many people watch real TV. I don't – other than *The Walking Dead* and football games, I don't remember the last time I watched TV, and if I want to watch *30 Rock* or something, I just click onto my computer and watch a few episodes in a row. That's what everybody does.

"Does anybody sit there and make popcorn and watch *New Girl* at 9:00 p.m. on Tuesdays? No. Everybody watches it whenever they want. I don't know anyone who would still say, 'I make TV commercials, and that's the only thing I do.' I don't think anybody who does is going to make it.

"The TV ratings are not still up. They're *relatively* still up. But when you have 300 channels instead of seven, you're not going to use the same share. It's about nuance, and to have a breathtaking film appear on a show that gets a million viewers is always going to be a thrill. In the past, the show might have had 30 million viewers, so it's still thrilling, and the average creative doesn't think about the numbers or make a class distinction because of it. TV isn't going away, but it's being controlled in such a fashion where you don't have to watch commercials to see it.

"I love *30 Rock* and *The Simpsons.* I watch those shows now whenever I want to, and I stare at the little pre-roll commercials before they play; everything adapts and finds its place. Most TV commercials I've seen have been in a small box on my laptop while I've been waiting to get to the content that I've clicked to and, in a weird way, that's exactly like waiting for CBS to do its flight of commercials so I could watch *The Brady Bunch.* Nothing's changed."

⤺

Brad Berens, "The problem with media properties right now is that they're built for scale, and scale is going away. That's why any magazine subscription you want (with only a handful of exceptions) is probably ten dollars a year. They had the great hope that tablets were going to save them, but it's not working, and tablets are only a temporary device right now, anyway. So, rebuilding the whole company around tablets is a mistake. The race to commodification is always going to be a big problem for agencies and media companies. The digital media folks are also in trouble because unless they can convince people that their product is so unusual that it's worth paying for, then a lot of people are going to be saying 'Alright. I'll just go elsewhere.'

"You know *The New York Times* is involved in this longitudinal experiment at the moment saying 'After 20 articles a month, we're going to make you pay.' The problem with this is it's really easy to game the system because you simply go to a different browser [and you get another 20 articles]. What they are hoping for is that eventually they'll prove their value. Kind of like the

NPR strategy where they guilt people into subscribing by saying, 'You listen to *All Things Considered* every night. You should cough up ten dollars a month in order to keep us in business.' It's not all that compelling, but the real issue is more that if *The New York Times* goes away, if all of the newspapers and the news sites go away, what are the people on *The Huffington Post* going to be blogging about?"

~

Brian Solis, "What I study is how disruptive technology is impacting customer behavior and then how that, in turn, affects businesses in every aspect of it from sales and innovation to service, marketing, etc. Social media is one of those disruptive channels, but one of the biggest misconceptions of social media is that it is a solution for more effective advertising and more effective marketing in general when, in fact, it is one of its greatest traps. It is something that is underestimated by advertisers and marketers, in general, as simply a new channel to do the same old push, dance, and switcheroo. They try to link social media to traditional advertising as a way of bringing in a lie to be part of the conversation, when in fact there's really no aspect of the conversation involved with this at all. It's just merely marketing guised as social.

"With advertisers, it's how they begin. How the whole process works. How they sell, and how they make money. It's all based on an idea, and that idea is based on a pitch when an RFP [request for proposal] is put into place. Agencies commit and they pitch their best idea based on what that campaign goal is. So already you're starting off from the wrong position. For example, if something is driven as a campaign, that means it's a facet of the bigger movements of the organization or the brand. It's finite. It could be product launch, it could be an event, or it could be a season. We're already looking at a sliver of customer engagement. And when an agency or an advertiser or creative professional is given that task, it is now less about an overall strategy for the organization, the brand, and the customer relationship and more about 'What is that story we are going to tell for this instant?' and 'How can we link all the media properties together so that we can bill our clients and make our percentages back in terms of media buying?'

"It's just the model of the business as it exists. It's very difficult to look at a continuum when you're literally trained from the outset to have a campaign mindset because some campaigns *are* brilliant. They *do* involve story-telling. They *do* evoke imagination. Some of them will make you cry and make you laugh, and it's still an art form that's very much valuable today. But when you look at how they integrate it with mobile and television and wherever else these things might try to look integrated, you start to see that there isn't a greater view for the way that a new customer aligns with the brand for the long term. That's now out of the advertising agency's control. That's out of the creative professional's control."

⌒

Dave Whittle, "The most obvious dramatic change with audiences is their access to the Internet with a mobile device... you've got a whole generation who knows nothing different. For them, all of this is normal. That is driving the market, and then they become these amazing advocates and evangelists.

"The relevance is really personal. There are so many people who have never and will never have a laptop or a desktop computer. They will never know anything but desktop computing. We're coming to this age of relevance: a marketer's nirvana, where we should be sending fewer, more targeted messages into a market. We don't have any excuses not to because we have all this data. In this new Age of Relevance, it's going to be a really interesting time to be in marketing and will mean that economic and time wastage – which is currently *massive* – will be cut back. If you think about it, the nirvana is that marketing will become so relevant, it becomes a service.

"People talk about advertising as an interruption, but what if marketing was so relevant it became helpful? That's where we will end up one day. It's just a matter of how much time that takes to transition operationally and culturally – because the technology is already here. The question is, 'How long will it take for consumers to build that expectation?' To have an expectation that a brand doesn't have an excuse to send them an irrelevant message."

⌒

Diane McKinnon, "Not that television isn't still a meaningful part of the mix, but it's the multiple screen, the three-screen life: the phone, the laptop or tablet – and then the TV. For people under, say, 30 years old, the

TV screen is only enabled by the computer screen. There's no appointment television. From a big-agency standpoint, that has got to be the most massive shift, because it changes the media equation. Whether the channels are digital or not, given the multichannel nature of our business, is the implied consumer choice of how you now can absorb and consume information and advertising. *That* is what the shift is. People are very willing to consume advertising in a lot of different forms. It's not that people don't want ads, it's that they consume them in different ways."

ᔦ

Neil Leslie, "The Internet was already in existence when I began my career, so my day is much the same as it was. What I have noticed is that I use my TV to access the net via my iMac and stopped watching terrestrial TV completely about two years ago. I also find that I'm often online when I'm watching movies at home, so my attention is almost always divided. And of course, I have a smartphone on me at all times, so that I can get online as and when I need to.

"I can only assume I'm not the only person watching three screens at once. Which means that our work has to be more arresting than ever before."

ᔦ

Steve Street, Creative Director of The VIA Agency in Portland, Maine and former Senior Creative for Ogilvy Sydney, "I know when I watch telly, I'm flanked by a smartphone and a tablet. As soon as an ad break hits, I'm reaching for one of those devices quicker than a gunslinger at 20 paces. That's if I can hold out for the ad breaks. Content consumption habits have definitely evolved, granting audiences greater control. What this means for us advertisers is that we better be on point. We better be entertaining, meaningful, and relevant, or people will redirect their attention to something that is. Who can blame them? For too long, we've been peppering them with crap.

"Now, couple this with the growing expectation that brands should offer meaningful experiences instead of simply shouting advertising slogans, and you've got a playing field for which a totally new playbook is required. How do we engage people and keep them engaged across multiple platforms at the same time? What can a TV commercial trigger on my smartphone or on my tablet, and where will it take me once I embark on this journey? Will it unlock an offer? Will it unlock exclusive content? Will it unlock both? Will I be connected to other adventurous souls, who, like me, dared to be guided by Brand X to some unknown destination? These are all questions that can possess some bloody exciting outcomes... if they're considered in the first place.

"Then there is the crowdsourcing model, where control is deliberately given to an audience to guide, shape, and/or create a particular outcome. A powerful approach if executed well.

"A current and ingenious example of this is what Beck did for the release of his latest album. Twenty songs, never before recorded or released, unveiled as sheet music only. Yep, sheet music. By providing the basic foundations, Beck is essentially inviting the public to embrace, interpret, and compose his new album. There is no right or wrong approach or genre for that matter. It's open for interpretation. You want a spoons solo on track three? Fire up GarageBand and head straight for the kitchen drawer. More cowbell? Get Gene Frenkle on the blower.

"You can bet your sweet arse that people will be sharing their creations. Not just with Beck, but with the world. Will we see incredible unsigned talent emerge? I'm sure. Will established artists get in on the act? I'd like to think so. Will Beck ultimately collaborate with the people behind his favorite song interpretations? That would be good, wouldn't it? This is an idea that has not only engaged Beck's fan base, it has empowered them, and many others who may not have listened to Beck previously, to embark on a musical journey of discovery. It sounds magical because it is."

⌒

Kult3D's Business Director and former Client Services Director for M&C Saatchi, Natarajan Vytheswaran, "I laughed when I first heard about Facebook. I said, 'Who will be stupid enough to tell their friends what they are doing at every moment of the day?' Guess who is not laughing now? The fact that smartphone technology has the ability to feed me, entertain me, stimulate me, keep me connected to the world in every shape or form wherever, whenever, it has become the 'can't-do-without' life tool. What excites me most about smartphone technology: I can be an island without actually being an island. Human contact without having to actually make conversation when you don't want to."

⤝

Dave Whittle, "Irrelevance is the enemy of our industry, and it's happening more and more and more despite the revolution in technology. And tremendous media fragmentation means that there are more messages to be irrelevant [mostly thanks to the devices we carry around]. Because of this, there has never been a time of greater waste in our industry. Advertising would have to be one of the most inefficient industries in the world."

⤝

Paul Kwong, "I ride the train home right now and everyone has some kind of digital medium in their hands. Whether they're texting, writing emails, listening to something, reading, or watching a movie or whatever... each one is holding some kind of digital device.

"I'm happy that I can watch ESPN anywhere my laptop goes. I'm sure some are the same with their iPhones, which I don't have. Everything is pretty instantaneous now. What's the name of that restaurant on Denman Street in Vancouver that has handmade noodles? Well, you can get that answer. Who played what part in that one movie for the directors that did *Fargo*? You can find that out in an instant. Remember that beach in Hawaii we vacationed at? You've got photos of the whole trip in your pocket. Even figuring out what the name of the font that's being used in something is instantaneous. Audiences have changed in that they are exposed to more. Ideas now have a tougher time surprising them.

"Audiences have changed tremendously in recent years. They are harder than ever before to reach en masse. They are constantly distracted, hyper-informed, and increasingly skeptical of advertising in all its forms. From what I can tell, they'd rather listen to and trust one another when it comes to deciding what products and services to buy. I'm still not entirely sure if the rise of social media is feeding off or fueling this."

⤝

Thierry Halbroth, "In this world, if you can't see through the phonies, maybe you should quit your job. It comes down to there being brilliant and intelligent people who are able to scam others into believing something they don't understand. A lot of the clients don't understand it, so if you can walk the talk, then it's great. Because you actually drum your clients into believing whatever you want. Social media, for me, it's how you want to understand it. It's a bridge between human insights and technology. It's human behavior at its very best. Psychologists make very good social media experts, I'm pretty sure."

⌐

Bob Hoffman, "The question is, what works and what doesn't work? What pays out and what doesn't pay out? We know that for the most part Google and search are probably the most effective uses of online dollars. What comes after that, I don't think anyone knows. I really don't think anyone knows. Is it display? Is it content? Is it social media? Is it Facebook? What is it? I don't know what the answer is. Look, if you're a small direct marketer, then Facebook can pay off for you and probably display banner ads can, too. But if you're a major marketer, which of these modes work? I don't think anyone really knows. I don't.

"I don't believe people are looking for entertainment and amusement from Campbell Soup. They're looking for good soup, no other reason. I don't believe they're interested in Campbell Soup's content as far as online media does. I don't think they want to have a conversation about the brand. There's plenty of entertainment in the world. There are a thousand TV channels. There're a zillion entertainment web sites. There're movies. I don't think people really care much for entertainment or utility from marketers. What they want from marketers are a good product, a good service, and a good price. That's what they want and a fair deal.

"The idea that marketers need to be in the entertainment business or provide utility other than a good bowl of soup is specious. I haven't seen evidence of it. Every now and then something breaks through, something that's terrifically entertaining or terrifically utilitarian will break through. That's one in 10,000. The 9,999 other marketers who're trying it are getting nowhere. I am not fully bought on it. I have not yet been convinced that the strategy of providing those things online to individuals is necessarily the most effective way to spend marketing dollars.

"The idea that social media is some kind of magical thing... it's like having a business card now. It's a cost of doing business. It's like having a web site. One in 1,000 web sites really makes a difference. One in 1,000 social media programs really makes a difference to the business. It's like having a sign on the door. You got to have it. But if you think that that's going to make you successful, you're losing your mind. There's nothing wrong with repackaging something and a new way to deliver, a new way to find – that's fine. But don't bullshit about what it is. Don't pretend it's something that it's not."

⌐

Jim Speelmon, "It's people who get it in the first place; people who become so excited about social media. It's like a first date how I'm excited about social networking. Social networking was first started to be researched in the '50s, for god's sake. It's nothing new. It's just the tools that people use to do it have changed. It doesn't matter what they are. Whether it's Facebook or Twitter or Tumblr or Flickr or whatever the hell it is, if you just use it as a tactic, then that's what it is. It is just another channel to put into your media plan. Without having some kind of coherent strategy for how it applies to your business, it will never be anything more than that.

"I always think it's funny when people say, 'We're going to pilot social media.' How do you pilot relationship building? Twitter, YouTube, all of those things, I really don't consider them any different from broadcast media in regards to how people are approaching the ads. When you go out on Friday night and you don't want to invite that one person, he always comes and does nothing but talk about himself. It's boring! You hem and haw and finally say, 'You can come along.' Like an ax, that's how digital is being used even today. In Asia, it's getting worse and it's, 'Please help me tell my story,' without any kind of, 'Let me get some feedback from you so I can fine tune my story.' Some people do it better than others, but in general I would have to say that digital is still very average."

⌐

Steve Hall, "You have the rise of different kinds of stars now. Social media hit the map five years ago, and now you have Scott Monty who's over at Ford doing an amazing job in that world. We're all focused on what's happening in social, but creativity fuels what's happening in social media as well. Monty said that social media is not a campaign, it's a commitment and really marketing should be a commitment, not a campaign. For a very long time, marketing consisted of several campaigns over time. We would flight them and then we would see what worked and we would retool. But still, there was this mentality of, 'We're going to do this really cool thing so that we can up sales this month.' That's very different from, 'We're going to do these really cool things so that this company will become successful and stay successful forever.' There should be more thought given to what can be done to guarantee that we'll have a 3% increase in sales every single month. Of course, that can't go on forever. But it should be a goal."

⤺

Andy Flemming, "How we will be consuming information in the next 5 to 10 years and how we can actively participate in this conversation is a scary thing, it's a good thing, but at the end of the day, I share a belief with Jeff Goodby: the people are suckers for stories and you should start there. It's good you can engage with someone very quickly. You can tell a story that they visually respond to. Either they can find it funny or find it sad or find it shocking. As an agency, sometimes we think people are absolutely desperate to hear what we want them to. We need to engage with them, we need to grab their attention, and they need to be motivated enough to actually follow the story through. It sounds old fashioned, but you can do that a hell of a lot quicker with something like Old Spice or *The Three Little Pigs*, which get the message across in a very short period of time."

⤺

Shane Ginsberg, President of EVB, former Senior VP of Corporate Development for Organic and former Managing Director of AKQA San Francisco, "In the last ten years, can you give one example of an agency that's really driven a change in consumer behavior? The whole agency business is always predicated on a kind of magical insight into what a consumer would do, so that they could position a brand or product and come to them at the right time. There was this ability to see just a little bit into the future. That's changed pretty dramatically because a large part of it now is not necessarily about media consumption, but rather about consumer views and behavior. It's different. I'm not consuming media on my smartphone, I'm using my phone."

~

Brien A. Daniels, Business & Planning Director for The Blood Group in Singapore and former Heineken Group Head for Bates Advertising, "The future of marketing and advertising will shift from a push to a pull approach. As more and more consumers evolve to a 'whatever I want, whenever I want, and wherever I want' frame of mind, brands that intrude or push their products and services to consumers do so at a great risk. Consumers dictate how they would like to interact with brands, and what was once tolerated will be looked upon unfavorably.

"Brands that invite or pull the consumer into the conversation clearly state their beliefs and purpose and do so in an engaging manner will get ahead of the game. You could call this shift 'advertising in reverse,' where it will no longer be about features, benefits, and the USP, but about brand values translated into a brand story that is in turn delivered in the form of unique experiences and content."

~

JWT Singapore's Chief Creative Officer, Valerie Cheng, "What's been lost in the explosion of technology has been brand-sensitive ideas. Technology is what you apply to an idea to bring it to life; therefore, everything must start with an idea. Many creatives and clients start from a wrong place when they just want to create the next app. I always begin by asking:

1. Who are you targeting?
2. Is there an insight about your audience?
3. How can this insight spark an idea?

"Only then will you explore which technology or media is most appropriate and best for the idea."

↜

Tobias Wilson, "Brands are terrified of social media because they can lose face very quickly. It's obviously the most explosive medium out there. Digital ad spend in Singapore is 8% of annual marketing budgets. Social is a very small percentage of that. They are a lot more scared of taking bigger risks on the off chance that they might fail or cause the company to lose face, get terminated and have to go and find a new job and be 'that person' that fucked up that social media campaign for that brand. Digital is so way behind over here, but the flip side is that when it works here, it *really* works as it's such a tech-savvy market.

"The thing is, there's no data around it, or there is not enough data around it as far as engagement nibbles and what people are spending time on, how they're spending and marketing magazines have just regular, daily email. They've only now stopped putting digital over in the corner and having your mainstream front and center. It's only just starting to be recognized from that perspective. You're talking Internet penetration of 70-80% and from a Social perspective, Singapore is the second most engaged social audience in the world."

↜

Global Vice President of Marketing for Vans and Dell's former Executive Director, Consumer and Small Office Marketing, North America, Fara Howard, "I think the premise of using YouTube and Facebook and Twitter and other social forums to get perspective on input is brilliant. We should be doing it more. I think that companies and marketers are daunted by how powerful the social ecosystem is here now, it's happening, you should probably embrace it. It's free."

↜

Barry Wong, "The new 'app-based culture' certainly is an exciting one, especially since I live an extremely digital lifestyle. I've always used technology to my advantage to make my life easier. I tried to find ways to articulate what that was, but didn't have a single word to sum it up. Then in 2004, I stumbled upon an article that encapsulated it for me beautifully – *utility*. Yes, digital and technology is about providing utility – doing something for the consumers and making their lives better.

"As a consumer myself, I could clearly see the relationship between the consumer and digital technology. I understood it, and the next task was to have clients understand that relationship as well. It was not an easy journey trying to educate them. Clients clung to the broadcast bandwagon, didn't want to do anything for their consumers, and stood firm that they only needed to communicate how good they were. That was 2006. Up 'til this day, there are still brands and clients that still believe in the single-direction broadcast methodology rather than making their consumers' lives better through the offering of a brand utility.

"Will brands ever realize that in this ever-changing digital world, they need to step up and become enablers instead of remaining in their cocoons? Can brands cross the chasm? I really don't know. But I am consoled that there are many like-minded people out there with the belief that true brands close gaps in people's lives, making them easier and more convenient through the smart application of technology."

⌒

Leo Burnett's Regional Director of Social on the Samsung account, Suresh Ramaswamy, "It's noisy online. With more people online and connected to each other, we are chatty beyond our immediate circles. We share more. Sometimes over share. The cacophony of chatter online can make a fish market seem like a library.

"Amidst the chatter, Brands could do well by promoting themselves less like they do with broadcast media. Inane chatter doesn't cut it. Focussing on creating a feature, content, offer, experience worthy of sharing works better.

"It's hard. Needs money, talent and commitment. The upside side for brands – getting it right and winning over an individual equates to being in a position to influence their network."

⌒

Clara Lee, "The audience has definitely changed since the '90s when I started my first job in an advertising agency. The consumer of today is empowered to broadcast his or her point of view at the click of a button. He or she has a much greater ability to influence and shape the point of view of others. In fact, a successful marketer of today *must* find out who are the most influential spokespersons in their business within the digital space (we call them key voices), create meaningful contact and interaction with them, and make sure they are always engaged so they will provide meaningful word of mouth for the brand and its activities.

"Companies and governments that have yet to grasp this gnash their teeth and quiver at the bad reviews or musings of these key voices while those who have mastered the art of engaging them revel in the positive vibes they generate."

〜

Tim Leake, "Audiences have changed in three fundamental ways:

1. **We are informed.** Knowledge used to be scarce and expensive, but now it's plentiful and free. It's ridiculously easy for us to learn nearly everything worth knowing about your product before they make a decision to buy. Chances are that information is not coming from a TV ad. The TV ad is mainly a stimulus to put an idea on their radar, and then they'll turn to the Internet to learn 'the truth.'

2. **We've developed an 'on-demand' mindset.** We used to be passive about receiving information. We watched TV shows when they were on. We experienced ads when we were subjected to them. We saw lectures whenever the speaker scheduled them, but everything is on our terms now. We can watch a lecture or take a class online, whenever it's convenient for us. We can tune out, skip, or block advertising we don't care about. We can engage in content whenever we like.

3. **Our voices have become amplified.** We've always been able to yell at the TV or curse an ugly outdoor board as we drove past in our car, but nobody else could hear us. Now it's easy to put our opinions out where anyone in the world can see them. (For better or worse, it's also easier than ever for uninformed people to find other uninformed people who share their uninformed opinions.)

"The audience isn't 'in control' any more than marketers are. What's changed is that everyone has a voice now. Everyone has the power to influence, but nobody's actually in control. That's scary as hell to an industry that desperately wants to continue to be able to control the message. Those days are gone. If we're lucky, we *might* be able to wrangle the message a bit. But the audience now has the power to wrangle it, too.

"I suppose this is bad for us as marketers because we used to have more power. But it's good for us as a society because it raises the bar of accountability and transparency. It's very difficult for brands to lie now since it's so easy for a lie to be exposed. Products and services have to be as good as we make them seem now or they'll fail. It's an old advertising truth that 'nothing kills a bad product faster than good advertising.' Still true. Now it just happens even faster."

Chapter 11: When Digital Did Matter

Brands used to be able to control their message because the agencies arranged it that way on their behalf. Of course, it didn't hurt that there were only so many major outlets through which it could be received. In the early days in the United States, there were only four national radio networks, and two of them were owned by the same company, NBC (until one decided to run off and become ABC). Even that small number began to fall when television broke through in the 1950s with only three commercial broadcast networks, making radio less relevant instead of turning it into an amplifier. Newspapers, magazines, billboards (Burma-Shave, anyone?), there really weren't many options compared to the endless channels available to brands today through new media technology—a thought that should send a thrilling chill up the spines of creative marketers. Imagine! You can reach people in so many new and fascinating ways, which was especially true back in the mid-90s when they began to appear. At every turn was an opportunity to actually invent a new tactic, strategy, or platform where none had existed before.

A reluctance to experiment with a client's budget is not only understandable, it's admirable. Eschewing, belittling, badmouthing, and walling off a universe of potential effectiveness that is only limited by your own creativity is what we in the business call "baffling." Especially considering the notion that advertising is a leading-edge business that employs types who like to push things, engage with the audience, and excite them. Those people definitely populate the agencies, but for much too long a time, the structures and processes forced segmentation and isolation between the experts responsible for each medium. In many places, those walls are still up, but intense pressure from all sides is causing them to begin to lose their integrity—a condition that is very appropriate.

〜

Craig Mapleston, "The first obstacle to overcome is the term *digital*. Consumers never differentiated ATL from BTL. The ad industry did. Consumers never differentiated digital from traditional. The ad industry did.

"We've created an enormous rod for our own backs and, tragically, we've convinced clients to think this way, too. Once we stop navel gazing and start becoming consumer-centric, channels will only have relevance in a media plan. We need to think the way consumers do and focus on points of engagement opportunities, rather than trying to bundle stuff that only has meaning to the industry.

"Once that is overcome, the rest is a lot more simple. Of course, production is a specific skill, and we'll need specialists to build stuff – TVCs, apps, final artwork, events, but that's always been the case."

⟿

Torrence Boone, "Today, the dialogue is very different, and digital is acknowledged as a core part of the consumer experience. Technology, I would argue, is ahead of our creativity. I don't miss the early digital days, although it was admittedly a heady time. I much prefer the dialogue Google is *now* driving with agencies and advertisers: one centered on brand storytelling and tapping the vast potential of technology to reinvent the way brands connect with consumers experientially.

"I noticed digital becoming more of a player when I was at Digitas in the 2006-2008 timeframe. While we were still very much fighting for budgets and a seat at the table in general, we began to see clients recognize the power of digital in unlocking insights that could drive a deeper brand-engagement dialogue. We started to get more brand-oriented assignments, and the bigger brand dialogue became a jump ball. For the first time, digital agencies could become a brand AOR."

⟿

David Shulman, "I, personally, never understood digital as a siloed activity. The industry we're in created this notion of digital, but users and consumers never had that definition in their minds. You don't go through life thinking, 'Now I'm going to engage digitally. Now I'm going to engage in an analog fashion. I'm now going to engage through a traditional channel.' It's not just the way we think or act. The industry created this idea, this very notion of digital. But it never really happened. There wasn't a year or a month or a date where things became digital. It was more a matter of agencies serving clients. The best agency partners leverage digital to build engaging customer experiences for clients. For others there is a, 'Holy cow, there's this new thing out there. We can build web sites for them. We can create banners.'"

⟿

Andy Greenaway, "I was telling the world about the advent of digital as far back as 2000. The problem with predictions is that they never quite happen as fast as you think, or, on the flip side, they happen much faster than you imagined.

"My predictions back then were scorned by many, and the revolution that is taking place right now has been a long time coming. That said, we have now reached a tipping point, the digital world is going to dominate our industry going forward, and it's going to do that at an accelerated rate. Anyone who thinks otherwise is probably a printosaurus."

⤶

Aden Hepburn, "There's nothing better than seeing the thing that you were interacting with, or clicking on a banner ad, carried over to the next web site you're on reminding you plus now it has a 10% discount. That's genius marketing, and with the way things are, it's actually really, really simple to do. But the impact of this 'retargeting' is like telling the right story. When you do follow them around the Web and you continue to market to that specific demographic, you can evolve the story and continue it. Don't just repeat the same banner everywhere they go. [Digital gives us significant opportunities to be successful if we don't trip over ourselves.]"

⤶

Jeff Cheong, "The introduction of new technologies actually shaped up the [advertising] industry and finally allowed mature creatives to create things for people to use. Technology is useless unless it's being used for the benefit of people – and accessing that usually requires an interface. The UIs that we create for apps these days have to match up [in quality and usability] with mobile giants like Apple and Samsung."

⤶

Angeli Beltran, "Digital was always a very poor sister to advertising. In the early days of digital in the early 2000s, I only had a few clients who were a bit more visionary and a bit more brave and decided to go for it. Like Honda, when they launched an entry-level car. The first thing the client told us was, 'We don't have much budget for this car, so you guys decide where we're going to do, but understand that we don't have money to do any above-the-line advertisements.' They said, 'Let's go digital because it's cheap,' or 'If we're going to try to reach the youth, let's go digital because most of them are online. It's only the young people using the Internet.' Those were those days.

"The car was the Honda Jazz, and they were going to launch in three months. They needed to get people excited about it and reserve cars before then. So they held an expo. The only thing they had at that time was one sample car to show. Just one model, and we had no media budget.

"The vehicles were going to be delivered two months after the show. Our KPI [key performance indicator], our desired result, was to get reservations at that car show. It was going to be, 'Okay, we did it through digital' at a time when Facebook hadn't existed! But we had Friendster and lots of blogs; Multiply was still around and big during that time. We found out through research that previous owners of the Jazz were hardcore advocates. What they would do was they would accessorize their Jazz and bring out their own personalities through them. We picked up those insights and created a web site that allowed people to 'jazz up their Jazz.'

"The idea sounds so common now, but during that time, it was the first in the Philippines. We invited the brand advocates and editors of the car web sites to do 'jazz up their Jazz' online first because they were the opinion leaders, and people listened to them. We invited the editors of the car web sites to try it, write about it, create their own Jazz, and post it in their sites, post it in their Multiply, send it to their friends, etc.

"If you were one of the first 150 or 200 people to do it, you'd get an exclusive invitation to see the new Honda Jazz in the car show. It seems a very simple strategy now, but then it was unheard of. Nobody had ever done anything like that, so the people came.

"We got so many reservations during the launch such that they were able to hit three months of their sales targets on that event alone. Everybody started using that case study. Everybody started to believe in the power of digital and word-of-mouth. It wasn't even called social media then; it was called 'word-of-mouth' marketing. Those were the early days, and it was fun.

"It was very typical to have to take your creative direction from the above-the-line agency and sort of execute it as the below-the-line agency. We would get the idea from the ATL. Some clients would even think that we just needed to take the ATL visuals, put them in a site, and that was it. We had to fight to get them to understand the fact that the medium is interactive. It's not one-way. We pushed for clients to understand that digital is not your brochureware or taking your TV commercial or your magazine ad and sticking it in a web site; so a lot of education needed to take place.

"What was good about the Philippines is that we had a very strong industry association, IMMAP, the Internet and Mobile Marketing association of the Philippines. It was composed of all these digital practitioners, which included agencies, publishers, technology providers, and clients who knew that we needed to come together to push the industry forward. We knew that the only way the industry was going to move in that direction was if the clients were educated enough about digital to understand its benefits and what was going on in digital elsewhere.

"Every year, we still have the huge conference, the IMMAP Summit. We showcase these great case studies, not just from the Philippines, but from overseas. We get clients inspired, and they start doing more digital work and become braver with executions. Much of the development in digital in the Philippines ad industry is driven by this strong association.

"Another aspect of digital is that the number of touch points is increasing and the number of new technologies just gets bigger and bigger every day. You had these new specialties where you've got people coming in saying, 'Hey! We're the SEO specialists,' or 'We are the guys who do mobile apps,' or 'We're the people who can help you with location-based services,' or 'We're your interactive point-of-sale people.' It's impossible to have everything in house.

"Dentsu Möbius was the company I helped set up before I left. The whole idea was we needed to bring clients to appreciate a digital solution not just a touch point. Many of the agencies tend to push a specialization. It's, 'mobile is the answer to everything,' or 'search is the most important aspect of everything.' We know that's not true.

"What we did at Möbius was to look at key areas of what a complete solution can look like; so we look at it as a customer journey. The idea was to go through paid, owned, and earned media opportunities to be able to help clients move customers. From attracting them to paid media, bringing them to their owned media, and being able to capture information about them so that we were communicating with them on a regular basis, which is CRM. We could also help customers have a good experience so that they would want to share the information.

"It was always within a framework of, 'How are we going to get the customer to move seamlessly through this journey?' We had the core expertise in-house, but there were still aspects such as application development where we knew there was someone in the Philippines who could do it a lot better than we could and a lot cheaper, too. We partnered with them on web site development doing the back-end solutions: we did the front end, we did the design, we did the user experience, but for the actual development, we had our partner.

"Anything that allowed us to deliver core solutions we did have in-house, and we did have partnerships for other services because the scope was just so broad and so deep. We couldn't possibly cover everything. We didn't keep programmers in-house. We had maybe a couple who could help us with the HTML5, but for the hardcore programming, we would have preferred partners who we would work with. What we would have are about five or six partners, each one varying in their capabilities and also depending upon the complexity of the client's requirements.

"We had suppliers who could do really, *really* good, very flashy, and very engaging web sites to multi-country corporate sites with a CRM capability. It varies. I had a person who was in charge of technology, and part of his role was to have a roster of partners who we could work with us on varying project sizes, technical requirements, and budgets.

"We forged relationships with the Chief Technology Officer. Our head of technology worked with most of them in the past because he came from both a telco and a digital background. We met during events like the ad:tech and iMedia Summits. A lot of networking goes on here in Singapore. We also had Web Wednesday when those of us in the industry would gather at a bar each week and exchange war stories.

"You really needed to have a good roster of and understanding of the range of capabilities that each one had so that you could bring the best-of-breed solutions to the client, based on the size of the requirement and the budget that they had and the complexity of the technical requirement. There were several ways to find them, so we had those that were based in Singapore, we had some based in Thailand, [some] in the Philippines, [some in] India. It was and is a global economy.

"For me, digital is the best platform because it has no borders. We also had technical partners who were coming from Sweden and some worked with our agencies in Germany. For us, it was whatever the client needed and required – we should have those capabilities, if not in-house, then within our roster of partners.

"Dentsu knew that they needed to improve their digital capabilities in ASEAN. The clients were asking for it, and in some places we were losing some business to competitors because we simply didn't have the capabilities to service them. My role was to raise the level of digital capability and also help develop the digital business. It was a combination of hiring the right people and training the organization. We did hold a lot of training sessions to improve the capabilities of the current staff. It wasn't a bit difficult... it was *very* difficult! It was very difficult because of the structure that Dentsu had then, which was each agency was run on its own. While I was working on a regional level, I was part of Dentsu Asia, so I only had a small part of the budget of Dentsu Asia, which was a contribution from the different agencies.

"While digital was said to be one of the priorities, there were all the other priorities that Dentsu Asia to allocate budget to. I had to focus my small funds on what would help raise the capabilities little by little rather than drive a radical change. The difficulty I also encountered was many of the heads of agencies, while they had the willingness to do digital (they knew how important it was), it was very difficult for a traditional advertising agency head to embrace it; digital was alien to them.

"Digital capabilities then also require very expensive resources to build. The people required are specialists, there were a few good ones, so their asking salaries were not within the same range as traditional agency staff. You've got to spend when getting a digital team. As a traditional advertising agency head, you really have no idea how to run it, but your clients need it. At the same time, at the end of the year, you are evaluated by your P&L, and the largest contributor to the budget – your revenue – is still advertising. Digital's contribution was only 1-2%, and then the costs were also much higher. So as a traditional agency head, it was very difficult to really invest the right resources on digital.

"That was the challenge that I faced when I came in, and I had to go through each and every head of agency to really help them understand where the potential was. The way I talked about it was, 'We know that this is where the future will be. Secondly, you don't have to hire everybody in-house; we're assembling some partners who you can work with on preferential rates so you can provide those services without having to hire everybody today.' Plus at the same time showing them the numbers where the digital business of the client was going.

"Digital business with our clients was going to other agencies so I would say to them, 'If they can enter the back door (digital), they might take the whole kitchen and the living room, too. We better close that door by being able to provide these services, too.' Slowly, but surely, we were able to get them in that mindset and that's when the digital business started to grow. It wasn't growing at the pace that it should have, though, because the funding was a bit low because it was a small share of Dentsu Asia's budget.

"What Dentsu did was to spin out the Dentsu Asia digital division into an independent agency, which was given the responsibility to grow the digital business Dentsu Möbius was fully funded and was independent: it could run on its own. It could get its own clients outside of the Dentsu roster.

"We knew that the best way to penetrate new accounts or accounts that were non-Japanese was through digital because everywhere in the world, the big accounts had a global AOR agency. Normally, in the region clients wouldn't have a digital AOR, so that was the back door we could enter to penetrate these businesses. It was important for Dentsu to diversify its client base because of its huge dependency on Japanese accounts.

"When Tokyo's economy gets sick, Dentsu will also not do well. One of the strategies to diversify the client base was to set up Dentsu Möbius to penetrate these new accounts, and before I left, we had done quite well in that area: we were able to win, for example, Marina Bay Sands in Singapore. We won business through our digital unit and because of our good relationship, we pitched the traditional media business and we won that as well. We won the Apple online store business. Normally, it was Dentsu Japan that would give Dentsu Asia new business, but this time Dentsu Asia was able to give Dentsu Japan business, so it was doing really quite well. We won Kraft (now Mondelez), and we opened up business with P&G. The strategy was working.

"We weren't planning to go head on with the Goliaths of this world, which have an army of people just in search alone, for example. No, where we saw the opportunity was the fact that clients would work with so many different digital agencies. They would work with someone on search, someone on social, and then they had their creative agency: it was all so fragmented.

"At the end of the day, marketing clients don't just do digital, they worry about many other things like distribution, sales, etc, so the proposition that we delivered was because everything was in-house, they only needed to talk to us and we would look after their business from a results point of view rather than a channel point of view. Clients are willing to pay if they see the value that you deliver. Because we led with strategy and desired results, the clients saw the value."

~

Jeffrey Dachis, "I don't believe digital was the catalyst for the entire advertising industry changing for the worse. Let me just say that I think that the evolution that's occurring within ad agencies anyway is independent of any huge catalyst. But suddenly in the mid-'90s, along comes this thing called digital and, in essence, they didn't know this then, but you started to see, first of all, the platform independence where you could create an idea and look at distributing that idea across multiple platforms. The Web being one of them and then mobile, of course, being another – and then PCs and TVs and all of these different screens. The media business used to be so highly fragmented. You'd buy a magazine, you'd buy print, you'd buy television, you'd buy radio, you'd buy cable, and they all had their own departments. They all had their own production and distribution means.

"You have to have people who were experts at creating cable television slot ads versus people who were experts at creating print ads. With digital, you leveled the playing field where production and distribution sort of got to be homogeneous. Not necessarily 100%, but you started to see the idea of the fully integrated campaign. You also started to see something that pushed brand building further down the purchase-intent funnel.

"Instead of building pre-purchase intent in digital, you're really building purchase intent and purchase or post-purchase intent. After 20 years in digital, it is excellent at finding something once you know you want to buy it.

It can facilitate mood. As a facilitator, you can search for something, and most of the time what you're looking for, you can find right away. You can click on it and in a matter of seconds buy the thing you were looking for. Fulfillment is a key component.

"On the other hand, digital has really sucked at brand building. I'll just say banner ads suck. You know, building brands in digital is almost impossible because nobody is really thinking about the considerations set, or they're not in this tradition to be influenced at the pre-purchase stage in digital. The formats are bad. The environment in which you're receiving brand-based messages in digital is crappy. I believe immersive product demonstrations are outside of the realm of pre-purchase intent.

"Brand building has, from an advertising agency mix perspective, thrived in the traditional agency because I don't think digital has really undermined in any way, shape, or form the ability to express the branded pre-purchase intent big idea, if you will, that advertising agencies are so good at.

"Twenty years ago when we started Razorfish, I thought for sure, in a matter of like two years or three years, that our advertising would move online and that you'd have this rich-media environment where people were interacting with brands and interacting with messages online and that TV, in fact, would dramatically shift right away. That's the way brands got built on TV and would shift right away. But that didn't happen."

⮌

Nimal Gunewardena, "We saw digital as another opportunity for a revenue stream and an essential area where we needed to maintain our credibility and leadership as an IMC [integrated marketing communications agency]. We had been doing bits and pieces, but a year ago, we set up a small expert team to drive it. We've had to learn and experiment. We're determined to take it to the next level and integrate it into the heads of everyone in the agency team and our overall campaign strategy planning.

"We're working on finding a framework that will do that. We realize that we will have to take clients along, weaning them from their ingrained habits with traditional paid media and overcome their diffidence with this new media. We've learned to be evangelists."

⮌

Ken Mandel, "I first noticed digital in 1994 – not so much in the context of advertising, but in a much wider context of what digital could be. I believe to this day that was the healthiest way to be exposed to digital because I always knew from the get go, it was way bigger than just 'digital marketing.' I was excited, but in the early days, especially after the dot.com crash, I became exhausted by the constant evangelizing. I felt like a Jehovah's Witness fundraiser: as you approached a home, the lights suddenly went out on the porch, the kids were shushed, and the dog muffled. It was like the dark ages and was a very hard slog until about 2004/5 when the age of enlightenment came upon us: yes, Web 2.0, when the promise of the technology caught up with the reality of what it could offer and social media began to catch fire."

⤸

Harish Vasudevan, "Digital accelerated a lot of this stuff and in many ways removed the mystery around a lot that the agencies were doing and made everything a little more transparent. Suddenly, clients felt that they were able to reach out to their consumers, and, of course, a whole different world has emerged.

"Complications of digital have emerged, but at least they get the sense that they were able to reach out to consumers, talk to them, put messaging in front of them without having to go through a whole complicated process of briefing an agency and waiting for six months or something to come back, which they didn't like, and then go back again. So digital, in many ways, opened marketers' eyes, and because many of them have burned their fingers by going down wrong paths, at least they've been able to understand a little more about how things work in the marketplace and are able to get feedback much faster than they would have in the old world.

"Maybe we would have gotten here if digital wasn't around, but digital has hastened the pace of change, and that has put pressure on the holding companies to pass at proving value because, using the old favorite tale of when two guys in a garage are able to do it faster (and with measurable results) than the big holding companies, they need to find a way to justify the millions of dollars of fees. Digital definitely has accelerated it."

⤸

Chris Kyme, "I first became aware of digital in the latter half of the '90s, but it wasn't scary at all. You just took it as something else you needed to get your head around in order to make it work for your clients. It's exciting. It opens up all sorts of new possibilities and adds to the mix of what you can get up to.

"Having said that, I've never really been particularly turned on doing digital work as I always have loved and still do love film. If that film is designed for digital media, then fine. I don't care because it's the product itself that I get excited about, not the media. I'm not crazy about integrated viral work myself, but that's just me. It's brilliant how the world's been opened up by it.

"I have never felt that digital was just a fad. If you keep evolving in this industry and embracing the new. you are never under threat. You're only under threat if you're not any good."

∽

Åsk Wäppling, "Digital is a really hot thing to do, at least it was five years ago because it was easier for young creatives to get a bite out of some production and for film. You can't get close to it in certain big agencies when you're new, but if you were in a digital department somewhere, yeah, boom, you've got six films going. Basically, digital is the fresh blood in the dying body part. Because digital isn't just the films on the Web. Not many people watch the films on the Web.

"Remember when Fallon's *BMW Films* came out? They put Madonna in one of them and they were like these long-ass films? Half of the world went to watch them, and it was because it was the first time it had been done. It wasn't because they were *BMW Films*; it wasn't because Madonna was in one. It was because it was the first time it was done and maybe the combination of those. Now you're doing the same thing for AT&T and nobody's watching that shit. We don't have time. You have to watch how the user is using the media. How they are consuming the media. It evolves constantly, and it evolves very fast.

"They should take a step back and go back to the '60s again or the '70s when it was, 'Okay, we have a base problem. We have a brand, but how do people talk about brands today?' They say brands have a soul, that brands have a personality. But brands don't have a soul, and they don't have a personality. They have a goal. When the goal is usually sell *x* more to *y*, and this is what we're going to figure out. Where *y* is, why is *y* there, and how do we talk to *y* in the space – and that's where you have to start. You can't start with, 'Oh my god, social media is the hottest shit!' But that's where they are. They sort of get distracted by all these shiny things. They forget where they are. They always have to start with themselves, and that's where agencies have to start, too.

"We have to look at what we're doing. We're solving a problem for a brand. The brand probably doesn't even know what their problem is. They probably have a marketing director that reads way too much *Ad Age*. He's going to say 'Snapchat is the best thing ever!' I got a brief once in the '90s where they had asked me for a double-page spread for a soft drink that was going to be sold to skaters between 16-23 in the national newspaper.

"Okay skater kids between 16-23 do not read the national newspaper. As much as I would love to do it over a page spread, they don't read this newspaper. We have a problem there, and that's how the briefs always arrived to me, and that's how the briefs are arriving today. They're saying 'Oh my god, you have to talk to this 40-year-old on Snapchat.' Oh god! Go away. That's not going to happen."

↜

George Tannenbaum, "I recognized the power of digital relatively early on because I was at Ogilvy on IBM and IBM is not a consumer products company. It really is a business-to-business company where you speak to niche audiences and, as much as broadcast was important, we all understand that one-to-one selling of the machine, as opposed to people, was going to become more and more important.

"Probably in the late '90s, I began realizing the importance of direct selling, although I'm not sure that if I were working at Pepsi, I would have come to the same conclusions that spawned the *Pepsi Refresh social charity campaign*. Certainly on something that is targetable, which things were on IBM. It seems like a pretty compelling proposition to me. The advertising funnel: awareness-consideration-response.

"They did a great awareness job and it was left to the online and, back in those days a decade ago, even direct communications mail to fill in the consideration and response, but certainly things like direct mail have completely fallen out of sight with teams in favor of digital communications.

"Without having coined the phrase 'engagement' or 'trial' or 'usability' or anything like that, we were ahead of the curve in letting viewers see the value of products and services. I've always worked with this model in my head that I call the three Ds, which is a brand needs or a person needs to define who they are and what they do. They need to demonstrate how it works. They need to put themselves in the hands that can sell and then they need to disseminate that information across channels to get into as many hands as they can to get people doing work for them. We understood that early on. It's not really that complicated."

~

Dirk Eschenbacher, "I decided it was going to be really big when I first realized what the concept of an email was and what a web site was. It was very obvious that digital would become really big. Being a person who really likes new, uncharted territory, I learned it… or learned by doing, rather.

"When it all started out, normally, the digital responsibility for the client was clearly with the IT department and not with the marketing or any other departments. They were not necessarily looking for agencies; they would look for people who could build web sites. Most of those people who could build web sites couldn't design, so they all looked very horrible. They realized that there were digital agencies that could also design, so they came with the right brief to the digital agencies. That brief didn't normally come from the marketing department who all worked with the guys in the traditional ad agencies.

"At the outset, there were these two parallel lines of business, and it just slowly merged. The discussions really started when clients took the digital lead out of the IT department and made it a marketing concern. Only then did the briefs come into the agency, one level higher at an integration level. Even then, it took a while. It wasn't just, 'OK, now it's a marketing department concern.' First, it was the CRM manager in the marketing department, then it was really only five, six, seven years ago that the Marketing Director started to make become more integrated."

⌒

Steffan Postaer, "My agency is a little bit of a hybrid [of a traditional and a digital agency]. Gyro was a B2B thing that now has bigger aspirations and we deal with very complicated, high-tech businesses in Silicon Valley. TV is the exception, not the rule here. The thread is a Web and people get caught up in it, rightly or wrongly. I would say when the dot.com madness happened in the '90s, there was culpability all around.

"It isn't just an agency holding on to old ideas. For clients, the fear probably starts there and in many cases, they wake up in the morning saying, 'I've got to get social. I don't even know how to log on to Twitter. I thought Facebook was for kids,' and so these 42-year-old CMOs freak out. They just fucking freak out, and it pushes that fear and insecurity into the C suite at ad agencies, and then the freak-out becomes a pandemic. A bunch of reactionary bad decisions are made like buying as many things as you can, investing in business models that don't really make sense. So that follows the way an epidemic does when it quickly gets out of control, and eventually reality sets in and things settle down. Like the dot.com thing came, and now you have the winners, the Amazons, the eBays and countless others and a jillion losers, which are already forgotten into the mists of time.

"Agencies are just reacting to their clients' fear, and I see that now like never before when you look back at it from above and look and recall things. When they were in real time, we were all sort of thinking, 'I better get my act together.' That's why I jumped into the digital pool as soon as I was scared and realized the old way was ending, I thought, 'Oh, my gosh.' The day you realize that newspapers weren't really going to be relevant anymore because the news was too old and you can get it online is an epiphany of sorts. I'm just glad I had mine sooner than later so that I didn't become like one of these 40-something dinosaurs that keep talking about how, 'I used to cut film with a razor blade.' I actually remember that stuff. But I've got multiple blogs and all kinds of fun things going on. I know more about a number of platforms than my kids and can take them to school on them and of course, they can do the same with the ones that they prefer that I don't care for.

"At first, the interesting thing was I became acclimated to all of that emerging stuff because I became a creative director of businesses that were doing a lot of work below-the-line, promotion event marketing, direct marketing. Like every preening creative, I looked down at those below-the-line services as sort of like second-, third-class citizens, and I was arrogant.

"There was a kernel of truth to junk mail [spam]. There's junk mail, there's junk mail, there's junk mail. There's no question. But I also accepted that there was good money there, and I wanted security. I liked fishing where the fish were and chasing ever more elusive and infrequent opportunities for television and other mass media. I went in and took jobs and responsibilities with businesses that were spending more and more money at Leo Burnett, at Euro RSCG, and below-the-line marketing. Some only in those things exclusively and those became digital faster. A bank that was doing a shit ton of junk mail quickly got into email and other things, and I was there at the beginning. Sooner than most, but after plenty; I was still in the first quarter of that. If it's a football game, I got into it during the first quarter, but I wasn't there at the kickoff.

"It was the mid-'90s. Indeed for me, Altoids is my creative calling card, and I just had the great fortune of this little assignment where they didn't have any money and no one at Burnett cared about it because it didn't feature television or national media. But as an ACD, with my partner Mark Faulkner, we get this little assignment and for whatever reason, we are told to do posters and we said, 'No money, but that just means we'll create propaganda and maybe it won't cost much of anything. We'll just be able to do terrific ads in a medium that we always use at home, billboards, signs, posters.' and that's what we did.

"Altoids became a coffee-table-book case study to end all case studies on how to get maximum impact from a minimum budget. That is one of the many high phase cards of digital. This idea that videos don't cost anything and social media is free with maximum impact, minimum dollars. In many cases, you fail miserably when you try to design some social campaign and it's transparently insincere. It doesn't go anywhere or do anything. It has the potential to do things powerfully well without big budgets. Mass media became real clear to me for the two reasons I've just said, 1) my big takeaway from Altoids and 2) because I was working with other clients who were below-the-line and who went digital long before mass media did.

"I held onto Altoids for the creative magic, but I took a bunch of other clients who were just merchandising and below-the-line stuff and I combined the two and parlayed what I knew from one for the other. That's how LB Works started – the agency created within Leo Burnett. I had Altoids to forever keep my reputation good. I was totally spending a ton of time winning, writing, creative directing, and selling work for clients who would end up as a commercial or something like it, and it was neat to have that combination. I was a hybrid. I became one. When I did that and when I left the classic structure of: you work for a group creative director, and there're 10 or 12 of you and each have a partner, and you each get one or two clients, and sometimes you compete and sometimes you don't. I walked away from that whole model in the mid-'90s and was doing this other stuff. I was encouraging new ways to work, and I would divide up a brief for everybody. I'd give everybody an opportunity – I called it a 'hit off the opium pipe.' Everyone in my group had a chance to do a nifty poster for Altoids, but at the same time, they all had to be very productive in these less glamorous clients, and also that whole scheme was contrary to how Burnett used to run their railroad. It was untraditional, what I was doing, and I had as many fans as haters for being *that* guy and doing things my way and *that* way."

⌣

Paul Ruta, "'We want a viral campaign,' says the client, 'like *The Subservient Chicken.*' Oh, you want one of *those*. Okay, but first let's agree that 'going viral' means that because of the random magic of digital molecular combustion, the campaign gains uncontrollable popularity at warp speed, defying gravity and logic, leaving even market research professionals unable to identify an area for improvement. The campaign is globally adopted and adored. It is petted and shared beyond any normal brand-consumer relationship. It is spoofed on late-night television. And it sells the product.

"Or, in this example, it *unsells* the product. *United Breaks Guitars* has a gratifying David & Goliath story: United Airlines lost $180 million in value, while singer Dave Carroll [who produced a hit viral video with a catchy music video telling his side of the story of United breaking his guitar and not seeming to be too concerned with remedying the situation] came out of it with a hit single and a fully booked lecture tour. If you are what you click on, Carroll slew the giant on behalf of 12 million cheesed-off air travelers.

United Breaks Guitars, 2009 by Dave Carroll, disgruntled customer-musician. His music video protest of United Airlines has turned into a social media speaking tour, a web site, more music videos, a book, and a huge public relations mess for the company. http://www.davecarrollmusic.com/

"The campaign is a star example of the democratizing potential of the Internet, how the right message from the right brand delivered the right way can win over a lot of the right people. In this case, it was strictly brains over budget, though it's always nice when you've got plenty of both to play with – just ask *The Subservient Chicken* folks. You can't just type the word viral into a box on a briefing document and expect anything special to happen. Going viral isn't a request from the client; it's a reward from the customer."

〜

Peter Moss, "There was a whole era of creating digital trash for download. I've not thought about this for quite a while, but that was a sad era. It was like having a bucket list of things you must have done, like a screensaver.

"We were all very positive and excited in those days, but without direction, to be honest. It's like the gold-rush mentality. Nothing you do is wrong because no one has actually done any of it before. What took a back seat for quite some time was measurability. People were doing things and that was all right, but they weren't quite as handcuffed to the results as they'd been previously."

⟜

Thierry Halbroth, "Digital is not a world on its own and apart. For me, it's simple. If you are a traditional creative, you need to look at traditional things and figure out how they translate to digital. This is always the question that a lot of people can't get their heads around. It's like how a print poster can translate in the digital environment.

"The *Mobile Medic* piece is a good example of how a poster can come to life, how an idea can come to life in a different environment. With a smartphone, the poster becomes a test for students interested in becoming medical officers in the Armed forces of Australia and can actually run a diagnosis on a situation that you may be faced with in the service. Things from PET scans and x-rays to checking vitals to running every single thing, basically [by] using your phone.

"Crossover is very, very important, but let's not forget that today in advertising, if you want to produce good ads and good creative, we are in the business of entertainment. We are now looking at two ways of seeing digital becoming very utilitarian. If you look at the mobile, you can see it's very useful. It's got a purpose, and it's a utility tool. It's not really entertainment. I don't want to go and use the trendy word gamification. The time of having a virtual beer actually empties your cell phone. It's becoming very utilitarian. You still have a need and a craving for entertainment, I would say. Now we are moving more and more into the space of entertainment, and content entertainment not just bridging a gap.

"You have a platform with digital that's been enabled to reach as many people as possible. There is still a role for traditional things because we live in the real world, we still walk around, and I'm still appalled by walking in a subway or around the city and seeing crappy advertising. It's just disgusting. There is still a role for improving it. I still think that despite everything we say about the CRT and the flat screen, TV is still very, very important, and in the reach, there is actually almost a renaissance of TV. The way it's being reborn, it's very different. Also, the way it's being consumed where people sit down and watch the entire series of *Breaking Bad,* for instance, from start to finish with no ads.

"It's the beginning of the next revolution, and I've seen a little bit of was what ad agencies like Party are doing in Japan. The potential for interacting with your TV is really the next thing where we won't have to take a leap. But we're going to have to get some serious expertise in terms of what's happening there.

"In Hong Kong, you can do this with cable channels. There are little buttons you can press. Press *here* if you want to order, press *here* if you want more details, all that. I don't think that's the way forward. That is very direct marketing, and it's traditional ABC. People still want to do that, but they don't understand that when you are at home, you're alone to be entertained. When you watch TV, you watch to be entertained. Even the news, even if you want to keep yourself informed, it's still an entertainment in a way. The TV is sacred in a way that is like our Mount Parnassus – it is really the magic box; but only in a proper size, not in a 4½-inch screen.

"I still think there is magic in this. What you want to do is be entertained, and if you're looking at what will be the future, Samsung and Sony are building us platforms trying to converge the dream in your home with the TV and how you can interact. This is only going to work if it's based on entertainment. It's not going to work if it says, 'Press here if you want to buy.' It's not even going to work where people can have fun by seeing things happen on their screen immediately. They will desire participation in it and to actually engage.

"There is still a thing that's being done in Japan that is unbelievable. They have a show that is broadcast on TV. A show where users – and we're talking hundreds of thousands of users – can actually engage in and shape and model the show the way they want it to be.

"By making scenes happen, by making a set explode, or where they can create dialogue that is repeated by a commentator, and by having their tweets displayed on air and then integrating the tweeters by name in the credits when the show is over. This is the thing we are seeing, and when you look at this, you go, 'I don't think you can do this over here. Oh, my god! Only in Japan can you do that.'

◠

Richard Bleasdale, "It's hard to bolt digital skill sets onto the side of something and expect the change to happen. It's hard. My gut says it's way too late for agencies that haven't already made the move. It's not just this little thing anymore, so your challenge now is that the shortage of really good talent is major, and if you're going to change, you are going to need to change in a way to attract that talent – and it is going to be really tough. Almost all the disciplines and agencies these days have become digital.

"When you say digital it's, 'What're you talking about?' Because pretty much everything is digital, even the TV and radio signals these days. That definitely raises an issue about are we seeing the rise of the digital master agency, like a SapientNitro or R/GA, that is now going to start looking at acquiring traditional agencies?

"Digital specialist agencies have traditionally been executionally extremely strong. More are getting stronger in the strategic area, but not particularly creatively strong or ideas-driven and, at some level, they haven't really come from that heritage anyway. It's a bit like the creative agency and media agencies that, bit-by-bit, are coming back together because one without the other has never made any sense. I have no idea why anyone in the industry let that happen. It was such a bad idea anywhere. It's a bit the same with the creative agencies and the digital agencies. The ability to ideate and think creatively at a big level is exactly where the digital agencies need to be going."

◠

Rob Martin Murphy, "Certain people who've gone through the business, it's good for them to have an understanding and to appreciate all of the different elements of digital. They might be able to become stronger in certain areas of it. They might even decide to go and write some simple code and build their own stuff. It's another skill. I think that probably you're still going to have a really core skill that is really strong that I don't think is ever going to go away.

"In advertising, there's good and bad advertising, and with the digital platforms, there's good and bad as well. There's still room for smart people who can think really well to create quality work. There's always going to be a need for quality."

～

Jeffrey Yu, "The profitability of a digital agency is higher than that of a normal agency. I still have a lot of people asking me whether if helping their digital colleagues will mean they will be losing their above-the-line revenue. I still hear that sort of question. However, I do believe that everybody knows digital is essential. Digital is an everyday part of our lives. It is part of the communication propositions we are offering. I don't think we are still trying to suffocate digital. I don't think that at all.

"In the early days because we didn't understand, we tried to protect our profit. We now say that advertising only sort of brings the client into the door. We make no profit at all or barely a profit. The profits are coming from digital and from activation."

～

Paul Kwong, "I came upon the digital world back around 1995-96. That was when folks started putting portfolios on the computer or on a disk, not having to carry big black physical portfolios with laminated work anymore. It was also when the office went to email. I don't really have any negative feelings or thoughts on digital, except the feeling that knowing the lingo and how to run programs doesn't qualify you to be a creative.

"It was a gradual process of bringing in the digital work. I can't say it was one big thing that changed everything. In fact, FedEx was probably a bigger impact in terms of speed and turnaround. Instead of waiting a few days to get something to the client, it was overnight. Deadlines were now a lot quicker and timelines were crunched. Digital only became important as clients requested it. Or being able to instantly send edits or scripts or print ads via email."

～

Scott Morrison, "We've always been really firm believers in leveraging technology. That's how we've always been fixated. As I went through the years working with different ad agencies, owning my own spots, what I found going on industry-wide was a fundamental break in how the client-agency relationship was working. It was fundamentally flawed. It was antagonistic. A lot of times, trust was rare when that happened.

"It's partially the advertising industry's own fault. A lot of times, creative types fixate on what's the best creativity, how things should work, what's cool, what is whiz bang, and what thing is the latest and greatest. Clients don't think that way. At my last agency, we wound up hiring a person to write our proposals that was an MBA. Because we realized that we were creative people trying to write proposals to people who were not in the same industry we were in. They couldn't digest what our recommendations were because, to them, it was like almost a different language.

"Since they had a level of discomfort, they had a level of mistrust that was inherent. Also, as much as there is a science to marketing, there's also the art, and the art is imperfect. All it takes is a bad agency working with a client that does a poor job, wasting a ton of money, and then that client is jaded about creative types from that point forward.

"Print work was much more trusted. I would say, definitely, if you were talking about the red-haired stepchild, digital was definitely higher on that plane. It was not clear what worked. It was pretty easy to know if you put a DM out and you got a 7% response rate because everybody's patting you on the back since 4% is the expected rate of a DM. [It's] 2% now, but at the time, if you got 7%, you were getting a promotion.

"I would be surprised, looking forward, if we didn't see it start to move to a 50/50 split in the budget between online and offline because I'm starting to see more and more conversations automatically including the digital component as part of everything, including the rebranding. The branding proposals are starting to incorporate how the brand should be applied digitally, whereas before, that wouldn't even come into consideration."

〜

Subhash Kamath, "India is still a newcomer to the whole digital game compared to what's happening, say, in the US or UK. In India, we focus on some of the largest vehicles simply because of geographic size and the number of consumers you need to reach at any point of time for larger advertisers. Though the Internet platforms are increasingly becoming bigger and bigger and more populated, it's still not enough to call it a true mass medium. Therefore, television continues to rule the roost when it comes to advertising messages. Unilever, for example, which is one of the biggest advertisers here, will have maybe 10% or 12% going towards – and I'm using the word loosely – digital.

"Eighty percent is still reserved for television. I believe that the next big change is going to come from mobile phones because in India, you have a subscriber base of 900 million mobile subscribers, and I read a report recently that said 600 to 700 million of them are actually really active users. The percentage of smartphones is very small today. It is still about a maximum of between 30-50 million of them. Now 30 to 50 million as a number on its own is very large, but looking at it as an overall penetration, it will still be considered a very small figure. It's galloping, and what is happening is there're a lot of price players that've come in now that are bringing down the price of smartphones or Internet-friendly phones.

"That is going to be the next boom in the next five years. It's not about only access to computers. In a large part of India, computer access is still through offices and Internet cafés. Personal computers are on the rise, but only in the larger towns. Broadband access is still not where the government wants it to be. They have taken up a plan to have broadband connectivity overtaking China over the next 10 years, but that's an ambitious goal. I don't know if they will be able to succeed, but the intentions are all there. Now if all that happens with 3G and 4G services becomes more popular, I believe that the next digital revolution is going to be on the small screen, which is mobile."

⌒

Harish Vasudevan, "Television is the primary medium in Africa. Television in some markets, and in some others, radio actually dominates the marketplace. For example, in Uganda, radio is two times the size of television. In other markets, television dominates. Newspaper readership is really low. It is a combination of illiteracy as well as the cost of buying the newspaper and the quality of reporting. Digital is big, but from a different perspective, which is essentially mobile phone access.

"Given the fact that about 35% of the population is under 25 and mobiles are the way that they communicate, digital is big, but not in the way that one is used to in Asia or everywhere else where it is a desktop or a laptop or even a tablet access. Here it's telephone access. The other thing is that smartphone penetration among all mobile phones is under 10%, so they're using old-fashioned feature phones. That will change soon since it is a function of price because only the Chinese companies are here and they started launching smartphones at between $40-$60. That'll see the growth of smartphones, but otherwise for now, it is mostly feature phones.

"Mobile advertising and smartphones will have to come. The issue is that because of the image of Africa: poverty, security, talent, environment, all of that, it's not unlike other markets. Getting high-quality talent into this market is always going to be hard. Any innovation that comes up will have to come through local talent or brave people who are willing to move here.

"There will be innovation, but it will take some time for it to happen. Kenya or Nairobi set up an IT hub, and several markets are trying to do that, not unlike Malaysia setting up their multimedia corridor. There are countries that are trying to do that and can carve out a silo to offer security and internationalness. They give people a feeling of, 'Why don't you come here and do what you're doing, say, in the valley or wherever that is,' but it will take quite a long time for that to happen.

"I would say it to be at least 5 to 10 years, but a particular uncertainty complicates life. There is a huge amount of corruption in Africa.

"What is happening now and what could drive the pace in which I am saying 5 to 10 years and not 30 to 40 years is the fact that so many companies are moving here. Historically, campaigns would manage Africa either or out of South Africa or out of Dubai. That's how they would run. It's just like how people would run China out of Hong Kong.

"What we're seeing over the last virtually 12 months is that a few companies are saying if they really want to make a difference, they need to be in Africa, not South Africa. Coke has already moved their regional headquarters to Nairobi. Nestlé has moved into Nairobi, as well. They can't do this remotely anymore. These clients are often coming with international experience, so they will start putting pressure on the local agencies to incorporate digital, but it may take a while. At least to think big ideas, to think in the classical communication sense and not here as a 'let's-get-an-ad out' thing.

"Television is still lagging behind like how we don't have landlines. It's quite possible that we leapfrog into tablets and smartphones being the way people access information and entertainment. It's possible. That does require the infrastructure and investments, though.

"The thing is that for telcos, the investments and infrastructure are always at risk of some terrorist attack. I honestly don't see them investing big time here purely because of all the political consideration more than anything else. Unlike China, which is one country where you can pay off the government centrally and they'll allow you to get in and start doing business, here half of the countries are run by dictators and despots, and the other half are some sort of a democracy, but rife with extreme corruption.

"Africa is a continent of a billion people, but it is still a continent compressing about 30 or 35 countries, all with different languages and different cultures, and there is not one economic zone. They will drip feed into some markets such as Kenya. Typically, the marketing people look at Kenya, Nigeria, Tanzania, Uganda, and Ghana, which are politically stable. I don't think they will be putting in a ton of money. The guys are doing really basic stuff. Like Unilever is selling soaps and detergents. It will take a while.

"We have about 70 people out of which, maybe, three or four have worked in multiple markets. Everybody is either from an African country or has moved in from India. They are not used to working within a large agency's processes. What's the big idea? All that stuff just passed them by.

"We just hired a digital creative director from South Africa. He came in two weeks ago and before him, we had an executive CD who had moved in from India, but these guys are used to working in office with 15 or 20 people. We've grown about 50% over the last six months, and now that there are 70 people, there is a completely different dynamic. Now, we actually are an office. There are bunches of people who've been here for the last seven to eight years. One guy from England has been here for over 19 years or more.

"It is a very sales-driven culture. It is all extremely transactional. It is extremely hard for people to think brand. Special offers, special deals, those are what dominates this marketplace. It is a very amazing dynamic. The advertisers are trying to go for the mass market, which is why all the functional communication around the one buck you saved or you'll get one free or whatever it is because people's needs are very basic at this point in time. The big MNC [multi-national companies] players haven't really come in here and invested a lot of time and effort in building this market. They have been distracted with shiny objects like China, India, Vietnam – places where it's easier to do business. These people have succeeded there.

"Unilever was here and they left. They shut down many of their plants and they left, and they're not coming back. Many people came here, dabbled, and said it's too hard and left. We are only now slowly seeing some of the bigger players getting in and, for them, I don't think they're seeing a place where they can sell a million bottles of Coke and that's great. They are not trying to make this a million-bottle market because it is extremely hard, and there are other places that are easier.

"The other markets got saturated, the honeymoon in China is over, and India has its political challenges. The only market left for them to grow now is Africa. We will slowly see them paying more attention to Africa and, once the quality of marketers improves, the quality of marketing will improve, and then the quality of advertising will improve. Otherwise, it's just going to be the same old, same old."

ᜉ

Tobias Wilson, "We just built a system for our automotive clients, which was called PRM for Prospect Relationship Management. Basically, we used our heavy programming skills to build a back end, then we built the front end and wrote all the strategy, hosted it in the cloud, which has about three-and-a-half-thousand pieces of creative served automatically through customers or prospects of anybody who engages with Toyota, Lexus, or Suzuki.

"Anybody who engages with them digitally is now captured in the system, and then based on the content of the five data points that we ask, they are then marketed to instantly with an offer. Everybody has an entry. Every piece of creative has an entry URL. If I send a print ad, that print would have a campaign-specific URL. When they come to the landing page, it's obviously branded and designed to match the print ad and then when they get their

'Thanks for registering,' the offer that is contained in that email is exactly the same as what is in the print ad. It's all unified and seamless.

"Then we serve our content and all that jazz. That system has a maximum consideration phase. The longest people could be in that system is some two years away from their date of purchase, and obviously they're not going to get bombarded with emails talking about the newest offers and trying to get them in to a showroom. We're talking more to them about the car or the brand and what it's like to be a Suzuki customer. We're sending them reviews and the maximum of emails over that two-year period was nine, and they were in quite different intervals. Sometimes, we don't send an email for three months. Sometimes, we send them six in three months if it's closer to their purchase date.

"That system is automatic. It will just keep growing eternally as long as you keep paying server costs. People coming through the system get served up their requested pieces of creative, and they keep going until they purchase or opt out. If they update their details, they go back on a roundabout. If somebody has triplets halfway through their cycle and move from a 4-door to a 6-door, they can update that, and obviously, the whole marketing plan will realign to their needs.

"With PRM, it's not a static eDM. It looks like a standard electronic direct mail piece because there's the header image, there're the content tabs on the right, etc., or here's the click-through and here's the footer. Each eDM is actually made up of eight separate pieces of creative. The eDM is built dynamically seconds before by the system, seconds before the clients receive it.

"If you come into the system and you've seen a 20% off offer in a newspaper for a Suzuki, and you come in and you register for Suzuki Swift and your purchase intent date is 30 days away, then you will receive an eDM with a Suzuki Swift header, and it's got much juicier content in it. The tone of the eDM is going to be a lot more fear of loss and sense of urgency, and you will have your offer there as well as something extra because you're 30 days away from purchase intent date. Whereas if you come in and you register interest in a Suzuki Swift and your purchase intent date is two years away, it will build the same eDM with the same image, but the content and the copy will be quite different.

"What I've also found is when I have engaged a traditional copywriter to start thinking this way, they walk off the job. They're on strike. 'This isn't a headline. This isn't a Cannes-winning prospect. I'm sorry. I'm not doing it.' It wasn't too hard to get the copywriters to write the sentiment that we needed for that project, it was just different to traditional copywriting. Then when the senior client marketer from Toyota left and we had to train their new team, it took another three or four months, and because of that, the penny takes a long time to drop. It's a long fall."

Neil Leslie, "I always thought digital was going to be huge. That's not to say I knew what form it would take on and when. It just made sense to me that the only thing stopping digital from total media domination was limited bandwidth and understanding. And I was about to have my first taste of just how painful circumnavigating these limitations could be.

"While at Bates, I became good friends with John Lambie, a key creative guru up at [their interactive agency] XM Asia Pacific. He invited me to help him develop a digital campaign for the regional launch of a new Nokia handset (the Nokia 6600, if I remember correctly.) It was the first time I'd worked on a digital campaign that wasn't simply an extension of ATL work.

"Our idea was to highlight the phone's many advanced features by putting site visitors in the shoes of Agent Gemini – a James Bond type who was required to complete a tongue-in-cheek series of spy-like tasks. Our approach was to use video footage of a model to narrate the scenarios and guide the user through the phone's features. However, once we'd built the site, it became apparent that it would take days to load with the then-standard 56k modem. This led us having to employ a team of students to work round the clock for over a week to turn every frame of footage into vector files.

"This may have made the site faster, but it certainly didn't make it prettier. Even then, we had to create simple mini games to keep visitors distracted at various points to disguise hefty loading times."

Åsk Wäppling, "Online advertising, in general, has been in a messed-up place for a really long time. It's a hyper bubble that's about to die. Facebook went up to the stock market pretending to be really valuable when nobody ever clicked any of those ads. Ever. People are realizing that it doesn't really work for them and this isn't what ads are supposed to be. Ads used to be information in the right context. My city on Facebook is 'Fucking, Austria,' because I think that's funny. But all the ads are now talking in Austrian at me. I would obviously never click on those. It's never actually worked.

"Remember, advertising is information in the right context. In London, you used to be able to smoke, both on the buses and in the subway. Then, suddenly, they banned the smoking on both. Nicorette gum, at the time, was saying that it was sort of the smoke break that you could no longer have, which was a really clever way of positioning their gum. I'm in the subway, pacing up and down, realizing I can't light up a cigarette and this is really annoying. I see these beautiful, enamel signs against the tile walls where it just says, 'No Smoking' and right underneath it in really tiny text is, 'This would be a really good time for Nicorette gum.' I think that's brilliant. That's what advertising is all about. It's coming up with the product information at the moment you need it. We've been able to do this offline forever. Why can't we do this online?

"There was also this ad on Chat Roulette about HIV and condoms. It was somebody that was going on Chat Roulette, where teenagers hit on each other for a little bit of naughty time, and then she holds up a sign that says, 'BINGO. I'm HIV positive,' [Don't play Russian roulette in real life. Condomerie.com.] and I was saying, 'That could actually happen to me, when I'm out and about.'

"These are the ideas that only come from creatives actually using the same stuff everybody else is using, which is the only reason I have SnapChat on my phone now. I am not a teenager, but I have to use that thing to see what on earth they're doing with it. It's like this problem-solving curiosity. We'll pick it apart, see how it works, and see what other people are doing. The problem that I find is that we're always chasing that school of fish today. We're not actually saying, 'This is where the school of fish is going to go.' We have all these specialized people, who are planners and strategists and everything, and we still don't know where the school of fish is going to go. That amazes me because we used to know where they were going to go.

"Maybe the consumer has been sorted into two different categories: the push-button school fish on the Web and the people who actually buy things and will be continuously brand loyal. The Web is hard to reach because there are online and offline, different types of people, like my neighbor, who is a total hippie. She only buys based on recommendations."

༆

Vice Chairman and Chief Strategist of The Brand Consulting Practice for Ogilvy Public Relations, Beijing-based Steve Bale, "Digital? What's that? I've never been quite sure. Don't tell anyone.

"Fast rewind to a well-known advertising agency in London at around the time of the Atlanta Olympics in 1996. The lengthy morning meeting with the client and creative team was about to conclude when the subject of 'new media' cropped up, thanks to the diligent junior suit who had put it on the agenda. It was the last item. 'No problem,' soothed the Art Director, 'I'm sure the print ads can be adapted.' Everyone agreed that we should talk to our new-media chap about this following the meeting. In the meantime, we got back to the important business of trying to persuade the client to invest more money on the TV campaign that would give his brand a much-needed fillip.

"1996 marked a significant year in the development of new media. In the US, first-quarter revenue from Internet advertising hadn't quite reached the paltry sum of US$30m. In the last quarter, it had leapt to US$109.5m. Perhaps significantly, the Internet Advertising Bureau (the source of these figures) began life that year, but was 1996 the key year of the digital revolution, or was 22nd January, 1984 the defining moment? That was the day that Super Bowl viewers were treated to a blonde-haired, white-vested Anya Major hurling her sledgehammer at the screen image of Big Brother. That TV ad made an indelible impression. It also had quite an impact on the fortunes of a company called Apple.

"Then again, when thinking about defining moments, it's hard to argue that the first salvos of the revolution were not fired on 4th April, 1975 when Bill Gates and Paul Allen founded Microsoft. On the other hand, some may argue that the digital revolution didn't really get going until the launch of Facebook in 2004, on the basis that a 'revolution' that doesn't make a big difference to your day isn't worthy of the name.

"One thing is for sure, 2000 wasn't a great year for the revolution. That year, believing that the dawn of the millennium would signal a brave new digital age, I joined a start-up e-education company in London that was part of *The Times* educational supplement. It was a sign of the times (if you'll excuse the pun) that a publishing group that had been around since 1785 was investing heavily in e-commerce. Alas, before the IPO could be launched, the dot.com bubble did what bubbles naturally do – *it burst.*

"The man or woman in the street – or, more to the point, in his or her sitting room watching TV and occasionally surfing the Internet in 2000 – didn't flinch. The same repeats appeared on TV and (most) favorite web sites were still there. Emails arrived and emails were sent much as they had been in 1999. The much-touted fireworks of the new millennium digital revolution had been a damp squib.

"In China, at the start of 2001, digital was being treated much as it had been in London in 1996, as a supplementary medium for advertising, company information, and sales brochures. As far as the advertising agency creative-brief was concerned, it continued to be an afterthought at best.

"A look at the Internet usage figures at the end of the year in 2000 illustrates exactly why that was. Back then, Mainland China had a mere 22.5 million Internet users (out of a population of close to 1.3 billion). Not unreasonably, most mass-market advertisers didn't have much time (and much of a budget) for digital, as they were too busy making TV and print ads for the mass market. Trustees of mass-market brands that targeted women were even more reliant on non-digital channels because 7 out of 10 Internet users were men.

"In the summer of 2002, Internet users were pretty much doing things the way they had been doing them in the summer of 2001. Then... [cue dramatic pause] ...in September 2002...[second dramatic pause] ...the digital revolution started in earnest. You may be surprised to learn [third and thankfully final dramatic pause] ...that it all began with an alien invasion.

"Thankfully, the aliens hadn't done their homework. They had underestimated the earthlings, who were packing their very own 'alien technology' in the otherworldly form of a Nokia 7650. This futuristic technology not only incorporated a camera (useful for capturing little blue men in the act), but also the means to email the incriminating evidence to newsrooms (so that the breaking news of the alien invasion could be broadcast to the general public).

"Prior to the launch of the advertising campaign, few people had any idea that this technology was even on the drawing board. Indeed, a few months before, in Beijing, I had listened to the Nokia 7650 product briefing open-mouthed. 'It does what?!' I exclaimed. Colin Giles, then head of Nokia's Sales and Marketing Group in China, again went through the list of what it had and what it did: camera (zoom function; standard, portrait, and night settings); image uploading; send and receive multimedia messages; send and receive emails; browse WAP pages; download Java applications and... the phone could be used as a modem. In short, Colin had unveiled the future.

"I wrote two words in my notebook: 'Alien technology!' And, mindful that the Chinese translation of 'Human Technology' (Keji yi renwei ben) was much appreciated by Nokia users in China, I added two more words: '...for humans.'

"We then talked about what the technology could do for people, and how it could make a difference to someone's day, or even their life. We also talked about how this technology would bring people closer together, and how it could help and even inspire them at play and at work. This being a Nokia meeting, we also talked about the importance of technology being in-tuitively easy to use.

"I then tried to encapsulate this in a line that I hoped would inspire the creative team, in a way that was underpinned by Nokia's mantra, *Connecting People*. All phones connect people, but what I had seen at the Nokia 7650 briefing was something that promised so much more: something that would be enthusiastically embraced by an increasingly idea- and experience-hungry Chinese phone-buyer. Hey, that's a thought, what about: 'Connecting peo-ple... to new ideas and experiences.'

"At that briefing, I realized that the world was about to change and that mobile technology would be the catalyst for that change. Technology was at last being designed to fit into people's lives, to help them to run things on their own terms, and to make their day that bit easier and more enjoyable (set-top-box manufacturers kindly take note).

"The more people realize what mobile technology can do for them, the more likely they are to embrace it. Inevitably, the more influential converts there are, the easier it is to persuade people to join the conversation. This virtuous circle continues to widen, drawing in ever more people who want to be part of this incredible social revolution. All of this has been made possible, of course, by the advanced technical-weaponry of the continuing digital revolution.

"What a wonderful time to be a brand trustee, as long as you're invited to join the conversation that is; and as long as you've got something to say that people really want to hear. Only then will it matter how and where the brand's story is told."

❧

John Lambie, "During the entire dot.com boom, the standard ad agency response was to pretend it wasn't happening. The typical responses included:

- It was a fad that would soon blow over.
- There weren't enough people online to matter.
- There wasn't a broad enough base of consumers (beyond the geek set) to matter.
- People just didn't spend enough time online for it to matter as a medium.
- It couldn't deliver a full-screen TV-style video experience, so it wouldn't work.
- It didn't deliver a full-screen, high-res print ad experience, so it didn't matter.
- People would never open a personal email from a corporation.
- You could never convert a virtual customer into a physical one.
- 'Because I've never clicked on a banner ad, that means no one else has either.'
- Calls-to-action are cheap, gimmicky and sound like we're desperate.
- 'Buy Now' buttons are cheaper, more gimmicky and even more desperate.
- URLs on print or TVCs or – gasp! – radio spots waste valuable space and destroy the integrity of both the copy and the art direction.

"Such was the antithesis to anything digital; the dot.com crash was one long vindication party for the agency naysayers. Their head-in-the-sand approach had been triumphantly justified and validated. Now, let's just get back to the important business of TV, print, outdoor, and radio, shall we?

"But the boom was a big enough boom to allow at least a few grudgingly placed seats at the table. Or, more than likely, down at the kid's table. These included:

- The importance of a corporate or brand web site as a repository of 24/7 accessible information.
- The need for visibility on a search engine or directory listing.
- The value of an email database as an adjunct to a brand's snail mail one.
- The validation of the banner > microsite > email database as a customer acquisition tool.
- The positive effect an awesome user experience could have as the user navigated between and within this process.

"Sure, this digital stuff would never usurp 'real advertising', but it did earn some minor merit badges. Now, go back to your basement office and stop disturbing the big boys, will you? We have some important thinking to do.

"Ironically, the dot.com bust was the worst possible thing that could have happened to ad agencies that adopted this thinking. And it was the best possible thing to happen to the digital agencies that held on for grim death and made it through the fire. Not only were these few hardy, battle-scarred veterans older and wiser, but they were also leaner and definitely meaner.

"Mistakes were made, lessons were learned, and all the flighty speculators had been driven from the market – they had other bubbles to inflate and burst. Brands, too, had learned from their excesses, and for the shrewder brands, there was some serious marketing to do.

"They were now viewing digital as:

- An important part of the overall marketing mix.
- A great way to engage consumers in a more personal way.
- A highly cost-effective way to reach not just entire markets but hitherto unidentified and unreachable niches.

- A new way to reach audiences no longer limited by the geographical constraints of traditional media.
- Exciting possibilities to scale a campaign quickly and cheaply.
- A way to capture peer-based customer endorsements to strengthen a brand message (via ratings, reviews, and recommendations).
- A way to engage a customer during that vital 'interest' phase of the sales cycle – when they were actively searching and researching purchase options.
- An ongoing opportunity to converse with a customer who could be enacted across multiple media and touch points.
- An ability to leverage one's own customers to broaden the reach of a campaign (i.e. virally).

"In other words, turning everything they'd learned about mass communications on its head. For some, this was too big an apple cart to upset. For others, it meant a golden career opportunity, wide open before them. Resistance from the old guard would be stiff and hostile, but ultimately futile.

"The old formula of [Attention = frequency x reach] no longer computed.

"A new variable was now in the mix: Engagement.

Web 2.0: Brave New World

"As we shall see in later chapters, the dot.com boom was merely a false start and the dot.com crash a mere hiccup. The turn of the millennium heralded the dawn of an entirely new era – a starting point for a massive shift that would change the art and science of marketing forever. And for the better.

"In the crucible of the boom and bust, a couple of world-changing ideas were spawned. Sometimes, it would be a generic technology breakthrough refined by several competing companies. More often than not, it was a blinding flash of innovation from a single company that created a massive and permanent disruption.

"Of course, this is only a sampler of a much larger and tastier menu. Some, like Flash, have already been superseded (by HTML5).

"These disruptive innovations combined to create an entire ecosystem where the whole was far, far greater than the sum of the parts. They converged to deliver a user experience that could be enjoyed anywhere, anytime, with a richness only dreamed of just a few short years before.

"The geeks did not inherit the world. They created an entirely new one. And, ostrich-like, ad agencies still had their heads in the sand, smug in the self-delusion that digital would remain a fringe medium. A prescient few could sense what was, and still is, going on with the audiences they were trying to connect with."

⁓

Head of Strategy and Associate Partner at Goodby, Silverstein & Partners New York and former Chief Strategy Officer for Havas, Tom Morton, "I think the Cannes Cyber and Titanium Lions made a difference in digital becoming accepted by 'traditional' colleagues. They created a legitimate world stage for digital creative ideas. It meant a lot that Dan Wieden was one of the pioneering champions of the Titanium Lions as an award back in 2003.

"It took a few years for the novelty factor to wear off. *Cyber* and *Titanium* sound like outsider language for describing the bright, shiny techno-objects of digital campaigns. The 2006 Titanium Grand Prix went to a Japanese designer who made bar codes in funny shapes, rather than to a game-changing idea.

"It's interesting that the Titanium and Integrated Lions have now merged into one awards category. It shows that digital has become the integrating force in campaign development."

⁓

Paul Tan, Creative Director at social media agency Pool, "We've spent years daily educating ourselves and trying to educate brands, but I can understand how it's difficult because it's uncomfortable for a traditional business to deal with something like digital. What the hell is that? How do I measure that?"

⁓

Harish Vasudevan, "You can see a lot more regret around measuring an agency's contribution to the business. At this point in time, agencies are ill equipped to handle that conversation, but they will need to get themselves sorted out because clients are going to demand to know what they're getting for the $100 million they're paying. Those metrics will finally be the way that the holding companies will be able to prove their worth and also help justify any acquisition that they make in this space. We'll see that's a very simplistic approach to measuring contribution and will need to evolve. Maybe we'll see a growth to a whole new different industry where people are helping clients define how to use data and make good value out of it."

⤻

Andy Greenaway, "A lot of the stuff we broadcast [on TV] in the old days was absolute garbage. People were captive in their living rooms and so the work was effective (in a brainwashing sort of way).

"The consumer definitely has more control now. But that's good. It gives the agency much more leverage to force clients to buy great work because everything is now measurable; clients, as well as agencies, will live or die by the results. I believe that great work delivers better results. Bad work gets dismissed and ignored by the consumer – and thus delivers poorer results. We are about to see a new era of heightened creativity (although that may still be off by a fair few years)."

Chapter 12: Minding the Data

It's easy to be confidently glib to a client about the robust results they are going to get from a creative idea you really believe to be strong. But before digital, there actually wasn't any good way to tell how effective a campaign had been that couldn't be heavily skewed by assumptions and positive spin. Those of us who were being honest based our conviction firmly in the faith we had in the concept, which in turn was bolstered by our past experiences because there was no way to determine if a person had looked at an ad in a magazine or on a billboard or heard a spot on radio or television and decided to follow the call to action. Having prospects recite a coupon code, call special phone lines, keep logs of what they listen to, or install measuring equipment on their televisions are ways of getting a snapshot of how things might be going in general, but are no more useful tools than the artificially constructed environment of a focus group. Many things could be inferred, surmised, or otherwise wishfully thought into a post-campaign analysis report, but the fact remains they were not fact-based, they were anecdotal and may explain why clients changed agencies so frequently.

Since the late 1990s, agencies and brands have had a way to track and measure how every aspect of their branding and marketing campaigns are performing in their real environments with actual customers engaging instead of imagining they are or keenly aware that they are being observed and will need to explain their reactions. The Web has always allowed those hosting content to see where visitors are coming from, what they interacted with when they arrived, how long they stayed on each page before moving on, where they continued to and what they did, and if and when they came back and performed a specific follow-up action. Over the past couple of decades, these instruments have continually been refined and added to such that now we are at the point where there is no piece of data that can't be captured and analyzed against any precise customer segment or path from Web to mobile to app to social and beyond, especially as the lines blur between the offline and online worlds.

Now we have the ability to see campaign results and fine-tune them on the fly by changing the words and images that are seen by potential customers that fit select criteria, but that does not mean we will execute or interpret it properly. There is always room for those who don't like what they see and prefer to always give their supervisors good news instead of the reality. Those who don't want to spend the time getting to know the medium or channel and how to be most effective within it, armed with what the data is telling them.

〜

Brad Berens, "The reason that big corporations are investing in big data and big automation is that it is the only way that they see themselves reclaiming scale because it involves relatively little human effort. Fifty years ago, during the *Gunsmoke* era in the early height of television, the marketing department of a consumer package-goods manufacturer could get in front of 80% of the women who were going to be making purchase decisions about Tide versus some other detergent. You had an audience that was bound and gagged in front of you, and you could tell them your message and move on. Big data is a substitute for that scale. That's why they're investing in it because they want to get back to the day when you could get to that level of audience with that region, that frequency, all without having to do 75 campaigns."

⌒

Jeffrey Dachis, "The thing that I am most enthralled with in digital is the fact that you can actually measure the conversations, content, and engagement activity that's going on in social. If you can measure it, then you can know where to spend your new investment. I can tell exactly what's working and what's not working with your engagement activity in social, whereas I can't really tell you which of your print ads are doing well versus the ones that aren't doing well. I can't really tell you how many people saw your billboard on the side of the road. I can't really tell you how many people heard your commercial on the radio and are taking action because of it. I can't really tell you which GoDaddy commercial on the Super Bowl created more value for you. The supermodel kissing the nerd: a good commercial that I found highly entertaining. Lots talked about it in the office the next morning. Does it benefit GoDaddy's brand? Is it more brand love or brand awareness or mindshare or advocacy for the GoDaddy brand because of the $4 million they spent on that 30 seconds?

"I'm not here to tell you one way or the other, other than to say that what I can do is measure the value of GoDaddy's engagement in the marketplace. Measure how effective it is, how impactful it is, and measure the lift in GoDaddy's brand when it comes to terms of satisfaction or passion or reach or conversation strength. Those are things that I can actually measure in the social universe. Those are brand-building efforts that then I can apply my investment criteria towards.

"Social, for me, is something where we're not talking about the number of tweets and things; we're talking about an aggregate worldwide. What is happening with brands in social is measurable, trackable, traceable, and amplifiable, whereas what is happening with brands on television is not. The measurability of this medium or this shift is what I see as the huge opportunity. It depends if you are measuring the right stuff. There's a lot of data, but you have to able to make sense of the data and derive insights from it. That's what my firm does now, so I'm going to say I've got a horse in that race, but I've got a horse in that race because it's the thing that's going to be the most effective and make the most difference, period. But doing your job and having an effect are two different things. You can do your job and you can keep your job or impact an organization.

"It's a brand-new world here in social, and so if you believe that 'likes' and 'follows' are a valuable measure of building your brand and you're getting compensated or your boss thinks that you should create more 'likes' and 'follows,' then you're going to. If you put tits up on your page, people are going to like it, but that doesn't mean you're building your brand. If you offer somebody 90% off your product, people are going to like it. That doesn't mean you're building your brand.

"The nascency of the social metrics and people's hunger for a standard have created some confusion. Nonetheless, people have to get smart about what engagement marketing means and what are those currencies of engagement and how do you value them and then focus on what's going to drive brand value in this new social world where the massive communicators can impact your brand in such an outsized way. You have to figure out how to do it. Yes, that's new for a lot of people and yes, that's hard and yes, we're not used to talking *to* people. We're used to talking *at* them.

"It's so chaotic in the ad-tech universe right now, trying to get to the last click attribution, etc. It's going to be chaos for quite some time. That said, I do believe there is going to be some standardization because for Facebook to be a viable company, there has to be some standardization for people to actually spend money on engagement. I believe there has to be some form of standardization for the normalization of engagement currencies in order for social to live up to its potential. The tweet, the re-tweet, the like, the follow, the pin, the post, the check-in, the rating, the review, the star, the tip, the blog comment, all of those engagement currencies have to be put into a currency clearing house and normalized for brand lift. Without that, you can't see media dollars shift from a $200 million reach and frequency buy to a $200 million engagement buy. That will be the key to unlocking the power of social brand building."[12]

∾

Steffan Postaer, "Data analysts think because you can see a spike and how many people click through a banner that sort of quasi-specific ROI will translate into everything, and if it doesn't, it's because everything else was bad and the banners were good. That's a specious argument if ever there was one.

"You can count how many consumers clicked on a banner and bought something. That is true. But who's to say if you didn't do the banner at all and something else instead that you'd even have more? You just couldn't quantify it right then and there. No one looks at the qualitative. They just want that sort of quantitative thing and its tactics where you can say, 'This banner got 450 hits between the hours of 9:00 and 11:00. Therefore, if we do one every morning at 9:00 and 11:00, we're going to get 450 customers,' and you can make that argument and look them right in the eye. But who's to say you couldn't get 450,000 customers if you tried something more amazing? It's crazy to limit yourself to a single tactic when there are doubles and triples and home runs that are still possible."

∾

Peter Kim, Chief Strategy Officer & Principal Analyst at Constellation Research and former Head of Global Digital Marketing for PUMA, "What's going to change the industry is big data. We've had data for years and years. We've seen Google try and not succeed when it came to changing the nature of radio advertising and print advertising. If Google can't do it, then who can?

"Go back further than that. You've got the marketing mix modeling firms like Hudson River and MMA – advertisers have been using their data

---

12 Josh Sklar, "In the 'traditional' digital world, years before social was even an idea, we had display banner ads on heavily visited online properties that were measured by clickthrough rates (CTRs). All that meant was that someone touched the ad unit. On purpose? By accident? What was the value of that banner versus another type of advertising?"

for a long time now, for decades. While social and big data may start to change things or offer more consumer insights or more behavioral direction, it's not going to be enough to change the industry, not the way people get fed and paid and compensated.

"I see two issues. The first is the marketers themselves. They tend to be right-brained. A lot of marketers and advertisers get into their field because they enjoy the big idea – the creative, emotional part of it. The right-brain creative side of things. They're not good with data numbers to begin with. The marketers who are good at that are the ones that go into banking. The ones who deal with RFM (Recency, Frequency, Monetary) analysis and the quantitative side, they're the ones dealing with market-optimization models and the left-brain side of things. That's not where all of the media and advertising dollars are getting spent today with the majority of brands. So we have a skills and inclination problem to start with.

"Then moving on from there, let's say you get a marketer who can do things with the data. Then you start to get regulation involved. We start talking about macroeconomics and, I'm not saying these are good or bad laws, but I think they are what they are. You've got safe harbor in Europe.[13] You've got things like California privacy laws, and you've got your Delaware laws.[14] Age limitations and how much data you can store or where you can store it, that sort of thing. You start getting governments involved, and they start putting restrictions on how to use the data.

"Let's say you're able to use it. Then you start getting restrictions because consumers push back. That flow is the evolution of the industry to actually using data in a useful way. Finally, what you've got is the availability of marketers. How to use the data because you've got a balanced left brain and right brain. You can get enough useable data beyond government regulation, technology cost to collect and analyze and parse the data. You've got a problem with the legacy of the organizations themselves. That makes it difficult to actually be able to act upon the data because, in theory, we talk about the importance of real-time marketing and being able to make real-time decisions

---

13 A provision that specifies how one should behave to ensure a regulation (e.g., a code of conduct) isn't being violated.

14 Legislation that protects college and post-secondary school students and employees from being required to turn over social media and email passwords over to the schools when asked by administrators and employers.

with the data. But then you're falling back into the whole traditional advertising model. We're talking about developing two campaigns a year and, maybe, if we're really good, we can do it on a quarterly basis or even more frequently than that.

"You have got people holding up examples like Old Spice's *The Man Your Man Could Smell Like* with Isaiah Mustafa, followed by their YouTube effort with the *Day of Video Responses* by Wieden+Kennedy. That's wholly unsustainable for the way marketing departments and advertising agencies are set up today. Maybe in theory something that's interesting and an example of how the world could be, but we're just so far away from being able to act like that for most brands because you've got those other barriers involved.

"The second issue is that there's the temporal factor of where people are in their careers. Where are people trying to get to when you start out as a junior copywriter on the agency or the marketer side; you start out as the email marketing manager today or the junior traffic manager. People are trying to get somewhere in their career. If once in a while we craft out everybody's career, once in a while you get a big breakthrough hit.

"Maybe there're a few outliers that are big smashes on the right hand side and there're many more people who fail in many little ways every day on the left hand side. Maybe it's like a power curve, right from high on the left to low on the right, from increasing amounts of success instead of a bell curve. How do people get motivated to take those risks? To put faith in the data? I had friends who graduated from business school who went to work at big CPG brands and brand management, and it was a catch-22. You're a new brand manager. On one hand, you go to this great company like P&G, General Mills, Kraft, or Coca-Cola and you want to work on Coca-Cola or you want to work on Tide or you want to work on Cheerios. But as a new employee, you learn the ropes on a small brand. One of them told me that it's the worst thing in the world that can happen, to get on a big brand, because then your job is to just don't eff it up. You don't want to be the one known as the guy who destroyed Tide. I think there's the element of career and risk and timing that go into to this as well. It's hard to account for that when we're talking about trying to move the ball forward."

Aden Hepburn, "Maybe everything does come down to subjectivity, and if somebody doesn't like your idea or doesn't agree with or has a different opinion on what the proposition or the outcome could be, then they're going to challenge that. Most of the people that have business here at VML would suggest that metrics are brilliant for us because we believe we're pretty damn good at our jobs. And we would far improve on and outperform nine out of 10 KPIs put against us that are driven by tangible metrics tracked by analytics software."

⌒

Oliver Woods, "For all the huff and puff about the importance of data in advertising, there is little appetite for it in day-to-day work. It is only in recent years, particularly amongst ambitious and dedicated clients, that even 'small data' as started to inform marketing.

"The vast majority of advertising, even in 2014, is not truly data-driven. Ad men may use it to inform elements of strategy, but it is nearly always used to retrospectively justify existing creative ideas. Digital Strategists like myself are often tasked to find data that suits an existing conclusion. Otherwise, the only time data crops up is during reporting of marketing performance, which inevitably ends up being presented after all other items to a chorus of yawning faces.

"All this being said, things are improving. Most agencies and clients expect basic analytics for their digital campaigns. Social media monitoring, originally oversold as a big data panacea, is starting to provide real value by giving live feedback on products, campaigns and brand health. It is a testament to many of the older senior figures in agencies that they have wholeheartedly begun to embrace data in our chaotic, creative discipline.

"A recent campaign I worked on where data was a genuine part of our digital strategy process was Schweppes Australia's *Cocktail Revolution.* We used Google Analytics, social listening & user engagement to plan out our content creation strategy, and to continually optimize how we shared that content. We took a big gamble by saying that we would use data to plan our creative, but it worked – and got us some great results."

⌒

Jim Speelmon, "I was reading the trade media today with interviews of people who say they are the social media experts where I don't think they are doing themselves any favors. Social media, in my opinion, is a lot like statistics. You give me a stat without any context, and I can make that stat tell you whatever it is that you want to believe is true.

"I was chatting with a creative director in Hong Kong yesterday about how he'll be in a brainstorm session and people will burst into the room with the latest facts about how many Facebook 'likes' the brand he's working on got, but what does that actually mean? It's almost like the law of high numbers. As long as you got a big number there, you're doing a good job. Qualitatively, what does it mean? Because of the piecemeal way that a strategy has been done that the campaign plan has been done but the execution is rolled out, there is no way for you to make each media choice do what it's best positioned to do. For example, what does a 'like' on Facebook mean in regards to the success of a campaign? Is it selling more products? Are people signing up for something?

"If he had really truly thought about what he was doing, he could do message trials and find the number of 'likes' versus whatever can give an indication of how people are responding to a position or a message that could use it for message testing. Build off of those things, rather than starting with TV, you might start with a concept on Facebook or Twitter. See what the response is, and take your winning response, and use that for the rest of the campaign. There are tiny things that you could do.

"If you look at the media industry, for example, you have the sell-side platforms, the demand-side platforms, the real-time bidding; so it's all going to be about data insights. From a media perspective, far more technology-driven. That's going to bring in a whole new cast of characters because at one time you never would have thought about Microsoft and advertising in the same conversation. That certainly has come to fruition.

"There will be more of the technology so the casts of characters will change on the data and the insights. Like the media agencies always say, 'We are in a power position because we have the data.' The media agencies' problem is they don't understand how to get insights. The creative agencies just don't have the right people. Creative agencies, the ones who are going to survive, will be the ones who have an outstanding creative product staffed by people who are able to work with data partners to get the insights to drive the creative process. They're really going to be just executional. I don't think that this is so far in the future. It's happening now."

෴

Susan Kim, "Lack of transparency led to fragmentation of media from the traditional agencies. The big thing is that agencies are not concerning themselves enough with how much money the clients are making, but I will say digital is pretty good about that. When I went to Advertising.com, I was floored how every single day we got an update on exactly all the ads that were running, how much was being paid, how many people were clicking, how much revenue was coming from each particular ad, and how much profit margin there was for each particular ad. That's amazing, right? And the joke used to be, 'Hey, how effective was your TV ad?' The traditional creative would answer, 'Really effective! I got three job offers after it. I got all these people interested in me after it ran because it won an award, blah, blah, blah.' I'd say, 'No, no, how was it for the client?' And they'd shrug and reply, 'I don't know, but it ran.' There was no way to measure it, so they were just in it for themselves and just promoting themselves. They took full advantage of the fact you couldn't measure it.

"A lot of the online ads used to be more static. There wasn't movement, and we found that just by having slight movement would get a huge increase in clicks. Just putting in some subtle movement made a huge difference or making the button look more 3D or just having a very clearly defined button. Once, we accidentally made the whole banner clickable. But after looking at the data, we couldn't figure out why the banner was doing so much better. It turned out it was because the whole thing was clickable. We'd have to ask ourselves why we were spending all this extra coding time to make just the button hot when making the entire banner hot gets it a huge bump in clicks.

"You don't have to make it that much better. If you just go from 0.3% to 0.9%, well you've increased by 300% and so you can buy 300% more media, or if you can just get the click rate up a little bit more, you could double or even triple improve it by doing something fairly simple. And that's why A/B tests are important. But not everyone is doing it.

"You probably know you shouldn't be eating junk food and you and your wife should be sitting down doing the monthly budget every – and maybe you do all of that. Because there are a lot of things you should do, but since everything is not falling to pieces when you don't do it, you don't do it. When I was at Advertising.com, despite getting all of this feedback, there was still no testing until I came. They said, 'Yeah, we know we need to do it, but when you don't have someone overseeing the whole thing, it doesn't get done.' Because you have the technical people really concerned with optimizing the one ad that you are running, and that actually was easier for them.'

"Sometimes I talk to clients who don't even know if they have installed Google Analytics in their site. A client I'm working for, right now, they use Constant Contact for emails, but they have never even looked at the open or bounce rates. I said, 'Holy crap! I don't know how they are not like blacklisting you right now because you are sending this out and 10% are bouncing back.' They replied, 'We've never cleaned out our list.' There were people that were asking to be unsubscribed and it was going into a black hole. It's unbelievable sometimes that because you have the data, you would think this wouldn't take that long, but people still are not doing it. They know they are not supposed to eat super high calorie foods or they know they should be working out and they don't do it. This is the same thing like with all human nature.

"When ad banners first came out, the clicks per rate was 5%. It was because people were like, 'What? Wow! Look at this!' They were willing to click on anything. Then it started going dramatically down because of experience and fatigue. Now, it has come to the point where it is just wallpaper and so people don't even see it anymore. That display ads have still been able to not go to 0.0001 shows that it's working because people do nothing but get more and more jaded all the time about ads. It's going to get to the point, though, where we will see far fewer ads just because the clicks are rated. Even with all of this, there is only so much you could squeeze. There is only so much more you can optimize. When is the last time you clicked on an ad?

"Everyone is jaded and that's what everyone says. Everyone I've interviewed said, 'I don't see prostitutes and I don't click on ads,' like it was equally disgusting. It's going to go away and there will be some ads, but it won't be like what you are seeing now and occasionally there will be interstitials. Instead, you are going to see a lot more sponsorship of the page where it really organically makes sense. You are going to see more of that because we are getting to the point where we cannot optimize them anymore, and the younger you are, the less likely you are to click on ad, so it's going to be going away."

⌐

Jeff Cheong, "Some things do not change. In the early days, clients (and agencies alike) were obsessed with collecting people in databases. Now, we've just migrated that to the collection of Facebook Fans, Twitter and Instagram followers. We have the tendency to make new media old overnight."

⌐

Former Group Account Director for Wunderman New York, Alex Eisenberg, "What is useful about digital tools is that people who are passionate about something tend to comment on things, so if you use something like Twitter Velocity to monitor the velocity of commentary, it acts as an AWACS early warning system – and I'll give a specific example. We had a launch for Nokia where the strategy was written by five agencies: the media agency, the in-store retail marketing agency, JWT, Wunderman, and Tracey Locke for retail marketing. For this particular launch, I argued vociferously that the strategy was off base. It was not well thought out. It was wrong. It was not going to be successful. I lost that argument. So, at some point you just say, 'Do it for England.'

"Of course, what happened is the campaign launched, and it was quickly apparent that it was awkward. We had a task team that was constantly monitoring Twitter actively around keywords for Nokia. And what we were able to do is we were able to pick out specific comments relative to this new handset we were launching that said, 'Wow. This is great for this reason. This is really good for this reason.' There were three or four features that were rising to the top of the discussion. These were the things that people were liking. What we did is we used that to inform the brief that we wrote – to *completely* redo the campaign over a weekend. We didn't do it with animated GIFs. We used research from comScore that said static banners will give you an immediate lift over your existing campaign by a factor of about 15%.

"We were seeing the biggest jump on Twitter from moment to moment in terms of interest. Things the people were retweeting and so forth. As soon as we launched that, we saw a 40% increase over the other campaign. We had a team that was on a weekly case to monitor what people were saying using the Radian6 launching tool. There are other tools out there now, but we had a team that was on a weekly case of monitoring, measuring specific topic areas. 'What are people saying about our future set?' 'What are people saying about our advertising?' 'What are people saying about us vis-à-vis the competition?' We get the data in from the prior week. We evaluated it for two to three days, we had an internal meeting and then, on the following Monday, a week after the data came in, we had a very short 30-minute presentation to the public relations people and a few senior marketers. It was kind of a like reading the paper. It wasn't a whole lot more complicated than that, but it did allow us to have a flash report of marketplace issues or accounting issues, any kind of competitive activity that we needed to highlight to management. And because the PR people sat in on it, there was a channel up to the head of the North American business unit. There was a channel from this information into the executive suite."

⌐

Tony Surtees, Board Member of Commercialisation Australia, Co-founder of Zeetings and former VP and GM of Yahoo!'s Commerce Group in the USA, "In my view, television is not dying, but it is changing. Television will now be increasingly bought programmatically. Old world assumptions about broadcasting are also dying. Soon there will be little need to rely on guesses about where to place display ads because of engagement metrics that track user engagement.

"If one wants to think about how technology is transforming the media and ad buying industry, think about how it had transformed the investment industry. The stockbroking industry used to be dependent upon the advantage of information asymmetry. Brokers knew more than investors. and some investors knew much more than others. Then the playing field got substantially leveled. Today, investors have easy access to so much more information and most of it is available free of charge. Everything pretty much is knowable by everybody. Charles Schwab introduced the concept of low-cost broking that depended upon the consumer being way more informed.

"Ad technology (ad-tech) is having a similar impact on advertisers, so advertising is now going through a similar transformation. The media buying industry (and in fact the media industry) has also been dependent upon information asymmetry. It is the world of digital display media that has changed. Now advertising agencies use 'trading desks' to drive much of digital media buying, a concept that has been inspired by the experience of investment industry.

"Today, programmatic media buying is a key tool in the digital arms race that is media buying. Driven by data, this powerful new tool adds much more precision to the challenge of ensuring the right message is seen by the right people at the right time for the right cost. Marketers increasingly do not just buy media anymore, they buy audiences. Programmatic media techniques are the way they do this. The real-time bidding or DSP [demand-side platform] and DMP platforms add intelligence to help develop and then apply consumer insights. You can now target your audiences with great precision almost irrespective of what media they are exposed to. Interestingly, while programmatic was really developed to be used in digital media it has become such a popular and effective tool that other forms of advertising are being bought that way. Advertisers and media buying agencies now want to apply these programmatic buying processes to media such as television and radio where it's never been used before. These new targeting technologies and big data software are radically disrupting survey and sampling based marketing techniques."

⤶

Diane McKinnon, "I would say business analytics and media metrics are our biggest drivers. Sometimes, we can connect the dots all the way to sales results. We can usually show how the kinds of things we do typically are driving the pipeline. Sometimes, a lot of it is about partner engagement: getting materials out to them, getting them trained on products and services that are being offered, so there're engagement metrics. There's also web metrics. We do put stuff up for awards and some clients state specifically, 'We want our work to win awards,' and therefore, those can be a measure as well, but we're much more focused on what the client success metric is."

⤶

Andy Greenaway, "The brands that will find success in the future will embrace and implement a form of CRM (whether that's through social media, an application, or simply via email or SMS). Communication will be a continuous conversation in an always-on world, across multiple devices. Everything will be measurable and thus tweakable. Brand communications of the future will be a concoction of promotion, content, social, and technology. A big brand idea will still be the glue that holds it all together."

⬿

Martin Howard, "If the past is of any record, we can't trust brands to self-regulate. [They need agency partners to advise them.] The thing is, there are too many [independent] disciplines involved at the moment. In marketing, there's an overlap of the mathematics database, management, and creative. There are all sorts of people in the pie, and there's the media themselves. Now what we've seen when there's a problem that occurs is finger-pointing instead of self-regulation. The television companies will say, 'Well, this is what the public is demanding. That's why we are doing this. This is why we are showing this television program,' or 'We think this particular advertisement is okay because the people love it.' When it comes to big data, the government doesn't really understand the depth of that problem, the pace at which it's emerging. The legal fraternity might be just becoming aware of it, but it's just moving too fast for people to, first of all, make an ethical judgment about it and then begin a grassroots movement to change it before eventually seeing government intervention.

"They are going to be coerced. There'll certainly be financial incentives for people to hand over data. We've seen this with loyalty cards and the points that you get on your credit card. There's a pattern of people accepting giving up that all for a small incentive. They're okay to give more data away. We're already seeing that people are making a choice to step away from that mechanism and they're seeing how that will impact them financially. There has been a fringe group in that space for a long time, but there are increasingly more and more people who are either marginalized because they don't want to or can't access those advantages or those incentives and then the rest of us, in the mainstream, are just seeing that pattern on a gradual basis.

"I just don't think there are enough people watching and with the access to the data that's being used. There's the CCTV cameras all across the city – a lot of them are being used inappropriately. And you don't know when they are being used to target a girl with a low-cut dress or to follow a person that has been profiled for all sorts of different reasons. So no one's watching the watchers.

"When it comes to the big data, the amount of data and the pace at which that area is moving is too fast for us to create the safeguards that need to be in place. You'd probably do best looking at a place like Europe where they are more aggressively monitoring it and understand what's going on. The horse is going to bolt, and it might be too late to control it. It's going to be a problem.

"The biggest thing is using 'big data' to predict people's shopping or consuming patterns with advertising as a means to tap into them so that the marketer will know exactly when the best time is to screen a potato chip commercial in order to make the cash register ring. They have got complete control of the timing of that, and they know when the shops are going to be open and when most people are going to be hitting them. They're really using the data.

"David Ogilvy was one of the first guys to really consider that level of feedback in the ad in the creative process and, although as a designer I resist that level of interference – you can't argue against his approach if a particular layout is going to sell 20x more than another layout. But it was still fairly radical in its time because art directors really wanted to own their patch. If someone came and said, 'That's a nice layout, but it's going to sell 20% less than this other layout,' then it was hard to refute – but still annoying. It was a case of overriding the creative side with facts.

"Ever since then, I've been a realist when it comes to creative work, and I've tried to find the best of both worlds: creative layouts that actually sell. Overall, that is the most powerful dynamic, and there are different ways of using it. Obviously, online is being used now very actively, predictive behavioral profiling and tracking, and it's the heart of all the major campaigns today[15]."

---

15 Josh Sklar, "The sophistication of these toolsets is breathtaking and breaking new ground in delivering the promise technology had always made to businesses, but rarely fulfilled, yet not every client has goals that require them."

⌇

Scott Morrison, "What does a web site metric mean? I've got a prime example of how it's relative. Eight or nine years ago, we did a rebranding and a web site for an investment firm that does a special kind of investment work called mezzanine financing. Now, they explained to us who their audience was. They had a good budget. It wasn't a great big brand, but, hey, it was a good project. We started seeing the metrics coming in. We ran a digital ad campaign in terms of some web banners. We ran a print campaign in magazines that were for accountants in Canada, and when the metrics started coming in, I literally stared to sweat, because, in my eyes, they were awful. I was thinking, 'Oh my god. What did we miss here? What has happened? Did we completely miss the audience? Did we say the wrong thing? What has happened here?'

"Well as it turned out, our client called, and they were ecstatic. We had exceeded their expectations in terms of the feedback from people coming to the web site. In our eyes, we were only getting hundreds of people coming in, not thousands. We said, 'They're going to be furious.' But in their world, it was amazing, because one key question we had stupidly forgotten to ask was, 'What does success look like to you?' That's a question I ask every client now because of this experience. We were panicking that the traffic was so low. But there are only 20 of these types of investment deals that go on in Canada in any given year. Not just with this company, but all of the deals in the entire country of Canada. Twenty of them per year. Getting a couple of hundred hits a day to this web site was unbelievable for them. They were over the moon while we were shaking in our boots. We were completely panicking for nothing.

"Eight or nine years ago, metrics weren't being tracked the same way. We did the BASF web site just before that, and I'm not even sure how much time and effort was put into SEO work at that point. It wasn't even a conversation. We didn't start learning about SEO until a year after we finished that project. It's ridiculous. In hindsight, what were we thinking? But at the time, the client didn't mention it, and we didn't think about it, and it wasn't part of the strategy."

Chapter 13: Breaking into Digital

For the first five years of the existence of interactive digital marketing, most of the companies that advertised for positions in the field required that candidates possess at least eight years of hands-on experience. People knew so little about the area that they didn't even have a clue as to what the requirements should be for vetting those who ostensibly did. In response, all sorts of characters have emerged throughout the years who purport to be wizened digital masters or the modern version (with the title that makes most in the industry shudder in revulsion), social media gurus.

How could anyone have the chutzpah to claim to be an expert in a brand-new arena such as those? We are only just now beginning to understand some of the science behind attracting desired audiences, leading them down prescribed paths to purchase funnels, and developing online relationships between them and the brands. We talked a good game, but for a very long time, we were no better about tracking and measurement online than we were offline. It has taken nearly two decades for the research and development phase to begin to transition to a hopefully more consistently effective one where we have the platforms, tools, analytics, years of learnings, and refined best practices that can get us there.

Beginning back circa 1994, those first years were incredible times for those who managed to recognize the immense green field opportunities in front of them. There were many roads that led them there, and the most successful people were those happy to admit what they didn't know, ask questions, or try and fail on their own until they got it right.

⤸

Valerie Cheng, "My digital experience weirdly began in a small post-production company. I was then employed to assist my boss in photography and videography, but during my spare time, he handed me the Macromedia Dreamweaver version 1 manual to explore creating the company's web site – my first. I was totally self-taught, which proves that anyone can start to pick up digital if they really want a better career in advertising."

⤸

Ken Mandel, "In 1994, Nicolas Negroponte's *Being Digital* was my first peek into what I wanted to be when I grew up. Later, in 1997, I was working in a traditional advertising network, Bates, based in Burma of all places, and I would travel to Singapore for regional meetings at the Bates Indochina office.

For whatever reason, there was a section of the office partitioned by 'groovy' beads where Josh, the creative director, and Kenneth, the art director, worked on web sites in what had been called Bates Interactive for the first two years.

"I was fascinated by what they were doing, and I would always pop in when I was in town to see what they were up to. I then started to read what I could about this graphical Internet called the World Wide Web, which was non-existent in Rangoon. Shortly after that, I was transferred temporarily to Singapore, where I immersed myself further by reading and spending more time on the Web.

"In June 1999, I was living in Cambodia when an opening came up to work at the much-grown Bates Interactive, by then renamed XM (short for Expanded Media) Asia Pacific. I leaped at it and moved to Singapore. I had no formal training – it was all on the job and using my general management skills from advertising.

"That was the beginning of my digital career path, and I remained with XM for six years. The early days were amazing. We were literally pioneers breaking new virtual ground at every turn. We often took briefs where we only knew about 50% of the solution and had to invent the rest as we went along. It was exhilarating and scary at the same time. We were the very opposite of the commodity service the rest of advertising had become.

"Today, digital has unfortunately moved closer to the commodity edge. That makes it less fun than it was back in the day. Selling digital back then was both harder and easier. Harder, because the people buying it had no clue. Easier, because the people buying it had no clue. You could get a meeting with just about anyone because you were the shiny new thing. Getting them to take the risk and reach deep into their pocket for dollars versus dimes was tough.

"It's easier to sell digital now because the industry has matured, but there is also a lot more competition. Talent continues to be a challenge and likely will always be a challenge, especially for agencies, because life in the agency is hard and younger folks are finding better options elsewhere (e.g., Facebook, Google, etc.)."

～

David Shulman, "Coming out of school, I had accepted a job with a really interesting technology startup. As the first one in my class to accept a job I was relaxed and ready to enjoy the last part of my senior year. Then they lost their funding, and I lost my job. So back in 1991, I got my first taste of what can happen during a bubble.

"I ended up with this psychology degree, which back then was something that really barred me from being able to interview with a lot of companies in the marketing space. They said, 'We don't want people who haven't studied business. We want people who have advanced marketing expertise.'

"I don't take credit for having the foresight to know that I would be the CEO of a leading company that's focused on how to engage and create great experiences for people. But I have to say that having a background in psychology could not have been a better foundation for understanding people, and it defines how I behave and how I lead. It's a very important part of who I am and my background. That is absolutely key to my understanding of user behaviors – what drives people to do things."

⌒

E-commerce entrepreneur and former Senior VP of Wells Fargo's Internet Services Group, Eskander Matta, "In 1994-95, I kept hearing about these people who were going into the digital space, and then some of them were actually showing me the capabilities of the true Internet. All these companies like Yahoo! and Netscape and so on going public started to permeate the consciousness in a way. And so what happened at that time is I got really fed up with the whole investment banking *Liar's Poker* thing I was doing at the time, and I just up and quit because I couldn't work a hundred hours a week in that type of a culture and environment. It is not me and how I like to treat people or be treated by people.

"Then this buddy of mine calls me up and he's working for a company called Organic. He tells me, 'We're growing really fast, we need some people to come in and build a strategic services practice for us. We're really much more strong on the media side and we have these creatives and project managers and engineers.'

"He said, 'If there's a creative brief from a traditional agency, then we can execute, but right now we're starting to have companies come to us and tell us they want us to build a digital business – and they don't know how. They don't have a strategy. They don't know what they want. We don't have any brief to work off of. So we need to get someone in here that has some actual professional services and consulting experience and do this for us. Why don't you come on maybe as a contractor and help us out with this client management piece and try out this digital stuff and see if it's interesting for you.' So that's how I got into the industry.

"The thing that blew my mind was we had built this web site – I think it was called Fragrance Counter or something like that – and it sold perfume and cosmetics over the Web. Someone showed me the administrative console of the site. Just how much stuff you could see about the customer, what they looked at, what they bought, how they bought it, if you did *x* then *y* happened; and so I just really started to see the power of the medium actually from looking at it from the back-end piece of most of the experience, the data view. That just blew my mind. How much you could know about the customer, how much marketing you could do, how much you could do to close the sale, all the experimentation you could do while merchandizing. That, for me, was huge.

"I started really to see the power of it as opposed to just you can go on and read some news story and compose an email and whatever. Then I could really see how this thing was going to be a monster game changer for commerce. I was off to the races from that point."

⤻

Peter Moss, "I never really knew much about anything I particularly wanted to do. Not having much idea about anything, I learned to program. My year was the first year in school that had Computer Science on the menu. I came out the other side having learned to program. It was with all the intent of doing my A-levels with no real direction after that, and the lecturer there was teaching people how to program for the next two years. He said that it was a waste of my time being in his class and I'd be better use working in his little software shop. During the lessons, I used to go run errands and develop little bits, like digital signage at the Wigan Rugby Grounds for all the cheers and wave things. That was odd. He said, 'If you don't really know why you're here and why you're going to university, there's another one-year course that takes you straight into a company. You place there for about six months, and there is a very good chance they'll give you a job.' I did that and they did. This was in '83. There was an Apple in the office. The Apple //e was on its way, and the IBM PC was just arriving in offices and businesses everywhere as a trophy wife.

"Anyway, I moved around to a few different places and by 1993, I was on client side, where the job climate changed from raw coding, which I really enjoyed, to migration from legacy systems to Unix-based operations. Everyone was already panicking about the Millennium Bug[16] even in 1992. I was going through thousands and thousands of lines of code checking out date routines. I decided that I had enough. I got bored very quickly and was spending way too much time in the clubs of Manchester.

"I had a friend in Hong Kong and I said, 'Look, I have had enough of England.' The other thing is if you do well at a certain role, it's not very easy, and certainly wasn't then, to take a different path. That's why I ended up in Hong Kong with no job and £200, which lasted me all of a day. That was a good incentive to get up and find a job.

"When I walked into Ogilvy & Mather Direct in '93, it was into a department full of very, very talented teams of art directors and copywriters who had at their disposal a studio of people who could actually use the tools: the Photoshops, good drawing skills, and everything else. We were not writer-dominant, but our smarter people were writers. Our ideas were very logical. Not boring ideas. They were very thoughtful ideas, though not very visual ones."

⤳

Torrence Boone, "I left Bain as a Senior Manager to join Avenue A/ NYC. Everyone thought I was insane, but there was such a sense of possibility then. A sense that the Web and digital were redefining everything."

⤳

---

16   In order to save space in databases, programmers in the 1960s and 1970s truncated years from four numbers to two (e.g., 1975 was listed as 75). The big fear was that in the year 2000, the computers would think "00" meant 1900 and many critical systems around the world would crash – as in airplanes falling out of the sky. Programmers had to go through millions of lines of code to manually change them back to four numbers, but couldn't get them all in time for the year 2000. Still, planes did not fall from the sky.

Sean Lam, "I started by pursuing a diploma in Electronic Media Design (EMD) at Temasek Polytechnic in Singapore. As much as I enjoyed graphic design, I felt that EMD was more interesting. It was pretty much unexplored (they called it 'new media' then), and it appealed to my inner geek. My interests in computer games and music seemed a good match with what the course was offering, so I dived into it.

"Back in those school days in the late '90s, the Internet was pretty much still in its infancy. I remember spending more time on IRC than surfing web sites over a painfully slow 28.8k modem. Lessons were mostly centered on designing CD-ROMs with Macromedia Director. There wasn't much emphasis on learning HTML to create web sites. However, by the time I graduated in 1998, CD-ROMs were no longer in demand. Instead, things were heating up on the Internet side.

"I picked up Web development skills on the job. Learning HTML tagging, how to optimize animated gifs, etc. as I went along. It wasn't until I discovered Macromedia Flash 3 that things got really interesting for me. I love interactivity beyond just clicking on a banner and I really have a thing for animation, so imagine my excitement when I discovered that I could finally apply my skill set on the Internet. Although already in its third version, Flash was still a format not fully explored, and there was a very good chance of being the first to do something unique with it. I took advantage of that, and it helped me get where I am today.

"Today Flash is in decline, and like everyone else, my portfolio has diversified to mostly HTML5 and jQuery-based projects. I do miss the ability of Flash to create unique web sites due to its 'blank-canvas' nature. More and more web sites are looking alike these days because of the current web standards.

"That said, it's still the vision and idea that matters most. Creativity really shouldn't be dictated by technology. Thanks to the demise of Flash, I've come to discover new ways of using and applying animated gifs as well as getting creative with the simplest of HTML to make sites that automatically function on various screen sizes. I've come to understand that they call this responsive design.

"I would say that I started out as a jack-of-all-trades, and in a sense, I still am one. I used to be able to complete projects as a one-man show, but these days, I leave the heavy lifting in terms of programming to trusted partners. Ultimately, my expertise lies in creativity, craft, and aesthetics, and in a way they aren't really affected by the changes in technology. If anything, the ever-diversifying nature of digital only provides more opportunities and challenges for me to hone these skill sets further."

⌒

Martin Howard, "I was working outside the normal agency as a consultant. I saw that the agencies weren't very interested [in new media], but the advertisers themselves fell into two groups: one who understood the proposition of the Internet and the digital space and they wanted to get it done. They were okay with the budget, and they were okay to have that creative driven by me as a consultant. Then another group who was really confused by the whole thing, very suspicious of it, unable to commit serious budgets to it, and unable to assess the creative.

"There were a lot of marketers in that last group category, and a lot of my experience at that time was educating them. I had to create my own resources to educate those advertisers and businesses about what the Internet was, what the promise was, what the capacity was, what they should expect from digital.

"Fortunately, the technology was so primitive at the beginning of the Web, and Adobe was one of the first good products out in the market for that. I knew I didn't want to be a programmer, so I had to wait for a decent desktop application to come out in order to build my web sites. It was primitive enough in those stages that I could keep myself up to date through bulletin board systems (BBSes) and emails, newsletters, videos, or material that was being put out by the vendors.

"Beyond that, as things developed, it was much the same thing. I was able to keep enough ahead of the curve and develop my skills in software to the point where I was ahead of what my clients were looking for.

"Currently, I've decided that the future is in content management systems rather than being a Dreamweaver guru. That what clients want is a good reliable web site that is creative, but doesn't have the massive front-end development that we used to do. We've been able to maintain pace with the market and keep the emphasis on good marketing web site as opposed to most of the competition, which have been driven by technical things like the Flash fad. It was a great fad, but it was always a specific technology that was overused. It's one thing that clients connected with and they engaged with, but it was done too much, and it was irrelevant to the creative marketing message. But it was a great fad. In many ways, it might've been Google that killed Flash. From a search-engine-optimization perspective, it presented a whole bunch of content that's just is not searchable. But it was a good technology. It's still a good technology. Every other good format has disappeared because of the constraints of being dominant."

⌒

Neil Leslie, "When I arrived at DDB in 1999, they already had a digital team of about five folks in place to help them develop small sites, banners, and eDMs [electronic direct mails] for various clients. My role was largely to act as a researcher for integrated campaigns and pitches. As a result, I worked with them on and off throughout my time there identifying new approaches and technologies that we could consider for our clients.

"At around the same time, some old school friends approached me to help them set up a dot.com by the name of Rocket8.com. It was through my involvement in this company that I really started to see the potential of digital. Rocket8.com used a point-based auction system to incentivize young people to interact with brands via research, advertising, and sampling.

"More importantly, users could earn additional points by referring their friends to the site via email. Seems obvious now, but at the time, this was considered to be among the earliest examples of viral marketing – one of the early iterations of what we now call social media. The results were amazing. We attracted well over one million registered members in just over a year without spending a penny, which in turn led to us being able to attract numerous investors and large clients such as Microsoft.

"We'd all be rich for sure – or so we thought. Unfortunately, our site became a victim of two key shortfalls: our inability to keep up with the hackers who constantly found new ways to game the system and up their points to preposterous levels. And our inability to keep a million-plus members involved in an experience where most people left empty-handed because only the most active users won. Eventually, the dot.com crash caused our investors to pull out, and the company disappeared almost overnight.

"So much for my dreams of dot.com millionairedom. That said, I learnt a great deal about the power of the medium, the fickle and demanding nature of people online, and the unforeseen difficulties that often arise in the digital domain."

↬

Bob Gebara, "Oddly enough, there was a time when the term digital referred only to watches with phosphorescent numbers, especially in a place I lived far from Silicon Valley called Brazil. In the early '90s, our economy was beginning to open to foreign markets, and the access to new technologies was still very restricted.

"Like everyone in my generation, I was an analogical guy who transmuted into digital. I was a young copywriter at McCann Erickson in São Paulo and had no idea where the digital adventure would take me. I still don't.

"I was the first connected professional at McCann Brazil and one of the pioneers among all agencies in the country. I still wrote my ads and scripts on a heavy Olivetti Lettera[17] when I got a PC from my brother with access to bulletin board systems. That made the difference.

"A short time later, already totally addicted to interactivity, I got a night job as a trainee in one of the first digital production houses of the country, Da Vinci New Media. I worked at McCann during the days and late into the night at Da Vinci.

"There, in the early days of the Internet, I was one of the copywriters of a web site called *Brahmaland*, fully created using Macromedia's Shockwave. An almost irresponsible daring at a time when nobody had any idea what [web browser] plug-ins were and modems only supported connection speeds up to 14.4 Kbps. The site told the story of a person who had lost his Apple Newton, another technological luxury at that time – and the first mobile tablet!

"There, I was also in contact with AlphaWorld, a 3D virtual world where I built my house: a crystal pyramid where I hung and exposed people

---

17   A portable mechanical typewriter.

to my favorite paintings, with the links of the museums where they were in the real world.

"At that time, only one journalist used to speak about the Internet on the Brazilian advertising vehicles. We got in touch by email, which was also an unusual thing, as almost no one even knew what an email was. He scheduled an interview with me in front of my pyramid! Good times. Unforgettable.

Blender, the interactive magazine on CD-ROM, May 1995 issue.

"I devoured each issue of *Wired* and *Blender* CD-ROM magazines, anxiously waited for each new Shockwave 'hot site of the week' from Nike. I was thrilled to see the anthological animation of the colored beach ball when FutureSplash Animator, the forerunner of Flash, was released.

"The same month, I got a Lion at Cannes for a TV commercial, so I quit my job as analogical copywriter and launched Thunder House Brazil. Together with around 10 brilliant young programmers and designers, such as André Matarazzo and Rico Villas-Bôas, I created one of the most innovative and award-winning digital agencies in the world (at a time when the division between traditional and digital agencies still seemed to make sense).

"The campaigns that marked me the most were created then, in the beginning of the Web; maybe for nostalgia, or maybe because at that time everything was new and anything was possible.

"The web site created by Thunder House for the Laramara Foundation, for example, simulated blindness by relying on sound alone to guide the user to a philanthropic solicitation, at which point graphics and text became available. The major advertising festivals awarded the piece because it persuaded the user through a sensorial stimulus.

"The brand that understood and benefited the most from the Internet boom was Nike. It coincided with an era when the brand was expanding throughout the world, engaging in sports outside the United States, and the Internet worked out nicely for them. The sites, campaigns, production, it seemed it was simply a matter of applying Nike's logo and everything was already cool.

"It was a mixture of ingenuity and daring on the Internet. The Internet was a new field, and nobody knew where it would go. What was remarkable was the total lack of fear to meddle, to take risks, and perhaps even to get hurt. There were sites whose purpose we couldn't figure out and others that we didn't even know how to use. But all of them were very nice.

"Today, I am convinced that a good idea transcends the platform. The idea's application is what is specific to the environment. It's not just a matter of 'Saving as...' For the idea to get through, it takes an understanding of the environment, whether in print, on the Web, or for a mobile app. It's not just applying, using the same colors, the same typeface, including the illustration, and saying it's ready because all media is covered. It's important to recognize the backbone of the campaign and sometimes subvert the idea, so that it has the same effect in any medium. Translating text doesn't mean only changing the words."

~

Jeff Cheong, "I first noticed digital becoming more of a player in the dot.com era, when brands started to look at response mechanics, loosely termed as Client Relationship Management. We saw an exponential increase in new business from banking, FMCG [fast-moving consumer goods], and mobile phone brands requesting direct-response campaigns. The cost per acquisition and ROI surpassed that of a traditional process. When the management saw almost 100% of revenue retained in a digital business, they started to invest more (we handle all the production work in-house, unlike the advertising model where there are many third-party costs).

"The age-old battle between 'traditional' creative vs. 'Digital' creative still exists. That will never go away until we send both parties back to school and retrain them.

"I was very fortunate because I grew from graphic designer to advertising art director and made the switch to the interactive craft. I spoke the same language as the traditionalists and introduced new lingo to make them see how far the idea could travel and solicit a response from a consumer.

"As a young traditional creative, I started work at a design studio that required me to do typesetting with bromides and Cow Gum and set squares. I finished the work and discarded the 'leftover' bromide unknowingly. Needless to say, when the boss found out about it, I was kicked out of the studio – *on my first day of work.*

"After that episode, I started to look for a more forgiving environment to work in. Through an IT Consultant friend who needed help in creating web pages, I dived headfirst into the world of World Wide Web and never looked back.

"How I constructed my first web page:

- Designed in Aldus PageMaker.
- Screen captured and transferred over to Photoshop.
- Created a spinning logo with FutureSplash Animator (which became Flash after Macromedia bought it).
- HTML was put together using Windows Notepad.
- Found out about image optimization with DeBabelizer three months later.

"Limitation breeds better the thinker. That was the environment then. We were working with limited tools and dial-up modems. We had to plan way in advance before delivering a fresh experience. The lack of resources pushed us to innovate. I remember creating 'video' on Flash before Flash video actually happened.

"Some flashback memories that bring a smile on my face when I talk about them.

"Three nostalgic sounds I miss:

- My US Robotics modem dialing
- The chime on my Eudora mail
- Badly looped midi background music

"Three nostalgic requests from clients:

- Blinking text in a paragraph to highlight the message.
- 3D spinning logo (some still ask for it today).
- Visit counter on the main page of sites."

↶

Barry Wong, "It was in 2001 when I first joined an agency that was setting up a digital department. I was fortunate to have a general manager who was very open despite being very new to the digital scene. I did get a lot of respect from my GM then, but she was probably the only person who ever took my presence seriously.

"The Creative Director would hardly give me the time of the day, always leaving the digital component to the very last, believing that digital would never be a driver as a channel. I would get instructions to design an entire site that was due for creative presentations in two to three days. There was little championing of digital, very little understanding of technology, zero belief in system and information architecture. It was very difficult. I had to work in conditions like these between 2001 and 2006.

"In 2006, I joined a digital agency that was part of a bigger network. It was then that things started looking up. Every brief was a standalone digital brief that was developed by the client digital marketing team. There was little requirement to synchronize with the above-the-line efforts, and the client believed in the concept of engagement and participation. They just weren't too hot about us getting overly creative with the experiential process.

"When there were requirements for a holistic 360 campaign that happened once a year, the traditional and digital creative directors worked together to develop an idea that could transcend through-the-line. We, as the digital agency, were involved from the get-go, from strategy to brainstorming to concept development. We were extremely delighted that two years out of three, it was the digital idea that led the entire holistic campaign. This was perhaps one of those rare opportunities that came along.

"Since leaving that agency in 2009, it has pretty much come back to square one where the above-the-line teams still come to the digital teams I've led and dump stuff on us as a 'by the way.' Isn't that the epitome of regression?"

Jim Speelmon: "I worked on these projects with humongous budgets. There's nothing worse than a project where the client says budget is not an issue. It's just, 'Christ! This will take forever and cost a fortune!' Half a million dollars on homepage concepts. It was ridiculous. Because of the nature of the projects that I worked on, the Web Outfitter Service, for example, was supposed to be software- and content-optimized for the Pentium III where they have these key areas. There was photography, gaming, and stuff like that. Quirky, niche areas.

"I wasn't really that involved with how you would drive people to the web site. For me, it started with when someone arrived because at the time, and even today, this happens a lot. The media brings them to the front door. After that, how you get them to the room they want is a lot of how you organize things on a page.

"When I first started, nobody had any idea what a wireframe was. You just designed the site and it would look pretty. Then you touch it and it doesn't go anywhere – it falls apart – so helping clients understand that the first step to building even a campaign site is to craft what the user experience journey is supposed to be. When I would do that work, this is one of the things that I brought in to add sense to it: you would start at the point of contact. Our job was to build the user; I would always insist that we start at point of contact. It might be somebody comes in through search, so we plot what the journey would look like. If it's through your banner ad, this is what that would look like from their perspective.

"Because your user journey will vary depending on what the frame of reference of the person coming in was and depending on what they saw right before they arrived, it is all going to have a huge effect on what we deliver in order to meet someone's expectation, which is why I have always had a problem with a 'we-will-just-pilot-this' attitude. If this is supposed to work with everything else, I can certainly understand wanting to trial something, but what's the point of trialing a tactic without having some larger strategy that you are trying to achieve? People get very wrapped up in the things that you could do without actually thinking about why we would be doing them in the first place."

✍

Angeli Beltran, "It was those early days of direct mail with letter shop-ping, database, list rentals. What I loved about it was that you could be very creative and at the same time know exactly how your creativity was having an effect on the business and making impact on the people you're commu-nicating with, as compared to going into advertising, which I felt was a bit too broad. There weren't really many tangible results that I could hang on to. Sure, there was the goal of building brand-awareness, but it wasn't really related to the direct results of the business, and that's why I was always keen on direct marketing and CRM.

"At American Express, I was in charge of the list brokers and cleaning up the database to make sure that we had the right communication going to the right people. I liked the whole idea of individualized marketing, and at that time we could only do so much.

"I got introduced to CRM [customer relationship management] when I was in Ogilvy, and they were pioneers of this area. I can say that OgilvyOne led with this idea of relationship marketing. As technology became less ex-pensive and more powerful, it was very natural to transition CRM into digital. Since you can communicate directly one-on-one, you can target your messag-es. You can do the statistics with analyses on steroids instantaneously due to everything being automated.

"I remember before I used to get a statistician to go through all the numbers and then I had to choose which list to prioritize because we didn't have much budget for sending out mail shots. Today you can communicate with practically everybody one-on-one using different, targeted messages – and that's how my career transitioned naturally into digital."

✍

Todd Ruff, Group Marketing Director for Dell and former Client Part-ner with Avenue A | Razorfish, "An introduction to digital really began for me in 1994 when the agency I worked for pitched and won the Netscape account. At that time, we were an advertising agency that was at the forefront of technology, and [we] had earned our stripes introducing the world to file/print sharing through NetWare and to the idea that a chip was the 'smarts' of a computer. But the world really opened up for me as I watched our company start to learn about and launch this funky little browser.

"Prior to this browser and our understanding of what it could do, we simply sat behind the walls of corporate America and were wowed by our ability to be able to simply send information digitally and receive feedback without getting sucked into an hour-long meeting. The world at this time was moving pretty fast, as we all were just getting our arms around email and its ability to open up instantaneous communication that didn't require typing a memo, printing it out, getting into an elevator or car, and hand delivering to a recipient.

"The Web browser transformed everything. We could actually create a true customer experience with a brand that could potentially deliver a brand story from start to finish. All we had to do was contain the story in simple, navigable frames that didn't completely bog down an i486 processor-based machine."

⤚

Aden Hepburn, "When I first started working, I was put in the back behind the IT guy in the room with no windows because that's where the web guy goes, right? I did become really good friends with the IT guy, so I got access to all the things that are normally locked down for administrators only, which helped me do my job. Digital there started as just me.

"It was a really interesting combination of me being quite young, very early 20s, and chatting with midlife 35- to 45-year-old creative directors about what the web site should look like once the project was done. Them potentially markering[18] out what it should look like versus me designing what it should like and trying to explain to them why their web site design just couldn't work and why it couldn't be built. Or why they couldn't have full-screen video of their TV commercials back then.

"It was pretty difficult because I was young and it was new technology, and these were some very high-paid, very senior creative directors who thought what they were designing was, of course, the right way forward. At that point, 10 years ago, it was a generation gap – at least in Australia for digi-

---

18 Drawing what something should look like with colored markers.

tal – and it took a year or two for them to be able to trust the fact that I should be giving them guidance on what they needed to do for a digital project.

"At one stage, I got to do the front end of a really big e-commerce platform before e-commerce was even big in Australia. When that site came into the building and we did a proposal for it and some strategy around it, we laid down what it needed to do. They realized at that point, 'Holy shit. This digital thing's a different game. It requires totally different thinking than what we thought it would be.'

"We didn't go into tender and presentation with big creative ideas or anything like that. It was wireframes and theater sets and documentation around what we were doing and why we would do it. It was at that point that the creative agencies went, 'This digital thing is completely different.' I probably got a big tick mark at that point and a bit more respect for helping to guide digital for the rest of the people in the business.

"The first year, I just found my place. The second year, I started to do work. By the third year, I was working nearly 24 hours a day and never went home before midnight. Because during the day, I would be meeting with the clients and working with the various creative teams to sort of structure how digital would work and what was required. Everyone would leave at 6:00 pm to 7:00 pm, and I was there then to design and code by night to make it ready for the next day.

"Halfway through that third year, I finally called the General Manager into a meeting on a Saturday and I explained my job, what I did, and all the projects that I was working on. At that point, she was like, 'Whoa. Well maybe you could use some help. I can't believe you're doing all this work and we're making money from it,' because digital was not tracked as a separate item or as a separate job number, so there was no reconciliation of any money that I was making for the business. Until I pointed out the projects that I was working on that were digitally focused, and from that third year on, we then separated out interactive job number codes.

"I hired one person and then I hired two people and then I hired five people and then suddenly another two or three years later, we had 20-odd people and we're turning out millions of dollars in digital. That was the catalyst, that one conversation with the General Manager at that time, sitting down with her and nodding it out when working through the actual jobs that were digital versus not digital and where the money was coming from. And then getting that support from her to get a single person to help and then build it from there.

"For the first time ever, there was a staff meeting where over half the presentation was digital work that we've been putting together for the last couple of months. A lot of people in the agency were surprised to see that we were actually doing digital work and it wasn't just concepts. It was the creative and the build and it was live animation on screen.

"I do remember in one of those when Joan McCoy, the Executive Creative Director at the time, was presenting all of this work, getting applause or a standing ovation where they went, 'Look at all the great digital that our agency is doing.' So they were pointing at me and saying, 'That's this young guy down the back. It's him and his couple of guys who live up the back of the agency. If you don't know them, go and say hi.' It took about three years of work to get to that point."

〜

Instead of absorbing these new skills and services into the offering of the main agency, most of the holding-company-controlled networks saw it as another excellent excuse for more fragmentation. Internal units were spun off into standalone digital agencies and even digital networks. The clients were told that the above-the-line agencies have these excellent sister groups that work with them hand-in-hand, and the leaders of the agencies were told they have to hit their monthly revenue targets at all costs. Without a steady stream of work from the ATLers (even with their demands of "family pricing" and even "at cost" rate cards), the upstarts were forced to find their own clients and priorities and, more often than not, to break off and go their own way.

Chapter 14: Digital Agencies

In a survey conducted by RSW/US in the summer of 2012, nearly three out of every 10 marketing directors said they had moved a minimum of 50% of their marketing budgets from traditional to digital advertising over the past several years. Two out of three have shifted at least 30% of their spend the same way, while a meager 4% have not altered their mix at all.

Overall, 44% of advertisers say that digital and social, in particular, now take up at least half of their marketing dollars and the percentage keeps sliding that way, quarter by quarter by quarter (by quarter). They may feel this is prudent because 57% of the respondents said that they are on the "cutting edge of understanding, working with, and maximizing their presence in the social and digital media spaces." Back in 2009, only 44% of them felt that confident and comfortable with new media.

Strangely, another survey conducted in the very same period by PulsePoint indicated that the majority of marketers were actually the opposite of confident and anything but comfortable with their digital abilities — proving that few traditional marketing executives have a handle on this transition yet and are likely too afraid to be honest with themselves, let alone surveyors. However, at least their board of directors and revenue targets give them the impetus to investigate and learn about these new directions, even if their ad agencies choose, for their own reasons, not to lead them down the path. Advertisers have little choice but to evolve if they are to retain their markets, whereas agencies believe there will always be marketers who want what they offer, what they've always brought to the table.

For those who broke into and embraced digital within the confines of these risk-averse agencies, it was becoming less of an option to stay under the roof of organizations that didn't understand what they were all about and often even resented having to employ them. Hey, when a relationship begins to turn abusive or even uncomfortable, it's best to leave and make your own way, taking what you've learned and making what you offer the world even stronger — hopefully, not repeating the mistakes they made that drove you out in the first place.

⌒

Ask Wäppling, "You watch everybody – and this has been happening since the '80s – you watch kids who grow up as creatives into major creative directors at large agencies that are owned by Omnicom and WPP and whoever. They start saying, 'This place is so uncreative. They're dinosaurs. They suck. Let's go out and start our own thing.' They go out as copywriter, art director, and account management. They are basically the cells of the dinosaur. They're just replicating the same structure. They're going through the same process in becoming whom they didn't like, and they tend to sell out to the big holding companies if they become successful. And it starts all over again."

∽

Bob Hoffman, "I entered advertising 1,000 years ago when it was an industry that was led by craftspeople and entrepreneurs: people who were either copywriters or art directors or account people or researchers. They would work in an agency for a while and say, 'These people are stupid. I'm going to start my own.' And they'd start their own.

"The agency world grew that way, metastasized, if you will, with craftspeople deciding that they were smarter than the people that they were working for, and they would open their own place and somewhat be successful; most wouldn't, but that's the way it grew."

∽

Mike Langton, "The guys who start their own companies or businesses have got to be very clear with their ethics, with their culture, with their vision, so that they will have great people wanting to work with them, who will be looked well after, and great clients will come and work with them. And, in turn, be looked after well by them."

∽

Shane Ginsberg, "We're not just an agency. Our clients see us as partners, collaborators, and facilitators. Our business model is different. Our entire approach is different. There's nothing left to compare us to what an ad agency traditionally does."

∽

Aden Hepburn, "When people ask me what I do, I say I run a digital advertising agency, and most of them go, 'What's a digital advertising agency?' Some people think it's like a media company, that I might sell banner ads or something like that. More and more we're talking about *experiences*.

"Maybe that's just a buzzword. I'm not quite sure at the moment, but we're definitely talking about experiences – end-to-end experiences that include advertising material – but it's largely focused across other areas: the mobile experience, the desktop experience, and the tablet experience. It's how you interact with banners online, it's the advertising material that's out there in the marketplace. It's how everything comes together to deliver that communication piece, and we call that an *experience*.

"When I first started in Australia, there was a digital shop called Fantasy Interactive – and First Born was another that just did some amazing stuff. They were two of the ones that I'd spotted way back. Their work and what they do and how they put it all together inspired me.

"Our creative teams are still quite focused. There are digital-concept creatives, there are digital-interface creatives, there are user-experience creatives. Those guys do a little bit of storytelling, but they're focused more around the technology at the moment. Where we're going to branch out is by hiring more traditional storytellers into that mix to help bolster the team from a storytelling perspective, and then mix those guys with the creative technologists, the technical engineers, and the technical directors to create bigger, better, more intricate experiences."

෴

Alan Schulman, "SapientNitro started from technology consulting roots where they were really much more embedded in the enterprise; That's the way the world is moving as technology and marketing intersect. The funnel has collapsed between brand communication and transaction. An app on your phone can take you from awareness to purchase in about four seconds. Many companies come to SapientNitro either through the digital experience door, the physical experience door, or the Agency of Record door and discover there are different types of offerings.

"What's unique about the company is that it is really literally the only company that fuses technology and brand marketing in a combined offering that's purpose built for where we are right now – at the intersection of brand storytelling and technology. Many agencies are just starting to wake up and say, 'Well, we better start learning about the marketing stack or what a CMS is or user experience is.' This is a company has been there for quite a while and does an outstanding job at it.

"Sapient is not following the holding company model of using the cash flow from giant media spends at 2.5% to fund other businesses or to generate cash flow in the hundreds of millions of dollars to keep smaller below-the-line companies afloat.

"In the early days of digital, my challenge was the casting. Many agencies getting into digital took direct marketing people, brand people, and web development people, and they threw them in a room and called it a digital agency. Half the problem was they didn't know the role of account management at that point; they didn't have real brand planners. They had digital strategists, but they didn't have account planners. They didn't really do a good job differentiating strategy roles.

"A big part of the problem of being a creative in those days was you'd be working on a web development assignment to build a brand site, when you'd have people from direct marketing who were just wrong muscling in on that job. Conversely, you'd be working on a marketing campaign, and you'd have web development people working on that job that knew nothing about advertising. A lot of it in the early days was just getting the casting right.

"What's fun about digital is that it's truly multidisciplinary, which, frankly, above-the-line advertising agencies are not. They've got a copy function, they've got a strategy function, they've got a visual function, and some production function. It's not nearly as much of a challenge as sitting with a technologist who is a developer. Real left-brain/right-brain types of disciplines come together in connected thinking. Getting the connected thinking you need in a digital shop, where you've got user-experience people, you've got developers and people who really understand the language of interaction and how to build it.

"Then you've got real idea people who are in the business of differentiating one product from another through a big organizing idea. That piece of what we do is still the fun bit that gets me out of bed in the morning. As we move towards more and more quantity and big-data conversations, the world shouldn't forget that algorithms don't feel; people feel. We can't forget that we're still trying to make people feel, not just think, through this thing called digital.

"Remember, not everybody is leaning forward and thinking, some people are still leaning back and feeling a lot of the time. The challenges that I enjoy are the multidisciplinary aspect of it and the different skill sets required as well as being able to vary my thinking from, are we trying to get somebody to feel here, or are we trying to get a lean-forward person who is in a thinking mode to act on something? Those are two very different things from just driving awareness."

∽

David Meredith, former Chief Talent Officer and Managing Partner of Bates Advertising, "Bates was one of the early adopters of digital, having established XM, the very first digital advertising agency in Asia [originally Bates Interactive before it became Expanded Media or XM – and now part of JWT]. In Asia, with Nokia as the founding client in 1995, it was based out of Tokyo given the advanced nature of the Japanese and Korean markets, particularly as mobile was growing at such a fast pace. 3G-penetration was so high there. But it was soon transferred to Singapore to act as the regional hub for digital because of the need for talent and English, plus many regional brand headquarters were based on the island.

"Our challenge was how to embed digital thinking and practice into the heartland of the traditional Bates agency. Digital had turned out to be a *very big deal,* and in 2007, our approach was to launch a cross-agency training program. We allocated a number of specialists in our Asian offices to prepare decks for a digital boot camp, whereby digital natives representing all of our offices would assemble for five days' intensive training and then return to spread the enlightenment.

"Topics included:

- Introduction to the digital ecosystem.
- Asia digital information – an update on the state-of-the-nation in each of our offices. A benchmark to establish exactly how digital were we.
- A full day on digital creative.
- The keys to emerging platforms.
- Digital point of sale.

- User-generated content.
- Digital media.
- Client engagement

to name but a few.

"The problem was that digital proved to be largely unteachable in a classroom style. The subject was weighty, suffering from data overload. It appeared ponderous and techie and out of date by the time each deck had been completed. And every office and every individual was at a different stage of development and understanding of technology.

"Years later, we eventually came to adopt a two-prong approach: using the WPP online self-teaching kits that are updated regularly, coupled with our internal forums, blogs, and Facebook pages to inform staff of the great work we'd done or best-in-class examples and case studies by others. Plus news, developments, and insights from around the Web.

"Our HR strategy was to hire digital natives as they graduated and teach them the advertising business as they built up their CVs. At 25, the WWW predated them. They were online in their formative years and were raised on gaming, music, video downloads, and Facebook. They will naturally be the ones to drive digital thinking so that it permeates all levels.

"Our 'change-engage' strategic model forces technology into the heart of our approach – to problem-solving and solutions thinking. And information is online for teaching: from a basic primer to the most recent case studies."

⌁

Paul Kwong, "Everyone wanted to work at an upstart digital place. It was a chance to get rich quick. Work at a start-up, grow it, sell it to a conglomerate, and get rich! That was the biggest thing. *See Razorfish*.

'The hardest part of working with a digital place was getting their people to understand the brands, the concepts, and the strategies. Much of the thinking was, 'We could do this and this, and it will be cool!' Yes, but it's not on strategy nor does it fall under the concept."

⌁

Chris Kyme, "Obviously, there are some good creative digital agencies out there doing amazing work. However, there are also lots of small outfits set up by digital specialists who, truth be known, are neither creative nor strategic. At the end of the day, clients come to you for the thinking more than anything. Just because you are great technically does not mean you are the total solution.

"A good digital creative agency should be good creatively and strategically as well have the digital knowledge and expertise to make it all happen."

Åsk Wäppling, "In the early days of digital, revealing that you understood the Internet meant you were soon relegated to a corner of the office and you were pushing pixels for the rest of your life. It was like this limbo you get in certain direct mail departments. I'd like to cough and say 'Ogilvy' here because they're totally like, 'If you're in direct mail in Ogilvy, you will never leave.'

"This was always a problem, and it's that media doesn't come before the idea. The idea has to come first, and digital is just one part of the execution. Today, everybody's talking about 360 campaigns, but very few people are sticking to the same proposition or base strategy and tone of voice in all the media that they're currently occupying. If you have a brand in all these different media and they're bubbly and funny in social media because that seems to work on Twitter and then they're somber in press ads, this makes no sense.

"Online was the ginger-haired stepchild, if I may mock my own color. It was really misunderstood. There were some people who saw opportunity in it, who really tried to do things. They had to fight people at bigger agencies to even try to get something done. It's no wonder that in certain parts of Europe, like Scandinavia and Holland, where Web agencies went so much further than ad agencies in the digital realm, they were either bought up by ad agencies… or bought ad agencies.

"When I was with Saatchis in Copenhagen millions of years ago, back when Mosaic was the only browser, there was some guy who came to our office to show everybody what this Internet thing was about and only installed it on one single computer in the entire office. Everybody's hovering around this computer, including the Creative Director, watching what was going on, and the first page on Mosaic loads, and it's taking forever.

"After about 15 seconds of this, the Creative Director behind me says 'F-this! Way too slow! Never going to take off!' And he walks out of the room. I laughed at him, and that very night, I was the only one who stayed late at the office just to mess with that computer, and I did it for the next six months, and soon after that I launched *Adland.* The difference between him and me is that I run *Adland,* and he's retired. He really missed out. He was impatient, and I saw that a lot in many people at that time.

"I kept looking the way chess players do, several steps ahead. I was getting engaged in these debates in small online publications and advertising publications about direct mail (i.e., spam) back then, and that we should outlaw it immediately because we will ruin the communication medium of email. People said, 'It doesn't really matter,' and 'Nobody uses email anymore.' That's because of spam. It's impossible. Everybody runs away from the spam.

"I've been looking at it – and I complained about it years ago on *Adland* – there are so many campaigns that are based on funny viral movies. Today, it seems every third campaign is based on a funny viral movie. It's like creatives are sitting around, browsing online all day just taking ideas. Come up with your own ideas!

"I was posting a couple of ads today that came out of Deutsch L.A. for Dr. Pepper. They're so proud of the fact that they're doing one in a million, we're all individuals, yada yada, that sort of thing. They have a non-celeb campaign where it's like, 'We're individual drinkers of Dr. Pepper.' This ad looks like all other campaigns for soft drinks that were ever made, so it's not an individual thing at all. Then interspersed in that are the clips of the little Asian girl who flip-flops her bike, which we've seen for like six years now. The guy with the jacket made of toast, he runs around on the beach being eaten by seagulls, and it's like I've seen all these videos. I hang around *Reddit,* man. I am a really popular user there. I'm really bored with this. People disrespect advertising a lot, and I can see why because it seems like the people who are getting paid for creating it are really getting paid for just reading *Reddit* all day.

"It's very lazy. Also, there's another trap I discovered when I was working for a makeup company (which is boring as shit). It was sort of like an *Avon Calling* thing where we made a catalog for 38 different countries. We had to fly to Belgium all the time to present these images and sketches to God knows how many representatives from Russia, from China, from wherever – and they have to approve everything we drew.

"I used to draw these things. This is how I started in advertising. I drew this stuff and now I'm doing it in Photoshop. The way to do it in Photoshop is to alter existing images. I'd cut the head out of a L'Oréal ad and then the hair out of an Estée Lauder ad, and then I'd put them together and present. They'd say 'Well, her ears look a little wonky' (because I spent five minutes on it in Photoshop.) Or, 'Could we have the model's ears not look wonky?' They'd say, 'We could get a better Photoshop artist.' And I reply, 'No, actually, we'll take a picture of our model and it won't look this wonky because I'm just presenting to you what she's supposed to look like' and – oh my God! You don't realize that I've cut together different pictures here. It's the laziness within clients. You have to show them stuff all the time. Clients can no longer accept your ideas if you use only words.

"Something definitely happened. Somebody stepped back and said, 'We will have to help them visualize it,' and this became the norm. We shouldn't show them things. It's like that thing where we started showing them three campaigns so they can pick the best one. You know they're not going to pick the best one; they're going to pick a piece from each one and then make one really mediocre campaign."

↪

David Paterson, Chief Innovation Officer of World Vision and former Global Chief Strategy Officer of XM, "Back around the late '90s, I had the good fortune of being headhunted from Arthur Andersen into an emerging digital agency called XM, which was globally headquartered in New York City. Cordiant Communications Group (CCG), one of the global advertising agency holding companies, was just about to merge the disparate digital agencies it owned – and that had popped up organically around the world in Bates Advertising offices – into a single global network. My first task as Chief Strategy Officer was to help the CEO figure out how we were going to pull these 14 outfits across 11 countries together into a cohesive international offering.

"Apart from the expected trials and tribulations of weaving together the firms from different countries, there was another big challenge around the corner we weren't expecting: the infamous dot.com crash, which hit us shortly after forming XM Worldwide.

"Breaking into digital brought heady times, and I had entered an amazing outfit. Upon formation, XM qualified as one of the ten largest global digital agency networks of its day, due mainly to some great work in the Singapore and London offices. In fact, XM was the most and second-most awarded digital agency in Asia and Europe, respectively, but when the crash hit, it was as though someone had opened the door of the space shuttle whilst in orbit. The oxygen was sucked out of the digital space faster than you could say, 'so much for my share options.' One by one, we watched various competitors deflate and eventually fold. In relative terms, XM held on pretty well – principally due to the fact that most of its clients were larger corporations with relatively sound digital business strategies, rather than puffed-up dot.coms with flimsy business models. Whilst we largely held our ground as others fell around us, we did struggle to grow, and the dreams of IPO'ing were as dead as Pets.com and its sock-puppet mascot.

"Obviously, the key lesson was that business fundamentals still matter. Yes, the Internet does radically change some of the economics of information, but the other rules of the universe remain largely the same. Most people intuitively knew this even before the dot.com crash, but irrational exuberance took over and entrepreneurs were hoping to make a million or ten before others found out. XM did okay because it erred more on the side of rational exuberance, but inevitably became partially irradiated from the fallout happening all around it. Now it's a part of Ogilvy and JWT, depending on the part of the world it's located."

⮌

Patrick Low, "There was an agency in Singapore in the early-2000s, named Kinetic, continually winning major global awards for their digital work. Nobody paid much attention to it then, but today it has grown into a successful full-fledged agency.

"Traditional agencies began offering digital know-how not because they believed in it, but because the revenues through traditional means had become stagnant and to some extent eroded. Like planning, digital became the new opportunity to increase profit. Unlike planning, which is really an old book in a fresh cover, digital is new and uncharted, and is easier to sell.

"In 2007, I was invited to judge the Cannes Cyber Lions, but before I left for Cannes, I read as much as I could on digital advertising to get myself up to speed. All that reading did not prepare me for what to expect on day one. The exposure I got from judging was priceless. Until this day, I haven't seen anything in Singapore that is remotely close to the standards set in Cannes in 2007. I believe that in the whole of Asia, Japan is the only country leading the charge in the field.

"When I returned from Cannes, I decided to get my creative department to embrace digital. We made it a point to incorporate a digital component whenever the opportunity arose. It went well for a while, but the clients kept saying they only needed TV and print, and eventually in the interest of time and effort, we went back to the old routine until about two years ago when clients began asking for it. Now they ask about the Web, viral, and Facebook.

"At about the time I went to Cannes, digital was beginning to gain importance; YouTube and Facebook were largely responsible for the popularity. At the office, everyone was watching YouTube and checking their Facebook accounts. Clients began asking for their ads to be online. One of our key clients wanted us to do web banners, e-cards, and invites, and we had to learn to do them quickly. Thankfully, most of my staff is digitally inclined because they had learned it in design school.

"My client's request, though unreasonable at first, turned out to be a blessing in disguise. To date, we are doing more and more online work, but I must add that what we provide is only conceptual. We leave the execution to the experts because we have no desire of becoming a full-on digital agency. Large agencies are fearful of the digital revolution because traditional advertising will eventually become more niche, and they can't afford to remain that way."

"Since I started Goodfellas in late 2009, I have made a conscious effort to partner with digital agencies whenever the opportunity presents itself. People I trust and like run most of these agencies. If the client likes their work, I'm happy for them because we are a traditional agency and don't pretend to be digital experts."

Steve Elrick, "Depending on the digital agencies involved, I saw some of them as competition… and they were. To be entirely frank, in some of the agencies, that's how even the digital departments were seen. In a big network agency the digital, direct, promo, PR arm, and whatever would all be run under separate MDs with separate P&Ls. Lunacy. Everybody trying to eat everybody's lunch!

"It was often highly competitive when we had to work alongside stand-alone digital agencies. Perhaps I was lulled into something of a sense of complacency early on by being severely unimpressed by their creative onus in the territories they were supposed to be especially good at. Our clients and we often found that the strategic and creative originality of many of the digital agencies was severely lacking, and the onus was put on the agency to deliver a strategic media channel master plan. We half-resented doing all the original thinking up front and teeing up the digitals with great campaigns to execute, and were half glad that it also proved we were creatively essential (at that time)."

Diane McKinnon, "Initially, there was an elitism issue regarding working in digital. It actually plays into our specific business model that we partner with Y&R sometimes and say, 'Hey, you are the big brand guys. You do TV and all that stuff.' But there's all this other integrated multichannel area that they're just willing to cede to us as an integrated marketing shop. There are a lot of digital agencies starting to embrace more strategic partnerships within the big agency networks. With Y&R, it's VML. With DDB, they've got their whole Tribal arm.

"A good example proving that bigger agencies are starting to embrace the reality is South by Southwest Interactive (SXSWi). The first time I went was probably 15 years ago, and it was a room at the Austin Convention Center with a few booths and a bunch of nerds. Now it's Kanye West and Ashton Kutcher and big brands that have nothing to do with technology. Every advertising agency and network wants to be there. There's a whole track this year around agencies and interactive. That tells me there are two different things going on. There is the creative approach of being willing to embrace digital, but then there's also the financial approach, which looks at digital's multichannel model as not as lucrative as the old-school TV model. That may be part of the reluctance: it's not necessarily the mindset of the creative as much as it is the business folks. It's not necessarily the mindset of the people; it's the business models of the agencies that are problematic.

"The example I can see is the way Y&R Advertising and VML go to market together in a way that was not happening even a couple of years ago. Now it's absolutely lock step. They're going into pitches, into markets, and into clients together because of everything that VML does and because Y&R does not possess the digital thinking."

Dirk Eschenbacher, "In 2001 when I came to Ogilvy Beijing, the top management was always strong on the importance of the Internet. I started to attend Ogilvy Interactive and OgilvyOne. When I got there, there were already 80 people! That was obviously in the heart of the dot.com time, and there was a lot of web site building, but that shrunk down quite quickly and quite dramatically. Overall, it was there, but nobody in the agency really knew what to do with it. It was all just a separate unit. The entire agency sat in a huuuuge room, and the digital department had a small side room next to the toilet.

"Normally, the briefs would come in separately, since at that time there wasn't a single brief encompassing everything. For me, very early on, it was all about personal connections. It wasn't really process driven or somebody holding up the digital banner. I was just this guy who sat in the first meetings and talked to people, although that wouldn't always be the case. Many people had issues with the digital ideas or understanding digital, but I always found a way around it with how I connected or communicated within the organization and found some common ground. Often with the digital guys, they were too nerdy, so that's why they isolated themselves a little bit from the traditional guys, too. That was always the case.

"By default, the digital departments within agencies were always at the cutting edge of technology and of digital culture, which was part of pop culture. Digital agencies or artists who operate in a multimedia environment mostly make that. There was always a link between digital creative agencies and let's say, Ars Electronica.[19] In Austria, where there were always great installations and CD-ROMs and multimedia projects, they were all mostly self-funded projects or private projects that agencies looked to for inspiration. They pushed it forward and created the digital pop culture. They were always a few steps ahead of what the client actually wanted.

"Many times, the digital agencies or the digital departments in agencies got lost in the complexity and didn't worry about the objectives (which nobody really knew at the time) such as click-throughs or the page views or the open-rate on emails. Everybody was really experimenting with what would work for many years. The push for innovation came mainly through the digital agencies."

↜

Joe Zandstra, "There is something scrappy about digital folk. We'll do what it takes. For a campaign I was doing for Nokia, the Account Director and I flew out to Finland to conduct some video interviews. We brought our newly purchased video camera, a tripod, a piece of green felt (our makeshift green screen), several rolls of gaffer tape and a couple of little lights. We did interviews with the top executives from Nokia in 20-minute sessions in about 20 different conference rooms around their Espoo headquarters. Happily we got a Cyber Lion for our efforts.

"Digital agencies are working in a challenging environment. Clients understood the desire of digital agencies to be seen as serious players. They can sometimes dangle strategic projects at us and say, 'Maybe you can get *this* if you do well with the budgets on this production work.' They got a lot of strategy from us for free.

"I've even been in situations where I've been asked to do some fairly high-level messaging strategy work for a client, only to have them present it to their incumbent traditional agency as an example of the quality of work they expected from them (they were unhappy with the output they were getting from them) – we didn't get paid for the work nor did we get any more strategy briefs.

↜

---

19 Said to be one of the most important digital art festivals in the world.

Peter Moss, "When people started to talk about digital and not just the Internet was when you started to get multiple touch points in there. We've got a whole arsenal of stuff now, which is digital. The biggest mistake I see that people have made is to talk about digital as a thing in itself. It's a range of stuff."

～

Partner in Cluaranach Consulting and former Head of Marketing Operations for Molson Coors Brewing in the UK, Scott Guthrie, "I think that turning technology into sales will become central. If we think TV has become fragmented, the digital world is in danger of going one of two ways: three or four giant owners (Facebook, Google etc.), or it'll fragment beyond having any meaningful purpose. Or could it become the ultimate personal communication route?"

～

Jeffrey Yu, "To a lot of us, many digital people out there still do not understand brand. They become suppliers of technical digital programs, which diminishes them to the level of technical supplier. It is still about how we can bring the brand people together with the digital people so digital can become a real path for the whole communication offerings. Now, it is starting to happen, at least in my agency. I can bring a lot more appreciation of brand to the digital people and also appreciation of digital to the brand people.

"What is the idea? It doesn't necessarily have to be a TV idea. The idea can originate from anywhere. It is not the idea; it is the understanding of the brand that we need to instill into everybody's head. It is still about talking to the consumers and telling them about one aspect of the brand in whatever medium we are talking about. You can tell a different story with a different way of expressing it. An idea can still be a digital idea leading them back to TV or an outdoor idea, but nowadays, we suffer from the fact that digital people don't think brand, and brand people don't think digital. It is still a scarcity to find people that actually understand both or are able to communicate well with one another and bring the whole thing together. We still suffer from that."

～

Tobias Wilson, "I started Accomplice and then added two creative partners in 2010. I approached the guys and sort of said, 'Look, there's a big gap in the market for high-end creative thinking at sort of mid-tier pricing and small-agency turnaround.' The idea behind Accomplice, the business plan, the strategy, was to never pretend to do everything under one roof. The big agencies will constantly say that they do everything under one roof and then go and hoodwink smaller agencies into really shitty margins and really shitty turnaround times, delivering at a massive margin.

"The whole idea was to do what we've always enjoyed, and we really got the most kick out of creative strategy. Sitting down in a room or at a pub or wherever and coming up with the campaign strategy and all of the creative. I didn't want to fill up an office with a shitload of kids getting paid peanuts and try to make all of that dough in the first quarter."

꙳

Mike Langton, "The way that Chris Clarke defined Nitro was so good. It was such a brilliant organization and it really added value. And he refused the overtures. He said, 'I would rather destroy the company and wind it up than sell it to any of the holding companies.' Everybody went, 'Yeah, you'll sell it to WPP next week.' He retorted, 'I absolutely never will.' He was approached by all of them and when he sold to Sapient, I thought, 'Yup, that makes sense.' The whole industry was like, 'What? He sold it to, like, a systems integration company. What the fuck's going on?'"

꙳

Torrence Boone, "Avenue A was differentiated given its ad-serving platform and the associated data and analytics was a source of excitement and promise: advertisers could finally understand in real time the ROI associated with their marketing spend. This notion of accountability really framed the dialogue then. Technology was so far behind creativity that it was really the only conversation to have: banners were embarrassingly bad; HTML emails were still on the horizon; search was in its infancy as was online video; mobile didn't exist as a viable brand communications vehicle. The promise of accountability saved the dialogue. It was a relatively easy sell, and there was openness to experimentation, but digital was still very much on the margins.

"I've always held AKQA in the highest regard. They manage to bridge first-class creativity with a level of digital sophistication that often transforms the brand narrative in super compelling ways."

↩

Andy Greenaway, "I first became aware of digital in the early '90s. Peter Moss (currently CD at Leo Burnett, Switzerland) and I worked on Ogilvy's very first web site in the Asian region. Our concept was fun and interesting, but eventually became dry and corporate as it went through the internal approval process. In those days, people viewed web sites as information channels and were myopic in their views of the potential of the medium.

"I was an advocate of digital early on. It was growing at such a phenomenal rate. I was involved in the renaming and rebranding of O&M Direct – our initial name for the new brand was OgilvyInteractive. Back then, it seemed a bit ahead of its time. We eventually settled on the name OgilvyOne, recognizing the fact that the Internet would become a powerful one-to-one channel. No one ever imagined how immersive the Internet would be in peoples' lives."

↩

Mike Fromowitz, "Many new digital agencies are springing up, threatening to displace the traditional ad agency, but let's be real: it's not about digital, and it's not about traditional approaches. It's about ideas, and the rest is only the medium.

"Reason? One only needs to look at the Internet to see how it is being misused. Very few Internet 'experts' seem to understand branding, nor do they seem to have any idea about how advertising works. Quite frankly, ads on TV, in the press, and on outdoor billboards are no better – what a terrible waste of good dollars.

"I believe no one buys when they're asleep. Much of what I see coming out of the digital shops is boring and trite. Why should the consumer think well of you when the messages are dull, boring, and off-brand? Many of these messages fall on deaf ears. Consumers can't remember them because they have no significant, memorable ideas. A good case in point is the telecommunication industry. The telcos are spending huge misplaced dollars and not getting the effectiveness levels they want. They're spending huge amounts of money fighting price wars that are doing nothing for their brands, save for turning their offerings into commodities. Consumers just don't see any unique differences.

"On the other hand, the Apple iPhone isn't a cell phone. It's an idea. Like great movies, like great music. The iPhone is a feeling. It's an emotional connection. It's iconic. For products, services, brands, and businesses to stay fresh, relevant, and in demand, they have to create the right associations at the right time with the right ideas that can enhance and accelerate core brand values. Everybody is falling all over digital like it's GOD, for heaven's sake! And most of them are getting it all wrong.

"In a curious way, a recession (like we are in now) should be a force for good, improving advertising's creative output – necessity quite literally being the mother of invention. How odd and depressing then that the knee-jerk reaction to an economic downturn by agencies and clients alike is to either cut budgets or produce 'low-risk' creative, a euphemism for boring, pointless advertising. What can be riskier than spending the little money you have on something guaranteed to not encourage the viewer to click, look, or zap away?

"In today's marketing and media environment, only the naïve and foolish confuse presence with impact. Gaining presence in the market is easy. Impact is hard. Impact requires creative ideas that bring entertainment value to brands. To win over today's consumer, we have to create ideas that elicit emotion and create connections. In the world of creativity, the real ROI is not the return on investment, but the return on imagination. Apple's sales results have had little to do with the financial investment and everything to do with its creative investment, aided and abetted by millions and millions of online viewings."

↫

Neil Leslie, "I've been lucky insofar as I've always managed to land in creative roles that allowed me to straddle a variety of media. My first creative position was that of a copywriter at Bates/141/XM Singapore. At the time, with great envy, I looked on at the ATL guys who got to travel the world making big-budget commercials with the likes of Dave LaChapelle, while I spent much of my time writing digital and BTL copy for various *Heineken Music* and Nokia campaigns. I have a whole new appreciation for the experience now.

"Many of the sites were developed by the very talented people over at Kinetic in Singapore and were far beyond what we could develop in-house. At the time, I still didn't realize how important digital was to become, and one of my biggest regrets is that I never kept screen grabs or copies of them. (I'm punching myself in the face as I say this.) On the surface of things, it seemed that the relationship worked well. They couldn't really manage events and ATL on such a grand scale. And, we certainly couldn't design web sites with the edgy visual style that Kinetic could."

〜

Tobias Wilson, "Speaking globally, there're too many fat cats sitting up in their ivory towers remembering the good old days with their hand on their balls watching *Mad Men* and thinking about how cool they are and how similar they are to Don Draper. There is certainly a groundswell, but there's only so much you can do from the bottom up. It really has to come top down, and you're going to need a changing of the guard. Sadly, the old guard is training the mid-tier as well. It's not even coming from the juniors anymore. It's coming from consumers because now they have a voice.

"With digital, everything's accountable. Now, it's not the junior exec whispering to his colleague at lunchtime saying, 'Man, we should tweet that,' or 'We probably should put a URL on that print ad.' It's not that at all. It's that consumers posting on a Facebook page going, 'How am I going to connect with this ad?' or as we saw with the Hummer in the US when they launched the web site that simply shows your thumbs-up in front of a Hummer. People thought, 'What? Fuck you, guys. We're not going to go off and do your marketing for you. What we're going to do is… we're going to do an anti-campaign,' and FUH2 was born. It was brilliant, and that's the consumers going, 'You know what? You fucked up.'"

FUH2.com

FUCK YOU AND YOUR H2   **SUBMISSIONS**   **INSPIRED WORKS**   **LINKS**   **FAN / HATE MAIL**   **MERCHANDISE**

Introducing the official H2 salute.

Welcome to FUH2.com, home of the official Hummer H2 salute. So...why all the fuss? Well, it breaks down like this:

- The H2 is the ultimate poseur vehicle. It has the chassis of a Chevy Tahoe and a body that *looks* like the original Hummer; i.e. it's a Chevy Tahoe in disguise.

- The H2 is a gas guzzler. Because it has a gross vehicle weight rating over 8500 lbs, the US government does not require it to meet federal fuel efficiency regulations. Hummer isn't even required to publish its fuel economy (owners indicate that they get around 10 mpg for normal use). So while our brothers and sisters are off in the Middle East risking their lives to secure America's fossil fuel future, H2 drivers are pissing away our "spoils of victory" during each trip to the grocery store.

- The H2 is a polluter. Based on G.M.'s optimistic claim that it gets 13 mpg, an H2 will produce 3.4 metric tons of carbon emissions in a typical year, nearly double that of G.M.'s Chevrolet Malibu sedan.

- The H2 is a death machine. You'd better hope that you don't collide with an H2 in your economy car. You can kiss your ass goodbye thanks to the H2's massive weight and raised bumpers. Too bad you couldn't afford an urban assault vehicle of your own. Or could you...?

- The H2 is a tax loophole. Under Bush's new tax plan, business owners can deduct the entire cost of their $55,000 H2. If you are in the highest tax bracket, that's a tax savings of nearly $20,000! The government rewards you more savings for buying an H2 than you'd get for buying an electric car.

So, if you see it our way, tell a Hummer owner what you think and show 'em the bird. If you do, send us a picture--we'd love to post it on our site.

--Your friends at FUH2.com

FUH2.com, 2003. A consumer site created as a backlash to the *Thumbs Up* marketing campaign for the fuel-thirsty Hummer H2 SUV.

Susan Kim, "Google wanted to get more ads on their display network, not just search, but that was before they were giving away $100 coupons to businesses. The thing about search is you actually see the results. All small-business people understand that. They know how much it is going to be for a click, and they are getting hipper to what an impression is. Most people don't even see the impression that is below the fold or even if it was there; maybe it didn't even load by the time you clicked on the page.

"It's the return that people are seeing that is a lot less, and I don't think people are buying as much branding as they used to. It will be around for a while because there still are some ads working, of course, although they tend to be the ads you don't like. For instance, when I was working at AOL's Advertising.com, Tim Armstrong became CEO and he went, 'Oh, my gosh! I cannot believe that these direct response ads are running on AOL. That's it. Get those awful things off.' He didn't want them tainting his great content on AOL, but Advertising.com had sold all of these direct response ads and their executives were aghast and said, 'We can't pull them!' He didn't care and said, 'Nope, we are doing it. Take them off.' So, that was it. No more direct response ads were running, and the revenue – not that AOL has ever been profitable – dropped dramatically. Because he saw that, all we had to do was say, 'Hey, sell more American Express ads. I want more blue-chip advertisers,' and the sales people were like, 'Holy crap! Don't you think we would have done that if we could have?' and 'Yes, we've badgered them to death, but the only people really forking out the money are the direct response people because they are measuring it.'

"The ads are now back on AOL, but it was funny how much revenue was sacrificed when we didn't have them running; those are the ones that seem to work the most."

⌇

"Everything has changed: consumers changed, marketing changed, budgets changed, technology changed. The only thing that hasn't changed is the agencies.
–Frederique Covington Corbett, Twitter's International Marketing Director and former CMO Lead for Microsoft Asia Pacific

Chapter 15: The Most Impressive Digital Campaigns

The amount of money to be made by agencies producing marketing campaigns on the Internet was fairly negligible compared to what their traditional media brethren were pulling down for the firms, holding companies, and even the ones doing the actual work. With less than 2% of a typical marketing group's overall ad budget allocated to digital, beyond the hardheaded belief that the rest of the world would soon see the light, what drove the pioneers working in these new media environments was the opportunity and creative challenge in conceptualizing and conceiving of tactics and techniques that had never been done before — and not only figuring out how to make it go, but also how it could achieve the goals of the client *and* the people interacting with it.

For the first time, creatives and strategists needed to think about the individuals that would be exposed to their ads in ways much deeper than whether or not they'd "get" the concept or could recall it later. They had to think long and hard about how to motivate different types of personalities into *inter*action when any online ad campaign would likely be seen as an interruption to and an unwelcome distraction from the reason the person took the time to come to the Web page in the first place. It quickly became a fascinating study into Web user behaviors; how people react subconsciously to movement, color, and layout and what exciting, new methods could entice them into leaving what they were doing and spend some of their valuable time with, of all things, an advertisement. A lot of the more successful approaches proved to be as inspiring as they were measurably effective.

‿

Alex Bodman, "The first digital campaign that resonated with me is the same for everyone; it has to be *The Subservient Chicken.* That when I jumped on. It was my first thing where I was saying to myself, 'How the fuck did they do that?' It's obvious when someone tells you, but at the time I said, 'What is this? Magic?' Then I just couldn't believe the aesthetic on it. I couldn't believe the fact that Burger King was doing something that looked like it was a basement-kidnapping movie. It was so low-fi, but it was coming from a major brand. The fact that it was incredibly clever, but that it made for a great experience... all of that really struck a chord with me. Where I was, 'So, you can do *that,*' and then I would say Burger King, for the next three or four years, pretty much every year they did something if not as revelatory, just as impressive.

The Subservient Chicken, 2004 for Burger King by Crispen Porter + Bogusky, site developed by The Barbarian Group. The visitor would type a natural-language instruction, and a pre-taped video of a person in a chicken suit would carry out the command (if possible), appearing to be doing it live. The site has had at least 100 million unique visitors and has been loaded over a billion times. Cannes Cyber Lion Gold 2004 winner. Creative direction by Andrew Keller, interactive creative direction by Jeff Benjamin, associate creative direction by Rob Reilly, copy by Rob Strasberg, art direction by James Dawson-Hollis, Mike Ferrare, interactive design by Rahul Pancha. http://www.subservientchicken.com/pre_bk_skinned.swf

"At that time, it was high fives, and with each success you grew bolder, but then with success comes hubris and then danger. We can see now that Burger King's business has moved on from Crispin Porter and apparently they're looking for someone else. They're number three now, and it is a really sobering thing to look a brand and say, 'heroes five years ago' and now they are saying they are not going to make that work anymore because it didn't perform for their business.

"One thing that's happened with the maturing of our industry is that people have to answer a little bit more quickly. Why would someone care about this? Or at least more often than not that they're having to answer that question. There was a period that a lot of digital creatives see as a golden age when they were getting these huge budgets, and things were getting green-lit, and they were making these incredible microsites that were very creatively fulfilling for a lot of the people involved. Ultimately, the client was looking and saw that 40,000 people came and spent a minute. I wouldn't go around singling out anyone in particular. It was the very impressive, brand-polished microsite and that's why, for most big clients now, that very word is toxic, which is a shame. The u-turn has been too severe, but for ages, it happened all the time."

↬

Peter Moss: "By far, the first digital campaign that stopped me in my tracks was *Nike+*.[20] For one simple reason: the site was an intrinsic part of the product. I had never before seen anything like how they managed to put the tech and the physical together. It took me some time to just sit back and think about how clever it was.

"The one thing that I took away from that was the power of the platform as something you can just continue to plug into and innovate around. When I look at *Nike+*, I see all the things I would love to do with an audience to get them to collaborate and participate and be receptive to product messages; to genuinely believe that you're as passionate about what they do as they are. It's not just about your shoes. It's an innovative kit as well a product innovation. On top of all of that, it brought together Apple and Nike. It's just awesome! It was a fundamental. It's the biggest game changer since the chicken, *The Subservient Chicken*.

"What I liked about *The Chicken* was quite simply that the stuff that works the best is the stuff that people get a chance to play with and really consider the medium that they have to play with – and the power of it. For the longest time, we couldn't get off our clarion and we were just broadcasting, but in a different medium. When things like *Subservient Chicken* came along, you began to see how this medium could be used in a much more powerful way. Albeit they did it in a fun way, a lot of people thought 'Isn't it brilliant

---

20 A device that sits in a Nike shoe measuring the distance travelled. It can transmit the data to a receiver plugged into an iPod or iPhone so runners can keep track of statistics such as calories burned, pace, and total distance. It also connects the user and data to a community of people via iTunes.

that we can get people's attention and involvement in this way?' That was a nice little thing to happen as well."

⤺

Sean Lam, "I can think of two digital campaigns that I like that had the ability to transcend the platforms: the Old Spice digital campaign and Uniqlo's *Uniqlock*. One used humor and the other, simple good design to appeal to their audience. It's easy to explain why Old Spice is a hit, as its appeal is pretty traditional. For *Uniqlock,* though, it's harder to explain. Traditional ad men would argue that it lacks any 'big idea,' but this is because they have failed to see that, in this case, the use of technology *is* the big idea. *Uniqlock* was one of the first really significant viral applications that gathered eyeball ratings that no TV commercial could match." [http://www.uniqlo.com/calendar/]

⤺

Neil Leslie, "My all-time favorite digital campaign is the *Tesco Homeplus Subway Virtual Store* [http://www.youtube.com/watch?v=nJVoYsBym88] created by Cheil in South Korea. I can see that approach being adopted by many companies in the future simply because it creates so much value for the client and the time-strapped commuters using it.

"I also have tremendous admiration for the work created by North Kingdom – a Swedish digital creative agency that works with top-notch integrated agencies and progressive brands all over the world. They're pretty good. Their two FWA *Sites of the Year* and Black D&AD Pencil lay testament to the fact."

⤺

Chris Kyme: "*Subservient Chicken.* It just led the way for everyone and opened the floodgates. Sure, there were many others, but that was *it.*"

⤺

Barry Wong, "The Nike Sphere viral ads created by the *H'OK guy* aka Jason Windsor, a California animator. During the time when the seeds of viral were planted, this came out and completely blew my socks off, along with everything else within a one-meter radius. [http://www.youtube.com/watch?v=cwZeSMiVfug]

"The illustration was just so left field, it was so ugly that it was beautiful. The animation was raw and felt incomplete. It felt like an amateur did it. (Who says you need to be able to draw to be an art director?) To me, this broke the boundaries and bent the rules. A digital initiative didn't need to be all square and boxy, all nice and perfect. It was then I realized that entertainment value and context was what nailed it. Since then, I've begun exploring the beauty of imperfections where flaws are seen as merit."

～

Brett Rolfe, "There were probably a series of four tentpole moments or flagship campaigns that demonstrated that things had moved on, but it took rolling them out for at least the next year before clients were inspired. The first one was *The Subservient Chicken*, which put Crispin on my mental map as an interesting agency to watch – as they've continued to be.

"That was really something that was beyond just banner ads and stuff. It was so into interactive and it had an idea in it. It was advertising in a digital way. That was pretty powerful. Sometime after that *Get The Glass*, which was California Milk Processing Board, part of Goodby's *Got milk?* campaign. It was a North Kingdom site that I think cost somewhere in the region of a million dollars and in terms of craft and production a bit of a milestone as it wasn't, 'We've thrown $30,000 together and we're going to make a little Flash game.' The level of effort that went into that was, I think, quite striking.

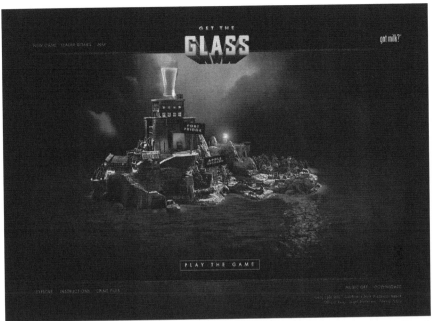

Get the Glass, 2007 by Goodby Silverstein & Partners for the California Milk Processing Board, executed by North Kingdom. Cannes Lion *People's Choice* 2007 winner. The second most-awarded interactive campaign for 2008 after Uniqlo's *Uniqlock,* according to the Gunn Report. Creative direction by Jeff Goodby, Pat McKay, Feh Tarty, Will McGinness, Ronny Northrop. Copy by Paul Charney, Jessica Shank, Katie McCarthy. Art direction by Jorge Calleja, Jessica Shank, Katie McCarthy, Brian Gunderson. http://demo.northkingdom.com/gettheglass/ – http://designchapel.com/blog/2007/04/05/designchapel-af-sverige/

"The promotional campaign for *AI,* the Spielberg movie, was one of the first ARGs (Alternate Reality Game). I think that while that's not necessarily something that's come to be an important tool for a lot of the advertising – although McDonald's did quite well with one a couple of years ago – I think this idea of transmedia storytelling and all those buzzwords really started from that point, and they're still really important things for us to be thinking about. Then the last one is *Nike+. Nike+* blurred that line between product and advertising, something that digital could do so effectively."

~

Dirk Eschenbacher., "The biggest impact on me was *The Subservient Chicken.* It was April 2004. At that time it was a wake-up call. It was just so simple. It wasn't just a web site, but for the first time, it was a digital ad. It really stood out, and all sorts of people heard about it. It took all the complexity out of things. It was approachable and human and emotional and funny and clever at the same time, so that did a lot. Before that, most things were quite technical and informative, and it moved it from the informational digital into the experiential digital.

"I never saw *BMW Films* as a digital project. I always saw that as a film project. It was a cinematic project. It was content, and content is *always* good, but that's not what normal digital departments did. They didn't just produce content, they produced the framework to hold content, which was normally given by the client and was very static. Content interaction only really started in 2005-2006."

⮌

Former Channel Marketing Manager for Electronic Arts and Strategic Planner at Wieden + Kennedy China, Fanni Ho, "I find *The Great Schlep* created by Droga5 to be one of the smartest and most engaging political campaigns in a presidential election ever. [And it was digital.] To post-rationalize the creative challenge will go something like this: Appeal to liberal (Jewish) grandchildren to convince their less liberal (Jewish) grandparents to vote for Obama.

"Rarely do we see such precise strategic thinking in this category. The same is true with successful advertising – it's not really what you say that matters at all, but how you make people feel."

The Great Schlep, 2008 and 2012 by Droga5 and starring Sarah Silverman. Cannes PR Lion 2009 winner. Creative direction by Ted Royer, Duncan Marshall, Scott Witt. Art direction by Jeff Anderson, copy by Isaac Silverglate and writing by Sarah Silverman. Directed by Wayne McClammy and edited by Josh Reynolds. http://www.thegreatschlep.com

Jim Speelmon, "There was *The Butterfly Man* by ninemsn [http://www.youtube.com/watch?v=kzVYga3vBD0], and they did some really cool integrated stuff where they had games. You could go to the web site and play a game. Then they had the theatre advertising. TV, Web. It was just a really awesome integrated package that worked so beautifully. There would be an event, and there would be the dude dressed up as the butterfly man. He would do something and hand out flyers and stuff like that. Then people could go and play this game online, and then you could win a year of theatre tickets or a gold pass to the movies, and the biggest prize was a car.

"One of the first digital campaigns I envied was a worldwide multiplayer contest. You had to do team things, but you had to find team members first. You would go and hang out on these [computer] bulletin boards and join these conversations to meet people who would be geographically close enough to you. Then there would be some offline event that you would then go to and meet these people, your team members, and then you would have assignments.

"It went through these stages, but it would be things like you need to go to this web site and put these secret codes in. It was a huge undertaking. I don't remember who did it. It was like somebody had an *idea.* You could just tell from looking at it. Somebody had an idea, and it was the amount of energy and effort and thinking to make that thing work was amazing. You'd have to have a client who had a sizable budget and a lot of faith in your abilities. Because it was a lot of stuff at the time, it would have been all very new, and it would have taken a while to put together because it was a three- to four-month campaign.

"You had to keep this engagement. You had to do these offline events. You would need to work with partner web sites to plant stuff on them so that people would have to go and find it in these treasure hunt kinds of things, and then they had prizes like 'round-the-world business-class tickets and cars and stuff like that. It was a big deal."

"Digital people were very, very good at integrated thinking. That's because they were put into so many positions where they were handed something that never was intended to be digital. They had to backwards engineer something that would work. For a period in the industry, the people who were best at this typically were in the digital space. That has gone away."

$$\backsim$$

Valerie Cheng, "The campaign that really was a turning point for me was for Hewlett-Packard that we called *HP Toyrama,* which was done in 2008. Even today, I would proudly say that it stands out from many other campaigns, maybe not in terms of an idea or technological advancement, but in craft and appeal. It's the project that reminds me every day that if everyone on the team strives for perfection, it will show up in the work. In fact, what you'll achieve is not a piece of work, but a piece of art. That's something we tend to forget ourselves – that we are creative people and artists, too."

$$\backsim$$

David Anders, "One of my favorite digital experiences of all time is *Take This Lollipop,* the 2011 interactive short film that showcases the power and risk of exposing personal information online. From a consumer's perspective, the simplicity and power of the storytelling is beautiful, albeit totally creepy.

From a marketer's point of view, the way the application seamlessly lever-ages Facebook Connect to cast the viewer as a main character in the film is absolutely brilliant. I think it's a shining example of how brands could create more emotional connections with people. Like any good live comedy show or magic routine, great things happen when you involve the audience. It's too bad how often we forget to make it personal."

Take this Lollipop, 2011 by Tool, Santa Monica. Written and directed by Jason Zada. Programming by Jason Nickel. SXSW Interactive 2012 Best of Show & Experimental winner and an Emmy Awards winner in the "New Approaches" category. http://takethislollipop.com https://vimeo.com/35781051

George Tannenbaum, "Too often, integration doesn't go much deeper than a replication as opposed to a deepening. That is how I would approach it. I would just unleash it because there's only so much you can do with 30 seconds, but the online world gives you a chance to do so much more and to deepen the story and the engagement.

"A lot of times the top-down, let's say, creative management who comes from a traditional campaign is just to sell the spot in as many places as you can rather than really bringing it to life. Some of it is maybe they thought there's a lack of trust in the people doing the pulling out, or they don't really want to do it themselves because they're focused on something else, or it's another team who they don't really communicate with.

"It's unfortunate, but it can be any number of things, and if there's a holdover from 10 years ago where TV was just part of it as an end in itself rather than the beginning of a deeper engagement, then that limits the view of what the communication can be.

"I used to say I somewhat feel like TV is the movie trailer and the movie takes the spotlight. It can drive people to something that's more of a complete examination, but that doesn't seem to happen a lot. Dodge had a commercial that was aired during this weekend's football game. They had a spot on the new way to buy a car. The new rules for buying a car and what they let you do is register for a wedding. You know, like when you register for your wedding so you get your china. Your mother-in-law will buy you china, and your sister will buy you tablecloths and shit.

"I had heard about it on *Agency Spy* or something and when I saw it on TV, I actually did type in the URL, partly because it's Wieden + Kennedy and I'm interested in anything they do because it's usually so exemplary. Of course, the spot crashed when it launched because there was so much traffic, which is a good problem to have in some ways, but now it's up fine. There doesn't seem enough of these going on. This is a good example, it seems to me, of working in a smart way. [http://www.youtube.com/watch?v=3U-H0aMd3igY]

⤺

Subhash Kamath, "Kevin Brown, our global engagement planning director here at BBH, once told me something and it stuck in my head so beautifully because it's changed the way I look at this whole digital thing. Kevin said, 'Subhash, we don't really need digital ideas. We need ideas for a digital world, that's all.'

"There's a huge difference because advertising agencies I've seen would do the typical soft-stuff brand ideas. They'd excitedly say, 'We've got some digital ideas as well,' which would turn out to be the same press ad put as a banner on the screen. If you think of it as ideas for a digital world, then to be the best agency in the world, the best fucking example is what Fallon did with *BMW Films*. It was not a digital idea. It was an idea. It belonged to the digital world simply because they understood that it was a film that they created, but they created it in a manner where I could consume it within the technology world that I was living in.

"I loved *The Subservient Chicken*, it's one of my favorites. But nothing changed my outlook the way *BMW Films* did. Yesterday, I was looking at content. It just changed the way I was looking at what brands were telling. It just made me think in a completely different way from what I'd learned. It broke all norms for me."

◞

Steve Street, "A great brand will build meaningful relationships with its customers. I'm not talking about 'like' my Facebook page for a chance to win some fancy shit, but in the meantime here's some thoughtless drivel for your newsfeed relationship. I'm talking about a proper two-way relationship that recognizes people as humans first and consumers second.

"'Hey hippie, we have to shift product. You know, move the needle, sell more shit.' Sure you do, but you don't have to be a prick about it. In fact, prove to me you're not a prick, and I'll start to take you seriously. Engage me on a human level, tell me something meaningful, crack a joke, give me an opportunity to respond, make me feel a part of something, and I'll probably have a gander at that product you're offering. Hell, I may even flick you a few bob for it. But you'd better be sincere because I can spot bullshit a mile off. So can my friends.

"In terms of the precise consumer outtake from a branded experience, I would argue that it doesn't matter, so long as it's positive. If, as a brand, you have people thinking, 'You know what, this brand really gets me,' I'll bet my left nut they'll be more likely to shell out for a product over someone who catches a glimpse of a headline somewhere. If you've got a decent product and you invest in the relationship that you're building with your audience, keeping it fresh and relevant, chances are they're going to stick around and purchase more from you over time. Great brands know that their message is in their actions, not a starburst.

"Nike, through its *Nike+* program, is doing a good job of engaging its audience and getting them to rally behind a common purpose. Philosophically, the idea of participating and pushing yourself, or 'making it count,' is, to many, highly motivating. Aid this tactically with a suite of products that help you track and compare your progress, and you've got a pretty smart program. There is also the community aspect for those that like to showboat or seek motivation from other sporting diehards, which leverages the usual social media channels. Of course, what better way to keep the fitness fires burning than to serve up inspiring content, training tips, and Q&A sessions with professional athletes.

"Whether you're a fitness nut or a weekend warrior, there's plenty here to keep you coming back, motivated, and proud to be a part of something positive. I'm sure they're shifting a shit-ton of product."

‿

Andy Flemming: "I'm still a big fan of work that can profoundly affect people. That makes them laugh or makes them think or change behavior – and anything like that will be shared. You can get an audience that is far, far greater than any media company could ever dream.

"We've seen that with, obviously, Old Spice. Where a beautiful piece of work didn't necessarily have a strong digital strategy, but more people engaged with it digitally than a lot of campaigns that have a vast sum of money put into them. The kind of people who move into the digital space sometimes – and I'm not saying that this is their fault – confuse technological advances with ideas.

"We've seen a rush of that. We've seen a lot of ideas that ask your permission to pull your Facebook data and some really great executions. Intel's *The Museum of Me* was a really great one. Droga5 did a really good one for Lynx, and there was something called *The Fun Audit* that came out of Saatchis. There was a very, very scary one called *Texas Money Pot*, which was about how easy it is for someone to get your personal details and stalk you. We've seen a lot of those, and it's really people showing off as in, 'We can make a story with you and your friends in it based on your Facebook profile.' That was a piece of technology that, yes, you should use and were nice ideas. They are the exceptions to the rule.

The Museum of Me, 2011 for Intel by Projector, Tokyo with Flash execution by Deltro, Tokyo. CLIO Awards 2012 Grand Clio – Social Media winner. Creative direction by Koichiro Tanaka, art direction by Masanori Sakamoto, interactive design by Ken Murayama. http://www.intel. com/museumofme/ http://youtu.be/qfd54nYPhXk

"Sometimes I have to ask myself the question, 'How many of these big campaigns (that I am very much a part of the demographic) have influenced me such that I actually actively spent time on their web site, played their game, continued the thing until I finally bought?' Because these things take a fair amount of time to engage with. The idea has to be simple, has got to be relevant, has got to be engaging, but there is just so much, it has become a confusing landscape.

"A lot of the clients are saying, 'We've got to be on Facebook. Maybe we can trust Facebook,' and obviously we will know what can happen when you give the public permission to engage with a brand on Facebook. Sometimes it's, 'All you fuckers have never returned my calls! You guys are the worst I've ever dealt with,' and then you get into the stage where you ask if we have to moderate this or do we allow it to be a free flowing exchange.

"There have been so many brands that have been bruised by social media, thinking they were playing the game and not realizing that the other team can actually take the gloves off. We've seen a lot of, 'Hey. Let's let the public decide something. Let's have the public create an ad. Let's make the public name the product. Let's let the people write a lyric or a song.' More often than not, it goes horribly wrong because there are so many people out there that actually enjoy fucking with companies.

"Mountain Dew crowd-sourced the name of their latest drink in 2012 with their *DubtheDew* campaign. The one that was in the lead when they had to kill the campaign was 'Diabeetus.' It was voted for the most (mostly by the infamous online group 4Chan). That's what happens when people are anonymous beforehand. It ends up like this and they all go, 'Fucking awesome, huh?'

"Top voted names for the 2012 Mountain Dew drink:

- Hitler Did Nothing Wrong
- Gushing Granny
- Fapple
- Moist Nugget
- Soda
- Sierra Mist
- DickButt
- NukaCola

"If you don't have the power to tell a story, the power to stand out, the knowledge of that standard, and the storytelling skills, then really all you're going to do is be capable of creating a very impressive Flash demo. That's what you're going to get to do. You have to understand the appropriateness of the technology that is being used as the channel. There are still people that seem to think that the classic 30 or 60 second TVC is dead. It's bullshit. It's the perfect size to share. The Old Spice 30-second TV ad probably got about 400 or 500 million views. A TV ad will be shared if it's beautiful and good."

Digby Richards, "The *Share a Coke* campaign is definitely the one that I would say I was inspired by the most in the last six months in Australia. Basically, 18-year-olds have grown up with no relationship with Coke because their relationship is with energy drinks. Coke was sort of seen as crap to them. The simple idea was, 'We'll give you the brand, here you go, it's your brand now. Have a bit of fun with it.' That was the simple thought and basically you could put your name on the label. Another thing it did at the storefront is it actually got people standing in front of the fridge, interacting with individual bottles, twisting them round, seeing what names were on there. I live right near a BP service station. You go in there at any hour of the day or night. There will be someone with the door open, twisting bottles around. From memory, there was another way to get new names on the bottles through an on-line voting mechanism. It was a great conversation starter for Coke that involved the audience, but released the outcome in a somewhat controlled manner befitting of Coke.

Decode Bing with Jay-Z, 2011 by Droga5 for Microsoft. This comprehensive transmedia campaign garnered 1.1 billion global media impressions. Cannes Lion Integrated and Outdoor Grand Prix 2011 winner. Creative direction by Neil Heymann, copy by Adam Noel and Spencer Lavallee, art direction by Jon Kubik, graphic design by Jon Donaghy, user experience design by Consuelo Ruybal.

"They're original thoughts that have been done beautifully. They've been thought through. They're digitally complete, those ideas. All of them are brand responsible. You think about the *Decode Bing with Jay-Z* transmedia campaign from Droga5, I thought it was great. I thought the *Buy the World a Coke* was very true to Coca-Cola, which was putting vending machines around world where you could actually buy someone in a different country in front of one a Coke. *The Great Schlep* I just loved because it really addressed the problem. Clearly, it had an impact on the 2008 US Presidential election. It was big thinking, that was simple, original and beautifully done."

↩

Andy Flemming: "I would say the best ad I've seen recently was for the Paralympics. *Meet the Superhumans.* [http://www.youtube.com/watch?v=k-KTamH__xuQ] It was one of *those* ads. People don't cry because they are feeling sorry for these people. They cry because they realize that they had misjudged them, and they give an emotional response. That 60 seconds is a fucking phenomenal achievement. I showed it to a girl over coffee the other day on an iPhone 4 through headphones and she just cried her eyes out. I hadn't ever seen her cry, and it just blew my fucking socks off. That's my greatest argument for how the landscape may change, but people are still the same. When you give them a complete, self-contained story, you get that kind of reaction, and I'm not discounting digital in any way, shape, or form, but you need to recognize how people will get emotionally involved with it.

"What I've enjoyed recently was Intel's *The Museum of Me.* I don't think it is a great example of a fully integrated campaign because it's just Intel showing off. It's showing off a piece of media that sucks in personal data and actually gave it back to us in a really compelling and very personal way. Everyone fucking shared that.

"*The Wilderness Downtown* work that @radical.media's Chris Milk did with Arcade Fire is extraordinary. That was one of the first examples of merging a music video, advanced album release, Google Chrome, Google Maps, Street View, HTML5, and all of the golden technology thrown into one to create very powerful pieces of digital communication that just so happen to be for a track for Arcade Fire. It just blew my mind.

"That was pretty fucking special because it is my own personal story being projected into the story of the song. That was very positive use using technology not for technology's sake, but in a very, very appropriate way that made me a part of the lyrics and the story.

The Wilderness Downtown, by @radical.media with Arcade Fire to show off Google Chrome's HTML5 abilities. Directed by Chris Milk. Cannes Lion Cyber Grand Prix 2011 winner. http://www.thewildernessdowntown.com

"There are far too many bullshit apps out there. I think CommBank has been remarkable and kicked off stuff that has been genuinely groundbreaking. When I was looking for a house, it was fucking valuable. CommBank's Property Guide app is a very, very, very, very useful piece of software.

Apps have just changed the way we live in simple ways. Ordering a pizza. Ordering a cab. The simple things. It used to be a phone call where you'd get 'your call is important to us,' you'd sit and wait and then they never fucking turned up. Apps have eradicated those little things that used to be annoying. And then you've got Yelp. Just honest reviews of places where people say, 'Just don't fucking go there, they're rude as fuck, and it's expensive or it's cheap and here's a good recommendation.' All these things we find ourselves just using and having, it sounds like fucking cliché, but we have a easier and better life because of them.

"When we're putting up app ideas for clients, we are very aware that they have to be an intrinsic part of the campaign. People are going to be motivated to download something or view something because it allows them to involve themselves in the campaign. It can be just a simple problem-solving thing that allows them to get a seat in an airplane quicker or get a beer quicker, or pays all the bills or reminds them of the bills that are due.

"All of those things can have a place in a campaign. When we did the CAN launch for example, we engaged experiential guys to get the message out there. We did some pretty crazy stunts that added to the story. We wanted to do something that got people's attention in some popular location that intrinsically linked it to the story we were trying to tell. But obviously, they were part of a much bigger thing. They hardly ever work in isolation because they just have such limited reach – unless they do something fucking amazing."

〜

Angeli Beltran: "Goodby, when they came out with *Got milk?* in the '90s, that was classic. It was epic. It's a really base idea. It's very, *very* good. You could go forever on a base idea. And they have gone on forever on that one."

Got Milk? by Goodby Silverstein & Partners for the California Milk Processor Board. Photographer: Dan Escobar. Clio Best in Show 1994 winner for original campaign's first television spot. http://www.youtube.com/watch?v=OLSsswr6z9Y

〜

Bob Gebara, "Among current projects that have captured my attention, I like the action to increase tourism promoted by Sweden, giving control of the twitter account @sweden to a resident each week, so that he or she can tell the world how his or her country is.

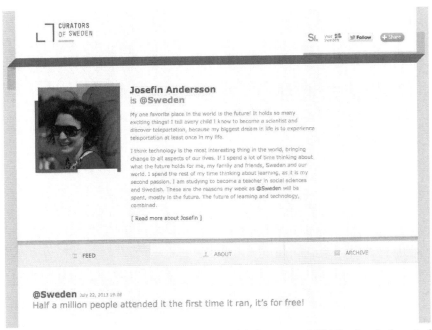

Curators of Sweden, 2011 by Volontaire for the Swedish Institute and VisitSweden, both part of NSU, the National Board for the promotion of Sweden. For a week, a regular citizen curates all of the tweets that are sent out on the country's official @Sweden Twitter account. Cannes Lion Grand Prix 2012 winner. http://curatorsofsweden.com/

"I would also mention Cannes Outdoor Grand Prix 2012 campaign, *Invisible Drive*. Is that offline, online? Does it matter? [http://youtu.be/uHWfFFi1k9Y]

George Tannenbaum: "I'm sure you remember the Axe Deodorant spot called *Susan Glenn* with Kiefer Sutherland. It's such a simple story about a girl who got away. I mean how is easy that? Who else has done it so elegantly? I don't why we've made creating ads so hard. I really don't.

Susan Glenn, 2012 by BBH NYC for Unilever's Axe. CLIO Awards 2013 Gold winner. Executive creative direction by Ari Weiss, art direction by Nate Able, copy by Peter Rosch. Directed by Ringan Ledwidge. Starring Kiefer Sutherland and Jessica Cook. http://www.fearnosusanglenn.com http://www.youtube.com/watch?v=YRB0i9-AUQs

Part IV: The Future of Advertising

What you have read in Parts II and III is not idle speculation or self-indulgent navel-gazing. The people in this book have all been working successfully in the fields of advertising and marketing for a very long time, and they have been through a number of shifts already. Although they naturally may have slightly differing opinions about where we'll end up or even what the catalysts were that have brought us to what many consider a low point for the craft and the industry, nearly everyone does agree that the current model is not sustainable or desirable.

They know there has to be a better way forward, and many of them have experimented with different models on their own and in concert with partners and even clients. Some have found what works for their talents, skills, personalities, and agency cultures, while others are still searching for something that allows them to do what they love and still send their kids to private schools.

If only they had been a little quicker on the uptake of what was going to be important not just to their clients, but their clients' audiences, they may have been able to control the situation more. The agencies may have been able to evolve more intelligently and gradually instead of requiring constant painful experimentation and then eventually facing great uncertainty and upheaval.

But it's never too late to start and take advantage of the new, powerfully effective (and trackable) channels, tactics, tools, and ways of being compensated.

Chapter 16: Agencies All But Ignore, Dismiss and Mislead

For most ad agencies, when new media raised its awkward head in the mid-1990s, it was a cute little tactical annoyance. It might have been good for one or two campaigns as a novelty, for the right brand, but otherwise it had nothing to do with storytelling and was considered akin to a brochure or point-of-purchase wobbler. At best, support material. At worst, gratuitous. Clients were not asking for it (aside from the rare hip one); creatives rightly thought it looked like crap; no one knew anything about how it worked and could care less. Because it sure didn't seem like they could charge much for something no one was requesting and had such a relatively small audience that no one was sure could even be influenced by anything they saw online. This was before e-commerce existed, folks.

The truth is, the majority of agency people had barely heard of the interactive field and of those who had, the only interest was personal. It may have piqued the intellectual curiosity of some, but very few of those cared to look into it on behalf of their clients because it was too hard a sell, too hard to become expert at, too hard all around. Anyone who had suggested CD-ROM projects a few years earlier had mostly lived to regret it, and this seemed like more of that: complicated expenditures without a clear and successful ROI. Frankly, the job is hard enough without having to add something that seems very technical and involving on top of it, especially when the return is so very muddy and therefore risky. Agencies get beaten up so much even for good work that they tend to avoid risk. Hey, it is very expensive and stressful to run an agency. Don't kid yourself.

Brand managers and gatekeepers thought so little of the Web that they didn't care if sites and online ads violated guidelines and standards. To them, it was a walled-off experimental garden — a greenhouse — where so few people would encounter the brand expression it would have no effect, positive or negative, and was of no concern. Digital staff who cared enough to ask for brand implementation guidance were told politely to figure it out for themselves. The brand gatekeepers were busy doing real work and couldn't be bothered to help with an experiment. The Web folk were perplexed by this attitude. They were under the impression that their area was the future and therefore necessary, especially as the new channel was attracting more and more people and attention. For their part, the Luddite counterparts couldn't understand why there were so many nerds in the office.

⌐∽

David Sable, "Agencies looked at digital and saw it as something technical. They saw it as a technology. It's not like anybody looked at a television back in the '40s and said, 'Holy shit. How the hell did Jack Benny get in there? That's technology. I can't do that.' They looked at it and said, 'Wow, this is great.' The 'Wow, this is great' then became, 'Okay. Now how do I use this?' They experimented, and they failed. If you look at the early TV spots, they were nothing more than people standing in front of radio microphones – static – and then they learned how to use the medium. They did all of it: they knew it, they learned it, and it became just another part of what they did.

"For some reason, with digital, the industry abdicated. It's really interesting to me; even my own company, which when you go back to 1994, you'll see we built the first web site any agency had ever done. We also did the first interactive TV, and we won an award for it. No one had ever heard about this before. We won an award for it, and then it just went away. Everybody stopped. It was like it didn't exist.

"What happened is you got all of these digital startups that came in, all of whom were charging millions upon millions of dollars to do what today a three-year-old does with a 50-cent software package. None of them knew shit about marketing, and they also didn't know how to use the Web, which is even more interesting. What happened was you had this influx of money that was just being wasted on bullshit.

"The big agencies said, 'Shit, how do I counteract this?' so they started doing bad work. They thought the way to counteract it was just to do this goofy shit work for clients who walked in with bags of cash. To them, being digital was to do sock puppets and all kinds of other shit like shooting gerbils out of cannons. Things that were so anti-anything you believed in. And by the way, didn't do a thing to drive anyone's business.

"Everybody thought, 'The sock puppets are so cool. It's really digital, it's really cool.' Here's a super insight: people are serious about their pets. They're fucking serious about their pets. Who is going to buy food or anything for the pet that they love, which they care for like a child, from some goofy, shitty-looking sock puppet? Some of them were mainline agencies. Really serious agencies.

"The work promoting the dot.com companies wasn't even online because there was no such thing as online yet. It was online commerce. The holding-company-owned agencies were just doing drive-to-web. They thought that that's what they had to do. They thought that the connection was just being goofy. They just didn't get it, so clients started to lose confidence in their agencies.

"Now they're paying these specialist companies millions upon millions of dollars to do web stuff and way more and at a way higher margin than they're paying their ad agencies. Then these guys said, 'We can do advertising, too.' So they started doing advertising.

"You had that going on, and then you had the holding companies coming in and buying up all the agencies. So then price became a bigger issue, there was commoditization of the product, plus the loss of confidence in the agencies, in the industry, and in advertising because everybody was saying, 'Advertising is dead. Television is dead.'

"Then you had the resurgence of, 'Wait a second. Maybe it's not *so* dead. By the way, turns out these digital guys really aren't driving a lot of business. They're helping us and they're doing important things, but they're really not changing our business the way we thought they would.' You had this perfect storm of shit: a perfect storm that created confusion, that created distrust, that created lack of credibility – and therein lies opportunity.

"Nothing is first; the same with digital. It always amazes me. I was talking to someone the other day who said, 'The best part of Amazon is Amazon Prime. That's brilliant.' You realize that Amazon Prime is as old as direct marketing? Like Sears was offering Amazon Prime in the 1800s? Do you understand that?"

⌒

Shane Ginsberg, "If we take a longer view of this source, digital obviously has been a very slow catalyst. If we look at general agency models, there was a time they made print ads and had billboards and radio. Then television changed that dramatically, and then direct did the same thing. We've always seen this massive shift. What's more interesting here is that no one is slower to catch on to this consumer behavior than a general-market agency. Their continued behavior has driven most of the interesting kind of innovation and almost few changes in consumption, and agencies haven't driven that at all. Not a single agency drives the adoption of Facebook or Google. Not a single one. Not a single agency, arguably, drove the adoption of smartphones, and then most of them said, 'The ad looks muffled.' The last people in the room to know or to drive consumer behavior as an agency. And that includes digital agencies by the way."

⌒

Steve Elrick, "With hindsight, of course, one would always wish that they got ahead of the curve earlier... invested in property, Apple, whatever; but the reality early on was that digital often wasn't relevant to our projects because the client simply wasn't buying into it being a serious channel, and they weren't putting money behind it.

"There's a great irony today in that the clients are now bemoaning the fact that some traditional agencies were slow to move – *harrumph* – but as little as three years ago, some major brands I worked on had no more than 3% of their annual budgets earmarked for that strange little thing called digital."

⥲

Nick Fletcher, former Planning Director for Euro RSCG London and Head of Account Planning at Wunderman, "I gave digital its due the second someone turned on a 9600 baud modem. It happened way before Facebook. What was clear very early on was that digital (in whatever incarnation) would be a very significant, if not the most significant, advancement since the industrial revolution.

"It might be interesting here to divide digital into digital marketing and doing business digitally. I think companies started doing business digitally much earlier than using it as a marketing tool. I worked on the UK launch of Amazon. In spite of being one of the poster children of the digital business, we didn't use the Internet to advertise; we used posters and billboards. Why? Because the general public was not using the Internet, and there was no point advertising on their own site.

"I also worked for United Technologies (UTC). Again, they did not use the Internet for marketing services, but they had developed an online auction site for industrial hardware. I think clients got interested only when they personally started using the Internet (clients love the self-referencing sample of one).

"In terms of briefing, my recollection was that I tried to use a normal brief at the start. I then started to develop a more digital brief, which culminated in an integrated brief that any comms agency could use. It was designed to get to an idea that any discipline could use, and in retrospect, it was a little naïve. I don't think there was one moment that digital became part of the brief. The use of digital in the brief began to emerge. The best briefing documents today clearly reflect that. They are much more open, allowing for wider thinking."

⥲

Aden Hepburn, "In late 2008, it started getting really, really quiet. We lost a lot of clients, the agency had shrunk by 50 people, and there just wasn't anything coming in that was exciting anymore. I spent a lot of my time trying to find good digital creative examples so that I could fuel my passion, further my career by seeing what was on the cutting edge. I would spend two hours a day, maybe more, trying to track anything interesting down, anything that I could find.

"I would go to all the global advertising industry web sites, and none of them had a digital section at that time. I couldn't find it. You'd have to scroll through their portfolio archives, and you would find one piece of digital that wasn't even current. When I came into work every morning, I wanted to see something new, and literally no matter how hard I'd search, I couldn't find something new that was posted and summarized.

"I didn't realize until I moved jobs and ended up in an agency with 150 people in it how much I knew in relation to a lot of other people in the business. I think digital is one of those things where to get to the top and to make a difference, you need to be a jack of all trades. You need to be a hybrid because as the technology base expands, it's more and more important to know how everything fits together. If you are just the interface designer or programmer, you no longer have enough exposure to all the other various aspects of the business to integrate them.

"I was really lucky doing a little bit of everything that I was good enough to be able to work with the right people for different projects, bring them together, and oversee them. I was in a position to be able to have valuable input in every different type of project that came along, and I found myself at the point of being able to sell big projects and manage the delivery of them, overseeing the creative and input on strategy and get really hands-on across the board. I was able to nurture digital within the agency to build it up when it wasn't easy to sell an agency to a client, but it was definitely pretty easy to sell digital 10 years ago. It's really interesting when you think about that, because now should be the easiest time in the entire world to sell digital to anyone. To a degree, it's not easy to sell digital anymore; it's just more common, and there's more requirement for it.

"You have to work a whole lot harder to sell it to a client now because everything is bound by metrics, it's bound by scopes of work. Budgets are tight, margins are small, but back then, if the client saw some digital or needed some digital, they were just happy that you could actually do it because no one was doing it, certainly not agencies.

"You'd have to go down to the little corner shop to a random one- or two-man digital brand where you weren't sure whether they were going to be there tomorrow. Big agencies just didn't have that skill set, so the client would just go ahead and spend their money with the smaller guys."

~

Bob Hoffman, "After 15 years as a mainstream medium, television had created hundreds of brands in dozens of categories, successful brands of peanut and mayonnaise and milk and aluminum foil and shampoo and toothpaste. Now after 15 years of the Web as a mainstream medium, what brands of toothpaste and shampoo and peanut butter have been created by web advertising? I can't think of any. I can't think of one. Not one. Where is the effectiveness here? Where is the marketing? I understand people want to make connections and engagement and all stuff, but where is the brand building? That's what marketing is about.

"Sales promotion is not hard. Anyone can do that. They lower the price, and you can sell more stuff. But where is the brand? Building the brand is the hard part of marketing because that has legs. Once you do that, it achieves momentum and then it rolls by itself. You can be like Apple and not do sales promotions. You don't have to lower prices. You don't have to do all that crap.

"Where are the brands that have been built by display advertising? Where are the brands that have been built by social media? Okay, Zappos, there's *one*. Where are the rest? It's 15 years. I'm waiting, and I'm not convinced.

"Here's what has happened. The advertising industry has taken what it knew about traditional advertising and tried to graft it onto the Web unsuccessfully. Traditional advertising has been good at creating demand for products. That's why people advertise. They wanted to create demand for their products, and they thought that they could take what they knew of traditional advertising, graft it onto the Web, and create demand for their products on the Web; from my point of view, that has not happened.

"What the Web has been good at is fulfilling demand, like the yellow pages used to do, not creating demand. Once you knew you wanted a pizza, you went to the yellow pages to figure out where to order it from, and that's what's happening with the Web — and Google in particular.

"The success of Google tells me that the Web is much better at fulfilling demand. Once I know I want to go to Hawaii, I go to Google to figure out who has the lowest price for a flight. Once I've already made a decision or I'm in the process of making a decision to buy something, then I go to Google, and that's where the Web is valuable.

"People have really not figured out yet how to use the Web to create demand very well, and marketers are trying to graft the old traditional model onto the Web unsuccessfully. How do you use the Web to create demand, not just fulfill demand? The two biggest web entities? In terms of advertising, it's Google. In terms of sales, it's Amazon. And what are they? They're about fulfilling demand. They're not about creating demand whereas Facebook is still trying to. They're still trying to use the display ads on Facebook, and it's just not working on them. Big scale, yes, for small companies that can buy clicks at a certain rate and find that a clip is worth a little more, yes, that works. For major advertisers that are trying to create demand for their brands and who are not direct marketers, it's just not working.

"I try to be very practical. I try to recommend using the Web for fulfilling demand rather than creating it. I believe in search. I believe in certain display advertising on certain sites people are shopping where it's fulfillment, and so I take a very practical approach. The metrics are not convincing for any other mode of web advertising that I've seen. I don't think social media has proven itself to be a sales builder. It's great for personal relations. It's good for some kind of short-term sales promotion opportunities; it's great for the brand. But as far as brand building, it hasn't proven itself or long-term sales growth. It hasn't proven to me yet that it's effective at those. It's the same with content, so I try to take a very practical approach when clients ask me about how to utilize the Web best.

"If the people in the agency have dumb ideas, I try to steer them away, too. We all pretend it's very scientific with the metrics and all that stuff. It's as much art as science right now. We really don't know a lot. The things we thought we knew have turned out to be wrong. We thought interactive advertising was going to be so much more engaging since it's so much more effective, given people could interact with it. Guess what? Nobody wants to interact with it.

"Click rates are under one in 1,000. It's not interactive. Calling it *interactive* advertising was a delusion. Consumers don't want to interact with our ads. They're not clicking on banners. It's 1/10 of 1%, and half the time, the click is a mistake. It's bad cursor-eye coordination. We're deluded by a lot of stuff, not just about the Web, but also about all advertising. We're delusional about a lot of things, but because the Web is relatively new, we're a little more delusional.

"It's very tumultuous to me now. It's very hard to really understand the value of it and it's confusing. Five years ago, I would've said it's exciting because there's so much new stuff, and now *I'm just tired of the bullshit.* There's been so much bullshit in that everything that comes along is the new miracle and the new magic, and it's going to change everything. But it just hasn't happened that way, and you'd think people would learn that that doesn't work, but they haven't and personally, I'm sick and tired of having to listen to bullshit artists tell me what the new magic is. I know it's not magic. I can see it's not magic. Don't try and tell me it's magic. There's always some new miracle that's coming along, and it's gotten to the point where it's annoying."

⌐∽

Former Regional Director of Marketing, Branding, and Strategic Planning for Samsung, Shell Oil, and Nokia Asia Pacific, Danesh Daryanani, "A lot of people don't understand digital... so how do I say this. The guys that are leading large networks, they've obviously embraced digital because they had to. That doesn't necessarily mean they understand digital. You see the difference?

"They had to embrace it, but they may not understand it. If they don't understand digital, they're not going to understand how to start it, how to manage it, and how to make money out of it, so you take a guy who is in his 50s... I'm 48. I know and embrace digital. I know it is important and it will kill any company that doesn't embrace it, but that doesn't mean I understand it. I probably do better than most, I'm probably not the best, but if you look at the CEO of any of the big agencies today, does he embrace digital? Of course he does because the writing's on the wall.... but will he actually *truly* understand it or will old-guard guys? These are the guys making decisions and directing the ones who understand digital is important, but they don't quite understand the nature of the beast."

~

George Tannenbaum, "Why traditional agency types have trouble understanding or being inspired by the opportunities in digital is probably 50% they don't understand and 50% they don't want to bother. It's probably a little harder to do something complete. There's probably some reticence in the client who takes more work on their part. It's probably some bottom-line issues where the money goes, especially when we have different agencies with different bottom lines. Whether they're in the same holding company or whether they're in the same building or just totally unrelated, [they think it's just not worth their while].

"On the digital side, there have been a lot of pretentious failures where we create these baroque wild experiences that really are esoteric and no one uses. I'm also not sure that that experience is the way to go for every product. Then it would be harder for you to do the old detergent experience and the Dodge experience. My interest level isn't all that great on certain things. I have a hard time with all that. Maybe that's just because I don't really care about what detergent I use. There are a lot of brands that might be better served by doing great traditional advertising. Maybe it's just me and maybe because I never had to do this, but I can't think of what, say, Saran Wrap will do. I've seen some of these online things that demand so much time and care and it's, where's your ROI? Where's your advocacy? Other than doing something for creativity's sake."

~

Steve Hall, "Most every creative person still wants to see their work on TV. They still want that TV commercial in prime time or in the Super Bowl, even though the importance of that medium is becoming less and less (although it's still frankly quite high). There're different kinds of glory. You can create the world's most successful social media campaign, and yet it's still not as cool as having your ad in the Super Bowl.

"People can spend $3.8 million on a Super Bowl ad, and yet you could do so much more effective marketing with $3.8 million through content marketing, lead generation, SEO, all of these other techniques. They would probably build your business more than having a really cool-looking commercial on the Super Bowl. Of course, I'm not bashing Super Bowl spots because some do work, but it's a bit of a crapshoot.

"I generalize, obviously, but certain creative people are fueled by that glamour and glory of having their work seen on TV, and there's not much glamour and glory to having your ad seen online, even if it's a video on YouTube that gets seen by five million people. It's, 'Yeah, that's a lot. It's cool, but I'm not on TV.'"

⤳

Ken Mandel, "Did traditional agencies see digital as a threat? Well, more like the antichrist! On one hand, they never saw it as a threat to their business because they did not believe in it. On the other, they saw it as threat to their relevance because they could not get their heads around it.

"Oh yes, we in digital shops pushed back at traditional agencies – and hard – to the point of damaging our relationships in some cases. We were arrogant back then, to say the least. The only way to deal with their resistance was to develop our own client relationships. When the traditional agencies saw that we were winning clients that they could not bring in, they started waking up to the fact that digital was something different. It was still hard going, although it resulted in a sense of awakening for some."

⤳

Roop Mukhopadhyay, Managing Partner and Director of Strategy & Planning at The Thinking Machine and former Regional Strategic Planning Director for McCann Worldgroup in Indonesia, "In 2003, I was a planner with TBWA India working on the Apple business. Apple had just launched in India, and they were not willing to do any ATL (TV, print, radio) for their launch. The client wanted to leverage their global digital assets and wanted us to provide digital solutions. The Apple brief had a big effect on the agency. Immediately, the hunt for digital creative began within.

"In those days, digital meant more of finding a web site and banner-ad developer. It was a tough time for the creative folks within the agency since the client demanded creative solutions specifically suited for a medium with which the agency never had worked before. There was huge resistance from the Creative Director who had no clue how digital works. But it was the beginning of a trend that I observed, and going forward, I realized more and more clients would be asking the agencies for help."

⌐

Paul Kwong, "In a big agency, the digital arm was another way to get money from the client: 'Hey, we can do web sites or ads on the Web for you.' It took a long time for clients to see that digital work could actually sell more product for them."

⌐

Jim Speelmon, "To be fair, no one really had any idea at the beginning if this was going to pan out because clients and agencies both still get overly wrapped up in the tactics. Eight years ago, there was no Facebook. Then people got very excited about Facebook. People got very excited about MySpace, for god's sake, and Twitter, and who knows what's coming next, and yet people keep getting really excited.

"What they seem to be forgetting is that the channel might change. The tactical opportunities definitely will change, but the one thing that is going to be consistent, as long as there are people trying to talk to other people, is the fact that you need to create a message to coordinate across multiple people who have multiple opinions, using multiple channels. That's the thing that's going to be consistent.

"Rather than feeding the chaos and trying to hedge your bets, go for the thing that is going to be consistent. As long as you have people who are able to understand the business goals and business data so as to derive insights from the people you want a specific outcome from, you have this huge bank of experts who can tell you, 'Basically, all you need to do is have somebody who is able to go and give them the brief.'"

⌐

Joe Zandstra, "For the first time in my life I found myself working in an integrated agency. All of our account directors were traditional, but they had to sell or manage digital and they did it with a certain degree of competency. Because they were all of a certain age they understood digital from the point of view of digital end-users. This is what's changed over the past 10 years. At the very least now we have account directors who know what digital is. Ten years ago we had account people who had never really experienced the Web before.

"The issue now is we have the curse of 'a little knowledge.' Non digital marketers lack the depth, subtlety and understanding of digital – digital needs, digital opportunities – to be able to get in there and sell it properly. There's a touch of overconfidence in the digital abilities amongst traditional folk that masks the problem – the need for digitally focused people managing digital projects.

"Clients don't know what the opportunities are for them to extend and expand their businesses and to do better business through digital. And if we don't have the experts in there advising them, then we end up with a lack of true consultancy and the usual tack-on 'would you like banners with that?' digital solutions being sold as something to go along with the nice TVC.

"Selling advanced digital solutions is esoteric. It's not straightforward stuff. Where I worked, they held the client relationship very firmly. It was very difficult for digital people to get in there and connect with the client. I really wanted to hire dedicated digital account people because sadly I felt that the existing account team didn't really *want* to be trained.

"I want to hire based on temperament, interest, and desire. Frankly, if you don't care about digital enough in this day and age to be dealing with it, I don't think you're going to be a good digital account director. The people I was working with recognized the power of it, but they just were not personally enthused. It was not their thing."

Martin Howard, "I was using the Internet a bit before the Web, and I could see the potential of it fairly early. I was using telnet[21] to retrieve documents from archives fairly early on and using email before I knew what I knew.

"The big breakthrough in digital from my perspective was the use of JPEGs on the early web sites. This was when the web sites were gray and contained mainly text. When I saw that there was an opportunity for genuine creativity for us to be able to use richer graphics, that was the point where I thought this was going to really take off because then it had become more interesting and engaging to the mainstream. That's when it moves from the nerd realm to the public sphere.

"On the other hand, agencies ignored digital because they were dominated by business models. The way the agencies were set up, they were listening to their own hype and holding seminars about their own little world, while the Internet and the digital realm in their early incarnations weren't all that stimulating to view. There's been a pattern of new technology adoption with being able to write it off as a fad. People put the Internet and digital multimedia at that time into the same basket, but they needed to take it seriously.

"When it came in, people still treated it as a fad. We had *Time* magazine saying that it was some weird thing to be scared of, and other people were talking about emails as being like a CB radio – as something that would come and go. What paid the bills in big agencies in those days was media royalty and commissions. The people who were making the decisions in the big agencies were still looking at their revenue stream and protecting it. The technology wasn't quite strong enough early on for people to grab hold of and sell to the advertisers. The Internet had a slow start, but when it got over that initial technology hump or around the technology curve of getting to a point where consumers could access and engage with it, then people started seeing it, but by then, they were caught with their pants down.

"Being based in Australia, I saw this as a timeline that was controlled by institutions and critical mass. I began to pitch digital when I had a government client come in and say, 'I'm going to pay you $10,000 for a web site. I don't really mind what it looks like. I just want a web site.' That was the point at which people within government and the big institutions were reading ahead

---

21 A computer application and protocol that allows remote access to computers connected to a network like the Internet.

and beginning to say, 'Yeah. Let's grab this, and we can apply it because it actually saves us money, and there're enough people out there who are going to use this technology to make the cool factor worthwhile.' That was from the marketer side, and they were very progressive in their outlook.

"What I found in the mid-sized companies that I tended to be working for at that stage was the IT people were seen as the ones that could build web sites. There was so little understanding about what constituted the web site and what metaphor to apply your marketing model to. It was very difficult to get the attention of people who had these tech people on their staff who were saying, 'I can build a web site with [Microsoft] FrontPage or directly with HTML, and I can do it for half of the price that you did.' That attitude prevailed for a very long time."

⌒

Jeffrey Yu, "The digital agency I ran in China, XM Beijing, was in a big, big fight with me because clients were not spending enough money. Our clients at that time, despite saying they wanted digital, wouldn't pay enough money to do it properly. We were losing money left, right, and center. We were using our XM Singapore revenues to subsidize the floundering Beijing group to the point where, one day, after WPP had already absorbed both Bates Advertising and our digital network, XM Asia Pacific, I was put into the room with all of the Ogilvy global executives and was told, 'Jeffrey, Bates is not making money, and you are losing money. Your direct marketing agency, 141, is losing money. XM is losing money. You have to make a choice. You will be giving up 141 or you will be giving up XM.'

"I thought about it for a while and, well, that's when I had to part ways with XM. I was told by Ogilvy's CEO, Miles Young, that XM would have a much better opportunity to live within WPP's J. Walter Thompson because they had a bigger client base and Bates would still be keeping a share of the XM revenue. But the revenue was stolen. The company was stolen. Bates never got the shares, and XM was passed into the wrong hands.

"The story goes that these WPP holding company people were driven by pure profit margin. If, instead of ruining ourselves, we were able to invest in XM, then XM would be running the traditional agency, Bates, already. If we were allowed to grow XM at that time, it would be a lot bigger than Bates, and XM could have been the forerunner of everything. There would not be Digitas and all these other guys coming in. Even since Digitas came in to Asia, I see they have been fucking up. My colleagues in Publicis are still trying to buy up little e-commerce companies and do little digital workshops and everything that is available to just try to catch up. The times have changed. The agency people are now treating digital people as equals. We are learning to live with one another now.

"There is much more respect afforded to the digital people because, for example, within my Publicis agency, I am now trying to consolidate planning with digital planning and brand planning and below-the-line planning having them all come together because that's the only way it's all going to gel for the client."

⏪

Larry Goode, "Who exactly is a digital expert? There are literally thousands of digital companies in India alone. There are many that call themselves digital experts, ranging from huge agencies that will cost a fortune and send waves of account executives who only know half of what they are talking about, to your nephew pumping out web sites in his basement on the cheap. None will have a grasp on the overall strategy to incorporate the latest trends of digital into their marketing plan. Finding a true digital agency is tough, and it's tougher for those with little digital background themselves."

⏪

Chick Foxgrover, "I suppose many agency folk didn't embrace the new because they didn't feel they had to. They were doing well enough with TV (and certainly, TV viewership numbers, as far as we can tell, haven't really gone down). In fact, maybe TV's gotten a little bit more concentrated and more precious in a sense. But I think that they weren't forced to change, so they didn't, and it probably seemed like too much trouble.

"Right now, there's all this debate and all this angst about the difference between an account manager and a project manager. But once the work gets more process-oriented, how do you maintain the separation between creative and production? These are the sorts of things that, institutionally, agencies are just not ready for at all. It seems like too big an investment."

Token Digital Efforts

In the early days, like the mid-'90s, people were building web sites because their competitors had web sites. It wasn't because they said, "Hey, we have a need. We need to cut down on the people calling our support line by directing them to some place they can use self-service, and that will save us because each call costs us money. Then we can then re-channel that into marketing or infrastructure or something else." There's a real solid business case for it, yet marketers were building web sites for the sake of it. They were using Flash for the sake of it. It was all mostly gratuitous.

There came a point when it was the responsibility of the advisors of these marketers to hold up the opportunities of digital and say, "Here are the things that you should be doing online because people are here and people have expectations," or, "You have an opportunity to have a leading advantage here way beyond your competitors if you move now." There were many, many good reasons to do it, and it's clear that the agencies never did honestly think about it and provide real insight for their clients and what they should do. They just continued to create emails, banners, and microsite campaigns, knowing full well they were ineffective or not even bothering to evaluate whether they were or not because the budgets were so small and the clients weren't paying much attention.

That's where we find ourselves today with Facebook's explosion and social media craziness and all this frenzy: now they're paying a lot of attention to it because the budgets are moving that way. But they no longer have any credibility with their clients, who are turning to boutiques and specialists and inward.

$\backsim$

Jon Cook, "The skill of true account management is something that in some ways, with all this change, has led to getting rid of certain aspects of the job that never needed to be there anyway, duties that can be handed over to other positions. I don't want to sound old-fashioned, but I do believe that the art of the account leader is in danger of being lost. Being a strategic leader, a strategic force, a business driver, an internal motivator, all these things that are a key part of what makes and has made agencies strong.

"It doesn't matter what the role is called. I'm not trying to hold onto old agency models, just the act and the art of what used to be the glue and that needs to be there if you're to have something really good. I see that less and less of late in account management. The problem is in both digital agencies and traditional, all over. It's a profession that's unfortunately on the decline, and whether it comes through account management or it's supposed to come through the project management, it's missing."

↩

Angeli Beltran, "If there's anything that traditional guys need to learn, it's that digital is another touch point. It's just another way to deliver an experience to the consumer. If that's where consumers prefer to be, then we have to understand how that works. It's not like, 'I'm not digital. I didn't grow up digital.' It's more of 'Okay, the consumers are there. How do we use that so that they can have an experience of the brand.' It is how people should see it rather than 'I'll stick to TV' or 'I'll stick to this because this is what I know.'"

↩

David Sable, "The mismanagement of the digital piece has hurt the industry. I really do believe in what I call the *Harry Potter* effect – the magic wand of digital is going to solve all my problems. This has literally held back the full and powerful development of digital because it just made people wary.

"When the market reacts in the short term to Google because they didn't understand it and they don't get it, there's a diminishing return. How much can you get for a click? By the way, they're still getting 2%. That's the joke. The joke is that in all these things, the returns are much like they were in direct mail because guess what? It's not targeted like this. It's even less targeted from a certain point of view. The other one went into your mailbox. It physically went into your hand. Here, it goes into your mailbox where you can easily delete it without even touching it. Or it's some banner that comes up in the middle of an article you're reading, and you really don't give a shit because you want to read the article. Or you sort of pay attention to it, much like you do, and even less so than if it had been an ad in a newspaper page or a magazine because it keeps changing and it's just not in front of you in the same way. It's not part of the experience; it's off to the side where you can ignore it easily. Or because you print the page – *printer friendly* – and the ads don't come with it. Again, these are all things we're struggling with."

↩

James Koh, "I have seen many times where an agency will hire a head of digital. Not necessarily creative, just a head of digital. And that person would be in the role, but without much support. A lot of times, a traditional agency will sub out the production to another shop, whether it's a local digital agency or in some third-world country. Then a whole complication will happen because the traditional agencies don't have people who really understand the process, so things fall through the cracks for a gamut of reasons, things fail, and then their one digital person leaves in frustration."

⌇

Jeffrey Dachis, "It's true digital may have been ignored because the money was still in TV, and if you look at the dollars that are flowing into measured media via the traditional agencies, they're doing just fine. In fact, they're increasing their revenues despite decreasing viewership, decreasing consumption of measured media product, the falling off a cliff of newspaper subscription rates or newspaper's circulation and magazine circulation and consumption. That incredible shift in the dynamics of young people's media consumption habits, time- and place-shifting, and the widely available digital sort of universe that exists outside of the measured media outlets.

"Over that, people are saying the death of measured media or the death of television is right in front of us, and yet there's more spending going into TV now than there ever has been. Which means that the advertisers are paying more and getting less, but that's a whole other story.

"The market for high-quality programming isn't going to go away. People like highly produced slick content. There's no question about that, but the experience of receiving highly produced slick content on a PC or on a tablet or a phone has sucked for the last 20 years. Broadband wasn't a reality, why? Because telephone companies and cable companies had to pay off all their copper infrastructures, so they didn't put fiber in while they still were monetizing all the copper that they put in and years before that.

"Broadband only came about because finally the copper infrastructure got monetized and people paid up their investments and they could afford the capex to build fiber. The broadband universe should have occurred in 1999 and didn't. It took 10 extra years 'til broadband became ubiquitous, except in places like Scandinavia – and Singapore with Singapore ONE in 1999. In a country with four and half million people, you can do that. It will take longer for 310 million people to catch up, but they *will* catch up.

"Those inevitabilities are coming. You'll hear the people and broadcasters in the advertising universe say the death of advertising is highly overrated. The advertising agency world has been evolving since the '50s, and it's going to continue to evolve. Digital should have killed the advertising agencies, but [it] didn't, because it turns out digital is really great for commerce and bottom-of-the-funnel conversion into commerce activity and really crappy at brand building."

꣼

Kay Johnson-Suglia, "I want to shake people! I am continually advocating for folks to wake up and embrace where we are, where we should be. I cringe at their view that it's all very simple, a cut and paste of traditional."

꣼

Barry Wong, "Every other day in China, a new campaign launches that looks so much like the one you saw yesterday, and the day before, and the day before the day before, and the day before, the day before, the day before. You get the drift[22]."

꣼

Paul Ruta, "Traditional ad agencies once boasted full service even though they didn't offer much in the way of digital. It's not that agencies were specifically fibbing; digital just wasn't a big thing. This was a while ago. As deadlines neared, someone would remember that the campaign needed a digital component, and it would be sent out for like Mandarin translations or pizza.

"Agencies soon figured they could profit from the digital component by bringing the service in-house. These digital guys were still treated like pixel-fluffers, of course, but now they were on-staff pixel-fluffers. Such agencies were 'integrated.' The business and creative fruits of early integration tended to err on the side of underwhelming. Television was still being peddled as

---

22 Josh Sklar, "There is no uniqueness. No creativity. They don't care to do their best because it's irrelevant to them."

the brand-building medium of choice, and the whole digital thing remained officially a bit iffy.

"This was back when agencies still had the word advertising in their names. Meanwhile, standalone digital agencies continued to thrive as a result of having correctly guessed the importance of digital media, and they had the nerd power to make it happen. And digital got big. It happened fast.

"Having money, but lacking any real digital expertise, traditional agencies bought digital agencies. Then, having money, but lacking any real strategic capabilities, digital agencies began buying traditional ones. They kept buying each other until they all started looking and behaving the same.

"The evolution is ongoing, but these are the brand-new traditional agencies, and the smart ones know they still need people who can do some good old-fashioned thinking. Whatever the technology of the moment, digital has been mainstreamed. It happens to all the best media. It's a good thing."

~

Alex Bodman, "The elegance and simplicity of one bold idea or thought can sometimes fall to the wayside quite understandably because the digital agency will be tasked with thinking about things like loyalty or what users are going to do. Or thinking about things like gamification that can lead to a structured engagement and jumping onto a lot of things experientially or as an engagement piece that will make for fantastic digital campaigns. But it means that often it's not starting with that pure, simple, clever 'What is this one brilliant twist on the YouTube platform that could land this message about x?' That is one thing that the above-the-line agencies are doing really well now, and that is necessarily leading to great business results or digital engagements for their client, but it is leading to some really exciting cool work that just makes you go 'Aw fuck, alright!'

"It is what is populating probably a lot of the award shows right now. That really simple, clever, wish-I-had-thought-of it, well-executed idea often at scale. So clients are really attracted to that because they only have to do this one-time hit to get it done, get the attention, and have deeper engagements without investing in the platform. I do think that that is one place where the above-the-line model of the killer thought or that clever idea in a print ad is being more cleverly applied in digital. One of the reasons why they flourished and why so many big clients went to find their own digital agencies just because, too often, digital is a box to tick for traditional agencies.

"Often now, even some of the top above-the-line agencies that are getting the chance to do some digital still see it as a box to tick. They still see it as, 'We've got the engagement piece. Yup, that will do. Great! Let us work with a below-the-line shop and get that produced, and we've ticked the box.' If that was your only creative opportunity and you had this brief in front of you, what would you do? You know, if that was your only chance to affect your client's business, not just to win an award, but to affect your client's business, what would you do? If you tackle a brief that way a few times, then you might find yourself thinking about it a little bit differently.

"If I were a client right now, I would still want my own digital shop. I certainly would be listening to all of my different shops when it came to ideas. If I felt that my above-the-line guys were getting sloppy on the latest campaign, that would be up for grabs, too. I would work with great creative shops and look for ideas. That is what I would do right now, but that is probably because I do see the need to hedge your bets, since it's so confusing right now.

"You know, right now in New York, a lot of what were really hot digital shops a few years ago aren't winning awards simply because their only stream of revenue is work they're getting from above-the-line agencies that are winning the awards for themselves.

"For all of the bigger above-the-line agencies that are complaining about lower revenues and threatening at the same time that the replacements of digital agencies are coming to the fore, a lot of them have really become high-end production shops. They haven't been able to grow into the strategic full-service agencies at the same pace that they thought they would.

"There is the obvious threat to creative people, having to bid themselves that way, but aside from those issues, if I were a client, I would find it really exciting that you get the best idea without the politics. What could be missing for me is the apparatus that built up the traditional agency for a good reason: the strategist, a good account person who knows how to tell you when you are making a bad choice.

"A lot of the things that people have come to rely from their agency are potentially getting taken out of the equation. I would broaden that to say that that is not just true of new agency models like Victors & Spoils, but it's true of a lot of the media agencies that are creating content for brands. They're doing it without that understanding that comes with being an agency that lives and breathes brands, and lives and breathes the relationship with the client. It doesn't always lead to great work. It's not that in principle I'm against it. It's just that I have personally seen bad work come out of it. Though I am sure there are really good creative people answering those briefs."

⤿

Åsk Wäppling, "It's like consumers are a bunch of fish in a school, and they're constantly dodging stuff left and right. We can steer them if we just look at the big picture a little better. That's what we used to do in advertising, but we're not doing it anymore. We're not following the school of fish around.

"*Adland* brings in everything from every country in the world, basically. Everything was coming in from a bunch of early creatives who just wanted to make a name. They came from any kind of media. It didn't matter if it was poster or a film, they just wanted to make a name for themselves. You know that's how advertising worked. You couldn't score a job until you scored something. If you couldn't score an award, you would score some mentions somewhere. You would do the most outrageous thing ever. None of this was actually good branding. The good craft, the good posters, the good brochures, the good art direction, and the good commercials, they didn't exist during that time because everybody had to fight for a job. That boils down to the fact that there are always new teams, and most of them were never paid. This is difficult after portfolio school. Advertising has always had a problem cannibalizing ourselves.

"The ad execs don't seem to have the view of what the brand is really all about. They don't know what the soul is. It's the same problem we had in the '90s. It was, 'Oh my god! She knows how to do HTML, let's put her over here in a corner and push pixels.' Now it's, 'You don't do this so you will sit over here and work on the Instagram thing,' or 'We will hire you only to be the Nissan social media manager,' which is like cutting limbs off of a creative, which is just wrong."

⤿

Dirk Eschenbacher, "I remember a web site project for a local client. It was a wine company that was government owned, and it went through two years of redesigns, rebuilding it and revamping it before we even launched. It was a very frustrating process until we actually had a web site up and running. It took forever. The client just couldn't make decisions. We kept saying, 'Let's put it online and change it later.' No, everything had to be done beforehand. There was probably the misconception of the difference between e-commerce site and a web site. They were never really happy with it, and there were too many layers of decision making."

～

Paul Kwong, "About eight to nine years ago, traditional agencies started hiring creative teams who focused on online advertising. Also, the traditional agencies started to incorporate those departments with the creative teams. Before that, they were a different part of the agency, pretty much their own separate company. Much of their work was smaller and had a smaller piece of the total budget.

"That started to change as clients began to move or expand those budgets. You also started to notice that headhunters only had job offerings for *digital* creatives and that there was a shortage of good digital creatives. Job requirements also stipulated candidates needed to have both traditional and digital experience.

"The big wall you had to get through with recruiters was that they thought only digital creatives could only do digital work and no one but traditional creatives could do traditional work. Their mindset was that creatives couldn't think in both areas. Which is ridiculous. Digital is just another medium. Like film, radio, or outdoor. If you can think or concept or be creative in one, you can probably do it all."

～

Susan Kim, "It's important that the agencies can continue to make a fair amount of money from TV. Look at the Olympics. There's still a lot of TV opportunity, and even though I am not sure how effective print and radio still is, it's something clients can easily understand. Advertisers are *willing* to understand it.'

"With digital, much of it can be done cheap; not that it's good, but it can be done and, yes, some of it *is* good. Much can be outsourced. It doesn't take that long to create a digital ad even if it has video in it. The production values are just so much lower. So, that's one part, and that's really crucial because if agencies cannot make money off of digital, then they are not going to do it.

"And then we have the executives who will say, 'My friend's daughter just graduated from college and she uses Facebook all the time. She doesn't have a job. I'll let her handle all the social media stuff.' You would never let someone's daughter who just graduated be in charge of media buying and placement and strategy for television, but if it's social media or something like that, they will let them do it. So, they are really not going to want to pay someone a whole lot of money to do a whole lot of strategy for social media because, *hey, my daughter does it. Give it to her.*

"The agencies are not as concerned about digital's bottom line, which is just that's the way it has always been from way back when we first started. Back from the *Mad Men* days such that if the client really saw how much was being wasted, they would just cry. Agencies are never going to be as concerned as the client who is really looking at those revenue numbers. In the old days, the agencies didn't even care what their revenue was."

⤺

Rob Martin Murphy, "It's like the old criticism that an integrated campaign isn't just matching luggage. It's the same thing with digital or social platforms. It's not about going, 'Oh, let's just plonk the same idea onto Twitter like that and then put it on Facebook like that.' The best ideas understand how those platforms are used by people and then create content that is useful enough or entertaining enough to be promoted by those people. Like how Best Buy put their Geek Squad on Twitter.

"That was using a platform to help solve problems their customers were having with technical electronic stuff. That's not ticking the Twitter box. That's a great example of using that platform. That's telling a brand story, and it's not necessarily making it similar to that idea in another platform. There are a whole lot of brands on these platforms because they have to be, but they're not really getting the most out of them because they're not using them in the most creative ways they can."

Brands Don't Lead the Way Either

Jeffrey Dachis, "Nokia is a perfect example of a great opportunity squandered in every way, shape, or form. I did a lot of early Nokia web development for the Nokia online experience. We built a lot of Nokia's subsidiary's web sites at Razorfish, and I always thought Nokia would lead the way with the tablet and the phone and PC multi-screen brand experience.

"The fact is that they sucked at all of them and were wed to an economic model that didn't allow them to really innovate in that space. So was Ericsson, for what it's worth: the Swedes and Finns had a very forward-looking view of what mobile telephony and mobile computing would be. They should get a lot of credit for that. They did build their brands that way, but they didn't build them by buying banner ads online. They built them by creating a branded immersive experience demonstrating what their propositions were. Creating grassroots movements in communities, *showing* what they're doing instead of only putting out banner ads, emails, and microsites.

"The general world view of advertising on the Internet is that money gets spent there, but generally all of those ad dollars are wasted. The big agencies have benefitted from the fact that digital isn't a really good place or hasn't been a good place to do advertising and brand building. Over the last 20 years, we've seen digital grow into, what is in essence, giant search-marketing efforts. The majority of the money that gets spent on digital today goes to search.

"I'll start with saying that the democratization of the tools of self-expression that we've seen in the last 10 years, the ability to produce and distribute ideas worldwide for free in high def is the *largest shift in the communication landscape that we've seen in the history of mankind.* The move from mass communications as you know it to be from the church hundreds of years ago through the major media companies that we now know of today (that are highly capital intensive) and used to control most of the dissemination of information and ideas. The shift has happened in the last 10 years, where the mass communications have become a mass of communicators.

"The mass of communicators can share their ideas, their manifestos for government, their educational opportunities, their cupcake recipes, their kitty-cat photos, and their feelings about the way they interact with brands worldwide for free. The shift from mass communications to a mass of communicators has created an entirely new landscape for brand building or for the building of pre-purchase intent. Awareness, brand love, mind share, or advocacy. That shift not only represents huge, enormous challenges for the traditional ad agency you know today because they're used to creating the big idea, owning the big idea, and then distributing the big idea via mass media versus engaging with, connecting with, and communicating with their constituents. This shift from mass communications to a mass of communicators necessitates a shift in the way brands engage with their constituents.

"And social, broadly coined – whether it be in communities, whether it be inside Facebook streams, Pinterest, Twitter, Instagram, Foursquare, Youtube, Renren, Google+, Orkut, VK, or the 400+ other social networks that have over a million users – represents the largest shift in the communication landscape in the history of mankind and necessitates a shift in the way brands get built for the future. I'll say that right now, I'm more excited about the social revolution for marketing communications than I ever was about the digital revolution that we all helped pioneer 20 years ago because right now, for once, with ubiquitous bandwidth, increased processing power, great screen resolution, and the miniaturization and mobility of computing, we finally can realize the benefits of what we thought was going to happen in digital 20 years ago. It's really, really exciting to think about the fact that cupcake bloggers can have as big of an impact on the baking industry as Hostess once had.

"It's the democratization of the medium, and if you're going to build a brand (which is still powerful because you need to be thought of in the consideration phase), you really have to think about building it in a different way. It really involves connecting with constituents and engaging them, activating them, and advocating for them – and having them advocate for you. It involves a shift from outsourcing your customer service department to India and looking at your customer service department as a profit center."

⌒

SAP APJ Channels Marketing Director and former Nokia APJ Regional Digital and CRM Lead, Wynthia Goh, "In the early days at Nokia, the marketing team was huge and full of people who were very experienced in their fields, which ran the gamut from TV to print to market research to below-the-line to retail.

"Fairly, or unfairly, depending on the vantage point of those of us with a digital background, we tended to group them all as simply 'traditional.' The fact is, true integration of digital with all those various fields of marketing did not come until years later, and even now as I say this, many areas of integration and interaction continue to evolve especially aided by increasing adoption of a middleware innovation such as QR codes, NFC, or wireless that glue digital with other forms of marketing to provide a true interactive consumer experience.

"In the initial phase of my role at Nokia, most of the marketing people had a general position that Nokia was a leading brand and needed to engage with digital in a way that befitted its brand status. However, they were also quite happy to let the digital team lead that effort, especially all of the more technical parts of digital: site content, publishing, databases, and CRM.

"As someone who was focused on digital, it was a great time and a great role. The brand had five or six levels of product price points, clear product groups who had different positionings, extensive customer segmentation research, which meant we were developing digital marketing to serve a very broad range of campaign objectives. There were campaigns that were focused on utility values of product ownership; campaigns that were market- making to push new themes and consumer behavioral changes; and there were brand campaigns where we were looking for creative expression that was meant to represent Nokia's belief in innovation.

"Because of the broad freedom I had to manage the digital strategy and execution of the products and the fairly centralized management of the entire region's online presence and online consumer communication, I was also able to integrate the developing and related fields within digital. That was deeply satisfying for me as an Internet industry professional.

Some of them that I can recall:

- Integrated creative digital strategy and online media planning
- Designed and executed usability research meant to provide data-driven changes to online presence

- Partnered with media publishers to measure effect of online advertising by measuring against control groups
- Piloted contextual advertising on mobile devices

"Though, on one hand, I had a lot of freedom, it was a struggle to integrate anything we were planning in digital with what was being planned for in TV, print, and for BTL. The recognition that digital was a field of emerging importance was also met with a sort of benign neglect by the management. Great that it's there and we have people who know what they are doing looking after that, so we can continue to delay learning more about it ourselves.

"For the online/digital/interactive team, you could do fantastic work, but only to a certain level. From my perspective, without the buy-in of the leadership, digital remained too far removed from the core of the business and could not impact beyond the communications sphere. In my case, I knew the Internet was going to change the world and change the way business was conducted – as well as change business itself, so it was a *big* frustration for me."

~

Director of Rawstream and Former Saatchi & Saatchi's Regional Business Director, Jonathan Holburt, "We tried to get our HP client to embrace this new world of digital and the potential of Asia then. We were invited as a team to HP's headquarters in Palo Alto to present an immersion on Korea, Japan, and China. We started the presentation with a quote from the science fiction writer, William Gibson: 'The future is already here – it's just not evenly distributed.'

"At that time, China had over 100 million on the Internet; Japan was already big into mobile with highly decorated mobile phones and PCs; and Korea was big into camera phones. The presentations to members of HP's management took place in November 2004. At that presentation, we made a prediction: camera phones would be ubiquitous within two years. The then-head of marketing for HP's consumer division replied with a quote I'll never forget, 'Not in my lifetime.' ...I'll bet he's still alive, too."

~

Andy Greenaway, "I work with an awful lot of FMCG brands. Most of the clients I meet (and remember, this is 2013) haven't got a clue about the digital world we live in. It frustrates me when you see a client who is obsessed with the 30-second TV spot and just pays lip service to digital and social. To tell the truth, I can't see how they can survive long term (probably a prediction that won't hold up). Media companies who blatantly lie about reach and viewership exacerbate this problem.

"I did some work recently for a QSR. We convinced them to launch a promotion purely online. The results were spectacular (much improved over their traditional campaigns). They are now converts and have whole-heartedly embraced the 'new' way. Maybe it's about doing less talking and just proving to these Luddites that the new approaches make a difference. Do first, ask for permission later."

Chapter 17: The Ghost of Agencies Yet to Come

Because of its very cautious and conservative nature, the advertising industry has been comfortably predictable for long enough that there are many families with three generations of ad execs who can swap war stories around the holiday table (that the rest of the family, frankly, has no interest in hearing). Back then and for a long time if you wanted a safe bet, you'd get a degree in Marketing or English Literature, join an agency at a junior level, and work your way up via experience, attrition, and, inevitably, politics.

For most of the last century you could stay in the same agency for your entire career and, toward the end of it, easily hop from one big shop to the next or over to the client side to see how the better half lived. You didn't have to worry about finding a satisfying role somewhere. You could still get a mortgage on a home, buy a slightly-nicer-than-you-can-comfortably-afford car, plan family vacations, and, in a nutshell, have a stable life.

From the agencies' point of view, they had a firm grasp on the resources they needed to keep employed and could plan career paths and provide training to them as an investment in their own business. They could sell clients on the idea of a long-term relationship with these people who would understand the brand values, corporate goals, and the clients' own personal ambitions. Agencies had clearly defined services with roles and responsibilities understood by all parties and they could even forecast fairly well. But like Ebenezer Scrooge back when he was still grumpy, we have fooled ourselves into thinking no matter how much we and the world around us changes, the future will merely be an extension of the past instead of something much less certain and palatable. If we continue on our present trajectory we can be sure that the holding companies will have wrung out every last cent from the people who devote themselves to the craft and possibly continue to transform agencies into commodity production services that strive to be the cheapest, most efficient sweatshops in all of the land. Or maybe they will simply reinvest in another industry altogether. Who can say?

～ک

Bob Hoffman, "I don't think anyone has a clear vision of the future of advertising and marketing. It is murky. But that doesn't mean that these big conglomerates are going to fall apart. They have been very good at convincing clients that what the clients need are resources rather than intelligence, and these huge companies position themselves as being very resource rich.

Whether they're smart or not is a matter of debate, but they definitely position themselves as resource rich, and clients are afraid not to have that. That's part of why the agency business has become so consolidated. Clients are afraid not to have things, whether they need them or not.

"The industry's not going to go into the abyss. If I had to predict, I predict we will muddle along just as we have been for the past five years or so not really knowing what we're doing or why. I don't think we're going to be going over any cliffs. I don't think anyone can come up with magic answers. It's going to be more of the same, which is not healthy for the advertising industry or for marketing in general.

"We are the victims of legends and rituals. We do the things that we're used to doing, and we think about the way we're used to thinking about it, and we're trying to graft old ways of thinking onto new media, which I don't think is working. I wish I knew what the problem is. I wish I knew what the answer was. I see more of the same."

⤴

Ignacio Oreamuno, "Hell, I don't think change is coming. Change came, it's in the entrance of the agency, and it's been waiting for a coffee for the last two hours. No one's even paying attention to it. Me, the head of an awards show, doesn't have a TV, and we're awarding TV ads. That's evidence that the world pretty much changed, and it's pretty dramatic, and there's nothing that anybody can do about it. I'm seeing it by people quitting. It was a lot easier before. You made an ad and you could see it on TV, you could see it out in cinemas, you can see what you're creating, and now it's so much harder just to make sense of what we're doing."

⤴

Shane Ginsberg, "Some agencies that are adept at adapting have done pretty well, Goodby being a great example. It's like there's been a forest fire and digital has been the accelerant."

⤴

David Sable, "The sad thing is to say it's one thing, digital, versus the other, TV. My crystal ball is cloudy. My attitude is I just want to know what my clients, my customers, my users, my buyers, whatever are doing, and I want to be there. I want to add value to their lives in ways that are interesting: entertain them, inform them, educate them, and make them happy. We've created a new segmentation, which is there is no segmentation. You can talk about millennials, but at the end of the day, people are discovering that audiences online are very mixed. You think it's all men? You're wrong. You think it's all women? You're wrong. You think it's all kids? You're wrong. You think it's all adults? You're wrong. I really do believe in digital. It's awesome. It has created huge opportunities for us."

⌒

Dave Fleet, "Radio didn't kill the newspaper, TV didn't kill radio, and social is not going to kill anything else either. It's an additional piece of your marketing mix. And I think it's being too narrow-sighted to think that it's the only thing that matters. Anyone that's worked in this space in a really integrated marketing mix is fully aware that social, PR, advertising all have their own strengths and they all have their own weaknesses. Likewise digital.

"To be truly effective as a communicator, you need to be able to learn how to integrate the pieces that are within your wheel house with the other pieces in the marketing mix. And have all of the different people at the table rowing in the same direction. That's what makes a successful program or a successful communications campaign. It's not the latest bright shiny object. It's a communications team working together."

⌒

Torrence Boone, "There is a lot of bright-shiny-object syndrome among agencies and advertisers, given the explosion of possibilities associated with technology and the fragmentation of media. Storytelling and emotional brand building are often the casualties in this process as agencies and advertisers lose sight of truly breakthrough insights and the construction of seamless cross-channel experiences. Tech companies are also to blame by focusing too narrowly on tactical utility plays that don't deliver sustainable value at scale. Madison Avenue and Silicon Valley have much to learn from each other."

⌒

Brian Solis, "This isn't anything new. It's the next phase of the erosion of the platform that advertising agencies used to stand on. And the erosion started with the Web and digital. You saw a lot of specialist firms, agencies, rise up, get acquired, and become part of this ecosystem so that these holding groups had what they needed in order to effectively compete at every level. And that's happening here with social, mobile, and new media – and as social TV becomes more pervasive, you're going to see agencies rise to that medium as well. The way this has played out historically shows us that holding companies are holding companies for a reason and they're going to keep buying. Just as a relevant aside, we at Solis believe that the mobile is not the second screen, in some cases it's the first screen.

"That's all fine. But what's needed is somebody becoming a Steve Jobs, Elon Musk, or Richard Branson within the holding company. Somebody who's got great vision, temperament, and strength to talk about how to go about these acquisitions and the restructuring the inside of our organizations to better address the needs of brands as they struggle to evolve (because they're going to need to be taught how to do things, just like we had to be taught how to use an iPad and an iPhone). And I thought of how could it be taught to rethink how we manage our music. How we are taught to think about how we compute. This is an opportunity to change something. Somebody has to rise to that occasion; otherwise, we're simply going to see a lot of acquisitions, a lot of campaign packages, direct sales, and more campaign mentalities. But the minute that somebody starts to say 'Look at all these pieces that we have and you as a brand, you've asked us to do this. Here's what we can do, but will you love it? But what if we could do this? And this is what it looks like. And imagine this.' You know they'll say, 'That's great, but it's not what we're asking for,' but at some point, someone's going to have to take those ideas and champion an industry, which is what I do as well. Trying to get people to say, 'Just because it's not what you're asking for doesn't necessarily mean that you're on the wrong path.'

"It takes champions inside the brand to realize that how they're marketing and servicing their customers is broken. Everything inside the organization's broken. So is the way that the advertising agencies are selling into broken environments to begin with; therefore, someone has to be the champion to push thinking so that RFPs are to ask for the right thing. If a holding company executive isn't going to become that leader, then that means the brand executive is going to become that leader for the industry and start to retrain people how to think and how to form and craft RFPs. Which side of the dollar do you want to be on?

"If I were somebody at the top of the holding company, I would be on the circuit banging out what the new ecosystem and the new model looks like. There's this great fear that everything is proprietary, everything is brilliant within the shop, and you can't give it away. You can't give away this thinking. Everybody talks about how it needs to change, but the minute you start to show that for media, you've got an opportunity. Then it's your value proposition, your USP,[23] your construction of your holding company, and every brand underneath it, how you integrate everything – that becomes your value proposition. It takes a different leader and a different philosophy."

↩

Jeffrey Dachis, "I don't see the holding companies restructuring. What they tend to do is wait for new trends to mature to a point at which those trends are impactful to the potential bottom line. When that occurs, they then step in with financial resources and buy what they need to buy. The ad agency holding companies are really investment portfolio managers. They just happen to have an investment thesis that says we're going to invest in the marketing services world. To boost their returns they, in essence, will apply capital towards buying the higher returning investments when those investments are generating higher returns.

"I don't really see much change in the ad agency holding company structures. I do believe that the old advertising agencies are going to have to face some sort of existential crisis going forward because I don't think brands are going to get built in the same ways. They're going to have to either reshape the mix of the type of services they sell and offer while destroying the ones they currently offer or find themselves in a tough spot. It's just very hard."

↩

---

23 Unique Selling Proposition, a core advertising concept conceived by Rosser Reeves of Ted Bates Advertising in the 1960s. It is the one thing each company should be able to articulate that differentiates it from competitors.

Sarah Bradley, "I think there has to be an awful lot of consolidation in our industry over the next five years because there are so many agencies that have sprung up like a phoenix from the flames of this recession. I can't see how the market can support so many different agencies. I mean, there are 17,000 in the UK alone."

◌

Thierry Halbroth, "We're just sitting on a big bomb that's about to implode. But what's happening in the agencies I'm not going to blame it on them. Agencies are driven by clients, and I have to unfortunately shine the light on clients in terms of what's happening out there. Everybody is becoming shortsighted, very shortsighted. The business of advertising is turning to instant ROI or nothing.

"If you look specifically in Asia, building a brand takes time, but then everywhere in the world, building a brand takes time. You can't build it overnight and then suddenly have fantastic success. It ain't gonna happen. It takes time, it takes vision, it takes proper planning, and it's not something you can do quickly. In Asia, we don't have a lot of these brand things that happen. Even if you're looking at the long-term in this region, you're looking at three years to five years. What's happening is with the current economic climate, where everybody's under the pressure today to deliver numbers, everyone becomes accountable. Now it is a very well-known fact that the only real medium that can scientifically deliver value with these metrics is digital. There's a huge pressure on digital to get all sorts of metrics that are completely irrelevant.

"One being, we have 10,000 'likes' on one day or we've increased our fan base by 50%. What does that mean? This perspective, what does it mean? What are these numbers? The clients are saying 'We want to this, we want to do that.' But then they forget to ask themselves, why would you want to do that in the first place? What are you going to do with these people? Three times out of four the answer is, 'We don't know, we'll see later.'

"What's happening in the world of advertising is that we are driven now by clients who want metrics. They don't know *why* they want metrics because it's just driven by accountability. If they can go in a meeting and say, 'We've gained *x%* in our fans on Facebook,' someone will go, 'Oh, that's cool! That's great!' But what's the plan? How are you going to engage with these people? What are you going to do with them? What are you going to let them do to you because they can do things now, you know? You have to take that as a risk factor, especially in social media. What's going to happen then? How do you hedge your risks? That's the biggest issue that we are facing at the moment, that everybody's talking 'social, social, social, social.' That's why the web sites are disappearing, everything is disappearing, and everything is becoming social media or nothing. But if you look in the world, I would say 85%, if not maybe 90%, are not ready to let consumers take control of their brands. They're talking out of both sides of their mouths.

"That's really what's happening in the world of advertising. We basically struggle because everything is not really a digital strategy. You can talk about social media strategy if you want, but is it a platform? Is it a channel? What is it? For me, that's the biggest bomb there is out there, and it's a very, very dangerous one."

⤿

Alan Schulman, "The client organization is the biggest challenge to the change in the marketing funnel. The loss of time and space from awareness to purchase and the sheer control that has been turned over to the consumer by technology and devices has collapsed the client's ability to control that. They're organized for brand management and marketing in the old method, where if you're only spending 5 to 8% of your media on digital, then it gets delegated to the lowest person on the brand team. That person might also be responsible for let's say, shopper or trade marketing.

"As long as that organizational model, which I'll call the traditional brand or product management model in largely CPG [consumer packaged goods] companies, is the way it is, you're going to not get a lot of movement from pure brand communications to content platforms plus. Many of our clients are still entrenched in that old organizational model, the brand management model. Some of them have really optimized themselves to be way more innovative about the way they make decisions and push innovation. Innovation has become such a top-of-mind subject for them internally as they try to become more systematic about how they innovate instead of just allowing pockets of innovation to emerge randomly when no one is looking.

"What's their customer experience going to look like three years from now? Are they thinking about that? Are they organized for that? If you talk to a lot of the agency search consultants, they are doing searches, and the other half of them are working with marketers on their organizational models. What they're learning through the course of doing agency searches and agency pitches is that some clients are in an entrenched model of product and brand management that just isn't suitable for the digital age.

"I've come across many clients that are not prepared for the digital age and no matter what you offer them – the evidence, the case studies, the logic of it – they're not prepared to move. They're not prepared to reorganize themselves. They say, 'You have to work against our entrenched model. If you don't show a return on investment within the quarter, we can't do it, no matter what it is,' which shows you that they just don't understand the marketplace today. They're too big; they're too glacial in their change, in their adoption of technology. At least they're not alone; there are so many organizations like that.

"Most clients are still entrenched in the old model, and it's not that for a lack of wanting to challenge themselves organizationally. Some of them want to do that. They want to change, they want to innovate, and they want their agency partners to be cheaper and better. If they continue to commoditize the value of an idea to separate their product from their competitors, if they continue to organize only around brand columns instead of around what they can do to change their service experience through the transaction, if they continue to rest on the laurels of reach and not reach versus relationship, those are the marketers that will continue to just plod along.

"There are bigger marketers that shouldn't be faulted for trying to take risks, even though it hasn't shown up on their balance sheet every quarter. Jeff Bezos and the Amazon folks are one example of a client who has a longer view about what they build and what they invest in. Companies like Target – and there are lots of them out there – are just more progressive by nature, because they're not as married to that entrenched model."

⤳

Martin Howard, "For most advertising, it is being increasingly dominated by technical pre-programming. Unfortunately, you're going to see that there are particular structures for ads whether they are online, on TV or press ads, if they still exist. They're going to be increasingly pre-packaged, and they won't have much creative input. However, if you get that dominating too much, it's then easier to come in with a slightly more exciting layout and bust through the clutter of these technically driven ones.

"Overall, you're going to find math dictating to the creative group because creativity is a dynamic synthesis of a lot of different variables about the audience in a moment in time. Because of all that, there's still going be an opportunity for the Old Spice ads [*The Man Your Man Could Smell Like*] or something that's genuinely creative, but also opens the market and surprises people *and* performs on the bottom line."

~

Peter Moss, "I might as well just go the whole nine yards on this: one thing that has disappointed me, coming into this industry – and it's the same when I see how judges, jurors, and award shows operate – is how many artists we have judging artists. I don't care how cool it is. I do not want to see another visual analogy on a piece of paper with a tiny logo hidden inside. Honestly, I look at that stuff and I say, 'Well, that's art.' But we're in the business of *commerce.*

"As we move into what is going to be a digital future, or a future in which digital is pervasive, there have been certain tipping points. There was PC penetration, then Internet penetration, then broadband penetration, then mobile, then 3G, then smartphones. One of the next areas we are going to see, and the one that I am desperately waiting for as the next tipping point, is e-commerce confidence. Where consumers say, 'I feel totally happy whether I'm just waving my phone over a reader or whether I'm online and I don't have to go through twenty questions to make a purchase.'"

~

Mike Fromowitz, "In my time, it appeared that ad agencies were far more entrepreneurial or that they had the people who were. Today there's a greater need, more than ever, for ad agencies to be more entrepreneurial. *Or they will die.*

"Today's clients need their agencies to think more strategically and act more entrepreneurial. Strategic thinking is necessary in positioning a brand in the marketplace and creating its difference. The ability to effectively communicate with customers, vendors, and employees is imperative to providing greater customer satisfaction and improving business productivity. How well information is communicated both externally to customers and vendors and internally to employees is vital to long-term business success.

"However, to engage with clients in this way requires agencies to shift attitude to become more entrepreneurial, thus thinking like a true business partner. It's no longer about just making ads or how many awards your agency has won. You've got to be proactive and entrepreneurial. What separates the entrepreneur from the run-of-the-mill is an intuitive quality about consumer needs and consumer thinking, about being more visionary and seeing new opportunities before others do.

"Marketers looking for an ad agency partnership with an 'entrepreneurial spirit' need look no further than the people who are at the helm, those that run and manage the agency and drive its direction and culture. Are they entrepreneurs? Or do they just work for their salary and four weeks holiday every year? Do they have the following characteristics:

"**Motivation to achieve** – In almost every case, successful ad agency entrepreneurs are highly motivated achievers. They tend to be doers, people who make things happen. Often very competitive. They possess the sheer will to win in everything they do. They don't want to come in third, or in second; they want to come in first.

"**Hard work is a habit** – Running an ad agency, or starting one, is hard work. Let no one kid you about that. Unless you are prepared to work hard, you should not start an ad agency or consider running one. Not all heads of agencies are entrepreneurial. In fact, very few are. Many of them have never started their own business. In his excellent book *Winners,* Carter Henderson says: 'Starting a company is unlikely to turn a lazy oaf into a raging bull.' He also quotes Nolan Bushnell, founder of Atari, as saying it all comes down to one critical ingredient, 'Getting off your ass and doing something.' In summary, entrepreneurs are almost always very hard workers.

"**Nonconformity** – Most entrepreneurs tend to be independent souls, unhappy when forced to conform to bureaucracy. They are people who want to set their own goals.

"**Strong leadership** – Building an existing ad agency or moving it up the competitive rankings is a tiring and unforgiving job that can rob you of your personal life. Starting any business from scratch can be a harrowing experience full of uncertainty and risk.

"**Street smarts** – Shrewd or sharp might be better words to describe entrepreneurs. They always seem to make the right moves. Call it common sense, instinct, whatever you want. Successful entrepreneurs seem to have an innate or intuitive good judgment when making complex business decisions with their clients.

"Why can't agencies just carry on doing what they're supposed to do? Creating big ideas. Make wonderful, memorable ads that convince consumers to purchase brands. Maybe, if we followed that simple path, we'd have no need for re-engineering, and maybe, just maybe, our clients would be happier with their ad agencies? Perhaps the best way to 'regenerate' an ad agency is through the creation of wonderful advertising ideas that build client brands?"

"It's easy, if not fashionable, for many marketers and those writing *industry trade* articles to lay the problems of the advertising industry at the feet of creatives.

"With an ever-increasing focus on advertising awards, they are accused of many things including introspection, irrelevance, and arrogance. Neither planners nor account management are damned in this way. It's hard to find a blog these days that does not ridicule above-the-line creatives for awardcentricism, or for not being in the digital world. In particular, members of the new marketing mafia are their greatest critics, and most of them have never made an ad in their life, or for that matter, made it in a proper advertising agency, and consequently have a massive chip on their shoulders.

"Many agencies and their creative people still believe the use of creative awards is the only way to get ahead in this business. The worst excess of this of course, are all the 'scam' ads used to increase an agency's awareness, to strengthen their show reel, and to hopefully, influence new business to come their way.

"All this reprehensible behavior is merely the result of a bunch of agency people trying to be as creative as they can and as they have been trained to do from the outset of their careers. If this is no longer what marketers and ad agencies want from them, then we have to take some responsibility for changing the situation, rather than simply saying that traditional advertising doesn't cut it any longer.

"Many years ago, advertising had a very simple task. To tell a lot of people why a particular product or service was brilliant so they could make a purchase decision. Things started to get complicated with so many identical products and services competing for our attention.

"My point in all of this is really only to suggest that we have trained generations of creative people to operate in an environment in which most products and services were identical. Some, not necessarily any good. We left it to creative people to create the 'difference.'

"Is it any wonder then that they instinctively reach to TV to create the big idea? Is it still not the most popular medium with more viewing eyeballs, bar none? That they have an awards system that links ideas to commercial success? That many traditional creative departments do not fit in the new 'digital' brand landscape where products have to survive consumer scrutiny?

"What we need now is for ad agencies to perform their tasks differently. What we want now are creative people to have a new set of skills that include things digital. Is that not a cause for restructuring the roles and relationships of creative people, or for the deconstruction of the big ad agency silo mentality?

"At the end of the day, it seems the advertising industry is being sent an important signal that change is necessary for survival. Without regeneration and an entrepreneurial approach to client business, agencies will not be able to convince their clients that their business is staffed by professionals, by advisers whose counsel is credible and influential, and by creative people who have the ability to craft ideas into gems and nuggets of intellectual property worth a king's ransom."

⁓

Paul Biedermann, "The times are very exciting and the opportunities for creative play are plentiful. However, the rush to digital and social has also largely thrown the baby out with the bath water, as human nature seems to be continually over-enamored with that pesky shiny object syndrome. This has led to a plethora of work that is weak and one-dimensional, instead of the well-crafted, integrated, inspired creative solutions that make brand, marketing, and communications experiences truly compelling.

"Of course I am generalizing here, but together with the weak economy we've been experiencing, lack of budgets, and clients who've been afraid of their own shadow, the situation hasn't been exactly fertile for creativity to flourish. Instead, quick, flashy, but generally insipid solutions have ruled the day. With the technologies, media platforms, and vast array of ways to bring creative together in all kinds of new and exciting ways, there has never been a better time with this kind of potential to do standout work with broad reach and impact and the future is even brighter."

⤳

Neil Leslie, "I expect there will soon be a major shift that will see big idea development move from the ATL domain to one that is predominantly digital. This reflects our audiences' media appetites and the resulting shift in our clients' budget allocation. Shame we didn't lead the charge. If we had, I think our industry would be in much better shape today.

"I still feel that we are in a Wild West period created by a power struggle between above-the-line and digital interests. Many agencies, it seems, have an inherent unwillingness to steer clients away from their cash cows and merely supplement largely traditional campaigns with digital elements. For now, the West and Japan seem well ahead in that regard, as campaigns like Amex's *Small Business Saturdays* demonstrate. They, at least, seem to be catching on to the fact that big ideas need to harness the power of digital at their core to maintain the sort of results once enjoyed via traditional media."

⤳

Chris Kyme, "I wouldn't say that creative people have suffered. But definitely standards of professionalism have been watered down, in general. Creative product has suffered because the execution is now cheap and quick… creativity has become fast food."

⤳

Creative Planning Director of DDB Oslo and former Executive Creative Director of Bates Singapore, Petter Gulli, "As Darwin said, it's not the strongest who survive, but the most adaptable to change. It's sad to see so many of the best creatives in the industry disappear just because they wanted the world to stay the same. Or maybe their skills were not so great after all. Lots of digital agencies were founded by designers and tech people, which should be an opportunity for experienced creatives from the ad agencies. Back in 2005 when I was ECD of Bates Singapore, I had a discussion with Chris Schaumann from XM about the future of advertising, which included some shouting and lots of beer. But I remember very well his closing line: 'You know Petter, you and I are ideas and strategy people. Companies will always find a use for us.'"

"Chris made this simple point: if you really do understand how insights, communication strategy, and creative ideas correlate, you don't have a problem. You just have to translate your knowledge into the new language. Today, I have found that we have old-school digital players who need to change as much as those of us coming from the advertising side."

꩜

Jennifer Hoe, "Digital (technology) is an enabler. The Internet/mobile/tablet/whatever, is a channel, a medium, like any other communication channel or medium. I've never understood why those who call themselves marketing professionals simply cannot grasp this basic view of marketing communications. From the failure to understand this basic concept comes the failure to be true marketing professionals by being media agnostic and selecting the best channels for delivering a brand or product message and experience. Those who work in advertising have no right to call themselves marketers if they don't get this."

꩜

John Winsor, "The reality is that advertising has always been a bastardized way to get people to talk about brand. There are going to be way more direct ways for brands to engage with their consumers and their communities and build value. I think social media is a great example of that. Some people have done it well, some people haven't.

"If you look at the old-school brands, it's like they got stuck with their business models. Best Buy got stuck with opening brick-and-mortar stores instead of building a community of consumers and continually focusing on, 'How do you guys want to buy electronics? What do you want us to be? How can we help you?' All those kinds of things. They could've easily done that. I am sure they have with those rewards on the card. But if you are in a business like Best Buy's, you're a real estate company. They're all run by people who maximize the revenue per square foot. If you're in the business of maximizing the revenue per square foot, there is no way that you would build an Amazon. It just doesn't make sense. It's out of your conscious thought – it doesn't even register – like, that's crazy.

"Those agencies that can help brands to create more culturally relevant materials that spur deeper dialogue, that build communities no matter what way it is, by using RTB [real time bidding] methodologies and creating ways to prospect through digital tools or whatever that is, or creating explosive Web videos or big TV ads. Those guys are going to win. It's going to be the Walmart-factor. There are going to be a few massive global agencies that are going to be kind of Walmart, one size-fits-all, we'll-do-anything-in-the-world, and then millions of tiny little providers, and there will be zero in between. Everything else will go out of business.

"I think the really interesting thing about agencies is that because they are so amorphous, you look at all the WPP agencies and Sir Martin does a masterful job of moving things between agencies. When you own agencies like JWT, Ogilvy, and all of those other agencies like they do, on one side of the door it says Ogilvy and other side of the door it says JWT. Agency names have become kind of conflict resolution methods. You can get a Ford, you can give GM to Ogilvy. You could pretend, wink-wink, that they don't know what's happening. I think agencies and agency brands are going to stay around for a long time. I think they're just going to be gutted from the inside out. And I think it's really cool. I think we are in this evolutionary time, and the Facebooks and the Twitters and the Apples are slaying the older brands.

"Google may very well be the advertising agency of the future. I had a buddy who has a company called Trada, and those guys are the crowdsource SEO search company. He is a tech guy, so of course he got big valuation from the VCs and then he got Google to put in $5 million for a quarter of his company immediately. He was crowdsourcing keyword searches with a really cool model. When Bing came out, Google's response to the competition was 'Oh, we will just give away for free all the services that Trada is doing' [to incentivize advertisers not to switch].

"So my buddy's investor, who owns a quarter of his company through Google Investments, essentially made the market value of his services zero. It's not a very scalable model, and I think that's the thing. It's sort of the like the old days when agencies came from the media business where hey, if you owned a newspaper, you could charge extra for putting together ads. So you set up an advertising agency to manage the print ad production [and get more dollars]. Like them, Google, of course, is trying to get more advertising dollars, so they are setting up all of these ways to work with advertisers and then giving it away for free because they make so much money on the search side of things and with their other tools [and just want to keep their customers spending there].

"It is kind of like the revenues from the newspaper business. It is essentially this kind of a long slow growth curve to 2008 and then it is a collapse to 1950s level. It has gone from 1950 to 2008 to grow by a factor four or five. It has taken five years to go all the way back to 1950 revenue. It is happening in music and is happening in every creative service business. When everybody can participate, when you are an agency and you are competing in a free market on the Web, where you've got some kid sitting in Kuala Lumpur with a video camera who composed some crazy video with your brand on a mountain bike, and it gets five million hits... and you're fucked.

"Because there are passionistas that have responded because they love it. You are totally screwed. I just think that is the future. I think the only play that the agencies are going to have or to get into is that McKinsey space of being brand advisers and being able to curate all that stuff. It feels to me like we are at a tipping point."

⤸

Scott Morrison, "Unfortunately, the main agencies are going to largely die off. I really do believe that because the requirement for them is becoming less and less relevant. Hey, the guys who were working their asses off to sell Beta cassettes in the VHS versus Beta days – they fought right to the end.

Look what happened to HD DVD. The people who believed in it believed in it until the time that it died. Our position with our creative collective, The Bauhub, is that we will not go the direction of crowdsourcing agencies like Victors & Spoils in Colorado or eYeka in France, but I'm perfectly prepared to say, 'Okay, gloves off, boys. Let's go.' Maybe there's enough space for both of us. I wish them well. I don't wish them ill for what they're doing. I just personally wouldn't be interested in working in an industry where I take 21 years of experience and I parlay that into spending evenings and evenings of my time or days and days of my time to maybe get paid. You can't do that."

The Talent Drain

These days, with so many more career options available for people with a creative bent, advertising is having a hard time competing for new talent and staving off attrition of personnel. The dot.com daze of the late 1990s taught us all a valuable lesson about abandoning carefully constructed careers in solid fields to jump into the nebulous world of Internet-based startups, but the last 15 years has taught us that advertising simply isn't a stable profession anymore. Here for decades, gone tomorrow. Make too much, gone. Client realigns globally, gone. Project ends, gone. Fall victim to scapegoating and politics, gone. For people entering the job market who don't even have knowledge of those new realities, advertising still isn't seen as attractive as it was in past years, definitely not when compared with the new opportunities available to them now. The young can gain the experience they need by joining an established innovation factory like Google, Facebook, Twitter, or Apple, where they will be shown appreciation with stock, hiring bonuses, competitive salaries, and plenty of perks to keep even the shallowest of hipsters satisfied. Alternatively, they can get the experience by iteratively trying and failing with their own creative ideas — and without harming their reputation.

The available infrastructure provided by the Internet removes the need for spending money every month on any significant overhead. People can closely collaborate over free online platforms from different parts of the world. There's even plenty of investment capital flowing around now that mature digital businesses have succeeded in becoming multi-billion-dollar companies that are taken seriously by the most serious people in the business world. More to the point, there's yet-another Gold Rush happening. First, there was the actual mid-19th century California Gold Rush, then the Web Gold Rush with agencies trying to quickly produce what the Internet startups needed to build their brands and have an online presence, and now we can imagine and create for a very content-hungry audience that has more than warmly embraced the digital-device era. In fact, they can scarcely remember a time they weren't feeling phantom vibrations on their legs every few minutes telling them that there's something *new* to look at, in anticipation of the actual vibrations going off... every few minutes.

‿

Bob Hoffman, "The talent drain has already happened. There's clearly less talent in the advertising industry – on both the creative side and the marketing side – than there used to be. As the clout that they have has been diminished and they become more and more order takers, real good marketing people don't want to work in agencies anymore. They don't want to be account people anymore. Why would they do that? All account people get is beaten up and blamed for shit. They're not allowed to make decisions anymore. They don't have to find strategies anymore."

‿

Ignacio Oreamuno, "There are a lot people now that are leaving the ad agencies. In fact, we started a whole series called *Startup*, which is all about creative directors that quit their jobs to launch their own type of startup-like technology companies, Instagram, whatever things, and it always sells out in a week. It's crazy because everybody is thinking that it's no longer cool to make ads and work at the monster agencies anymore. I also have a lot of friends that used to work at big agencies that now are creative directors at a client organization."

‿

Jennifer Seidel, "I will say that the advertising business still has 30% turnover, and that's across the board. In some agencies, it's much higher, and a lot of that is because the industry as a whole (there are exceptions) doesn't do a good job of performance management, of career coaching, of giving younger people an understanding of what their career paths and options are. It's a really hard business. You work your ass off, and you don't get paid well in the beginning."

‿

Andy Flemming, "Digital has drained a lot of the talent that we used to get in the advertising business. They're now doing online stuff. They're creating stuff for the Web and mobile, and they have more freedom than they would in a huge ad agency. From the creative side, talent has been drained, and from the marketing side, talent has been drained.

"There is also a lack of writers. One of the biggest problems I've found is that I don't think people read books anymore. My generation, or maybe the generation after me, is the last one that actually got to consume books. Only by being obsessed with books and reading as many as possible can you write, really fucking write, and actually be able to understand how to do it, how it works. A lot of people can get away with it, but not very many people can actually do it really, really well.

"A lot of the young people coming in, we see their books and what they've been doing for the last five years and I don't think they have a voice of their own. I don't see a distinct personality coming through or even a portfolio that tells me that I'm getting old, and maybe this is now the way of things. People have told them that a great idea is a fucking big visual with a tiny logo in the bottom – and that's all it takes. But it is not what makes a good ad. It's just what makes an ad *look* like an ad. It looks like ads that you've seen before, but what I'm looking for is someone who gives me an ad that maybe doesn't look like an ad, but is a very different way of provoking me. Or making me feel something.

They generally give you what they think you expect, which is an amalgamation of stuff they've seen before. It might get them through the door for some people, but I want to see the next David Droga appear. Someone who just goes, 'fuck it.' What we're all after, at the end of the day, is to see a great piece of work. Someone that tells us we're old and finished. That's what I want."

↜

Mike Langton, "Will another Bernbach or Ogilvy rise in today's environment? Yes, but – and the 'but' should be in big, bold capitals – **BUT**, they have to do it in their own organizations and it has to be the way that things went for David Droga. What happened with the industry previously was that people would work for a big agency and they'd say, 'I have a great relationship with this client. This client really loves me. I love their business. I'm going to start my own agency. I hope this client comes with me.' The two get drunk in private. The client says, 'Okay, we'll give you the brand. Do good things with it.'

"The guy does well, and the client gives all their business to them. There are no global alignments so, ta-dah, you land up with your agency doing great work and making a healthy living. Global alignments fly in the face of you being able to set up a really strong agency with a major client, a big spender. You have to go with the larger local client who tends to be unsophisticated and very often a little scared to spend big money.

By the 2000s and onward, if someone set up their own agency and they were any good, a Sorrell, or one of their organizations would come snuffling around and say, 'Hey. Why don't we buy your company for $50 million and you carry on running it for the next four years and these would be your opening and annual pay outs.' And these guys look at the numbers and think, 'Ka-ching! Wow, look at all the money!' That became the thing. You would get rich by starting an agency and flipping it to a Sorrell or Levy or their minions, and people were like, 'Yay! I'm in the get-rich business.'

'No you're in the advertising business.' 'No, I'm in the get-rich business.' 'Okay, you're in the get-rich business.' There goes the quality straight out the window, and it's gotten to the point where people started to say, 'The madness has to stop. I'm going to start an agency. I'm not going to sell it,' or, 'I'm going to let a network have a relatively small share or an affiliation agreement so I'm connected to one of the networks so I've got air cover so I can get a big piece of global business in the door by having access to the big guns.' Because so much is globally aligned; unless your agency globally aligned, you can't get into the big business.

"What has to break down, and I do see it breaking down, is that the ad industry now produces so much crap in such large volumes that they are adding almost no value at all. Marketers are starting to say, 'Shit. I have an almost undifferentiable product, and the only thing what will differentiate it is great advertising. Where the hell am I going to get that?' Unilever has been putting business out with small agencies for more than 10 years. A project here, a project there to get great creative. It does work.

"What you're going to see is a lot of major players who will say, 'We're going to use some of these smaller agencies that were started by guys who've worked in the environment, understand our sort of needs, but they've gone off and started their own businesses and now they are producing great advertising that is getting cut-through in the markets. People are delighted by it, and we need some of that, so we're going to work with them.'"

‿

Thierry Halbroth, "The biggest issue we have is with talent. Agencies are not really ready to pay anymore for talent. They want people on call all day or they're happy to downsize and not get what they want and not pay for the money. It has got to do with revenue. It has got to do with what the clients, at least I'm hoping that's what it is. That it has got to do with what clients are ready to pay for or how the contracts are structured."

‿

Susan Kim, "My first creative director was at W.B. Doner & Co, and I don't know if it was because of digital, but he now does fine carpentry woodworking-type stuff. He left the industry entirely. Another creative director I worked with, Michael Monicket, is so funny and talented, but he was fed up and said, 'That's it! I've had it!' He was tired of putting all of his passion and blood, sweat, and tears into it, and he left for years. His dad had a photography business that he went to work for, and he was happy. But then, somehow after being out for several years, he got drawn back and he was doing a photo shoot. There was a client there and then… he couldn't help himself. He started art directing and then advising the client, and then he got sucked back into doing it.

"I don't know if you have completely given up, even if you do go to a nonprofit and you do say, 'Forget it, I'm getting out of this.' Once you are away from it, you start to get frustrated when you see people that are doing it so well, and sometimes you start doing campaigns and strategy in your head, 'If I were there, I would do this.' Sometimes you can't help it. Even the folks that do leave it in their minds, maybe they haven't totally left it. Unless you are doing it for your own company, it's hard to maintain the enthusiasm, the passion, and the drive because there are only so many times you can roll that stone up the mountain. If you are getting paid by the hour to roll it up there, who cares if it rolls down again."

⟿

Jason Ayers, CEO and Founder of Sector Five Recruiting based in Hawaii, "It's still sexy to work with movie stars to make a cool TV spot or print campaign. The same people are still attracted to the business for the same reasons as they've always been. But the business is different. There is now a focus on profits, and the holding company structure means people don't feel the same freedom. I guess the agencies don't make the money like they used to, and a lot of the perks are gone. They all want to go client side now because they feel like they'll be able to be the deciders. If somebody is really bright and they're frustrated with the way that the agency is run and they know that it's not efficient and they really care about the success of their client, then they want to be the client because they want to be able to make things happen. They feel like they're restricted. They're held back.

"The problem is, the clients don't want to hire people from agencies anymore because they think they don't understand important areas like supply chain. They don't understand about what happens with production and retail, and they're seen as people that can come up with cute campaigns, but have no clue about *real* business. They hire people from other clients – from other makers. Unless somebody's young, it's rare we can place somebody from an agency role to a client role, if they haven't already worked for that client."

⟿

Barry Wong, "Truth be told, I don't have the confidence in most of the teams, and I don't think I ever will. It might sound totally brutal, but it is a sad truth. The teams that used to work with me varied between the traditional guys and the digital guys. The conundrum in this mix is this: the traditional guys understood branding, messaging, and strategy, but had little desire to pick up new media. They've been brainwashed into thinking that digital has little room for creativity and almost it never had the multi-million-dollar budgets they're used to. The digital guys were mostly post-1980s kids extremely well-versed in technology and the digital space, yet possessed close to zero knowledge of branding, strategy, and messaging. To them, it was all about fancy animation, great little mouse-over effects, collapsing and expanding menus and navigation bars.

"As such, I've had to always get in on a project from the beginning, work with the team in delivering a sound strategy, build up the creative work, and sell that to the client. It sure as hell wasn't an easy thing to do since I had to be present at most creative presentations, doing the sell-in on my own. Very often a digital team, when faced with a client who understands strategy, branding, and messaging, would crumble. Conversely, a traditional team would be hard-pressed when trying to sell in a digital component to a client who was digitally savvy. As such, it wasn't so much of a budget issue for me; instead, I was more concerned with how ideas were presented and sold to clients, who also varied to great extremes."

〰️

Joe Zandstra, "It's this cyclical process where big ad agencies say, 'We need digital people and innovation directors.' And they get them in and they fail to use them and then they fire them. Then they're left without any digital capabilities and then they hire them again and it goes over and over again. Because there's this desire to get the end product without the understanding of the actual way of working that that entails."

〰️

The fate of most everyone you know in the business is likely tied to the large global agency networks. The big names like Ogilvy and McCann that have practiced what they sell to clients and have created bona fide brands known by everyone related to the industry and even familiar to a few civilians who pay attention. If they are unable to adapt in time and convince key staff and clients that they bring much more to the table than invoicing for renting a table with a 120% markup and three hours of project management time, then collapse they very well might. When they go down, so do the full-time-employment prospects of hundreds of thousands of dedicated people the world over. It will be the Advertising Apocalypse.

Every job related to messaging, selling, creating awareness, building a brand, managing an event, and so on will be immediately taken by whoever can call in favors faster than the rest of the desperate hordes watching their unemployment benefits quickly dry up.

The majority will either need to go back to school or otherwise reinvent by choosing a new career path that may be able to use some of the old skills.

❦

George Tannenbaum, "I'd love to see a chart that had the top 10 agencies from 10 years ago in size. How many employees they had 10 years ago. How much revenue they had 10 years ago. Where they are now? I want to see it because my impression is that in 2001 or 2002, Y&R probably had in New York 1,200 people. Now, my guess is they're down to about 300 – and nobody is talking about the seismic transformation of the industry. I've worked at some of the bigger agencies and you walk into them today, and it's like walking into a morgue, where it's supposed to be bristling with thoughts and solutions and ideas. Everything that they were disparaging digital agencies for should have been taken as best practices. That's essentially what they do, right? They look for the tried-and-true formula, which is neither tried nor true."

❦

Shane Ginsberg, "The other day I was looking around in San Francisco and thinking back 15 years ago. The largest agency here was FCB. The most venerable and second largest agency was Hal Riney. We had a very large Y&R office here, McCann was a fairly significant entity, Goldberg Moser O'Neill was big, Odiorne Wilde & Narraway was big... I can list a bunch of others that no longer either exist or have whittled down to shells. The ones that don't adapt die very, very quickly."

❦

Diane McKinnon, "The amount of information that's out there about any of these kinds of things, digital, mobile, social, whatever it is, is overwhelming. You can't be an expert about everything obviously, but you just gotta *learn, learn, learn.* Immerse yourself. My advice, my mantra for myself is: keep learning, keep digging, keep trying to find out more about what's successful.

"Almost five years ago, I gave a talk to the students at the Portfolio Center in Atlanta. They were asking me about what we are looking for, what skills do they need coming into the marketplace. My contention was you have to be a polymath. You have to have your passion and expertise if you're a copywriter or an art director, but you also have to be able to do research and critical thinking and writing and communicating and speaking and learning about new things. Probably the core of what I look for in people is some level of intellectual curiosity about the world and how it is changing, and about my client's business and about how Facebook might mean something to this client or Twitter to that. Whatever is, you have got to be intellectually curious.

"It's being willing to be a little bit tangential and just start with something like Yahoo! News that's an aggregator and to start following threads of interesting stories and see where it takes you. It's trade magazines, it's technology sites, it's news aggregators. I find stuff all over the place. I go on vendor sites, for example Radian6, which is the social listening platform and has tons of white papers about social media and how you set up social media strategies. Companies that are doing this work or are in the space and even agencies putting out white papers about this or that.

"You've got to be on these social platforms and play around a little bit, follow people in your industry. Take Twitter, for example: go out and look at trending topics. You have to engage in the platforms to have some meaningful ideas about what the platforms might ultimately do. You as an individual may not be the one who ultimately manages the Twitter account for a client or driving strategy, but you've got to play in the sandbox a little bit to have some appreciation for what those things are.

"I don't know how you keep up except to constantly ask questions. That goes back to that curiosity thing. I wish I had a magic bullet in terms of how to keep up with what's out there. It is tough. It's really tough. You have to work at it is the answer. You can be overwhelmed by trying to always stay ahead of the curve, but as a leader, you have to find the people who have that drive to really be latest and greatest and put them in a position to use that hunger to their best advantage. It's gauging who the people are who have that constant 'what's the next thing' drive versus those people who want to dig deep into a specific topic and really become more expert in it. You need both in your organization if you really want to be successful. It's hard for one person to do both. In any business, if you're not willing to learn and evolve, you're going to get overtaken at some point. Some of us are going to end up working for people who are younger than we are, and you see a lot of young Turks emerging in these chief social officer positions and such."

↩

Joe Zandstra, "Traditional agencies will learn to adapt. They'll downsize and then upsize again just like digital has been doing over the past 15 years, except they're going to be less prepared for it. I remember my old digital agency that I joined in 1996, Agency.com, had its Exchange Place building with five floors and they downsized to two floors, then one floor and then they moved out, then they got bigger and then they got smaller again – this kind of constant shift has been painful but I feel it's made digital practitioners more flexible. It remains to be seen how the traditional agencies are going to adapt. The big agency brands may live on, but the organizations are going to change. There are going to be layoffs.

"These agencies are so big that these are not entrepreneurial spaces. These are not areas where everyone feels like they have the ability to make new things happen in their little sphere within the big agency they work in. They are perhaps a little dehumanized. And I'll say, this is a symptom of size, not so much traditional vs. digital – but right now digital is more fleet-of-foot – perhaps by dint of its challenger position as a channel. Give it 10 years and I wonder if we'll see the same lethargic heft amongst the big digital brands. Large agencies are just sort of plodding along with ridged processes and a lot of momentum. The whole ethos of these big agencies mediates against the idea that you can wake up one morning and go against the flow. I think that at the root of it, this inertia comes out of a fear of losing the old business model. A certain defensiveness sets in and, I think you end up with a bit of a trench mentality in these organizations."

↩

Susan Kim, "I could not agree more with putting the blame on the agencies for not mentoring new employees in digital and for putting them in silos where they had no chance to learn strategy, research, and conceptual creative thinking. However, I'll tell you a conversation I had with R2i, which is what they shortened R2integrated to. They started by building web sites and then, by default, because there was just this vacuum there, they started doing advertising and digital marketing, and now what they have is a whole lot of graphic designers. They have developers and they have one copywriter who is just way, way overworked. Normally, they just make him do the long email copy and stuff. Forget writing any type of headlines or coming up with concepts. And so I said, 'Who is doing that?' They said, 'Either the designers have to do it themselves or it's the Project Manager that, just by default, has to come up with it.' I replied, 'That's hard for the PM to be responsible for the stuff he sends.' He said, 'Who else is going to do it?' I wondered why they wouldn't just get some more copywriters?' They said, 'We have this one, but he is already so overworked and he has to do the real writing, which is like for emails and e-books and stuff like that.'

"I suggested that they have a creative director and get a few more writers and they said theoretically, they buy it. They are like 'Yeah, that probably would be good.' But I can't believe this place. They don't have a creative director. They don't have anyone who oversees the things that are going to have a concept. That there is going to be continuity that once again, it's just not blue, or let's put in a QR code in it. Just to have like some spark, some wit, something that's creative and interesting besides whatever the project manager gets to do. They were just, 'Hey, we'll wing it. We'll figure it out as we go.' They still, though, think by far the most important thing is the development, the code behind it, and if you have time, that little, tiny thing of having a concept and a headline and making it all hang together would be nice, maybe, but you don't really need that as long as the code is working and it's working in all the different browsers and stuff like that.

"They say, 'Yeah, it would be nice if we ever get time, but how much is a creative director going to cost? That sounds like a lot – and to get another writer?' The other thing I get is, 'There's spellcheck now.' Like you don't have to worry about anything. Just type a bunch of stuff, and spellcheck will take care of it. The amount of importance they give to writing is unbelievably low."

⌐

Angeli Beltran, "There has to be a desire to learn. There has to be a desire to take the strength of the skills that they have and understand that, 'Digital is in demand now and you can demand higher pay, and if you develop yourself, you will add more value.'

"You should be saying, 'The younger guys are easier to talk with because they're natives and they understand and they have the desire to learn it.' However, with traditional agencies it needs to be part of the structural change. It needs to be done as part of the agency's thrust to prioritize digital. It can't be lip service. It has to be incorporated into the KPIs as well because otherwise all they will say is, 'Whether I do digital or I don't do digital, I'll get the same salary anyway, so what's the point?' Firstly, unless it's put in as a goal or part of their responsibilities, it won't be a priority. Secondly, there has to be a process in place that allows people to work together in an integrated way.

"A lot of the younger folks are more focused on execution of digital and falling into the trap that everything's quite tactical, or technology-driven. It's sometimes the shiny-new-object syndrome. There's this shiny new thing I want you to try, and it's really cool. Sometimes it tends to be short-term thinking, and what I find that's lost in digital with a lot of these specialists is that they are not very good on the brand side.

"I'll give an example. My client explained, 'We're going to do some banner ads, but we want to have these flashy things like starbursts that will pop up because that will attract people to click.' I replied, 'Sure, but you are a very expensive hotel brand, and I don't think your customers expect you to have flashy and blinky starbursts on your banner ads.' There's this fine line between doing what works because it will bring in the response in the short term versus building the brand in the long term, which advertising has done quite well. It's the brand thinking. Digital needs to have it and find the balance."

〜

Jennifer Hoe, "My advice to those that refuse to understand the fundamental principle of marketing channels and still view digital as an alien life form: resistance is futile. Adapt or die."

Won't Anyone Think of the Agency Networks?

Change is a very scary prospect. It's not unusual for multimillionaires, even billionaires, to speak about ways they can save themselves money using terms no different than a single mother of four might with supermarket coupons, freebies, and all. You'd be shocked at how insecure many of these super rich people are. As if any day they expect to wake up in a nightmare without end; an existence where they no longer have their money, privilege, convenience, and influence.

That same paranoia didn't happen to take hold of the global and regional networked agencies. They were not prepared for any sort of upheaval more earth shattering than having a few more women rise to leadership positions. They saw no looming threat to their advisory position with brands, not even from the management consultants. To the agencies, all of the fragmentation, the advent of new media, issues of browser compatibility, and so on weren't secondary or even tertiary areas of concerns or priority. Likely not even duodenary. They had plenty of other plates spinning on sticks that they had to keep going and while they may not have been maliciously holding back the digital side of the house, their headstrong attitudes didn't allow for much dialogue on the subject with those who might have been able to paint a realistic future for them — to help them see where they should be focusing their clients' attention and making investments in training. More often than not, a fantastic new digital idea would be cruelly crushed before it even had a chance to be built (and viciously mocked). Their attitude held that "real" ad men do TV, radio, and print and anyone working in these new-fangled areas were outsiders with specialized skills brought in to work on gimmicks (even if those same people used to work in ATL alongside them). They did not take it seriously and rarely looked up from their own work to pay attention to what it all meant. In effect, they didn't know what they didn't know.

⌒

Jeffrey Dachis, "There are huge factors working against agencies. They have a financial interest in maintaining the status quo. They're either going to embrace creative destruction – and those that do will make the transformation – or they're going to definitely cling to the building of brands in a way that reflects a mode of brand building that won't exist in the future. They're going to fight like dogs to show that TV is the relevant way to build brands. You will increasingly see the price of spots go up and yet the reach of those spots is down. There is no more ad inventory, and yet ad revenue keeps going up each year. Because they're charging more for stuff, that ad inventory goes up 3% a year, 5% a year; the up-fronts are still the way television gets bought.

"There are still enough people who believe in television on the marketers' side that they're just willing to invest. That is going to continue for some time because of this huge infrastructure that's associated with protecting it. But, it's funny. Go pull up a chart on Google about newspaper circulation rate or something. Pull up a chart for the last 10 years. Look at the cliff. The big media companies have blistered their position because all the networks are now owned by conglomerates that have the ability to do different things. I'm not saying the networks are going to go out of business because the production of and distribution of high-quality content isn't going to go away. I don't believe that Comcast or NBC, Universal, etc. are going to go out of business. The agencies that service the media buying and the monetization of those are going to face an existential crisis – and this time it's real."

Joe Zandstra, "The traditional agencies need to understand what they don't understand. I think there's been a lot of 'we got this – we're fine' attitude that has stopped them from growing and becoming truly digital. For me it's as much about a failure to embrace digital culture as it is a lack of knowledge or understanding of the practical aspects of the digital marketing space. I've seen an interesting shift in recent years where traditional agencies have gone from ignoring digital to whole-heartedly trumpeting 'integration' – but that has taken the form of forcing their traditional folk into 'doing digital.' These are often digital natives – people who know digital from an end-user point of view very well – but are sorely lacking in experience with selling and creating digital strategies.

"There's a need for training, but there is also a need for an internal structure where there's knowledge sharing and there's also trust, such that an account director can go, 'Hey I was at this meeting and this guy was talking about SEO. Can you give me a primer on this shit? Because I really don't know all that, the difference between SEO and SEM,' as opposed to them giving what they think is the often wrong answer. So, initially, before an agency can get a fully digital-savvy, 'integrated' team up and running, there's a need for a bit of respect and communication.

"I think that the clients will drive transformation in traditional agencies. I can already see them pulling budgets away towards digital and also holding up the purely strategic output of digital agencies as an example of the kind of *truly* integrated plans they expect from their traditional AORs."

Ignacio Oreamuno, "Big clients like big agencies. I always criticize big agencies for being sloppy, slow, and inefficient. But the reality is the big clients are sloppy, big, and inefficient. It is impossible, once you've passed 200 employees; there's no way that you're efficient. A big, sloppy client can only function with a big, sloppy agency. The agency has to mirror the client's organization. These are the people that need to have a meeting with eight people instead of just two people just hammering it out, making a decision and going, 'If your client likes to do that, you'll need an agency that likes to do that because eight clients and one creative probably will not work.'"

〜

Steve Hall, "There actually will always be, for the foreseeable future anyway, a place for an agency that's comfortable with doing just radio and TV spots. The way I look at it, there's always going to be car dealers and lawyers of the world, and car dealers and lawyers love radio and they love advertising. They love billboards. Yeah, they do some online stuff, too, but it's just going to take time for people to default to the new way of doing things. There are always going to be people who don't necessarily need the sophistication. There're going to be small, local picture shops, pet stores, and little retail clothing stores where the Internet at large, the new media, and all these technologies may not work well for them. Geography plays into that, too. If you're just trying to reach a town or two, then what're you going to rely on? You're going to rely on direct mail. You're going to rely on local newspaper advertising. Maybe some local radio or cable TV commercials. So for the foreseeable future, those media are going to continue to require creativity and agency focus. I don't think this traditional approach is ever going to disappear completely but it's definitely going to morph over time."

〜

Harish Vasudevan, "There will eventually be some sort of consolidation that takes place because while in the short term, it makes sense for clients to be going out talking to different people to find solutions to what they have, eventually it's going to be hard for them to manage all of these multiple people who are dealing with them. You have a digital agency, you have a creative shop, you have a brand consulting company, you have a design company, you've got a production company. It's all very hard.

"For the short term, it makes sense to do it because maybe you want to get the solution out more cheaply, but eventually they will and they'll finally come back to saying, 'I need a one-stop shop that does it all.' Then AKQA gets bought by WPP. You'll see things like that happening where the big holding companies buy out the smaller guys, but keep them as independent operations. They still get the income without the clients feeling that they've lost what they were getting.

"If they stay their course, we will see consolidation take place, with the smaller guys becoming part of the bigger guys and still retaining their identity, not getting merged into another large operation. The shape of the large holding companies will change from having a few large brands split across different silos into having a whole clutch of these small and medium agencies that are able to keep and hold on to talent, because they're keeping their independence, while at the same time, the holding company is getting the benefit of these peoples' skill that they can then leverage for other business. That's probably how it'll go again coming from marketers who do not want to deal with multiple agencies."

⌒

Richard Bleasdale, "My company's business model is what I describe as marriage counseling and matchmaking between brands and agencies, with more of the focus on marriage counseling. We've had the opportunity to be involved in our agency careers in quite a large amount of agency reorganizations, agency restructurings, agency mergers and acquisitions, or JVs (joint-ventures), and nearly 80% of those experience didn't go anywhere near as well as they should've.

"We feel strongly that in the agency space, there are some fundamental issues that need to be dealt with, and agencies really struggle to do it on their own because they never have time. They never have the manpower. They never have the budget. They never have the mandate, and it just goes on and on and on. What we found was that there were opportunities for a consultancy that was focused on the agency space and was focused on matchmaking and marriage counseling.

"We're not that interested in trying to get involved in the acquisition deal or the multiples or the numbers or any of that stuff because in all of our experiences, that comes down to bullies and accountants, at the end of the day. An independent agency is looking for external investment, finding the absolute best potential partner that can provide investment for them, or if an agency group is thinking about coming to Asia, which obviously we see a lot of. Finding the absolute best local partner that can be paired up with them to help them come into the region.

"We're also inside existing agency organizations, helping them restructure and reorganize or post-marriage, helping them the morning after the wedding and they realize, 'Holy shit, what've I done?' Having an independent third party that can counsel them through actually what it's like being in bed with each other, and how your life has changed, and what really needs to happen now. How, actually, are you going to make this succeed? People seem to be finding quite a lot of value."

∽

Peter Moss, "The whole agency model is change-averse. It's unfortunate, and it has very much to do with that old Darwinism about, 'It's not the biggest and the strongest, but the most agile that actually survive.' I think Ogilvy as a whole benefited from OgilvyOne spending many years getting to grips with digital. But at some point, we had to open the doors to everyone, and now digital is as pervasive in Ogilvy as creativity."

∽

Jeffrey Yu, "I want to believe that there is now a revival of the advertising agencies because we have learned to work with digital, with activation, and came together as a combined offering. I genuinely believe that agencies will reinvent ourselves and become sexy again. I see young people coming in, especially in China, where advertising is considered a sexy occupation.

"We have gone through the evolution the hard way, when we were considered the has-beens, and we are now sort of coming back. The consolidation is almost done. Now, if you look around, there are only three agency groups left. We have already gone through the survival of the fittest, the sorting out. We will not see a lot more companies, and the days of the closures

– of the DMB&Bs and all the others that are gone – is over. I do not want to defend the industry, but having gone through all these waves of change, I also see us coming through. Maybe the situation in America is quite different. In Asia, especially in China, it's cool to be in advertising. We are on the course of stabilizing already. We have gone through all the instability stage. Ted Bates is one of the last of the last of the agencies to die or get absorbed. There are no more real Bates agencies around, anymore."

～

David Shulman, "I joined Digitas back in '99 when it was still SIG, the Strategic Interactive Group. I joined during this interesting time where they went from Bronner Slosberg Humphrey to BSH to Bronnercom. There were the Bronner folks who largely came from a strong direct background, and then there were the SIG folks that were the pioneers in digital, the so-called – I hate this term – digital natives.

"There were a lot of technologists. There were a lot of people who had great user experience and design talent, and then there were a lot of consultant strategic types. It was a very cool, hip, progressive way to be, but there was a real clash of cultures. The Bronner folks said, 'Digital isn't a rocket science. We can do that as well. We have the foundation in our direct knowledge, and we can just as easily extend to what the needs are in any digital space.' Then you had the SIG folks who said, 'You guys don't even speak our language. You don't speak our culture. You're not going to be a fit for this.'

"I came in as an outsider to this process as someone with a very integrated background of digital plus everything else. I felt like I was at least trying to bridge the gap. However, what happened, which was fascinating, is that so many people who came from the Bronner side got frustrated and felt shut out and left. They went to digital jobs at other agencies or on the client side. And then the neat thing is that some of them came back for integrated digital careers. In 2000, the shop went public and in addition to rebranding, began to truly bringing those areas together. There was a recognition that direct, digital, and data was about one offering, not about siloed offerings. I give the shop credit for that.

"Integration was a scary word, but there was a powerful notion that this was not just about a digital silo. At one point, SIG was largely building complex web sites and doing banners and other online ads. We had a great strategic practice, too, but where clients were spending did not necessarily dictate a siloed activity. It was an uncomfortable six months, maybe a year, but then it just came together, based on the way we drove our scopes and drove our client engagements and the need to do the business.

"Think about the different competing forces. There are all these general and brand agencies that realize that they have to get in the game of digital. It's not just because they want to remain relevant and need to go where the money is going, where the minds are going, but they also want to retain their staff. If they don't have digital at the core of what they're doing, including marketing intelligence and all the components that are critical to the future of how we run our business, people will leave.

"In the meantime, you have all the pure-play digital companies that are saying, 'If we're a pure digital company, we either need to be a specialist that is really good at one thing that we do really well and can charge a premium for or we need to be broader in digital so we can have a seat driving the brand. If we don't move up in the brand category, we can't be anything more than an extension of what the brand agencies are doing.' Then you have tech players that are saying, 'We can come at it with not so much a boutique expertise, but actually a platform of technology that can be unique in how we position ourselves.' It's an up-for-grabs landscape.

"A good friend of mine who went to one of the top strategic consulting companies told me they're building an internal practice that will offer true creative services and execution, which is something that we've been hearing and seeing about for a while.

"I put less emphasis on the word digital when thinking about where Organic is and what the need is. Digital, to me, implies tactics. It implies execution. It implies channel focus, and it implies that we're doing projects, which is not the place that we are in and not the place where we want to be. What really is exciting is thinking about the connections between people, the *human connection* that we speak about, which is not about digital. Digital now gives us the power, the tools, the marketing intelligence, the insights we can gather and garner, but it's about how we apply this that makes digital so powerful. It can be a much more effective way to initiate conversations, to engage user to user, and user to brand. We have an edge in having a digital heart, but I don't think it's about being a digital agency."

~

Aden Hepburn, "I would say a couple of years ago, it would've been 90-10 or 80-20 in terms of traditional marketing directors versus ones with digital savvy. There's been a pretty significant shift over the last two years. Most of the businesses that we work with now have internal digital departments, and they've brought in ex-agency people or just digital savvy people to look after the digital marketing, then the web site and the eCRM platforms and all that sort of stuff. So, largely, we're pretty good, and the ones where we don't have that we definitely hope to get and can occasionally handhold. I don't see handholding as a negative thing, but really a quite positive thing because it's an opportunity to help bring that client into the digital age. So long as we have a great relationship with them, that we get some runs on the board for them, and we can help them show their bosses and their internal management groups the value of digital. We get a lot of support from a client that might be quite nervous about it. We are very conscious of that.

"I can't say we have any clients that we've worked on where you get digital wide open, because they don't get it. We definitely have them where they quite understand it, but they, as they all insist on pointing out, want to understand it, and they invite you in to help them get it across the line. That might mean we help create tools or presentations for them. It is a big shift. It's not a 100% of the shift, but it's the large majority now when we get put on pitch lists. It's from the digital department of a brand, which means that we're working directly with digitally-focused people who're responsible for digital within those brands.

"So, it's definitely different because you would be working with the overarching marketing director with digital under their remit, but it might be only 10% of their focus. They probably don't have enough time to dedicate to it considering how tiring digital can be. They want to, but they just might not be able to dedicate that time, so it's definitely made it easier to work through projects and to work on everyday clients when there is an internally-focused digital team on the brand side. Because it just comes down to a focus thing, in my mind.

"I would fully expect a traditional agency to be an order-taker from the digital agency. It will happen to varying degrees and in varying industries and various agency sizes. It's funny, because I always joke that it's really challenging for a new digital agency to start up. Every agency is trying to be digital and build up digital. They typically have the money and resources to be able to get a couple of good people in there. That's not to say that they can do a great job of it all the time, but they can get certainly people in there and with resources. They can win pitches.

"What I would say to agencies that are trying to upscale in digital is that they need to focus on the big idea. Focus on the content, but pull in and build up the user experience side and the digital strategic side of your business to help support those and guide the big ideas to come out of those sorts of agencies. That's where their advantage lies; it's in typically big, emotive brand platforms. If they can find a way, with the help of some really good digital experience thinking, whether it be a little bit of technical, a little bit of the user experience and a little bit of digital and social insight and planning, would actually create some seriously good content, some seriously good campaigns. They still can, at that point, outsource the production if they need to. Any one of the good agencies still does that. It's about selling them that big idea, and, if you can, make sure it's digitally-focused from the core of those ideas.

"If you look at some of the world's biggest brands, they set up that kind of agency village model where they have a best-in-breed digital agency, a best-in-breed PR agency, a best-in-breed above-the-line agency, a best-in-breed below-the-line agency, a best-in-breed events agency, and a best-in-breed media agency. And they have them around the table, they brief them together, they come back together, each of them presents back and builds out their specialism within the wide campaign. Your big alcohol groups do it, your big banking groups do it, and your big global brands do it every other day of the week. When it comes back under one roof, it's going to be very skewed. There's got to be a letting go from some of these big egos. Some of those egos will perish when they can't make the jump and others will succeed and amplify it and get bigger and better than they even were when they were at the top of the traditional game, for sure.

"One possibility is that everything may very well fall back under media companies. They typically now control client budgets to some degree. They are more and more hiring in strategists, creative, and technical guys and are starting to eat our lunch because they often have the first conversation with the clients. The media agencies, in my mind, have set revenue. They know their clients can spend $10 million bucks a year, and they're going to get that 3% margin, whatever that might be, and their way to diversify and to grow and increase their revenues is to find new ways to make money. That new way to make money is digital. It's social. It's experiential. It's content. It's all the things that other types of agencies do. Because they do hold the purse strings, and they do have large dedicated teams built around clients, and they have great connections to all the media platforms of all the various spenders they can build amazing presentations, they can bring in specialist people, and they bring in the guy from Google and head honcho from Facebook. They can convince clients to buy stuff without involving the other agencies in that village model. When I look at the agency village model, it's so important to have because media is the glue that does bring everything together, and you need that to be worked into all your creative concepts across the board, whether you're PR, you're digital, you're experiential, traditional, or below-the-line. They're the guys who're placing ads, they're the ones who are buying space, and you need to be able to work with them seriously closely to actually get the right spot for your idea. What is dangerous is when they leave the idea.

"I thought that crowdsourced ideas were going to get really, really big, and I'm pretty sure last year they were big. They were huge. I think they died off in 2012. I definitely haven't seen as many as I saw in 2011, and I don't know whether that's because I'm immune to seeing them now or I don't notice them as much anymore. But 2011 was definitely big, like everyone was talking about getting a crowdsourced idea and putting up something where people could submit something, vote, and we choose that one and make it. It'll still be there and it'll evolve over the next couple of years in terms of brands running competitions and things like that. But, professionally, as an agency, we definitely don't use it. We've never tried it. I don't see us trying it at this point. It could work, maybe for content-type businesses that just need hero ideas that can be sold in one or two slides as a very top-line direction. One where they could take it and you could definitely crowdsource it by putting a brief out to get 50 responses at $100 bucks a go. Out of that 50, you might get one or two really brilliant ideas, and you need to go work out how to make them effective.

"I would definitely agree that I do know a lot of people who say, 'Oh. Just put it up for $100 bucks on 99designs.com.' And you'll get 99 shit designs, but you'll get one absolutely amazing one from some professional freelancer that sits on there and smashes it. If you're a half good designer, you quit your day job, and you could make twice as much as money on 99designs.com."

⁓

Tobias Wilson, "We're certainly seeing a trend with marketers starting to trust the smaller agencies or the less-awarded agencies. I would love to one day be judged on our effectiveness, rather than how many awards we've won and things like that. It's a huge wakeup call for the industry that we do work with the bigger clients and we do take business from the bigger agencies.

"The ad industry needs to wake up because the clients are just going to say, 'No,' one day. They are just going to say, 'No' to this $10 million concept fee of an interest rate on a piece of toast which was a campaign from years ago. I'm down for a fairer industry where good work is rewarded, but not astronomically, not ridiculously, because nobody's going to able to afford that. If the marketing can go off and spend $100,000 on a campaign and get better results than they can on a $500,000, or a million-dollar campaign, then that's a pretty easy decision to make as a marketer, and as a CEO, and I'm looking forward to that.

"People say, 'You started Accomplice when it was pretty tough times.' But that was perfect for us because marketers were watching their pennies more and they needed to get more performance out of their marketing budgets for less. PRM (partner relationship marketing) is a prime example. The whole thing about PRM is that we don't want the client to spend more money. We want to sell more of their product for LESS money spent on marketing."

⁓

Chris Kyme, "We tend to work with outside digital specialists in order to execute digital campaigns. Hopefully, we'll change that as we grow, but first things first. I would never pretend we are digital specialists when we are not. However, we do get it.

"Having set up my own small creative shop, I find we have no trouble getting big-name clients who come to us for our experience. At the end of the day, clients want people who can solve their problems, who are grown-up enough to think for their business. If you're 25, hot, and a digital whiz kid, you still might not be qualified to lead an agency and be a grown up. Having said that, as an experienced creative director, you should always be taking young, fresh blood and grooming them. You can learn as much from them as they can from you. CDs who fail to do this will get left behind anyway."

It is of critical importance for agencies to learn from people entering the industry, whether they're digital natives or simply those with a fresh perspective and insight into what it is people are looking for from brands today. More important is to learn what they are *not* looking for and will repel them faster than a client can reduce an agency's signed scope of work.

These advertising n00bs[24] can also potentially give the inspiration a traditionally minded agency team needs in order to understand how to evolve from offering the same services everyone has, for the same type of remuneration, into something more appealing for all. A model with revenue streams that can be as exciting and interesting as a new-era startup in the mobile, social, or digital spaces. Something that can reignite the passion inherent in creative professionals, provide new sources of income for those running the shop, present existing clientele with flexible and leading-edge options for accomplishing their goals, and attract new types of clients and fresh talent.

---

24 Internet slang for someone who is new and inexperienced in a topic at hand. It is most commonly pronounced as "new-bee" (newbie), though sometimes as "noob" (usually by n00bs).

Chapter 18: If You Can Dream It, You Can Build It

People used to say that technology will free all of us to focus on what's really important while greatly adding to the quality of our lives. Yeah. Well, 50 years later, and we're still holding our collective breath waiting for the paperless office and world, let alone reduced working hours thanks to increased technologically blessed productivity. If anything, we now work longer and harder than ever in "always-available" mode, with "quality of life" merely a phrase we once heard blow through the window. It's doubtful that we will ever see the promise of this techno-Nirvana fulfilled in our lifetimes, but that doesn't mean the digital world has completely let us down.

In fact, we should be electrified at the potential new media give us. There's a world of people labeled "users" (but in the positive sense) who are actively seeking content, entertainment, news, and utility. They are always moving on, like sharks hunting for the next fascinating bits to grab on to, play with, consume, and share (not necessarily in that order). Steve Jobs proved that people don't know what they really want and need until you show it to them. Modern technological platforms allow us to continually create and demonstrate to them what we think they may want and need with little pain involved. In the old days, we would have to commit every resource to realizing a vision, and if it failed, it would have numerous dire implications for the company and the employees. Now, it can get up and running quickly, whether it's a mobile app, a responsive[25] Web site, an online campaign, a social media program, a network, or something that hasn't ever been done before. If it doesn't work out, it doesn't cost any more than your time to put up an iteratively improved version or take it down entirely and move on to the next idea. This is how we can regain the trust of clients and the talent we want to come back to advertising — choosing to invent the viable agency of the future.

〜

Ignacio Oreamuno, "Charles Porter told me one time that the agency of the future is not a gigantic agency up in Boulder or New York or LA with 500 people and everything. 'The agency of the future,' he said, 'is 50 well-

---

25 A Web site that has been programmed to automatically reorient itself to appropriately fit any device screen and resolution (e.g., desktop monitor, smartphone, or tablet). Sometimes, this simply involves intelligently scaling itself up or down and other times by presenting a template that maximizes usability and readability on the user's system.

paid, highly talented, creative professionals that outsource and just work very effectively with different specialists of all kinds.'"

↜

Paul Kwong, "Nobody can know everything, but you've got to be informed as much as you can. If clients know more than you, then own up to it. Ask questions back and learn from them. Meetings should be run by department heads or leads since they know more. It's a team effort. You can't expect the quarterback to know what the linebackers know because there's too much information, but at least know *some* of it."

↜

Gareth Kay, "Someone interviewed [Sir] John Hegarty and asked him, 'What would you do if you were opening BBH now?' He candidly replied, 'I wouldn't build BBH. I would build something that is akin to a members club where people pay membership fees every year to be part of it. One that will have a common working space where people can choose to work with one another on a very ad hoc needs-based basis.' That's a really interesting observation for two reasons: one, it's a very different model to what we have at the moment and two, it's being said by a guy who has run a hugely successful ad agency for over 30 years and has always loved his brick-and-mortar traditional advertising agency. Even he is thinking what a business would look like nowadays, if he had a blank sheet of paper."

↜

David Sable, "The way we look at it is very simple. We think every office has to be digital. They have to be able to do the basic digital things. They have to understand an idea is an idea and if they have an idea, don't express it only as a 30-second commercial or a piece of film. What's the idea and then what do I do with it? Most of what you see online is video. It's some video thing and everybody hopes it goes viral. Which is, *poof* – Harry Potter again – magic. You're viral! You've got to apply marketing to it. You have to think about the media it's going to be in online, the channels, which specific ones, where's it going to show up. Part of the problem is that you buy stuff, then you have no idea how it gets bought because it gets bought through exchanges: 80% of what goes out there just shows up. Then you say, 'Who can I make a real deal with? Should I be on NewYorkTimes.com? Should I make a deal with Gilt? How do I use Facebook? Should I even use Facebook?' Agencies need to learn that, but then there's also what I call enterprise digital. Enterprise digital is the digital strategy of a company. It asks how are they going to use their web-based presence. How does it get used in mobile? Not the creative that goes in it. How does it get used? What are you doing with it and why?

"We're all in a learning curve here, frankly. In digital, we're still at the era of the television commercial where the guy stood in front of a radio microphone. We really are. People think we're not, but we really are. Certainly, in mobile we are. Here's the problem, though: every time clients stop putting money into TV, their sales drop. That's the problem. We look at it the wrong way. TV's not dead. What does it mean when they say that TV's down? I don't know that it's down. If they watch it on digital… who cares where they watch it? Where they watch it is totally irrelevant.

"The question is: how do you attach yourself to video wherever they watch it? If I'm into *Homeland*, if that's my thing, then how do you follow me? If I watch it on delay, which I do, why should you lose the opportunity to advertise to me? By the way, remember: what's advertising? Advertising is just a way to pay for content. The fact is, if the content creators could get the money – if I'd pay them for it – they'd be happy not to take any advertising. The pay-per-view model is fine, so long as the producers can make enough money to keep producing the great stuff that they produce. That's part of the challenge. That's what everybody thought: everybody was worried that that's what would happen on cable. You'd have the HBO model where you pay enough and you get a big enough audience that you continue to watch and create great stuff, and then you lose all the opportunity to advertise. Then you have to think of other stuff to advertise in and around. I don't care where it shows up. I just want to figure out how to follow the audience.

"Television is online. It's the same thing, if you really think about it, but those people making webisodes want to get on cable. That's the joke. *Wired* still has a print version of their magazine. Here's this spokesperson-publication of our times and their print edition is still strong. It's because the content is great, people love the format, and it works. You can carry it on the plane, so during that period of time when you're not allowed to have your digital stuff on, you can read it. That's when I read it. Whereas Newsweek is now digital only."

～

Alan Schulman, "Where we sit now is a very interesting time. The tools and techniques of building digital things are becoming widgetized, open-sourced, and put out on the Web in ways that even the layperson can go get them and build from them. It's a continual struggle for any services-based company, whatever aspect of the marketing funnel or social landscape you're in. You're having to continually prove value. That value has to come from thinking first and doing second, as opposed to doing something for the sake of doing it.

"Seventy percent of the people in the digital industry do a disservice to marketers, including Silicon Valley. They are looking to make a quick buck by scaling something very quickly through advertising and then flipping it for as many millions of dollars as they can. They put them in a fearfully hysterical state of mind versus what I call a thoughtfully urgent state of mind, which is taking a thoughtful look at new technologies that are coming down the pipe rather than reacting to them immediately and saying, 'We've got to do augmented reality,' or 'Oh my god! We've got to be in Second Life,' or 'Oh my god! We've got to have an app for that.'

"The marketers that are looking at digital as something more holistic to their enterprise, and who have an enterprise digital strategy – not just in marketing, but using digital channels for many things – are the ones that are going to be better positioned to be thoughtfully urgent. As new technologies roll out, they've got a mindset and a framework for integrating those into their organizations. I would say those companies are the exceptions rather than the rule right now. Over time, the challenge for marketers is in organizing themselves to be thoughtfully urgent, as opposed to being fearfully hysterical about every new thing that comes up to give the consumer more control.

"Look at how widgetized television is right now. We're walking into another CES show about to look at a bevy of televisions that can do everything that an iPad can do. These migrations of convergence are just going to continue to happen. Those clients and marketers who have a framework for how to deal with it, and a process to be thoughtfully urgent rather than fearfully hysterical, won't ring up the agency right away and say, 'Alan, quick, make me a *this*! Because we need a *this*!'"

↜

Ask Wäppling, "We're really tired of all these apps that require us to give out information and stuff. [Giving agencies a great opportunity to go way beyond hanging messages in highly visible areas and provide memorable value to customers and prospects.] To me, apps and stuff are something that will enable the consumers. Basically, we're giving the consumer tools, and our solution to problems is handing the consumer things that they can solve their issues with. Apps, most of the time, are seen as places where you're going to put media, like Instagram is a place where we can advertise in, but that's not really what it is.

"From the beginning, it was to solve the problem of how do I share this picture of my toe or my new shoes with all my friends at the same time? You don't really need a special app for that, but if that's the problem you need to solve, you go for it. From a client's point of view, you have to look at where you fit in this. If you are Toyota, then Instagram is not for you because then you're just advertising in somebody else's media space. You can come up with something better than that. You can help them with something. You can make the Toyota Camry the bestselling car in America. I'm in L.A. now, which is car city, so how do you sell the car to the people here? I've studied the people who drive here, and they're really into the fact that they can push their little steering wheel things and talk to people on the phone without touching anything. I understand what they are doing and why; now how do I make an app that works for that? Wouldn't it be great if there was an app that's in your car anticipating stuff for you? 'You're 5.7 kilometers away from home. Should I turn on the air conditioner?' Why don't we enable our consumers that way?

"That's what word-of-mouth marketing via Tupperware parties held in homes was all about. You want to empower consumers. You want to tell them something that they can actually share with somebody. When you're doing your little jokey shit online, that's cute. It's great when you're funny on Twitter, so that it gets screen copied and put on Reddit or something. That's cute. That means you actually told somebody, who told somebody else. I get that. But, at the same time, you need to have something to say. When I tell her something like, 'Well, this tea really worked for me when I needed to sleep,' or 'This helps my tummy ache,' or 'This works for my hair.'"

⤷

Chris Kyme "Everything should be about an idea in the end. Apps are no different. If there is a good idea for an app, then great. There is trend for brands to want apps just because everyone else has one. Just like a corporate brochure. But, really, nothing should exist unless it's part of an idea... for a reason... that it fits the strategy."

⤷

John Winsor, "Wherever this kind of disruption happens, it's really amazing, but I think it's just super, *super* early days. I read this great quote from the guy who's running the Columbia journalism school, and he said, 'The idea of digital journalism is in such early days nobody knows what it's going to be.' And the same is still true of digital advertising.

"If you send a brief into a creative department, potentially anything could come out of it. I don't care whether someone says, 'Oh, we've got a brilliant concept where everybody can play Pong on all the buildings using the lights in the center of town.' Then someone else comes back and says, 'Oh, we've got another one whereby when a bus goes past, the high-frequency audio emitted reacts with your phone, and you get to watch a trailer for a movie.'

"All these are good ideas, but people in agencies don't know what to do with them: 'Which one should I go with then? What is the right one?' That's the big frustration now, but if you have a platform, then everybody knows what he or she needs to plug into it and where it's going to go. That is not handcuffs to me, it is really wings. Because you can focus on delivering the engagement you really want instead of having such a broad canvass to work with that you just get that horrible 'Where do I start?' and 'Where do I finish?' There's too much.

"We forget sometimes how difficult it is being a client and being shown an idea and thinking, 'My god. That's interesting, but is that really going to do it?' I'm not trying to force platforms as an issue because that's where we need to go, but we need the maturity. We've had a long time with all of this now. Smartphones and TVs won't get much smarter than they are right now. The computer won't get that much smarter. There won't be significant shifts. Iteration, not revolution, is what it is."

⌐

Heather Albrecht, Digital Marketing Trainer for Digital Connections in Australia, "The new marketing worldview is simply a contemporary one that recognizes how we interact with each other, with brands, with organizations, with media has fundamentally shifted to a real time, on-demand, one-to-one, one-to-many interactive model where we can be audience, author, and critic. We can now pull (and upload) highly personal content through four different screens when, where, and how we want to. This requires marketing to shift away from a push-based delivery of message via predominantly paid media on a campaign basis. The traditional marketing model is the antithesis of inviting participation in real time continuously via bought, owned, and earned media and offering content, conversation, community, and utility versus simply messages."

⌐

Aden Hepburn, "Digital convergence and experiential territory is starting to get play outside the digital area. It gets into PR, it gets into the traditional advertising, and it gets into the event companies. We have this massive advantage because we don't have traditional skill sets in the team. We have a group of problem solvers from varying technical and creative levels. From project management and strategy, as well, and we see UX [user experience strategy and design] very much as a strategic role.

"It's really interesting when you can pull in six or seven of those guys into a one- or two-hour brainstorm. The difference you get out of that as opposed to throwing an art director and copywriter is completely different. It's really easy to tell when we came up with an idea versus another agency, and you see the result at the end of the pitch. Or the client awards it to us and then shows us the competition's work later, and you're like, 'Wow. Okay, I get why we won.' You see that within the wider group and sets of agencies you get that more multi-diverse range of brains versus the traditional copywriter-art director combination, and the ideas come out.

"Sometimes, we might think it's such an exciting idea because of the data we get from it, the results we can pull out of the back of it, or how we can track that user for later, which the client doesn't quite find as interesting as a really cool piece of artwork."

~

Steve Hall, "There are so many interrelated mechanisms. You have the agencies who used to be charged with coming up with wonderfully creative ideas to help sell stuff. Then the CMO or, as they were called back in the day, the Marketing Director, was supposed to integrate that with the sales side of the business and make all these programs work together smoothly. The agencies started to be asked to do more, and they weren't able to do more, and I'm sure some of those demands were unreasonable. There's one particular agency in Boston that just announced, in effect, that it's converting to a software platform that will look at over 50 key performance indicators and be able to answer the CEO's question, which is, 'We spent $2.5 million on marketing last year. What did it do?' That is not an easy question to answer, and ad agencies weren't really set up to answer it. I don't know if they ever really should be because it's the Marketing Director's responsibility to coordinate all this stuff."

~

Diane McKinnon, "The most interesting work is definitely being driven out of the entrepreneurial app and digital space, not the big ad agencies. We've finally found a model, and it's around niche clients to make a successful partnership. We started this global tech practice, meaning tech from a client standpoint. We're seeing where agencies can bring collaboration and expertise around some specific markets or verticals. It's called Tech.Y&R.

"I've seen agencies who have shifted themselves and turned into social media agencies. Ultimately, that's limiting. If you put yourself in a niche, as a social media guru, or whatever, you're going to probably have some initial success. You can build a practice around that, but, ultimately it will become commoditized just like anything else. If you only do TV or radio commercials, you become commoditized at a certain point. Just the same way that mobile app developers will be commoditized, although not right now. There are some that are extremely successful and really good, but there are more and more app companies, so that service is already becoming a little bit more commoditized.

"Social media strategy and execution, it's newer, it's exciting, and not everybody's comfortable with it. Not everybody knows how to make it work. A lot of companies are not really convinced that they can monetize it, as a matter of fact. You're seeing some consumer brands even questioning it already."

∽

Scott Morrison, "I really believe that it's time to reinvent the industry. It's time for the clients and the creative people who can help them to forget about the past, reinvent the way we work so that everyone is happy and we can just get on with business. That's really what I feel."

∽

Co-Founder & Global VP Sales of eYeka, Alexandre Olmedo, "The duty of an agency is to embrace change before its clients do. So [with eYeka], we've decided to take the lead with a new agency model that integrates consumer ideas from the start. If you are in that mindset, your business will grow because you will adapt and you find solutions, whether it's about collaboration, whether it's about acquisition, whether it's about transformation – you can be in sync with your client and, if possible, ahead. If you're not, you are in trouble.

"We have 280,000 creators in 148 countries and so we tap into those people through competition, work with ideas for these, for positioning, branding, packaging, social content, etc. We moderate all the ideas that have been submitted. We give feedback to all those creators, and the brand then will select the best idea to offer the prize in exchange for the idea. For the people who are not winning, they get the feedback, but that's it."

∽

Jim Speelmon, "When I started working on HP, they had 85% brand awareness. Branding clearly was not the issue. They had 68% of the market for printers, with 80% penetration in the market. If you're them, are you going to spend all of your money trying to convert the 20% over a printer? Well, of course not. In that context, your smartest business opportunity is to encourage people to replace and upgrade. Nobody wants to hear about the technology of your printhead. People don't care about that. It is an education process that you need to go through for people who have really old printers. It's an education process about what's new that they haven't been paying attention to because it's not something they think about.

"You have to find reasons to make people think or to associate themselves with something in a way that's going to make them be receptive to what you want them to do. Social media lends itself very well to doing exactly those things. One of the main issues is that the clients have unrealistic expectations about what social media is going to deliver. This is an opportunity for you to really get into, know, understand, and display empathy with your customers. You take what you learn from there, and you use that to guide your broader communications tactic. Rather than try to use that channel also for selling. It's a very poor sales tool. It's a very poor place for you to run big messages that cost a lot of money to put together because it's very easy for someone to hijack it.

"When I worked on a major consumer electronic brand's project in 2009, their tag line was *Ideas for Life*. Samsung was taking over the market share, and times were tough. We kept doing these social media things, and it was not working. If I were Panasonic, I would get the engineers who design my products to come on to the Facebook page, either putting things out there explaining what *Ideas for Life* truly means. Which brings a whole new element to your brand message. It could have been so powerful and so useful. But they said no because they didn't see it relating to sales. If you're looking to see what the incremental percentage contribution from a Facebook page to your bottom line sales results is, you're going to be sorely disappointed.

"The people who are going to be very successful are the ones who are able to, again, step back and look at the bigger picture. If you're looking at things that we conceive coming in as being locally relevant, being able to have something meaningful to talk about, then create a reason for why someone would consider what you want to talk about. I don't necessarily see the move towards apps as making any difference there. If you want to be a successful planner in the future, you are going to have to be far more sophisticated in your thinking. That is going to be a huge problem for a lot of people. It is things like if you wanted to sell a candy bar or some kind of food product in Sri Lanka, for example. I was there sitting on this bus behind people who were complaining about the fact that there was garbage everywhere – and a significant portion of that garbage was food-wrappers.

"We ran into these people again at this hotel and this woman was still going on about how these people don't care about anything. There's garbage everywhere. I said, 'To be fair, not that long ago, if you were going to have a snack or something for eating on the go, it was probably going to be some kind of rice-based dish wrapped in a banana leaf.' So, is it really the local population's problem that some multinational company has now introduced non-biodegradable food packaging for the first time?

"A future opportunity for a company like that could be something that locates the nearest trash can or provides some kind of useful social or functional utility. The first wave of apps is proving to be those where people are going for the obvious connections. The reality is that I don't use this app because it is specific to the company's product; I use it because I like that brand. It's more like the brand is sponsoring the app. It might have no direct relationship to the actual product, but it might be an excellent relationship with the brand personality.

"If people think that the media fragmentation of digital was bad, like what the hell are they expecting from apps? It will get to a point where the advertising is going to become all about letting people know about your app. Wouldn't it be easier for you to focus on doing a better job with your overall brand so that people actually start looking for you? If you look at the same tools that people use today, when they want to create a problem, the best way to really avoid getting into a shitty situation is to be more realistic about what people can do with the different communications tools to do a better job of your risk planning. But also to do a better job of assigning channels, application, or what feature is going to play what role in the overall effort.

"Where Martin Sorrell has really made his life difficult is going out and recreating Internet digital chaos with a reduced-sized WPP digital version. When somebody at one of the holding companies gets serious about making their different capabilities actually work together, then they will make some serious progress. They really all three have the same problem. At the micro-level, where you're with the individual person, they are generally too specialist. You're a specialist at the end of the food chain with limited opportunity to create the environment you need to do what you were actually supposed to be doing. For the agency, you have too many pieces, and you can't make any of them work."

⌒

Peter Moss, "There is something about high streets, but there is going to be a difference between the shopping versus the sensorial/physical thing that we all need. I'm really looking forward to a time when if you want to purchase something, you can do it without thinking about any particular place or platform. It's a big behavioral shift as well as one in the fundamental infrastructure.

"There's a lot of e-commerce taking place, but we haven't yet hit the tipping point whereby there's that global level of comfort. We have to find consumers that are going to lead this, and they're going to hopefully be the influencers that create that tipping point for the rest of the population. But we've got to be a little bit careful when we start banging around expressions like gamification. It all sounds nice. It probably came out of a planning department somewhere, but the point is, *life isn't a game.*

"I don't think that every time you want to get someone involved, there has to be a prize or a treasure hunt. Why would they want to spend so much time in a game? Gaming is powerful because they have figured out stickiness. When you go into Photoshop, you're in there and you're doing your stuff. When you're done, you exit. Gamers changed it to 'quit.' Total genius: one word. Instead of, 'Yes, I've finished, I now want to leave,' it becomes, 'I am a quitter!'

"If you look carefully at games and understand them and watch people play them, there are many bits of brilliance you can take away from it. To try and turn everything into some game is unrealistic. If you want to engage, not just through social channels, but in general, you don't start a conversation, and you certainly don't attempt to stop it. A lot of clients have not got their head around the fact that their world is no longer a calendar. They are used to doing things by the clock, by the calendar: 'We will run this for three weeks. We will run that for four weeks. We're in the Christmas period. We're in the back-to-school period...' Well, those things can dictate a skew of content and a skew of a story or a conversation, but they are not finite periods or finite timelines. Once you're in, you're in. That is it. You're on. You're always on. You must be able to do that confidently as a brand.

"How many Facebook pages have you seen where some manager excitedly says, 'Let's reach out to our brand fans.' And then on a Friday afternoon, they say, 'Have a good weekend,' and leave the office and the job behind. That's the kind of commitment they have and, subsequently, their pages aren't really 'liked' much longer. There's a lot of planning and organizing to be able to flip that switch in terms of:

- Do we have an online editorial team?
- Is our support center in place?
- Is our story clear?
- Is content mapping already there?
- Is the content that we will start with already produced?
- What are we going to encourage the people who get involved with this to produce?
- At what point do we stop dictating the play and start to react to the conversation that is taking place?

"One of the projects I was working on here was a real-time marketing model. That was attempting to monitor not only the social channels, but what blogs were saying about our brands in real time. I literally sat in a room full of screens with a good data person, a really smart editor – a real *Daily Mail* guy – who could go a little bit deeper and say, 'No, what they're talking about, the real story is *here*.' See, we could spend an hour or two and get a snapshot of the world of this brand and then turn content around – *video* content – within eight hours. We could reply immediately to the people talking about our clients and begin to lead a conversation in a certain desired direction.

"But agencies are not newsrooms. I got to a point where I was looking at how much we would have to compromise to make this doable. Because you could throw lots of people and lots of money at it, but that wasn't going to happen because no client would make that investment. Certainly, if you wanted the client to pay for this as a service, then it would work more like, 'We've done a live session on your brand, and here are five things that you should and can do.' It was almost a way for us to proactively pick up briefs."

⮑

Reporter David Kirkpatrick, Manager of Editorial Content for *MarketingSherpa*, "Things are changing so rapidly in terms of individual platforms and the way different channels work together. From the marketing agency perspective, and this is an old-school answer, I think there are two places where things are going. One, you're going to see some agencies that are going to specialize in one particular area, and some of that may be predictive analytics and dealing with some of the data, helping out on that side of things and then even specializing in platforms. You'll definitely see agencies that specialize in marketing, and you might see them get as granular as social and mobile, but you'll definitely see people that specialize in email. You'll see people focus on social and mobile together and maybe some people who're going to try to talk about being bigger and really integrating these things, putting all these different pieces into it.

"Then, two, paid search and SEO, which are still a huge part of all of these different things. Some people will separate out some of the inbound tactics with some of the social. Mobile's going to tie into that, although it goes to other places. Another side of that is going to be more paid search and some of the SEO things. You're going to have your paid search and organic searches. Those agencies are going to try and be holistic, while they're going to be a little more specialized in particular areas."

⮑

Richard Bleasdale, "For some of the digital agencies, it potentially makes sense for them to be acquired by a media agency for a range of reasons. We're seeing some of the digital agencies that we're working with now. But they're actually interested in being acquired by clients because they can see an opportunity to take their skill sets inside a client organization and have much more of an effect on the decision making of the client rather than potentially being acquired, for instance, by a WPP or an Omnicom or one of their sub brands and just becoming a part of the external service offering to a client.

"In the digital space, we're seeing that a lot of the specialist independents are very interested in being acquired by client organizations. There's a process at the beginning to try and help them define their best potential partner or their best potential future. When we agree on that, that's when we would start looking at alternatives."

↩

Torrence Boone, "I believe there is a seismic reinvention of the campaign development process still to take place – one that fuses elements from the Silicon Valley playbook of agile software development with the fantastic creative process already in transition at the top agency shops. I refer to this reinvention as Agile Creativity.

"In addition, I see agencies and advertisers better leveraging the power of existing technology to tell compelling brand stories as opposed to focusing on 'breaking APIs' or attempting to out-technology the most advanced technologies. A yielding away from technology for technology's sake to re-orient around the craft of storytelling and brand building with technology as an enabler. We saw this at Cannes this past June: agencies are becoming more facile with existing technology and building compelling, innovative brand experiences with technology in the supporting role as opposed to the lead. Nike Fuel Band[26] is a great example of this trend."

Going Beyond Headlines and Calls-to-Action

Thierry Halbroth, "It's just the beginning, and we're moving [to evolve what is considered 'advertising'] in the right direction. Mobile is the first platform I see where a brand can actually have a legitimate purpose, if they do it well. Because you can build tools not just an app. You can build something that is useful and get a lot more engagement from your target audience. From either existing consumers and non-existent ones. It's quite good at that.

"I'm was judging the Spikes Awards last month and, in terms of mobile, I saw there's a fine line between what is just a stupid app that is clever and funny and creative and going to the next step of what ranges from what can save lives. For example, if you look at the mobile application put out by the Red Cross that helps identify future paramedics to a very targeted, functional application that actually immerses you in a branded environment. In Australia at the moment, we're seeing a lot of this. For some reason, there's a

---

26 An activity tracker that wirelessly transmits a wearer's calories burned and similar info to a supportive Internet community via an iPad or iPhone.

huge attraction to mobile in Australia, much more than the rest of the world from what I've seen.

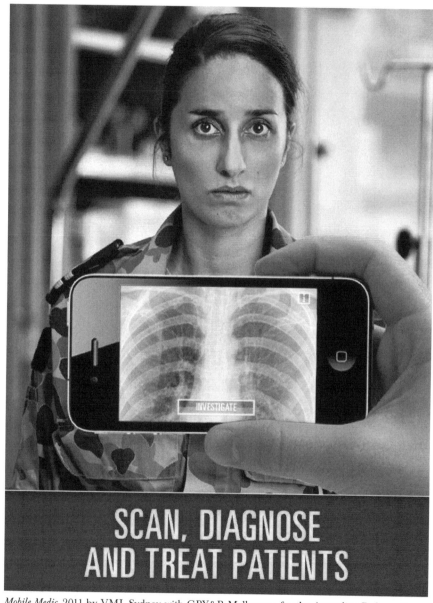

SCAN, DIAGNOSE AND TREAT PATIENTS

Mobile Medic, 2011 by VML Sydney with GPY&R Melbourne for the Australian Defence Force. Creative direction by Chris Northam, developed by Chuck Brandt, art direction by Jake Barrow, digital design by Janna Mamar, copy by Matt Lawson, photography by Hugh Peachy. Cannes Lion Gold 2012 winner.

"For example, there is a campaign that won a Gold Lion in Cannes and did well in the Spikes several times. It's called *Mobile Medic,* and it's a recruitment campaign for medical officers in the army. The Australia Defence Force. It was placed on a university campus; a very targeted campaign. It uses an app and four sheets of poster, nothing more complicated than that. The app is a test that students use on the poster to run an actual diagnosis for the exact situation it describes that you may be faced with in the field. Things from a PET scan and x-rays to checking vitals to running every single thing using your phone and that poster. Classic geographical targeting using technology.

"Now, I look at these kind of things and it's very inspiring, because it's, 'Let's do something that is actually true to what we were looking for.' Instead of, 'It's just cool to be in the army as a medic – and you're going to save lives!' This campaign is putting you to the test in the scenario, then and there. You're already part of the way there by engaging with it. It's an audio experiment, it's a visual experiment, tech experiment; everything is bundled into this. It's using what? It's using what you have in your pocket and what you see on the streets every day in the form of a poster. It was done by VML and George Patterson Y&R in Melbourne."

∽

David Kirkpatrick, "I think some of the gamification things that are going on, particularly in B2B marketing, are pretty interesting, and those bleed over into consumer marketing. Two B2B examples that really stand out from last year: one of them is a smart gamification element this company did internally to encourage staff to be more active with social sharing. They're one of the first B2B marketers that was really heavily using Pinterest. That platform has been coming on, though it's definitely seen more as a consumer space. Anyway, this B2B's CEO gives a yearly presentation to the entire company, so he challenged the marketing group to really one up each other over each previous year on how they put the presentation together. It was at the end of 2011, and they decided to use Pinterest instead of doing a PowerPoint slide deck. They created pinboards for all this content.

"It was so interesting and successful that they started using pinboards for external presentations people in that company were doing at different industries for clients. Early last year, Pinterest was still pretty young. It was still seen very much as a consumer platform and, at the time, it was 80% or 85% females between 25 and 55 in the Midwest, not even on the coasts. It was pretty much Oklahoma to Canada with most of the users in this very specific demographic, yet this company looked beyond all that and found a completely different use for Pinterest.

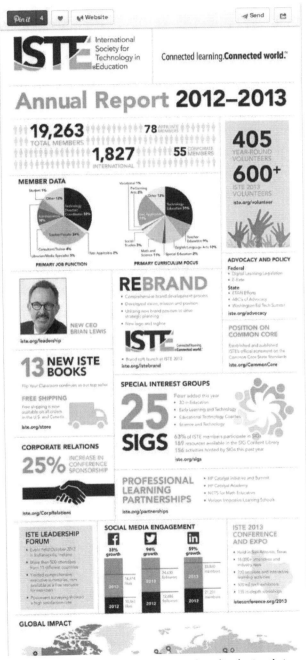

Organizations are using Pinterest for exotic purposes such as distributing their annual reports.

"The second example is one with a QR code. It was by a very large company that holds a yearly user conference that's also pretty large. This past year, they decided to go paperless. They had some paper available for people that did not have a smartphone or didn't want to do it, but they told all their users in advance that everything at the conference was going to be available on a mobile optimized site through QR codes. Everything from registration to the event materials like the agenda and all these various pieces, every speaker had a placard with their bio available through the QR code. Click on that, and go to their bio online. All their presentation materials were available on those mobile optimized sites.

"They were just about paperless. There was no bag to hand out to people. There was no paper involved in the whole thing. You showed up, and everything you did was on your smartphone. You found all the material you needed and accessed it all through QR codes. They drastically reduced their printing costs, and they were extremely pleased at the feedback they received from people and the sheer volume of usage they had. It ended up being a gamble because if you're used to going to a conference, you're used to getting a guidebook of some sort with the agenda and everything in it. You're probably used to going to booths, even at a user conference, and getting all kinds of collateral and schwag.

"It was a completely different way of looking at it, and they were highly successful. I'm not sure if everyone could pull it off. It was a tech company, and their crowd was tech savvy and was going to be carrying smartphones, but it was interesting, and I thought it was an outside-the-box way of looking at a traditional, in-person event and bringing in a very innovative digital element to it."

Alan Schulman, "I now enjoy working in a culture of possibility. People who come to work in a place where you can ask, 'Wow, we can build anything here! What should we build?' If you work in a culture of connected thinking, you have a little bit more room to stretch. That's why the innovation projects done at a place like SapientNitro are very different from what any typical advertising agency would do – be it redefining how people experience things in the physical world, or what a vending machine looks and behaves like, or with new kinds of retail experience innovations that just make people feel better about a brand."

~

Neil Leslie, "Smartphones present the biggest potential opportunity for brands and marketers moving forward. Whether it's via augmented reality, advergaming, social media, or location-based content.

"I'm also very interested in in-game advertising and expect to see big developments in that space in the near future. I see no reason why games like the *Grand Theft Auto* series won't be able to sell targeted or localized media throughout the virtual worlds that they create. Whether it's a billboard by the side of the road, a radio spot, or even in-game Web content. If it exists in our world, it will almost certainly exist in these virtual spaces in the not-so-distant future. And the games themselves will become even more immersive, surprising, and engaging as a result."

~

Jeff Cheong, "Difficult is worth doing. That is our mantra. Why do things when they're tried and tested? I have built one of Southeast Asia's best tech/creative squads, and our innovation arm is constantly trying out various technologies. We have a cupboard full of POCs [proof of concepts] we've developed before we shared the ideas."

~

Diane McKinnon, "Gowalla:[27] really cool app, interesting experience, but, ultimately they couldn't paint the vision of where that app was going to take people and what relationship they were going to have with the service or with each other. How was what they were doing going to be more successful than competitors? They lost the location-based arms race to Foursquare. Their vision of how this was going to make our lives more meaningful or better or whatever wasn't clear. In the end, Facebook bought them for their IP so they could integrate it into the larger social network [as they did more recently with Instagram and Oculus]. There are some challenges, but this is the normal process of younger people and new things coming in thinking they're going

---

27 A location-based social network.

to revolutionize everything. Some things are revolutionized, some things fall back to the core of a relationship between a consumer and a brand. That's the core of marketing and advertising anyway. The technology is the facilitator, it's driving a lot of change, but there's a part of it that needs to be the same."

～

Jerry (Yoram) Wind, "I think there are a lot of agencies pushing the boundaries and breaking new ground, though it's not so much the agency as an entity. It's more of the specific individuals in the agency. The old model of interruption advertising – as in trying to interrupt the life of the consumer by bombarding them with messages – is going to decrease significantly in its importance. The successful brands will be those who will be able truly engage their consumers in conversations – and that's a fundamental change. Another is instead of being in a traditional campaign mode to start thinking about the advertising agency as a newsroom. How do you provide information in advertising, but also entertainment and education? The whole combination of what advertising can be. How do you provide this in terms of ongoing 24/7 input as opposed to designing a campaign and then slowly releasing the commercials throughout the year. It's a totally different world when you think advertising as a newsroom. Think about on-demand advertising. Companies using big data and analytics to identify specific consumers in specific situations and then targeting them for the information they need, while they're shopping or searching for specific information. If you think in those terms, we can see some actually dramatic changes occurring in advertising."

What We Can Become Again — and More

Mike Langton, "I do think there's hope for the industry. It really does come down to a breakdown of the current malaise, and new organizations that will rise – you can't call them ad agencies, per se. They'll be content agencies. They'll have a content strategy, not a media strategy. It will be content production, not ad production.

"It does need to turn into a different business model and to recognize one thing: when you look at marketers, they don't want to have to deal with 16 different organizations. But they're not getting what they need at the moment, and that's why they'll look at working with 16 different companies. There's pressure to find, not the one-stop shop per se, but the two or three lead organizations that can be their content leadership mechanisms. And those content leadership mechanisms can reach out through project managers, content strategists and through content producers to the organizations that are talented at doing all of that.

"Management consulting companies have been talking this game for 15 years. I still haven't seen them do anything other than repeat what they always do, which is to perform a lot of expensive research, produce a large bound document that makes a great paperweight or a door stopper, but they are poor at implementation. It's a big blind spot for them. I've talked to a couple of them, and nothing came out of it that gave me any sense that they could understand in any way, the creative content development process.

"That point of contact, which understands the whole creative process, it will still have to be a sort of ideas leadership hub, but it will be very technologically advanced in terms of project management and engagement. It will combine data analytics around research, sociology, and media to get the insights that are needed. It will still have ideas at its core and the ability to come with up a campaign idea, an overall brand idea. That is very much a consulting-based model of defining brands and how those brands communicate as part of this new organization. What you will see, in essence, is a sort of creative hub, which is far more brand, research, and data savvy than any of them are at the moment. So the conventional agency model will be dead. What worked before hasn't worked in a long time, so there needs to be a different model.

"I don't know about systems integrators. What I see is that Sapient-Nitro was a phenomenal below-the-line organization. It started in Australia, on the back of the Mars business, with an absolutely brilliant player, Chris Clarke, who had never worked in an agency in his life. He built this phenomenal thing from scratch, the Mars guys poured business through it and eventually he sold it to Sapient. He was a brilliant man, who had built a brilliant organization and he refused to let it fall into the clutches of the holding companies. What has become of it post-Sapient is worth looking into."

Alan Schulman, "People [in places] like R/GA are going, 'Well, we don't want to be an agency anymore. We tried and that sucks. What can we be now? We're going to be a platform company because we build stuff like *Nike + FuelBand.* We're going to integrate products. We're going to be a product-design company.' Well, suddenly they realize that then they have to fight IDEO, and they're not really optimized to be a product-design company. They look at consulting and say, 'We're going to do digital consulting. We're going to do what Sapient does and...' It's all with good intent. With the Nitro purchase, Sapient fully embraced the digital AOR model; we just realized early on that that wasn't going to be the only piece of it that we wanted to embrace. We wanted the CMO's piece of the pie."

⌒

Ignacio Oreamuno, "If you are an agency now, you might be asked to do a store or an app or a game or an event. You can't dream to have that in-house, those specialties. Whenever you got to do that, boom, you go out and you hire. 'I got to do it,' so then the creative people you need to have are collaborators, people that work within that agency. You still need the agency. It's just the model of it is going to change. We're way beyond.

"The 'who's the copywriter/art director?' model is dead. That died a long time ago. We need another 10 years before that completely changes. It is like the Bernbach model is just gone. Because everything's changing. As long as there're big clients, they are going to work with big agencies. It's not like the world is completely falling apart. You're going to have those gigantic normal clients for a long time. A Unilever, FedEx, an IBM, whatever they are. They'll be begging a long time, but now you have companies like Kodak. Kodak went from gigantic monster, old school, everything to gone within four years because of technology[28]."

⌒

John Winsor, "My sense is it's still early days. A guy from Kraft Digital told me, 'Part of the issue with innovation is that the huge brands only care about the outcome and don't push their agencies to be innovative.' The reality

---

28 Josh Sklar, "Just because there are gigantic agency networks built over decades does not mean they can't likewise disappear overnight."

is with all the digital measuring tools, the ability to measure digital stuff is going to demand more real-time creativity. It's going to demand cheaper creativity with all of this real-time bidding stuff and DSPs [demand-side platforms – real-time bidding for keywords on different online properties] exchanging everything. At Digiday, I heard that now 30% of all online ads are being bought on these kinds of exchange platforms.

"You're in constant beta, and that means we can tweak creative and we can tweak strategy as we go rather than, 'Let's build it all into this great big expensive thing and hope that it works.' I think that is a really good perspective because agencies were built in a pre-production world.

"More brands have been going from pre-production to post-production. What does a post-production brand look like? It's all about testing and experimenting and all that kind of stuff. But that is a rapid change for marketing departments. If you are a senior vice-president of research and you are 45 years old without knowledge of the craft, you don't want that to happen. That is a whole different skill level. You have no idea how to do it. You are really good at hiring big agencies to do big demographic studies and doing big brand-planning sessions and taking months and weeks and years to plan things out and grow your brand, and that is just the opposite of kind of the meritocracy of market dynamics. It is almost like brands and brand value becomes another stock exchange. This is hyper-connected and hyper-focused. You think about the old days of stockbrokers, what they charged, and now that whole business of buying and selling stocks has become commoditized."

⤚

Joe Zandstra, "We're moving to a demand-based consumption model when it comes to media. We're skipping ads with DVRs, we're watching blockbuster TV episodes like *House of Cards* on Netflix when it suits us. Pandora's box is open – people are cable-cutting and are less and less prepared to be told what to watch and when. People want to consume media on their own terms and that means fragmentation, which means you're not looking at homogeneous audiences in the same place at the same time. And when it comes to commerce and services online, you're looking at a shift to freemium models, you're looking at people expecting things ostensibly for free, but then spending money in not so obvious ways. Musicians make more money from touring and t-shirt sales than from record sales to the point that now, many artists are giving their music away online for free. I'm currently working with a brand, and we're doing some content marketing work that's around helping people avoid back-pain with exercise and stretching – which to some might seem illogical as the client's product is all about relieving back-pain with an OTC remedy – but both the agency and client understand the value of trust. Definitely a new way of thinking about a marketing problem. Things are really being turned on their head. And this isn't all about digital per se, really – it's just about how we market within a new, fragmented, information-rich world. It's a world that I think digital agencies are prepared for... actually, not just prepared for, but have already been involved in for years.

"So, things are changing to such a degree that it means ATL agencies based on the old media and the old ways of distributing content, well, as those ways of distributing content disappear those agencies can become irrelevant unless they truly believe in and embrace that change."

↩

Scott Morrison, "As far as the future and where we should be moving the industry, I'm a big fan of Saatchi's *Lovemarks* approach for replacing brands. I believe that there is a transcendent element of creating a brand, digital, or otherwise that is about tribalism. It's about emotional association that defies logic. I feel good about buying Apple. Seventy to 80% of the people in any room have an iPhone, yet all of us feel unique for having one, even though there's nothing unique about it. They're everywhere. Most families have more than one, and you feel like you're part of something.

"The digital space is where tribalism has moved to from print and it's the communication around, 'What tribe do I belong to? What brands am I associated with?' It has moved to the digital space, and if companies don't respect individuals in there, it starts to break the relationship. I believe that that relationship is like a marriage. You and your wife, on a daily basis, you're fantastically attentive. You're home all the time. You take out the garbage on time, and you give her a back rub, she cooks you dinner, you guys are adding to the emotional bank account the whole time. If you happen to come home late without calling one time and she's totally pissed off because dinner's cold, she will draw on the emotional bank account that she felt good about for that last six months, and she'll forgive you very quickly or she won't get angry about it to begin with.

"I believe that the brand relationship is the same thing for businesses and people working together. Apple, even if I had seen them produce a really boneheaded ad, I still would've forgiven it very quickly, because it's Apple. Because they've built such an emotional bank account with me, they have to go a long way to piss me off."

∽

Chris Schaumann, Global Vice President, Digital & Social Marketing and CRM for Microsoft Mobile Device Marketing and former Nokia Global VP, Digital & Social Marketing and CRM, "Ray Kurzweil, the head of the MIT artificial intelligence lab, had an awesome talk at a TED conference about how technologies are actually accelerating us. For example, we've done more innovation in the last 15 years than in the entire history of human mankind. And we've generated more information in the last two years than in the entire history of mankind. We're living in exponential times, and that's a critical capability that marketing organizations and ad agencies need to adopt. The adoption and the change management, being able to constantly evolve to new environments and trends. That's the critical ability organizations need. In my previous role at Nokia, that was also one of the things that we continued to highlight in the organization: our constant need to adapt to new marketing opportunities and to the ever-changing consumer behaviors.

"I think we're entering a third wave. After the Industrial Revolution, we had the Information Age. The Internet has basically democratized information. Any information, for anybody, anywhere – and that's a fantastic thing. What also happened is we've democratized the creation of things and the distribution of things with the desktop printer – it created desktop publishing. Now, with 3D printers, the creation of objects is also democratized, and anybody with a couple of thousand dollars can buy one, but also the sourcing of hardware with China's Alibaba e-commerce sites and getting businesses to produce things. Through all these new communities and sites, you can upload your 3D model, and they can create it and build it for you. Vendors like the UPS Store will also offer affordable 3D printing services.

"Then there's this vibrant ecosystem of funding right now, like Kickstarter, where you can basically fill your order book before you start creating the product or even the company, yet. I think all that contributes to a democratized world where anybody can access any information, but also can distribute their products worldwide. It's a fantastic leveling off of the competing field for the creation of competition."

⌒

Thierry Halbroth, "In the advertising world, you'll hear both sides. This is really a split, but people say it's horrible what we've come to. It's all complicated. It's become so complicated, so manipulative, and it's just a matrix of ongoing paths that you have to take and to devise a proper creative idea for. We've never had it better than in the '60s or the '80s when we were working on radio and TV spots and print ads. You'll hear the other guys who say, 'No, there has never been a better time to be in advertising than now because anything you want to do, you can do it. Anything.'"

Chapter 19: The Industry Reborn

Imagine waking up bright and early in the morning, excited about going in to your office to jump on a couple of projects and experience the satisfaction of bringing inventively clever ideas to life. For much too long now, a good percentage of those of us who work in ad firms have come to loathe climbing out of bed to head to the decidedly uncreative factory atmosphere. Most situations we face are either soul crushing or mind numbingly wearisome, as the same sort of templated production work comes in and out and management insists that we do whatever it takes to keep the client happy, whether it's in their best interest or not. The beast (read: agency overhead) must be fed at all costs!

With that in mind, picture once again being empowered to come up with strong concepts that are fun to produce and can be sold to a client or even directly to targeted segments of the public. Rather than being saddled with coworkers who are constantly fighting your creative solution and opting for the safety of mediocrity, what if they rallied behind a single vision rooted in quality and pride in work, energetically supporting the team and the mission?

Fortunately, the so-called "digital natives," those who have grown up with the Internet and mobile devices as fixtures in their lives — the way television and transistor radios were for the previous generations — don't see things the way the old guard does. Since they didn't live through the era of strategic agency fragmentation, the walled off silos for different disciplines and media channels don't make any sense to them. (Of course, they don't make any sense to anyone who isn't motivated by fear and ego.) These 20-somethings coming into the industry are boiling over with thoughts of how to turn technology into desirable communication, even as they are too naïve to understand what is and is not expected or even appropriate these days. All they want is to get working generating ideas, learning on the job how branding and messaging really works, and it's time we let them.

Advertising: The Next Generation

George Tannenbaum, "My kids aren't going into the business, but, I'll tell you I must get 10 calls a week from people who want to break in. For the life of me, I don't really understand it because it's a lot of hard work and there's a ton of frustration. But people still want to get in and are willing to work for virtually nothing for the privilege. I don't consider it sexy, but I do enjoy what I do."

᠆

Mike Fromowitz, "Finding people is just as easy today as it ever was. Besides, there're more of them out of work. But finding people with the skills that we need is getting harder, as many are giving up on the business and going into teaching or working at Walmart. It's much harder to find really good writers and skilled art directors who think and create ideas of their own, rather than find ideas on the Internet and piece them together."

～

Steve Hall, "You've got older creative people who may or may not have the wish, desire, or ability to create for new media. That's going to be a cultural generational shift. I would say that there are probably a lot of very young creative people who don't give a crap about TV because they don't watch TV and everything they do is online.

"Agencies are going to have to restructure and have to sign creative people who see the value in where consumers are viewing stuff now and how they're consuming it. Creativity can still be creative. That's important. But there has to be a shift in the mindset and the value placed on where that creativity is seen. A lot of people are consuming content and are seeing advertising online, but, for some reason that doesn't seem to translate to the sort of glamorous success of having your work appear on TV, irrational as that may sound."

～

Andy Flemming, "These young guys that have done Award School and got a foot in the door based on how intensive that course was, after three months, they're generally in a pretty good position to be given a fair amount of work that they can handle. We're even talking to people from overseas. We like to have a fairly broad selection of individuals in the agency from a lot of backgrounds. The world has grown up. I'm not being patronizing, but having people who have been in the industry long enough to be able to handle a very big pitch single-handedly, that's very important for an agency of our size, but we also need those little fires underneath us to show us that we're old farts and, hey, here's something completely new and fresh. There is no particular type of person that we're seeking. We like a variety."

Jeff Cheong, "I look for adventurous, bold people with special skills and interests. These are qualities we look out for. What they do on a weekend pretty much sums up what they can do during the week. I love to employ young people. The younger, the better. They have a lot of energy and we are here to guide them and make them as successful as their potential can take them. But just so that we can relax? No."

Dirk Eschenbacher, "Maybe curiosity sets apart old-school creatives from TV and print and the new digital creatives. It's always difficult to learn new things, especially if they seem really complex. I reckon if you go into a bookstore and you face the wall of digital marketing and digital creativity books from strategy to social media to server side to email marketing, the topics are just so huge and so vast that many traditional creatives are a little bit turned off.

"On the other hand, they're now using it every day and they are exposed to all the great work. The biggest trouble they have is in understanding that they don't have to actually produce it; they can always find somebody to produce stuff for them. They just have to understand more about what is possible. Even sometimes things they think might not be possible probably are possible! It's really just about allowing yourself to dream in uncharted territory and then just put it out there.

"There's a lack of curiosity and bravery among traditional creatives, which is actually a shame because it's really not that difficult. The new creatives grew up with digital, so there is nothing for them to fear. They understand how all the processes work and they, of course, just lack the conceptual/ strategic approach to things and are maybe are not really good storytellers.

"Now, my ideal team is a senior writer, a mid-level hungry art director, and a producer. That's all I need. The writer would think about stories, about ideas, and about concepts. The art director can mock it up and put it together across different devices. The producer gets it done. That's how it should work. Right now, I don't have any teams, I'm a one-man show. I left Ogilvy in 2007, then I went to Tribal DDB where I was regional – I was a one-person team there. Then I stopped that, and I went to DDB Beijing for two years in a part-time role running the Volkswagen account.

"Those were hard times so I couldn't build the teams, and there was a lot of offline work to be done. There was much more offline than online. There wasn't that kind of dilemma there or that kind of challenge. Now I am back in Ogilvy in a part-time consulting role, so I still don't have a team. I'm a one-man show again. If I could hire, I would hire a senior writer, a mid-level hungry art director, and a producer.

"It doesn't have to be that many people. If you've got the producer, then you don't have to worry too much. It's the same thing in TV. You don't shoot a TV commercial by yourself; you always have 80 people on the set. It's manageable, you just have to understand what each person does. Frankly, I don't have too much to do with a database person. I roughly understand where we capture stuff. Another role that is good to have on the team is the user experience (UX) person. Even bigger, in terms of customer experience, or just people's experiences because more and more you create experiences across devices and stories across devices. That's a very important thing, if you can think in terms of satisfaction. How does the Facebook page connect with the journey to an offline event? How do we create a total experience out of it? That's a big skill set. Rather than managing a thousand people, rather than relying on a good producer, you have got to create a top-level experience."

⌇

Thierry Halbroth, "I would like to think advertising is still a sexy career choice, and that's why I'm fighting for it as the creative chairman of the Hong Kong 4As. I would love to think that we are still a very sexy industry. The reality is we're not. We're not because we are buried with work, we are working horrible hours, and we are doing it by passion – and that's the only reason we are in this business. Not because of the money because we certainly don't fucking make money. You can talk to a lot of creative heads and creative is just growing. It's the cherry on the cake that nobody wants to pay for, but they need the cherry.

"Nobody wants to pay for creative because it's tiny. The cake is a lot bigger. It's a lot more difficult to bake, it's running the operations, it's buying the media, it's doing all of that, but without the cherry, it's just a cake. The cherry makes it.

"It's a vicious circle. It's a seriously vicious circle, and I don't know what's happening, I don't have an answer. I don't know why we cannot develop our industry. I'm not saying we should be traders and we should earn millions of dollars and things like that. But today in the performance grand scheme, we should be able to change the model of our revenues. Maybe that's what is going to happen in the future. Everybody becomes a lot more accountable to what they produce. A great or significant part of this would be for risk taking. Taking risks is not something that's a part of many clients. Numerous people mention both on the client side and on the agency side that they should be allocating a portion of their budget to experimental stuff, but they don't.

"Take risk. That's what it all is. What drives innovation? This is what can separate you from your competition. We want to see this, but it's very difficult. I read an interview recently that this has happened at TBWA with their global digital lead. He got to go through 30, 40, 50 renditions of his business plans to set up a little 20-man unit who are basically dedicated to experiments, to building product it can own.

"Use clients to monetize their creativity. It's a no-brainer. The problem is even if you want $50,000 from a corporation to fund it, you can't get it. You can't. Even if you prove to them that you can sell it over and over and over and over and make money. You could be very bored and say, 'If I were a marketer or CMO today, I would take 10% of my budget and dedicate it to innovation and experiments.' It would motivate, a lot, any agency or any partner to work with to build a brand like that. But it's not happening. It's fucking gold, okay. You don't strike gold all the time. But when you strike gold, geez. It could actually pay itself back I don't know how many times over."

↩

Dave Whittle, "LinkedIn has had a really disruptive role in the recruitment industry. It's become classifieds for people, which is pretty amazing and incredibly powerful. We hire a lot of people through LinkedIn, and we find it really useful. We also hire a lot of people through internal referrals that we pay for. We've got a particular focus, at the moment, to use those channels to reduce our reliance on the traditional recruitment industry that has provided tremendous service, but is very expensive.

"We definitely use SEEK. We've been using SEEK for a very, very long time. SEEK provides a great source of recruitment leads and is a fantastic way to get the word out very quickly. But when we're looking for somebody with a particular type of skill set or pedigree, we'll approach somebody directly through LinkedIn or use LinkedIn to build a very short list of two or three people – and that's the case with the more specialist roles.

"To keep good people, we've got to continue to do brilliant work and ensure that people believe that they're part of something much bigger than themselves.

"To get people excited about working in advertising, they should keep making *Mad Men*. Roll out the 10th, 12th, 15th series of that show. That certainly will help. But in all seriousness, it's the work, the creative work. The marketing industry's greatest channel of promotion is the work that people see in their daily lives, the thousands and thousands of messages that people interact with every day.

"The best way to attract people in the industry is make it exciting to the general public in the same way that great architects do it. It's the same with any publicly viewable pursuit. It's no wonder the oil industry has such a dearth of talent right now. They're fairly invisible. I think that's one problem that advertising certainly does not have."

⌐

Barry Wong, "In 2006, I began exploring the possibility of a new-age creative team. I've tried doing radical things with my teams before, and most times, the result was bemused management faces. My vision with each brand account was to assign a heavyweight head creative, art or words, it didn't matter which they specialized in. What was crucial was an understanding of digital. This person would be client-facing and partnered with both a strategist and a business lead.

"The mid-weight creatives would get a change of titles and responsibilities. Art directors and copywriters would become user experience and content leads. An art director in digital needed to be more than just able to produce pretty pictures. Likewise, a copywriter today in the digital context needs to do more than just write a headline or web copy.

"What would the workflow be? The head creative sets the overall direction (creative / digital) and gets a sanity check on the technological feasibility via a creative technologist who also sits with the creative team. Then a UX lead and a content lead get assigned, and the four work as a team in delivering the project led by the head creative. That would be the ideal setup, and it's proven to work in a real agency environment.

"As for using freelancers and contractors in my team structure in China, it's hit and miss. More of a miss most times. I tend not to use them unless I am extremely desperate. I find that with the locals, there's an accountability issue. More often than not, it's about getting the most money in the shortest period of time, even if quality is compromised. And there is a high chance that the freelancer you engage is already overloaded with work from other clients."

〜

Erin Iwata, "I think hiring people is a nightmare that transcends our industry as a nationwide challenge. That said, I'm looking for people who understand digital, how it fits in to the rest of the mix and client objectives. I'm looking for people who think and operate in terms of movement. The trick is getting one of those who can write a coherent sentence that isn't in text shorthand. Or someone that doesn't think Facebook is the only place to go for news. Or someone that can carry on an actual phone conversation with a client and build a relationship. It's more about what seems to be the disconnect between being digitally savvy and emotionally intelligent. Based on my experience with digital partners, I don't feel comfortable allowing most of them to interact with my clients, so I play conduit. When I find one that can, I can hardly believe it. It's rare, but it happens on occasion. Thing is, those people are generally a bit older and more seasoned."

〜

Subhash Kamath, "If I looked at the top business goals in India, I don't think advertising is seen as a sexy career at all because, typically, advertising agencies only get to see candidates on the fifth or sixth day of campus recruitment. Also, advertising agencies have never been able to pay the kind of money that marketing companies or consulting groups are willing to pay today. When it comes from a business school perspective, I don't think advertising is seen as sexy anymore, either. But you know something, I'm fine with that. I'm fine if we have fewer MBAs in the fucking industry. For people who want to create, advertising is still a very sexy place to be."

New Revenue Streams

Aden Hepburn, "There are so many people who work here that have side projects or products that they're trying to make and market and sell. And we, as VML here in Sydney, are producing products that are outside the typical realm of an agency. We're building systems that we license to clients and we maintain those systems, we're improving upon them and charging licensing fees. Clients do love that because it's a software-as-a-service (SaaS) flat model, and they know it's going to be improved in the future, always guaranteed to be maintained regularly, and working because that's what they're paying for. We're trying that more and more, and we're getting more and more proactive at going to clients with a product-based idea or a platform that is going to change the way their business works.

"All of this is coming from the new breed of people that we are hiring into digital who are young, who are typically digitally native, who have that kind of hunger and entrepreneurial spirit. But it also comes from the dynamic of the people in the business, and those people come from different types of backgrounds with top skills. A lot of them would like to think that they could out there and build the next Facebook themselves, but they're stuck in a day job. It just happens that their day job actually allows them to facilitate a little bit of that for our clients."

~

Scott Morrison, "To understand the reason that design has had such a problem from the get-go with advertising, we need to go back to the '50s and '60s where advertising agencies made their money off of media buying and off of the commission on printing. Tons of things being printed in advertising were going into publications everywhere, and you worked with the top news agencies, you worked with the television stations to get your commercial on there for Tide or Downy or whatever, and you got a commission from it. The creative work was frequently thrown in for free. The ad layout was included in the price. It wasn't even a separate line item way back when. Then, as now, the ability to mark up printing or mark up media buying is not very difficult.

"Clients have caught onto the fact that there was tons of money being made. They started creating relationships directly with media buying firms or directly with the publications themselves and the same thing for the print space. I used to make 30 points on a print run; I can barely make 5 points on one now. In fact, sometimes I just introduce my printer directly to my client because if I can only make 5 points on it, I don't even want to be in the middle of the invoicing structure. I'm used to making tons of money of print commissions, but it's just not there now. By providing spec creative to try and win that business, we're sort of telling the clients, 'No, it's okay. You don't have to respect what we do. We'll give it away.'

"I'm not sure exactly when it did change. I mostly became aware of it six or seven years ago when we had a client that was being abusive to us. We would design the first run of a brochure, and then they would take it to the local printing company down the street where they'd pay someone $20 an hour to do all the changes that we would've done right before that. They were taking our layout and then handing it to someone else to do, which meant it went from being a $10,000-$15,000 project for us down to a $3,000 project with some other person getting paid to make all the other iterations – and that hurts. That makes the big difference to our bottom line.

"I went to the president of the agency at that time and I said, 'Listen, these guys are killing morale in the agency. We feel like we're not being listened to or respected for what we're doing, and this is not working. We need to fire this client.' His response was simply, 'We can't because we have our office space, our heat, our hydro, all of our overhead, and I can't replace the income.' What effectively it meant was we had to bend over and take whatever the client wanted to throw at us, regardless of how bad it was. Effectively, we had empowered them to do anything they wanted and we could only say, 'Yes sir,' to anything that they came back with. That was not healthy.

"The inspiration for The Bauhub came out of the fact that we need to reinvent the way the industry works, wholesale. We have really smart, great companies out there with fantastic people in them who need help to achieve their marketing goals, their business goals, whatever it is. We have incredibly smart people who're down to earth and understand what they're doing in the creative space. But the thing that's causing those two groups to not work well together is the infrastructure itself. Because if you take those people out of that infrastructure, independently, we've observed that they're great, smart, amazing people.

"However, the clients are dealing with the politics and the budgets and all these types of challenges, and the agencies are dealing with trying to be profitable and win this new business in a very competitive market space. It's very difficult. The idea behind The Bauhub was what if we could erase all of that? What if we could reset the boards and leverage technology, leverage the market trend, which is that big businesses are downsizing because they can't afford to keep people on staff anymore. So why don't we leverage the technology and the market trend that is happening right now to create the next evolution of work? That is, the self-employed knowledge worker as the ideal working method.

"One of our members had a friend of theirs come up to them and say, 'You're working freelance. Ha! When are you going to get a real job?' We thought about that and what is the answer? Why the heck would I want that? Why would I want something where I have to go to a set place to show my face every day so that someone knows that I'm working? I already work 14 hours a day right now. I'm a very hard worker, and I don't need to show someone else that I am. I don't need to be in an office. The thought was let's take all of these incredibly smart people and try to find a way where they can be matched up with the people who need their help. In a way that will build trust, will foster creativity, and be a more enjoyable working experience for the creative people and the clients who need to hire them. That's where the inspiration came from. The old way of working, it's just not working anymore.

"The people are the difference between a traditional bricks-and-mortar firm and what we're doing in the self-employed space. Now the funny part is that in most cases, it's the same people. But the mentality has changed 180 degrees. Let's run a scenario. Someone's been working at a business for 10 years. They're feeling burned out, they're feeling unappreciated. They're feeling under-compensated for what they're doing, and they feel powerless. They feel stressed because they don't feel they have control over their own destiny. They are doing a great job. Maybe they get promoted really quickly.

Maybe they feel they should've been promoted more quickly. A lot of people are unhappy with that.

"Now, there are some great superstars in traditional businesses that are doing great jobs, nothing against them at all. But the people joining us are the people who have either chosen to leave to go on their own because they're entrepreneurial by nature or they're fed up with what they've been doing and they need a lifestyle change. They need to feel better. They don't enjoy what they're doing.

"The other type of people are the ones that get downsized against their will. It happens. Great people get downsized. It's no reflection on your talent or ability. When an agency or a business is losing money, they take off the people who're making $30,000 a year and they take out the people who're making $150,000 a year. They keep the middle people and have them do more work. What happens, though, is these people go out in the workforce and they're looking around going, 'What do I do now?'

"We get calls all the time saying, 'I've wanted to go freelance forever, but I never felt like I could do it. I never felt like there was infrastructure that could support me.' What we're finding is when people leave a business, they also leave behind the employee-employer mentality. They now realized that their success is entirely based on their own ability to do something. There's a direct correlation to, 'If I do a great job this week, I get a $5,000 check next week.' It changes peoples' mindset, and it changes their attitude towards the work that they do. I have yet to experience a single member that we've worked on a project with who has said to me, 'Oh no, it's 5:00pm. I'm out of here,' or even insinuate that they were thinking that. I Skype with people at a regular basis at 11:00 at night because we're all there working, because we all believe in it.

"When I say it's the people that are the difference, it's actually that the people – when they leave the job and they know that they're under their own power – feel enthusiastic. They feel excited. They feel that joy back in what they're doing. There are ups and downs, like one of our members just called me today. He's thinking he might not be cut out for freelancing. It's too much insecurity for him. But the point is the people who are out of the workforce, the traditional workforce in this space are generally very positive, entrepreneurial, and outgoing people. They tend to be the ones that really understand they have to give their all.

"The trend in the workforce is that people just want to feel good. They want to enjoy what they're doing. Our experience so far is that people who have chosen self-employment exhibit more traits of feeling happy. The Freelancer Academy in the US put out some statistics on that in the *2012 Freelance Industry* report. The people that they polled specifically stated they held extraordinary high levels of satisfaction with their current work lifestyle."

"That's where The Bauhub comes in. Because part of what we're trying to put together is not only the work collaboration, but we have recognized that there are three major components to make the self-employed space operate. The first thing is you have to make sure the individuals you're working with are people you can trust. We're handling that by creating our recruiting mechanism which makes sure that people when they come in, are good at what they do, have the experience, and are someone you can work with.

"The second thing is an infrastructure to facilitate working and communication. Every large agency will have an agency management system of some type. But who's got a cohesive one that works for self-employed people? It doesn't exist. Basecamp[29] has it to a certain extent, but it's only designed to deal with very small groups of people at any given time. The last thing is we need to change the minds of the people in the client space and get them to see this is a group they can work with. It's not the, 'Oh... freelancers.' thing, anymore. No, this is a very large talent resource that you are missing out on leveraging."

"I can't speak to self-employment in general because there are fly-by-nighter freelancers who can disappear tomorrow. That's the reason we're trying to create a collective. We had a member, and I'm not joking with you, a great member doing great work. He had an upheaval in his personal life, something happened with him and his wife. We're still not even sure what happened, but I'm not kidding you, over a weekend, he sent an email to the three clients he was working with that were Bauhub-related clients saying, 'I'm not working on this anymore. I'm out of here. I'll give you all your passwords. I'm gone.' He literally joined a cult; he literally took off and joined

---

29　An online, collaborative project management software from 37signals.

some sort of reclusive kind of group. We don't even know where it is. He left his wife and he left his child.

"There's one in every crowd. We can't promise that we're going to have everyone be awesome forever. But what I can tell you is that even though we had one guy out of the couple of hundred who were involved, one guy who went a bit wing nutty, we were able to replace him within two days because the collective had more people who could replace his skills. Somebody could take off, anywhere, at any company. That happens in businesses, too."

⮌

John Winsor, "I am an old dog, but my sense is that all these holding companies – except for my boss at Havas, David – are run by pretty old guys, and all these big agencies are, too. If their whole being is affected by the *Hamptons Effect,*[30] then their attitude is, 'My horizon for retirement is four to five years. I'm not going to reinvent anything. I'm just not going to fuck it up, not on my watch. I'm not going to be the guy who blew up a big holding company. I'll just manage it and exploit the shit out of it and continue to increase revenues, continue to increase profitability by just keeping the screws as tight as possible.' But it's still super early days.

"I think it's a killer for the young guy that is living in Brisbane or in Kuala Lumpur that is passionate and can get all this free information out of the Internet and just putting himself in business by starting a [virtual or small] agency."

⮌

Andy Flemming, "The gaming industry is now what the advertising industry used to be. A lot of creative minds are basically making Angry Birds, and they're going out and they're creating the next big art form, which I truly believe gaming is. I think gamification is something that is definitely going to become very important [within advertising]. It attracts a lot of people, but it is a more complicated business now."

---

30 Abandoning work for a long weekend.

Reignition

Jon Cook, "I've feel I'm completely in touch with and have a pulse from a digital perspective. But the idea that you would truly write down and observe how people are consuming content and marketing in their lives is the biggest eye-opener that I have, whenever I need a dose of how impactful is this stuff that we're doing. Because we're not the old guys that don't believe; we're digitized people who are doing great.

"I still think that we need to go out and see it in action. If you go watch the world, then you go see how that person took that action, and you can kind of follow and trace it. You have to stitch together some of the steps in your mind, but that's what I do. I believe somebody who is in the position to describe would be better than any school. Just observe.

"What we're trying to do is we're trying to create choice of communication. Some of it takes some action. That's having a feeling about a brand, the persuading, and getting somebody to take an action. That's no different whether it is digital or whatever. To truly dissect in your mind how somebody took an action. Why do they do it? Why did they see that movie? Why did they bring three friends with them to that movie? How did they get those three friends together? Then you say, 'You just call them on the telephone.' Is that really what happened here? It's the most primal original force. I was merely looking at a medium agnostically in how did it actually happen? Some of them you can observe, some of them you have to extrapolate, but if somebody did that, it would be the best thing they can do, short of doing an internship or taking a job or going back to school.

"It's the cultural anthropology of how people are taking an action in this day and age and what led to that action, every aspect of it. What they are saying about how they are communicating their reaction to that, not looking for the digital things, just everything they do. You'd trace back the importance of digital through that exploration, and you would open your eyes, no matter who you are, to what it was. I think it's helpful to even the most experienced digital professionals."

﹌

Mike Fromowitz, "It seems that the skills of the Art Director are no longer needed because of the advances in digital technology and software applications that almost anybody can learn.

"When you think about it, almost everybody today thinks he or she is a writer or art director because they can 'do stuff' on their computer. There're apps for everything!

"That's why almost everything today looks so commoditized.

"Information on the Internet has become so ubiquitous that the Copywriter's job isn't faring much better than that of the Art Director. Advertising copy, especially long copy, has mostly disappeared from the ads we see today. We are told that, 'given the shorter attention span of consumers, the advertising of the day demands that communication be short and simple.' Oh, and don't forget adding the web site URL to the ad, just in case the consumer needs more information.

"By the year 2000, the term 'copywriter' seemed almost obsolete. Body copy? Forget it! Copy had taken a complete backseat to visual gags and headlines made up of two to five words. The role of the Copywriter had changed. The job had become far more visually demanding. It was no longer about a clever turn of phrase. It actually required the Copywriter and art director to work even closer together to find some 'Intrusive' idea. Award shows gave out gongs to the ads with the fewest words. The once-specialized and proprietary skills of art direction and copywriting had become commoditized. Anybody with a computer could create their own ads and be a copywriter – or so it seemed.

"My good friend Blair Currie, in one notable blog for *Campaign Asia*, said that, 'The (ad) industry seems to be alive with new types of jobs that have been created at 'progressive' agencies. One of them was for 'Creative Technologists,' a new type of creative person that blends creative with technology.' Technology people are more adept at experimenting with different options. This includes moving from The Big Idea to many ideas and by launching work and then improving upon it, the way software developers work, giving rise to faster turn-around and higher margins because more work is done internally.'

"The question: *Is technology making the Art Director and the Copywriter redundant?*

"The creative idea has always been the most important thing. There's certainly money to be saved if you hire one creative person who is equally adept at both copy and art, but is he any good?

"Some agency executives believe it makes more sense that an advertising idea person is teamed with a technology person. Others are moving to a 'cell' structure by teaming a strategic planner with a creative ideas person and a technology person. The cell then collaborates with the clients.

"Many large agencies are heavily invested in the old way of doing things and find it difficult to experiment or to change, and they continue with their traditional silos. As soon as they find yet another way to make some money, up goes a new silo. More and more, clients are finding this system antiquated and anything but efficient or creative. Lately, I've been following an interesting D&AD discussion group. A contributor to the group recently proposed a new blanket title for the Art Director: Content Strategy Director.

"'The term Art Director sounded great in the '60s,' he said, 'but now that term is so readily applied to a senior web designer. It's time to kill the old dog and generate a title that better reflects the modern usage of the role in advertising across all media.'

"One contributor to the discussion offered the following: 'It needs an expert in there somewhere because we need to compete with all the other experts, like social media experts, digital experts, etc.'

"'Concept Director' (for both writers and art directors) got a quick thumbs-up in the department of another contributor to the group.

"Another chap from the USA noted, 'For the clients' benefit, the term *content strategist* speaks to something tangible – content! I'm finding business leaders even scoffing at the terms 'creative' and 'conceptual.' Of course, this is the States, where anti-intellectualism seems to be very fashionable these days.'

"And lastly, I found the following contributor's statement the most interesting of all: 'It would be a sad day if the word art was stripped from our profession. Art is at the root of what we do, and it's one of the most valuable assets of our culture.'

"Personally, I believe that our industry still requires highly specialized craft people. The best creative work that I've seen over these past few years still comes from teams of copywriters and art directors. I don't mind teaming them up with a technology/digital specialist. For me, it's not a matter of whether it's digital or traditional or both; it's about the creative idea and what creative ideas, when activated, can do for sales.

"Advertising agencies and their clients are queuing up for digital like it was the only show in town. I wish for once they'd shut up and get on with focusing on sales. At the end of the day, we don't produce advertising or do social media marketing so we can say 'Look at the amazing ads we made.' We do it to reach people (or have them reach us) so that we can sell them something: a product, a service, a thought.

"From here, it's beginning to look like anyone with an iPad, a Twitter, LinkedIn or a Facebook account, and fluency in other digital mumbo jumbo, can get a job in advertising. The arrival of professionals with fancy titles like Social Media Mogul, Creative Technologists, Developers, etc. makes it darn near impossible to know who really does what.

"In the case for retaining the art director and the copywriter (and keeping their titles as is), there is no better argument than the recent article penned by Antony Young, the CEO of Mindshare North America, a WPP media strategy and investment agency. In his article for *Advertising Age Digital*, he said, 'We in the media industry are infatuated with the new… but digital marketers are investing in the old. How ironic, then, that when it comes to pitching for advertising dollars, being somewhat old school appears to be the formula to win over marketers' budgets. The hottest digital ad mediums are adaptations from old media.'

"'What's the fastest growing medium in digital at the moment? Online video or, basically, TV commercials,' adds Young. 'Example after example, we see that today's digital new media clamoring to sell us very traditional advertising solutions. But it doesn't stop with traditional digital media. Social media powerhouse Facebook sees its financial future in selling display advertising space, which is a decidedly traditional online advertising model.'

"Given Antony Young's assessment of digital media, doesn't that sound like there remains a need for art directors and copywriters? I would think so.

"Just yesterday, a creative friend and ex-colleague of mine, who now works in one of Singapore's newest ad agencies, wrote an email to me on the subject of advertising titles. He said, 'I've worked in an agency that threw a lot of people from all the fields, with all the new fancy titles into a room to do some brainstorming. By the end of the day, we had nothing. Then, my art director and I had to spend the next two nights creating a campaign the client would buy. Involving developers, planners, or the media team did not help ideas come to life. It only made things more confusing simply because they don't have the background skills to do what we know how to do. It's what we've been doing for more than 10 years together.'

"Certainly, the art of creativity is not mutually exclusive to the pairing of the art director and copywriter. Great ideas can come from anyone and anywhere, and it's about time that agencies realize this fact. Creative brainstorming should be based on collaboration rather than on teams. Involving other roles such as a planner, a technologist, or even a business entrepreneur can help bring different perspectives and ideas than those that may be brought to the table by the classic agency pair.

"At the end of the day, it doesn't matter if you are an expert in social media, in digital technology, in web site design and architecture, or an expert in SEM [search engine marketing]. The question is, can you make ads?"

$$\backsim$$

Thierry Halbroth, "I don't know if traditional agencies are in threat of extinction. I don't think so. We have a fundamental problem that we have to address. One is the inability to view our industry as a whole instead of in silos. That's the issue that we're all facing – and that everyone is still facing. Digital is digital. 'Oh, you want something digital? That's technical, so talk to these guys. They're the specialists. They belong to us, but you'll get a different bill for it. We can also do digital. We'll actually create the digital for you and then we'll use these guys to build the back end.' It's completely wrong. You want to create a strategy or develop a creative idea. It doesn't matter where it's coming from. It has to be understood by everybody, and everybody has to work on it. Until we start breaking down the walls of agencies and bringing everyone together properly: the nerd guys, the techie guys, the basement guy, we don't know who they are... everyone. They work through the night and until we break this down on the corporate levels. That is where it's the hardest part to break down, the P&L. Unless we figure out the P&L, the industry is fucked.

"Doing this is their reaction to what the clients are doing because the budget is allocated by silo. The clients say, 'We want to spend $x\%$ there.' And the agencies respond, 'I'm the ad agency, which means I want $x\%$ of this and

$y\%$ of that. Thank you very much.' Well, it doesn't work like that anymore. You'd be surprised how difficult it is to fix. Because it's a structural change within an organization. It's also a different way of working. I've talked to many ECDs and CEOs and we have the same conversation. How do you integrate? How do you do it? How many people? What is happening with the original copywriter-art director team combo?

"The first thing I've done, and I've always believed in, that is no good writer team combo is dedicated. Nobody is in a paired team. It doesn't work like that. You work in an agency, now, together. Everybody works together. One day working with John and tomorrow you'll be working with Diana. That's the first thing. I've broken down the teams as in an official team. Everybody gets to work with different people, get used to different behaviors, get used to lots of people. The second thing I've done when it comes to big integration or big projects where you have different channels involved like digital channels and traditional channels, it's a team of three, it's not a team of two.

"It could be a team of three or it could be a team even of four sometimes. It's a team in an ideal world, a situation. So, you'll have one digital person who is a digital art director or digital writer or whatever and then a traditional copywriter who needs to pick a digital head. A traditional art director who is here to look at how he's going to build his traditional channels. Hopefully, he is also able eventually, in the best way, to develop or think digitally. It will enhance the project, because what happens is that person understands best how the technology really can help. Or can enable an idea. In some cases, how the technology can become the idea."

Conclusion

For a long, long time, you could not do business without a handshake hard enough to be uncomfortable and a lot of time spent getting to know the clients and what their personalities were really all about. To help those folks build relationships with their target audiences, it was essential to first establish a strong relationship between the agency point people and the decision makers in the marketing organization. Only then would they trust you to dream up creative solutions using their budget and, quite often, that would lead to many fruitful years of working side by side. The best part: when the client eventually moved to another brand, he or she would usually summarily fire the incumbent agency and bring in the familiar one. The one that really *gets* how it's all supposed to work. The one that the marketing executive knew would make life much easier.

That sort of relationship-building doesn't come cheap. It takes a large investment of time, personnel, and hard-to-get tickets to ball games and concerts. Let's not even talk about the damage to generations of livers and marriages. However, without a suave, intelligent, and charismatic account director helping the client with his job, the account is not going to stay the agency's for long, and when you have dozens of highly paid professionals on your books and a modern, sophisticated office to maintain, you need to feel secure with long-term clients, each feeding in a sizable monthly retainer. To keep it flowing in means doing whatever it takes to keep the clients happy, no matter the cost to personal lives, personal humility, or even the integrity of what you're supposed to be personally delivering. These are the issues at the heart of the age-old war between Creatives and Suits.

Like many things here in the early 21st century, all of that is coming to an end, for the most part. While there will undoubtedly always be the need to woo the largest of the large accounts in the biggest of the big agencies in this time-honored tradition passed down from Account Director to Account Manager to Account Executive, the fact is, the majority of today's marketers don't have time for it. They would probably very much like to be able to sit across from the agency rep with a drink in hand and pontificate about all of their dreams, ambitions, and frustrations with the job, just as they would likely not mind adjusting and growing ad campaigns over a couple of years instead of, at best, a couple of fiscal quarters. It's simply not today's reality.

There are constant pressures on the marketing executives to deliver measurable results. In the past, there simply weren't good analytics that pinpointed what was effective and what was great in theory, but miserable in practice. Traditional media required a healthy serving of positive thinking and application of many unknowable assumptions that could give credit to the ads for driving an increase in sales (never mind better weather, competitions' failures, or other possible factors).

Today, digital footprints and social listening tools allow us to see everything and anything we'd want to know about a person's exposure to a brand's messaging. While the data has invariably been spun to seemingly fit corporate goals, it is becoming harder and harder to do as people become more educated about what information the data can relate for improving tactics and unambiguously delivering tangible, measurable ROI.

Thankfully, not only has the technology improved to the point of being ready for prime time, but so have the players. Around the turn of the millennium, there was no Dropbox, no Basecamp, no Skype, no FreshBooks, no Google Docs, no Podio, no one really accustomed to working primarily online. Even YouTube didn't show up until 2005, if you can fathom that. People had experience working to produce web sites, microsites, banner ads, email campaigns, and product demos, but mainly by doing so in traditional, analog ways. Items were still FedExed between offices, even if they were digital assets. Only a brave few souls in the agencies and client organizations knew about FTP (File Transfer Protocol) or had the patience to tie up their modem line with a ridiculously time-consuming download.

Here in the second decade of the third millennium, though, things are a lot different. Not only do all of those online productivity tools exist, they are relied upon heavily by everyone working in all types of business today, not just advertising. People are as comfortable using cloud storage services like Google Drive, Mozy, and box as they were with physical filing systems of the past. These are facilities that many people use in their personal life as well as their professional. There is no intimidation factor, learning curve, or confusion about how to work in a virtual, digital environment. That's a major change from even 10 years back, when people feared *the machines.*

If I wanted a physical office for Heresy with an impressive façade and lots of people running around, moving piles of documents between offices, setting up meeting rooms, and arranging client lunches, I could raise the rates we charge by several hundred dollars an hour just like the brick-and-mortar ones are forced to. By doing so, I could ostensibly give our clients peace of mind that we are a stable, committed, invested company because we take more of their money than we need to for their goals to be realized and put it into helping them feel better about their choice of agency.

We have no overhead. We have no full-time employees with benefits. We have no account managers. We have no project managers. We have no administrative staff. We charge clients for the time it takes the people doing the hands-on work to complete the job. Not even time & materials. Just their time. Depending on the skill, there is a transparent

15-25% markup on that time, the hourly rates are reasonable, in that we do not gouge the clients just because we can. Where a traditional ad agency might charge $600/hr, we may charge $150/hr for the same effort.

Companies come to us because they know we're a group of people who have worked together for decades at some of the largest agencies in the world. They know they're going to get exactly what they'd get at those $600-$1000/hr agencies for $125-$250/hr. They don't have to pay for our impressive office space or people running around shuffling papers and setting up meetings or for executive salaries tied to executive egos and career ambitions.

There's no reason to stay tethered to the old model simply because it's familiar and has been in place for a long while. There are many more flexible structures that allow the best work to be conceived and executed with the highest quality without having to bring it to a third-world country in order to make it affordable. By cutting away all of the unnecessary excess, the trappings, and not having to cater to the needs of a large group (i.e., establishing a human resources department, feeding the culture, resolving personnel drama, stroking egos, developing a hierarchy, enforcing rules, worrying about who has a bigger cubicle or more comfortable chair or better computer or a mobile device provided by the company, etc., ad nauseam), using the excellent, reliable, and dirt cheap online tools (or building your own), suddenly you can be competitive with Costa Rica and Mumbai. Only you can produce something that doesn't look and act like it *belongs* in third world.

The Industry of the Future

Andy Flemming, "Maybe advertising is still seen as wunderkinds wearing funny T- shirts that go to a lot of lunches, do piles of coke, and then fuck off to the Bahamas for shoots. Alright, there is that, and hooray! But admittedly, we've gone through one of the greatest recessions since the 1930s. Clients have changed. Mediums have changed. Agencies have changed - and those great pieces of work that would appear twice a year for Nike, Adidas, and Coke. They're appearing more and more – just in different channels. People are sharing the stuff they love and that's the yardstick. It's all about getting someone to say 'fuck me! Look at THIS!' I guess that'll never change.

᳐

Andy Greenaway, "It's an exciting new world. I love it. There are more opportunities in the industry than ever before. The world moves on.

This business is better than emptying bins for a living or even working in a stuffy corporate environment. I think one change we will see is a rise of people starting their own businesses. Why would you want to work for one of the big holding groups that restrict your pay rises to 10% every 18 months?"

❦

Chris Kyme, "The industry has been devalued. There is no self-respect anymore. Technology has also contributed to this. Anyone with a Mac can start an agency nowadays."

❦

Paul Kwong, "Advertising is probably still a sexy business to be in. Look at all the 'write-your-own-commercial' contests that are out there. People love to see their influence on brands. Look at all the folks commenting on client web sites and Facebook pages."

❦

Craig Mapleston, "We're definitely in a much more difficult business than ever, but also a far more exciting one. We're on the cusp of a new world order, and there will be fatalities. Big, international networks will die, and smaller agencies will thrive. The democratization of creativity and channels for creativity mean that the automatic authority that some agencies had, is now gone. Clients are seeing quality ideas and quality production from all over, and they are questioning the value of their agencies. That's a good thing."

❦

Paul Biedermann, "These are exciting times. Things have been moving very fast and perhaps that will only increase, but I also believe that a good creative will always have a place. There will come a time when the newest technological trick won't mean much anymore, and people will see the value in clever solutions and real entertainment again. I think that is already happening. There is so much boring work around, and what was new is not so new anymore. People will want more, and we will deliver."

↜

Martin Riley, "Let's be careful not to abandon great creative ideas and crusading messages for our brands that have been effective in traditional media as we embrace technology. The people we seek to recruit in marketing must have digital skills and must feel comfortable with what digital can bring, but they must also offer consumer understanding and curiosity about how to engage consumers in original ways that remain true to the brand's values. A combination of quantitative/analytical skills that can manage and understand Big Data and creativity that can enable them to use the data effectively by creating relevant content. I call this diagonal thinking.

"As current President of the World Federation of Advertisers, which represents the top 70 advertisers in the world, I can say that we all fully recognize the potential and impact that digital communication can have and that we must be mindful of how we use data and how we interact with consumers to avoid being too intrusive or interruptive, especially on sites like Facebook.

"I am convinced that we are living through a revolution every bit as impactful as the Industrial Revolution. I am currently reading a book about how the Industrial Revolution in 18th-century Manchester changed the world forever. All aspects of people's lives at every level of society were affected: social, business, and political. As we see how the digital revolution is changing every aspect of our lives, from how we socialize to how we purchase and how we find entertainment and jobs, it is clear what is happening in Silicon Valley today is as significant for the world as the mechanization of the cotton industry was in Manchester almost 250 years ago."

↜

Dirk Eschenbacher, "If you look at the Webbys, for example, which is a quite popular barometer for what people like out there, you have a lot of stuff created by agencies. A lot of work that really finds its way into popular culture. And that is why agencies, especially good ones, are really quite attractive places for younger people to work at. I see this happening more and more, actually. I talk to more and more people who are really getting excited about the industry again."

↜

Todd Ruff, "I think the economy is leading to a shift of the work moving more in-house. I guess it's still sexy based on what I see at SXSWi and other interactive media festivals and ad technology conferences, but even that seems more bullshit than reality. Hipsters who think they know. The need for big ideas will still be out there, but I see these coming from shops like Heresy. Smaller, leaner, more adaptable, where you partner vs. build."

⤙

Neil Leslie, "While the industry may have lost some of its shine over the years, I still think that advertising is seen as an exciting industry for those with a creative streak. Although, if you're thinking every day will be a blur of booze and illicit affairs as depicted in Mad Men, you're likely to be disappointed."

"I have high hopes for the future, though. Perhaps, when the dust settles, the clients and agencies will appreciate that they need to build entertaining and enjoyable content, applications experiences around the needs, interests, and behaviors of their customers.

"And that would make our lives as creatives even more fun."

⤙

Kay Johnson-Suglia, "Advertising is not a sexy world any more. It's long hours and hard work. It's frustration, negotiation, deliberation, and ultimately never really getting what you want, *But*, it's still exciting – the sale, the win, the rocking campaign, the awards, the highs that come with all that. The people in advertising are some of the best, brightest, most passionate, convicted, committed, and cantankerous!"

"Advertising, communication, or marketing, is at least one industry where any type of creativity will be encouraged and appreciated. So, one will leave in a hurry as long as what they do is not appreciated and there is a platform for them to express themselves, regardless of whether it is the digital world or traditional expression."

⤙

Jonathan Holburt, "I think advertising still attracts smart people as it holds a certain amount of glamour. Misguided, I think. But young people, as a whole, are less likely to commit long term to an agency or the career than those of my generation did. I learned by apprenticeship, and that is still true today. But it takes patience to be an apprentice, and patience isn't a strong suit of today's young people."

༄

John Lambie, "The beauty of the future is that it never arrives. There is only the here and now. While this is axiomatically true, humans are pattern-seeking creatures. We crave certainty and build entire industries around planning for, mapping out, and paving the way for 'the future.'

"The insurance industry uses past patterns of events to build probabilities for future events. On the trading floor, investors snap up futures in a range of commodities, from iron ore to pork bellies. Companies closely watch the sales figures of unrelated companies to detect hints as to the direction of future consumer trends. Trend hunters hang out where the cool kids congregate to be the first to predict where fashion, art, and music are headed. All the while, technologists keep pushing the boundaries of smaller, faster, and better.

"But advertising has lost its mojo. It's no longer the creative vortex that once sucked the brightest and most creative minds into its epicenter. Young audiences are disdainful and dismissive of advertising. They like to think they have the better of it and can see straight through its overt (and even covert) brand messages. The reason top talent is looking elsewhere is because that elsewhere looks more attractive. They're pursuing studies in business, science, and technology (testament to this is the ever-shrinking humanities departments at major universities around the world). They're joining start-ups. They have the desire to change the world and the self-belief that they can do it.

"Let's face it, today's talent wants more than what a traditional agency environment promises. They want:

- Meaning
- Purpose
- Involvement in something bigger than themselves
- Recognition
- Responsibility
- Autonomy
- Engagement
- Security

- Freedom
- Fluidity
- Flexibility
- Time off
- Sabbaticals
- Multi-skilling

"And here's what they don't want:

- Rigidity
- Hierarchy
- 9-to-5
- Geographical constraint
- Micromanagement
- Uncertainty
- Mediocrity

"Full-time long-term employment is rarely offered, so it's rarely even considered as an option. There are thirty- and even forty-somethings who've never held anything more than an ongoing 'short-term contract.' There is also the perpetual freelancer – the holder of a specialist skill set 'too narrow' to be ever be fully utilized within a generalist agency.

"To recap, *Digital Doesn't Matter* is essentially a book about the future:

- Your future
- Your agency's future
- Your brand's future

"At the risk of sounding glib and based on current trends, here's what that future holds:

- More fragmentation
- More disintermediation
- More technology
- More diversity and individualism in the market
- More complexity
- More change
- Less certainty

"Exciting, isn't it?! Preparing for the future means preparing for greater and faster change than ever before. The key to individual survival is to be like a bicycle wheel.

You can be an axle:
It's not what you know it's who. It's not about you; what it's about is your network and who. Seth Godin calls these people 'linchpins.'

You can be a spoke:
You do one thing and you do it well. Without you, the whole wheel would buckle. You are at the top of your game in your particular field, the master craftsperson, the always-in-demand freelancer.

You can be a rim:
You hold all the spokes in place. Your job is to keep everything in alignment and turning smoothly.

You can be a tire:
You are the interface between the wheel and the road. You're sensitive to every bump and divot. You're flexible, yet highly sensitive. You report your findings back to the rest of the wheel.

You can be a chain:
You are the energy that drives everything.

"The future agency needs people like these:

- Visionaries
- Connectors
- Sergeant-Majors
- Curators
- Craftspeople."

∽

It needs you.

Acknowledgements

I'd like to thank the many people over the past two years who allowed this book to come to fruition. First and foremost, John Lambie, my Australian friend and former agency creative colleague for the past 16 years, who agreed to help me get this beast started when I really needed someone to be responsible to. Without a client, so to speak, or a partner, I knew this would be a never-ending labor... of love, but, definitely never-ending. John tirelessly helped create the endless questions we threw at the numerous executives we spoke with and rallied many to the cause to contribute their thoughts and, in the case of the Kickstarter campaign we held for the innovative iPad app version, their dollars. He had to drop out as co-author shortly after the crowdfunding success in order to focus on Dextr, the burgeoning keyboard app startup he founded, but he was instrumental in the birthing of this tome and that I found my way up the mountain without him at my side was just... stamina.

Next, Tony Willoughby, who graciously allowed John, my son, Ethan, and me use of his family's ranch out in the wilds of Medina, Texas in July of 2012 so we could completely disconnect from the digital world that the ad industry has become obsessed with and concentrate on how to go about pulling off *Digital Doesn't Matter*.

There were 135 industry experts that generously gave of their incredibly valuable (hey, have you seen their hourly rates?) time and graciously allowed us to pummel them with a barrage of thoughts about the business and their careers. A few weren't able to make it into the book because of its already generous page count, but their interviews with us definitely helped influence how I organized everything to tell the story. Everyone we spoke to was of great help and assistance and, as you see within, made this book what it is through their personal anecdotes, experiences, considered thoughts and helpful advice over the countless hours of conversations we enjoyed.

My developmental editor, Ruth Mills, helped me streamline a manuscript that was *twice* the size of the final edit at a time when I was beginning to think there was no realistic path forward for me on my own. Her 1,000+ sticky notes made it tough to see my content, but by addressing each one — one-by-one — I began to see a way up and over.

Larry Goode and John Lambie helped create a striking cover while Michael Streiter crafted excellent copy for the back cover and Jakob Clark helped me design the sleek, modern look of the app. Allen Zuk professionally and quickly formatted the print and electronic editions and was an amazing find, while Scott Morrison of The Bauhub, with his crack technical team of Alex Spencer and Murtada Shah, devoted themselves to making my app vision and many features a wonderful, functioning reality, with Marianne Angeli providing PM support. Thanks, too, to Wilson Manalo and his tireless team of transcribers and, of course, *all of the backers* of the Kickstarter campaign for our incredible app version (look up the book title on iTunes!).

Finally, Ethan and my wife, Winy, for both having the infinite patience and understanding to let me build a new-fangled kind of ad agency during the day and spend too many nights on this book and the accompanying "reinvention of the book" iPad app. Next project: lots of quality time with my family!

Index

@

1

A

B

C

G

H

N

O

P

Q

R

S

U

Made in the USA
San Bernardino, CA
07 July 2014